Convergence of Project Management and Knowledge Management

Edited by
T. Kanti Srikantaiah
Michael E. D. Koenig
Suliman Hawamdeh

THE SCARECROW PRESS, INC.
Lanham • Toronto • Plymouth, UK
2010

Published by Scarecrow Press, Inc.
A wholly owned subsidiary of The Rowman & Littlefield Publishing Group, Inc.
4501 Forbes Boulevard, Suite 200, Lanham, Maryland 20706
http://www.scarecrowpress.com

Estover Road, Plymouth PL6 7PY, United Kingdom

British Library Cataloguing in Publication Information Available

Library of Congress Cataloging-in-Publication Data

Convergence of project management and knowledge management / edited by T. Kanti Srikantaiah, Michael E. D. Koenig, Suliman Hawamdeh.
p. cm.
Includes bibliographical references and index.
ISBN 978-0-8108-7697-2 (cloth : alk. paper) — ISBN 978-0-8108-7698-9 (ebook)
1. Project management. 2. Knowledge management. I. Srikantaiah, Taverekere. II. Koenig, Michael, E.D. III. Al-Hawamdeh, Suliman.
HD69.P75.C648 2010
658.4'04—dc22 2010014161

™ The paper used in this publication meets the minimum requirements of American National Standard for Information Sciences—Permanence of Paper for Printed Library Materials, ANSI/NISO Z39.48-1992.

Printed in the United States of America

Contents

Preface

Projects have been in existence for thousands of years, dating back as far as Egyptian civilization and the construction of the pyramids. It is only recently that project management practices have evolved to the status of a discipline with proper methodology, tools, and techniques. Today, the need for efficient and effective management of projects within the organization comes about as a result of the increased competition in the marketplace. Projects in organizations have grown exponentially in recent years due to globalization and open markets; today large numbers of these projects are carried out all over the world, both in the public and private sectors. Organizations are continuously looking for ways to improve their knowledge management practices and seek to deploy tools and technologies in the hope of gaining an edge over their competitors and at the same time protecting their investment. At the heart of all of this is an important and vital resource that is frequently overlooked or downplayed by the organization. Knowledge is an important resource, and it is essential to the success of any project within the organization. Managing knowledge in projects is essential not only to the success of an individual project, but also to the creation of best practices and lessons learned that will ensure organizational continuity and sustainability.

Knowledge management, which started to attract attention around the mid-nineties, has a great potential and adds value to project management in all areas and at all stages— initiating projects, managing projects, and assisting in completing projects on schedule, on budget, and with quality deliverables. At the project and organizational levels, knowledge management has emerged explosively, through an interdisciplinary approach, to address the knowledge issues in projects and project management. Knowledge management's operational approach has become invaluable in the area of project management.

In the project environment, there are many projects that could turn into "troubled projects" and end up as failures. Anecdotal and documentary evidence indicates that if knowledge management were applied in those projects, many of them would have had their risk mitigated and would not have become "troubled projects." Also, it has become clear that if knowledge is captured properly at every stage in the cycle of a project and that knowledge is shared throughout the project life cycle, the project will benefit and the organization will benefit. Knowledge management has shown the advantages of managing knowledge effectively in all nine areas of project management as specified by the Project Management Institute's *PMI Guide*.

Project management thrives in an information- and knowledge-intensive environment. Project workers have realized that knowledge in projects is power—only if readily accessible—acquired, organized, analyzed, and delivered to meet the project objectives. With the advances in technology applications, knowledge management has become a fundamental necessity in project management. The ability of knowledge management to focus on the proper access and delivery methods for explicit knowledge on the desktop and also concentrate on tacit knowledge of individuals, which is frequently difficult to locate and retrieve, will be extremely beneficial in project management. Effective knowledge management in projects has the potential to give organizations competitive advantage, increased returns, and innovation.

Knowledge management for the project environment, however, has a sticky wicket to overcome. Perhaps the greatest advantage to good KM in today's projects is that it creates advantages for the management of tomorrow's projects. The problem is that in concentrating on today's projects, it is all too easy to ignore or skimp on the KM practices that will bring advantages to tomorrow's projects. How does an organization get beyond the "one project at a time" mentality? That is a central theme that this book addresses.

This book captures the intricacies of managing knowledge in the project environment. Chapters written by experts in the PM and KM fields cover methodologies, tools and techniques, deployment issues, strategy issues, and relevant case studies.

Acknowledgments

We would like to acknowledge the contributions of the chapter authors. In this rapidly growing field of KM and its convergence to project management, this book would not have been possible without their full cooperation. We would like to thank them not only for their specific chapters but also for the insights, suggestions, and guidance they have provided for the editors. We also would like to thank Jayashree Srikantaiah, Luciana Marulli-Koenig, and Jacqueline Hawamdeh for their support and in assisting with the completion of the manuscript on time. We would like to thank Leslie Cerkoney for preparing the manuscript as specified by the publisher. We would also like to thank the editorial staff at Scarecrow, especially Martin Dillon, consulting editor, who provided valuable and timely guidance and support in the completion of the manuscript.

The Road Map to the Book

A Thematic Guide to the Convergence of Project Management and Knowledge Management

Probably very few readers other than the editors and the editorial staff will read this book in its entirety. Most will come to this book with particular interests in mind and with specific information interests or needs. The intent of this "road map" is to allow entry into the book by subject and theme, at a level of specificity much greater than that of a table of contents but broader and more contextually informative than that provided by a back-of-the-book index. This entry route also provides an analytical guide—a road map that allows one to use the book for researching a specific subject of interest as well as for browsing and pursuing serendipity, and doing either with a real feel for the terrain.

One note is that while the KM literature in general talks about knowledge being either explicit or tacit, we prefer the distinction made by Keen and Tan (2007) between explicit, implicit, and tacit. Explicit knowledge is that information or knowledge that is captured in documentary form. Implicit knowledge is knowledge that is not captured in documentary form but that in practice could be. An example might be the knowledge that despite what the organizational chart might imply, the real decision maker for that realm in that organization is Jane Doe. Tacit knowledge is that knowledge that is not in practice satisfactorily captureable in documentary form. An example might be the knowledge of how to shift a nonsynchromesh transmission. We feel that what is described as tacit in the KM literature is often not really tacit, but implicit, as it could well be captured. However, since we prefer not to rewrite what chapter authors have written, you will find both conventions used.

HIGHLIGHTS

- The K-Index, a single aggregate measure of the state of practice of KM in a project (or business unit) that is used at Infosys, discussed in chapter 9 by Latha, Suresh, and Mahesh. A questionnaire used for compilation of the index is included as an appendix to the chapter.

- The tableau of project management phases alongside appropriate knowledge action steps, and the tableau of the knowledge champion life cycle alongside the "nurturing action steps" that the knowledge champion should be undertaking, both in chapter 18 by Shobha and Potta.
- The delineation of the breadth and extent of KM activities at Infosys in support of project management, set out in chapter 17 by Srikantaiah. In particular, the discussion of Infosys's KCU (knowledge currency unit) for promoting and providing incentive for knowledge sharing bears examination.

CHECKLISTS

- Latha, Suresh, and Mahesh (chapter 9) provide a list of lessons learned, and this serves as a useful checklist.
- Sutton (chapter 8) provides a checklist for the possible uses of wikis and the types of information and documents for which a wiki-based system can be useful.
- Rao (chapter 19) provides a brief guide, bibliography, and description of a number of important articles relating to KM in PM.
- Shobha and Potta (chapter 18) provide two useful tableaus, one of project management phases with appropriate knowledge action steps, and the second a tableau of the knowledge champion life cycle with the "nurturing action steps" that the knowledge champion should be undertaking.
- Srikantaiah (chapter 11) provides checklists of the benefits of KM to PM.
- Hawamdeh, Srikantaiah, and Koenig (chapter 1) provide a checklist of potential KM benefits for project management.
- Srikantaiah's extensive list of "gaps and issues" at Infosys serves as a highly useful checklist of both problems and future directions (chapter 11).
- Sutton (chapter 8) provides an enumeration of the various kinds of documentation that should be anticipated in project management KM.
- Bedford (chapter 15) provides checklists for the information contents of a BOKOS, a business-oriented knowledge organization system.
- Both Koenig (chapter 2) and Jones and Stephens (chapter 14) provide lists of key social networking tools.

OBSTACLES AND STUMBLING BLOCKS

A number of chapters identify obstacles and stumbling blocks. A perusal of these chapters yields a useful checklist—useful either for the initiation of new projects or as an overview checklist for your organization to see where you stand overall in your capacity to support effective KM in the project environment.

- Tryon and Hawamdeh (chapter 6) identify a number of issues and focus particularly on inadequate training programs and policies and upon the importance of keeping the key assets, employees, unseparated, that is, not overburdening employees with multiple assignments, and in particular not simultaneously assigning project roles and general support roles. They also stress minimizing staff interruptibility.

- Kasten (chapter 12), in a related vein, points out the need for some slack in staff assignments; otherwise, attention to KM tends to fall by the wayside.
- Morales-Arroyo, Chang, and Sanchez-Guerrero (chapter 4) set out the difference between traditional projects and unconventional projects and in the process identify roadblocks. They emphasize in particular the failure to modularize and thereby reduce project scope as a major stumbling block.
- Fonseca and Fonseca (chapter 16) list and discuss obstacles to the creation of a KM system for project information at the World Bank.

ALIGNMENT: KM TO THE PROJECT

- Kasten (chapter 12) emphasizes analyzing the knowledge strategy of your organization or the appropriate business unit to see where the project fits, what KM is in place, and what supplemental systems need to be constructed.
- Neubauer and Barachini (chapter 5) provide a discussion of the KM tools they found to be useful in their project.
- White (chapter 3) discusses alignment in the context of requirements management and the impact of that upon the larger project.

ALIGNMENT: KM TO THE PROJECT PHASES

- Morales-Arroyo, Chang, and Sanchez-Guerrero (chapter 4) set out (1) a useful tableau linking KM processes to project phases and (2) a tableau linking the selection of KM tools for project management with project phases.
- Shobha and Potta (chapter 18) heavily emphasize alignment, and they provide a useful setting out of the project management phases alongside appropriate knowledge action steps.
- Latha, Suresh, and Mahesh (chapter 9) discuss the role of KM in specific project phases and how to fit KM to those stages.
- White (chapter 3) specifically discusses the requirements management aspect/phase of project management.

LINKING PROJECT KNOWLEDGE TO FUTURE PROJECTS

The theme that project knowledge needs to be captured and made accessible for the success of future projects and for the long-range good of the organization is a theme referred to frequently. That problem is highlighted in the introductory chapter by the editors of the book.

- Bedford (chapter 15), writes on developing a BOKOS, a business-oriented knowledge organization system, and discusses providing the framework to tie current project knowledge to the future.

- Shobha and Potta (chapter 18) put great emphasis upon developing project-oriented KM into a "knowledge ecology" for the organization as a whole.
- Fonseca and Fonseca's (chapter 16) chapter on KM development at the World Bank is entirely driven by this objective.

IMPLICIT AND TACIT: PERSON TO PERSON

Not surprisingly, many chapters emphasize the importance of the transfer of knowledge, particularly implicit and tacit knowledge, in a person-to-person mode.

- Swain (chapter 7) makes a compelling case for the importance of summarization (the "presentation or summary cognitive mode"), the technique of holding group meetings to explicitly present and review "where are we now?"
- Kasten (chapter 10) points out the necessity, insofar as possible, for the location of implicit and tacit knowledge to be identified and the consequent responsibility of the team leader to undertake that task.
- Koenig (chapter 2) stresses the importance of your organization's information stars, gatekeepers, and boundary spanners, for successful implementation of KM in the project environment. Specifically, he stresses the need to identify them before you assemble your project team to ensure that your team has at least one such person. He also emphasizes fostering and supporting your organization's information stars.
- Hawamdeh, Srikantaiah, and Koenig (chapter 1) point out the importance of capturing information at the time, or shortly after, events happen. Subsequent, more formal reports are often sanitized, embarrassing events glossed over, and the lessons learned obscured.
- Kasten (chapter 12) similarly points out the need to capture tacit and implicit knowledge "when and where."
- Srikantaiah (chapter 17) describes Infosys's techniques for capturing implicit and tacit knowledge, including communities of practice, coaching, mentoring, debriefing, and oral history.

SOCIAL NETWORKS

- Koenig (chapter 2) points out the utility of SNA tools to identify your organization's information stars, gatekeepers, and boundary spanners to facilitate the assembling of an effective project team.
- The use of wikis as collaboration tools for projects is increasing rapidly. Sutton (chapter 8) discusses the use of wikis in some detail. His chapter serves as a discussion, a review of the literature, and a call for action on research relating to the use of wikis in KM and PM.
- Jones and Stephens (chapter 14) provide a guide to social networking tools for KM use in PM, with a list of actions that should be undertaken to enhance use of social network tools in KM.
- Srikantaiah (chapter 17) discusses the use of SNA tools, particularly wikis, at Infosys.

- Both Koenig (chapter 2) and Jones and Stephens (chapter 14) provide lists of key social networking tools.
- Rao (chapter 19) also discusses blogs, particularly k-logs, knowledge blogs.

KNOWLEDGE ORGANIZATION PLAN

- Kasten (chapter 10) points out the need for a knowledge organization plan and discusses a number of issues in developing such a plan.
- Bedford's (chapter 15) BOKOS, business-oriented knowledge organization system, makes the same point and adds a checklist for the type of information that needs to be incorporated in a BOKOS.

KM ROLES IN PROJECT MANAGEMENT

- Latha, Suresh, and Mahesh (chapter 9) describe a number of key roles for KM in project management:

  - KM SPOC (single point of contact)
  - KM patron
  - KM anchor
  - KM prime

  Each of these roles is described in some detail.

- Shobha and Potta (chapter 18) describe the role of the knowledge champion at Perot Systems, and they provide a tableau of the knowledge champion life cycle with the "nurturing action steps" that the knowledge champion should be undertaking.
- Koenig (chapter 2) focuses on the role of the information stars, gatekeepers, and boundary spanners in facilitating knowledge transfer within the team and across the organization, and upon the importance of locating and assigning such persons to project teams before the project is launched.
- Kasten (chapter 10) points out the responsibility of a project team leader to locate where tacit and implicit knowledge is likely to be found and to use that knowledge to design the knowledge organization plan for the project.

STRATEGY DEVELOPMENT FOR KM FOR PM

- Neubauer and Barachini (chapter 5) provide a discussion of the KM tools that they found to be useful in their strategy development project.
- Srikantaiah (chapter 17) includes a discussion of the KM strategy management process at Infosys used to develop its extensive suite of KM applications for project management.

- Bedford (chapter 15) on developing business-oriented knowledge organization systems (BOKOS) is inherently about strategy to a high degree. A BOKOS can be, and serves well as, the basis for strategy.

STORYTELLING

- The chapter by Marek (chapter 13) is obviously about storytelling, but the theme appears and is emphasized elsewhere as well. She focuses on storytelling not just as a way of communicating knowledge and lessons learned, but also on the utility of storytelling as a tool to lead a group of people through a process. And, of course, one very cogent way of looking at project management is that it consists of leading a group of people through a process.
- Rao (chapter 19) discusses k-logs, knowledge blogs, as a tool for storytelling.

KM CULTURE

- Srikantaiah (chapter 17) describes Infosys's KCU (knowledge currency unit) for promoting and providing incentive for knowledge sharing and bears examination.
- Shobha and Potta (chapter 18) discuss the creation and development of a knowledge ecosystem, the creation of a knowledge-sharing culture, and extending it from the project domain to the larger organization overall.

MEASURING KM

How to metrify KM or its impacts is always an issue of great interest, but a difficult one to accomplish or deal with. The difficulty of measuring or quantifying knowledge impact is precisely why there is such emphasis upon storytelling in both the KM literature and in the practice of KM.

- Latha, Suresh, and Mahesh (chapter 9) present the concept of the K-Index, a single aggregate measure of the maturity of the state of practice of KM in a project (or business unit), that is used at Infosys. Appendix 2 to their chapter presents a questionnaire used to compile the K-Index.
- Srikantaiah (chapter 17) describes the KCU (knowledge currency unit) used at Infosys to promote and incentivize knowledge sharing.

VOCABULARY AND TAXONOMY ISSUES

- Fonseca and Fonseca's chapter (chapter 16) on KM development at the World Bank discusses these issues in some depth.
- Bedford's chapter (chapter 15) on developing a business-oriented knowledge organization system is centered on vocabulary and taxonomy issues.
- White (chapter 3) discusses taxonomy issues, particularly in the context of requirements management.

CASE STUDY DESCRIPTIONS

In addition to those specifically labeled as such in the table of contents, case studies appear elsewhere in the book.

- The World Bank is discussed in Srikantaiah (chapter 17).
- Swain (chapter 7) presents case studies from an unnamed business corporation and an unnamed university.

TRAINING

Training is an important issue for KM, but a particularly underrecognized one. That danger of underrecognition is particularly acute for KM in project management, where the pressures of comparatively short project life cycles and the inevitable tendency to focus upon the project and to not look very far ahead beyond the lifetime of the project often makes training appear to be a postponable luxury. The classic exposition of the underrecognition of the importance of training in KM is Koenig's (2001) reanalysis of a major study of KM implementation conducted by KPMG. The KPMG study revealed a very high failure rate for the implementation of KM projects, and it inadvertently, paradoxically, and compellingly revealed the underrecognition of the importance of user training and education for KM. The data from their analysis revealed the importance of user training and education, but the analysts at KPMG totally failed to see that importance. The reexamination of their data is supplied as an addendum below.

What jumps out clearly when the data is properly analyzed is that inadequate user education and training accounts for more KM failures than all the other tabulated reasons combined. Several chapters in this book address the problem of training:

- Tryon and Hawamdeh (chapter 6) emphasize the importance of training and identify inadequate attention to training as a major stumbling block.
- Latha, Suresh, and Mahesh (chapter 9) point out the importance of KM awareness for the project team and the need for specific KM training to create that awareness.
- Kasten (chapter 10) points out the importance of including training as a key factor in the knowledge organization plan for a project.
- Srikantaiah (chapter 17) describes the training undertaken at Infosys and Infosys's perception that KM should be more involved.

ADDENDUM: THE KPMG STUDY PROPERLY ANALYZED

The reasons for KM failure as presented by KPMG are shown in figure 1.

When it is recognized that reasons 1, 3, and 4 are all functionally the same thing—inadequate user education and training—then the table can be recast in a much more informative and compelling fashion. The revised KPMG study lists the reasons for KM failures (see figure 2).

The Reasons for KM Failure as presented by KPMG:

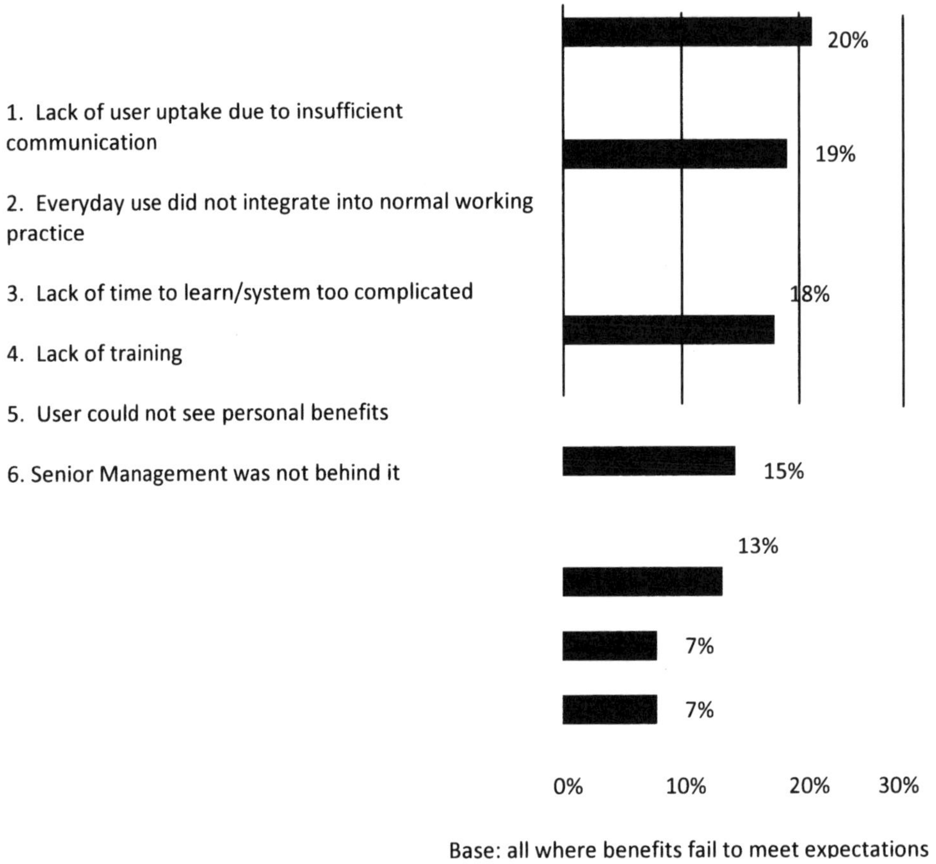

Figure 1. Reasons for KM Failure as Presented by KPMG

What now jumps out clearly is that inadequate user education and training accounts for more failures than all other reasons combined.

REFERENCES

Keen, Peter, & Tan, Margaret. (2007). Knowledge fusion: A framework for extending the rigor and relevance of knowledge management. *International Journal of Knowledge Management, 3*(4), 1–17.

Koenig, Michael E. D. (2001). User education for KM—The problem we won't recognize. *KM World, 10*(10), 24–26

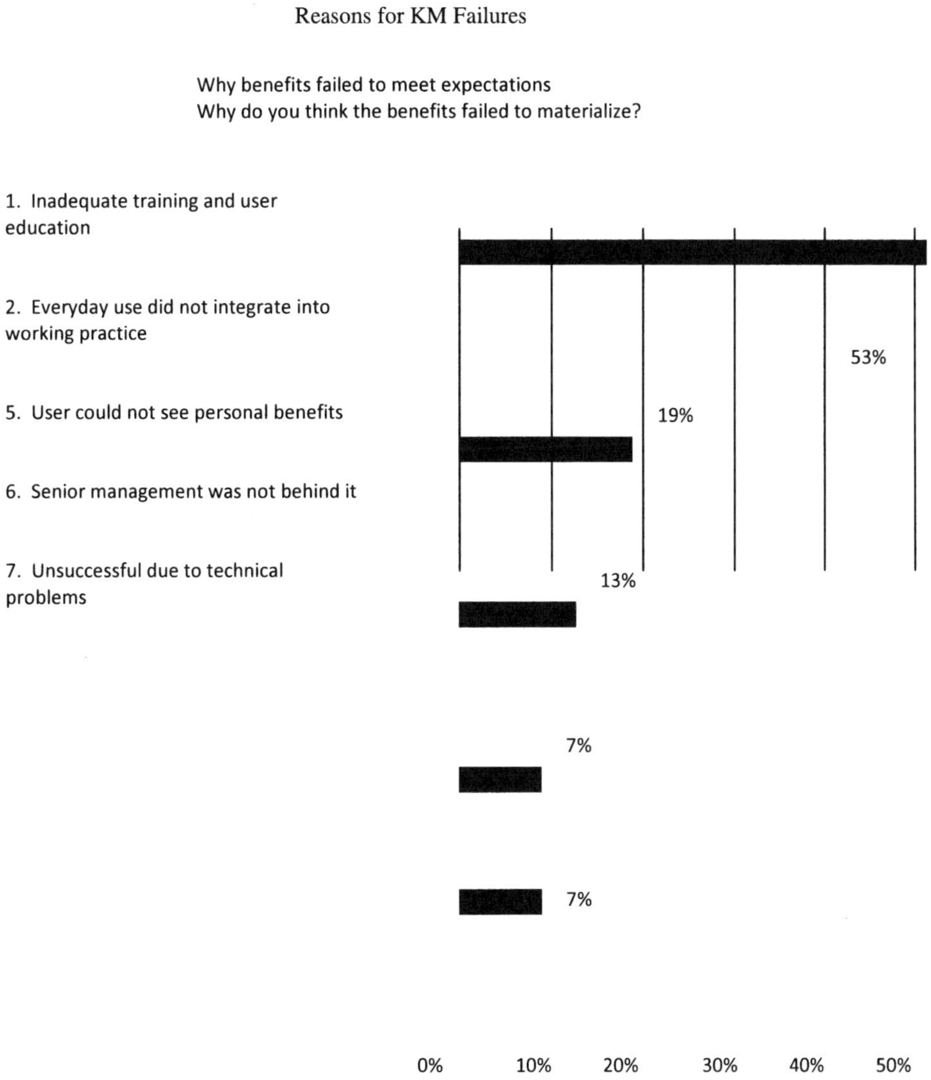
Reasons for KM Failures
Why benefits failed to meet expectations
Why do you think the benefits failed to materialize?
1. Inadequate training and user education
2. Everyday use did not integrate into working practice
5. User could not see personal benefits
6. Senior management was not behind it
7. Unsuccessful due to technical problems
53%
19%
13%
7%
7%
0%
10%
20%
30%
40%
50%

Figure 2. Revised KPMG Study

Companies and Organizations Mentioned in Chapters

ABS	Neubauer and Barachini (chapter 5)
Accenture	Rao (chapter 19)
American Library Association	Jones and Stephens (chapter 14)
APQC (American Productivity Quality Center)	Srikantaiah (chapter 11)
Avondale Shipyards	Marek (chapter 13)
Bank of Montreal	Rao (chapter 19)
Buckman Labs	Hawamdeh, Srikantaiah, and Koenig (chapter 1); Rao (chapter 19)
Chevron	Rao (chapter 19)
Context Integration	Rao (chapter 19)
Dutch Tax and Customs Administration	Tryon & Hawamdeh (chapter 6)
Ernst & Young	Rao (chapter 19)
Ford Motor Co.	Rao (chapter 19)
Fujitsu Consulting	Rao (chapter 19)
Google	Jones and Stephens (chapter 14)
Hughes Corporation	White (chapter 3)
i2 India	Rao (chapter 19)
i-Flex	Rao (chapter 19)
Infosys	Lahta, Suresh, and Mahesh (chapter 9); Srikantaiah (chapter 17); Rao (chapter 19)
Johnson & Johnson	Marek (chapter 13)
Matsushita	Hawamdeh, Srikantaiah, and Koenig (chapter 1)
NASA	Rao (chapter 19)
Oracle	Rao (chapter 19)
Perot Systems	Shobha and Potta (chapter 18)

Project Management Institute	Hawamdeh, Srikantaiah, and Koenig (chapter 1); Sutton (chapter 8); Kasten (chapters 10 and 12); Srikantaiah (chapter 11); Jones and Stephens (chapter 14)
Philippine System Products	Rao (chapter 19)
QAI India	Rao (chapter 19)
SAS	Rao (chapter 19)
Siemens	Rao (chapter 19)
Sun Microsystems	Rao (chapter 19)
Sun Microsystems Philippines	Rao (chapter 19)
Syngenta	Rao (chapter 19)
Tandem Computers	Rao (chapter 19)
Texas Instruments	Rao (chapter 19)
Union Square Cafe	Marek (chapter 13)
U.S. Army	Srikantaiah (chapter 11)
World Bank	Srikantaiah (chapter 11); Marek (chapter 13); Fonseca and Fonseca (chapter 16); Rao (chapter 19)
Xerox	Marek (chapter 13)

I

Introduction

1

Convergence of Project Management and Knowledge Management

An Overview

Suliman Hawamdeh, T. Kanti Srikantaiah, and Michael E. D. Koenig

Knowledge is crucial for development and economic growth. Much of what people do while working on projects today involves decisions that need to be made on the spot. Workers must now be able to acquire and apply theoretical and analytical knowledge. Workers need to think and learn because innovation and idea generation depend not so much on the volume of information as on the connections that link it and give it greater meaning. Peter Drucker (1988), almost universally recognized as the preeminent management thinker of the twentieth century, referred to knowledge as the only meaningful economic resource of the postcapitalist or knowledge society. The creation and use of knowledge in today's competitive business environment is an organizational challenge. Knowledge and expertise are normally dispersed throughout the organization and are often closely held by individuals or work units. In project-based organizations, the task of managing knowledge is even harder given the typically discrete nature of projects and their lack of continuity. One of the main obstacles to learning on projects is being unable to identify existing knowledge and build on it rather than reinventing the wheel. The ability to learn from previous experience and consequently to innovate quickly is key to enhancing performance and productivity and achieving competitive success.

Project management involves planning, organizing, and managing the resources needed to bring about a successful conclusion. The most important resources that need to be managed skillfully are the expertise, skills, and competencies of the people working on the project. Unlike most repetitive and permanent operations within an organization, projects are limited by time and funding. They are undertaken to meet certain goals and objectives and yet remain within the constraints of time and funding. Several approaches to project management include agile, interactive, incremental, and phased approaches. The traditional approaches to project management are built on a sequence of stages: project initiation, planning and design, execution and production, monitoring and controlling, completion, and project post mortem. Not all projects go through a systematic process or follow the typical project management stages and phases. The levels of detail in each step may also vary from one project to another. Most information or knowledge management undertaken to support projects is focused almost entirely on the information needed to control the project and remain on time and within budget. That narrow approach risks leaving important and critical details and thinking vital to successfully completing the project in silos unconnected to the project. More often than not, the results are project failure, delays, cost increases, and lost opportunities.

One critical aspect of project management is managing project resources. Project resources normally include people, equipment, material, time, and money. The most problematic and difficult aspect of managing project resources is managing people. Managing people requires having the right people with the right skills and competencies as well as a thorough understanding of what needs to be done on the project. The most important aspect of managing people may well be managing the knowledge resources, the tacit knowledge needed to get the job done. Managing people on projects is no longer a zero-sum game. To be successful, the manager will be required to "deploy" the knowledge resource (knowledge worker) where that worker's specialized knowledge can make the greatest contribution.

The twenty-first century paradigm of management will require business to do the right thing, and instead of there being one right way to organize an organization's structure, that organization will have to recognize each individual's own strengths and areas of expertise and find ways to make each person productive. It is now clear that the advances in information and communication technologies, the Internet and the Web, enable knowledge workers to adequately do their jobs less and less bound by the strictures of physical time and space. The production and utilization of knowledge can be perpetuated through workers in different time zones and locations without the need for a central office. The burgeoning of information technologies has enabled organizations to decentralize and focus more on meeting the needs of customers rather than maintaining physical structures.

Knowledge workers and project management professionals, on the other hand, are people who make their living using the knowledge they possess rather than through manual labor. Knowledge workers consider themselves "professionals rather than employees," which changes the way that organizations structure their projects, clearly shifting away from the traditional model of "boss and subordinate." The new generation of knowledge and project professionals identify themselves by the knowledge they possess. They identify themselves in terms of the field in which they work rather than the organization at which they work. This tends to minimize the hierarchy in the workplace, as specialized knowledge is increasingly valued no matter the class of the possessor. All these factors create problems for management systems that are currently in place. Many knowledge workers and knowledge professionals do not feel loyalty to the particular organization for which they work, but rather to their particular type of knowledge and the profession to which they belong. They might choose to leave a job if they feel that their skills are undervalued or that they will be better off at another organization. "Most of them probably feel that they have more in common with someone who practices the same specialty in another institution than with their colleagues at their own institution who work in a different knowledge area" (Drucker, 2008).

In the knowledge society, it is increasingly the case that the organization needs the knowledge workers more than the knowledge workers need the organization. If the organization persists in enforcing older styles of management and the knowledge workers feel that they are not treated fairly and with respect, they may move on to other organizations or to another project. Many organizations are realizing this fact and are slowly changing their management styles to reflect this change in society. An example of such a company is Google, which is consistently presented as one of the top ten places at which to work. As a practice, they allow their employees time during office hours to work on projects of their own choosing. Many of their projects, such as Gmail and Google Earth, have come out of projects that employees were doing for fun.

DRIVER AND ENABLERS OF KM

Managing knowledge in projects is gaining more and more importance due to the advances in information and communication technologies and the need to deal with information overload. Project management is an information-intensive activity, and information or knowledge generated during the project is either archived or by default often destroyed, or at best it becomes difficult to retrieve tacit information locked away in a silo. Information management during the project life cycle is extremely important. But it also important to remember that information is not knowledge unless that information is organized and processed in a meaningful way. Nowadays information overload is a serious problem. While technology facilitates generating and organizing information, it can also impede efficiency and affect productivity.

Managing knowledge in projects is important and critical for several reasons. One is the advancement in communication technologies, the Internet and the Web. Mobile devices as well as easy connectivity to the Internet have changed the way we do business and have altered working life. The benefits of harnessing this technology to manage knowledge have given a competitive advantage to organizations that effectively succeed in managing their knowledge assets. In today's work environment, our work life revolves around these technologies.

The second reason is the exploding nature of information, particularly online information. Gone are the days where we had almost all information packages in hard-copy format (on paper). With thousands of websites, search engines, e-mail programs, and so on, digital information is replacing print on paper in most areas. Digital information is growing each day and has become part of our culture. As the proportion of electronic information versus hard-copy information becomes ever greater, knowledge management has become a functional necessity.

The third reason is that organizations have to compete for their survival through projects. These days, organizations are acquired, merged, and claim bankruptcy if they do not successfully compete with others in their industry. Increasingly, many projects are operating at the global level, which poses yet more complex strategic challenges. In order to stay competitive and survive, organizations are making knowledge management a priority in projects.

The fourth reason is regulatory reforms at the national level, and in this fast-growing global environment, organizations have realized that the culture of managing projects should change from hoarding to sharing of knowledge. The knowledge management systems that are set up in projects are designed to promote a knowledge-sharing culture. Collaboration among various members of the project team in a synergic way increases trust and morale, resulting in success of the project. It also cuts costs and fulfills the goals and objectives of the project more effectively. Knowledge management plays a key role in accomplishing this.

The fifth reason knowledge management is so crucial is that in a project environment, organizations are influenced by the external economic conditions and internal political conditions (management styles). The current environment drives organizations to increase productivity using fewer resources. To do this, knowledge in projects needs to be managed properly. Knowledge management experts must set up knowledge management systems in projects to accomplish the objective of increasing productivity and collaboration even while resources are cut.

At the organizational and project level, knowledge management is attributed to organizational and project assets. Over the past few years, knowledge management has emerged explosively through an interdisciplinary approach dealing with all aspects of knowledge in the organization, including knowledge creation, codification, organization, and sharing. This has a wide application in the project environment. The knowledge assets in the project environment may include databases, documents, and policies and procedures, as well as the previously untapped expertise of individual workers.

Knowledge management addresses the problem of inaccessibility of knowledge in projects and their inadequacy, poor quality, and poor organization. It focuses both on the proper access and delivery methods for explicit knowledge on the desktop, and it also concentrates on implicit knowledge that is frequently difficult to locate and retrieve and whose existence is often functionally unknown. The knowledge management challenge and perspective in projects is to look at assets in a new way at the organizational level, which includes: employees and staff, customers, databases, documents, products, processes, and services.

Looking at project knowledge, Davenport and Laurence's (2000) continuum concept seems relevant. According to them, knowledge management starts with data, which is based on raw facts, figures, or statistics. When these raw facts are contextualized, categorized, calculated, corrected, and condensed, it leads to codification and becomes explicit, or information. When this information is applied by users through comparisons, conversations, and connections, it becomes knowledge. In other words, knowledge focuses on experience, values, and the context in which information is applied to a message and thus embraces both explicit and implicit knowledge. The last segment of the knowledge management continuum is wisdom, which reflects on sound and effective decisions made based on knowledge. Wisdom is a collective application of knowledge in action by wise men and women. In projects, decision making results from data, information, knowledge, and the experience of individuals, all of which are ultimately reflected in the decisions made.

The problem with the data-information-knowledge-wisdom (DIKW) hierarchy, or what some refer to as the knowledge hierarchy, is the transformation from information to knowledge and vice versa. Information is not knowledge unless it is fully understood and acted upon. It is the combination of actionable information, experience, and insight that enables individuals to make good and sound decisions. Decision making is a knowledge process that combines actionable information, experience, and insight. Knowledge, on the other hand, can be viewed as a competency that can be developed and improved over time. Appropriate investment in knowledge requires a keen understanding of knowledge management processes and practices. The ability to distinguish between information and knowledge enables organization to assess their return on investment when implementing knowledge management. Al-Hawamdeh (2003) used the utilization pyramid shown in figure 1.1 to illustrate the return on investment in knowledge management. Traditionally, organizations invest heavily in infrastructure such as information systems, networking, hardware, software; databases, and so on, and they invest rather less in activities such as knowledge sharing and knowledge utilization. This is largely due to the intangible nature of these activities and the difficulty in justifying expenses in these areas.

It is much easier for managers to justify costs for more equipment or tools for doing the job. It is harder to justify expenses in areas of an intangible nature such as knowledge sharing, best practices, and knowledge utilization, even though the return on investment in these areas is often much higher. While investment in steps 1 and 2 of the utilization pyramid is important, the return on investment in these areas is low. As we go up the ladder to steps 3 and 4, it becomes difficult for managers to justify expenses in these areas, although the return on investment is higher. Steps 3 and 4 are important to the organization's survival in the knowledge economy. Sustaining growth and staying competitive in the knowledge economy

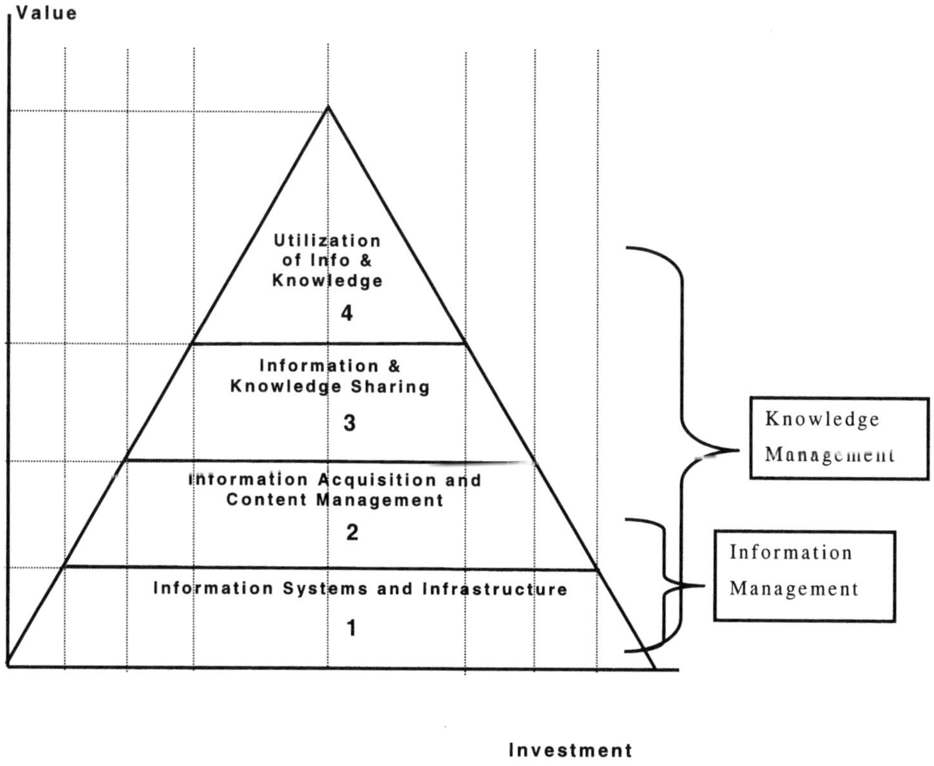

Figure 1.1. Utilization Pyramid

requires greater investment in less-tangible areas such as knowledge sharing and knowledge utilization. For such investment to happen, and for organizations to take advantage of the resulting growth, organizations need to have a better understanding of knowledge management processes and practices.

This is just as true in the project management area. Managers are normally consumed with the project details such as project scheduling, budgeting, material, personnel, and deliverables. It is easy to overlook or give short shrift to the fact that for the project to be completed on time and on schedule, people working on the project must cooperate, share information, and put their knowledge competencies to work. Most of the time, a project fails for reasons beyond the physical resources allocated to the project. Project failure most often has to do with people and the inability to manage the knowledge competencies needed to carry out the project. Knowledge sharing and knowledge utilization are key to effectively managing the knowledge resources in any project.

Realizing the importance of knowledge competencies in the new economy, organizations will start to embark on knowledge management initiatives to enhance their productivity and maintain competitiveness. In doing so, they will first require knowledge management performance measurements to help them assess the effectiveness of their knowledge management initiatives, and they next will require knowledge management professionals or champions who will guide the knowledge management implementation within the organization. Given the high value that can be derived from knowledge management activities, organizations hope to make these practices part of their daily operations. They hope to recruit new breeds of knowledge professionals who can help them maximize the return on their investment.

FOSTERING A KNOWLEDGE CULTURE

In this dynamically changing project environment where managers are expected to deliver more using less, one of the most challenging things an organization must do is protect and utilize its knowledge assets. The issue of the balance between protection and ease of utilization is a tricky one. Therefore, managing knowledge, both explicit and tacit, is an important function in project management. But before any change can happen, the organizational culture must facilitate and encourage knowledge management processes and practices. In particular, the environment must be conducive enough to facilitate knowledge generating, sharing, and collaboration. Duffy (1999) suggests that a knowledge-friendly environment should exhibit the following organizational attributes:

- Policies that encourage contribution and use of the KM system, according to the employees' learning styles;
- Procedures that allow use of employee's knowledge;
- Processes that enhance communication, collaboration, and creativity, which allow communities of interest to flourish;
- A management style that creates an open atmosphere whereby employees are sufficiently comfortable to question what is done and the way things are done;
- Business processes that embed, incorporate, and promote KM processes.

Most of the time, an organization's culture can be judged through structure, leadership, management style, and the organization's norms and practices. These parameters contribute significantly to the organization's overall behavior. Organizational structure reflects the arrangement of relationships, communication patterns, authority, and workflow within an organization. Organizational culture is normally reflected in the organization's structure, stories, norms, and practices. Multilayered hierarchies or flat structures say something about the core values that directed the organization's designers and the consequent expectations of its members. A mechanistic organization characterized by tall structure and narrow spans of control tends to be bureaucratic. Decision is centralized, and communication channels tend to be top-down. Such an organization is slow when responding to change, as information has to cascade down or up, level by level, often becoming distorted and delayed along the way. It is well recognized that steep functional hierarchies create cultures of distrust in which member participation is minimized and discouraged. Wenger, McDermott & Snyder (2002) classify this as an "anti-learning culture." In such organizations, communities of practice, one of the most important tools of KM, are marginalized and their effectiveness limited. Organizational hierarchy could hinder the learning culture that facilitates knowledge generation, diffusion, coordination, and control.

On the other hand, organic structures are less rigid and decision making is decentralized. Communication channels are less formal, and the flow of information is controlled and mandated only by the functional requirements and the organizational process. In network organizations, dynamic processes and fluid teams replace rigid organizational lines. This in turn promotes the knowledge sharing and collaboration that allow KM to flourish.

For knowledge management to be successful, management's commitment and continued support at all levels is important. Beckman (1999) highlights the importance of management support in channeling resources and giving direction. Unambiguous support from direct managers is an important enabler of knowledge sharing. For example, at Buckman Labs, the CEO created a knowledge transfer department and built K'Netix—a computer platform for sharing information. He appointed systems operators to monitor discussions in the forums and participated personally in these discussions. Buckman management also provided substantial financial support to the whole process.

Convincing people to come forward and share their knowledge is considered a daunting, nontrivial task due to the fact that sharing what one knows is often perceived to be a loss of power. The norms and practices of the organization play a significant role as they may serve to promote or destroy knowledge sharing. Culture embodies all unspoken rules about how knowledge is created, shared, and transferred. It determines who is expected to have what knowledge, who must share it, and who can hoard it or should maintain it. An organization's culture may condone hoarding knowledge, treating it as a source of power, impeding knowledge transfer and sharing among the employees. Culture determines the frequency and expectations for interactions needed to accomplish work (Long, 1997). These practices may consist of formal communication processes such as periodic face-to-face meetings, fairs, conferences, or unplanned interactions such as bumping into each other in the pantry or during a break. Regardless of how sophisticated a technological infrastructure is, without cultural norms and practices supporting a high level of interactivity, new communication channels will have little effect in knowledge transfer and use.

Davenport & Prusak (2000) highlighted several cultural factors that inhibit knowledge transfer. They include lack of trust, lack of time and meeting places, status and rewards going to knowledge owners, lack of absorptive capacity in recipients, belief that knowledge is a prerogative of particular groups (not-invented-here syndrome), intolerance for mistakes, or the expression of a need for help. They describe these factors as "frictions to knowledge transfer." They emphasize the importance of trust as a key element in knowledge sharing and knowledge transfer. The contributor of knowledge has to trust that the recipients will not misuse the knowledge and will give the contributor the rightful credit, while the recipient has to trust the credibility, competence, and good intent of the source of knowledge. An organization that practices fairness and transparency with regard to knowledge sharing fosters trust in its culture. Trustful environments will, perhaps inadvertently but very importantly, encourage people to share their expertise, facilitating knowledge transfer and organizational learning. This may be the most important by-product of a trusting environment.

Rewards and incentive systems serve as tools in molding behavior, and in most cases they are reflective of the knowledge culture within the organization. Rewards can take many forms, such as monetary, recognition, time off, empowerment, work selection, advancement, and so on. Rewards should come early and often, and they should promote desired behaviors, such as collaborating, experimenting, risk taking, and learning. Unfortunately, more often than not, corporations tend to reward safe, bureaucratic behavior rather than the risk-taking, individualistic behavior that is typical of innovators. Drucker (2000) and Horibes (1999) contend that knowledge workers having more autonomy and responsibility in their work are more likely to commit and contribute to organizational goals. Having a challenging and autonomous work environment creates the conditions where employees are intrinsically motivated to engage in productive and goal-oriented behavior.

Another important aspect of knowledge culture is the organization's ability to recognize workforce diversity and align work process to accommodate it. Can the organization adopt a working group culture in which people with different knowledge and experience come together to solve problems? According to Nonaka and Takeuchi (1995), an effective working group is one of the necessary conditions for knowledge creation. Organizations with good working group practices benefit from a larger pool of ideas, and that in turn prevents the group from falling into routine solutions to problems. They cite the success of Matsushita in developing its first automatic bread-making machines using the idea of a working group. Matsushita combined three product divisions with different subcultures, realizing that it needed the variety of knowledge possessed by those different groups. The new product combined the efforts of computer-control expertise, experience with induction heater technology, and rotating motor technology. The collaboration of expertise brought the new product into fruition.

For KM to be successful, the organization must be pro-learning. Learning facilitates the generation of new knowledge and promotes knowledge sharing and use. Organizations can support learning through formal and informal training, through experience, and most importantly, through learning from mistakes. Management support in terms of time and financial resources is a critical factor in creating a knowledge culture. A culture with high levels of trust removes major obstacles against knowledge sharing and collaboration. Trust must be built both at the employer-employee level and among employees. Since knowledge is power, the employee has to be convinced that the benefits of sharing outweigh the cost of losing "power." This needs to tie in with the reward and recognition system in the organization. The practice of rewarding and recognition is important to ensure the repetition of desired behavior, that is, behavior that supports sharing expertise and knowledge. The system must be visible enough for an employee to assimilate and should be one that rewards both individual effort and group effort, so as to bring people forward.

KM APPLICATIONS IN PROJECT MANAGEMENT

Knowledge management is applicable to projects and the project environment in several areas and stages:

- The first area is driven by IT and the realization of the importance of Internet technologies such as intranets, knowledge portals, and social software. Organizations, particularly the large international organizations, realized that their stock is information and knowledge, that often the left hand, as it were, had no idea what the right hand knew, and that if they could share that knowledge, they would avoid reinventing the wheel and increase profits. This resulted in applying IT to the fullest extent and concentrating on the intellectual capital and the Internet (including intranets, extranets, and so on). The key phrase here is "best practices" later replaced by "lessons learned." In many projects knowledge is still managed in this fashion.
- The second area is recognizing the human and cultural dimensions. "If you build it, they will come" is not sufficient. A too heavily technological approach could be a recipe for disaster if human factors are not sufficiently taken into account. With this in mind, two major themes from the business literature were brought into the KM fold. The first was a work by Senge, 1990 on the learning organization, and the second that by Nonaka and others on tacit knowledge. The hallmark of this stage is "communities of practice,"
- The third stage is the awareness of the importance of content, and in particular, awareness of the importance of knowledge organization. The theme in this area is "It's no good if they can't find it." The hallmark of this area is "content management," which includes taxonomies, ontologies, metadata, and so on.
- The fourth area involves the use of advanced tools and technologies to enhance performance and maintain competitiveness. Some of the tools of KM relevant for application here are competitive intelligence, environmental scanning, and knowledge auditing.

There are several phases to a project life cycle. According to the *PMBOK Guide* (Project Management Institute, 2004), projects can be divided into phases to provide better management control. Collectively, these phases become the project life cycle. Many organizations identify a specific set of life cycles for use in their projects. However, all project life cycles connect the beginning of a project to its end. There is no single best way to define the ideal project life cycle. Some organizations have established policies that standardize all projects with a single life cycle, while others allow the project management team to choose the most appropriate life cycle for the team's project. Project life cycles generally cover areas such as the technical work needed to be completed in each phase, deliverables generated in each phase, and the people involved in the planning and control of each phase.

Knowledge management activities as described above are part and parcel of each stage in the project life cycle. For example, the first phase of the project lifecycle involves identification of a problem or need. At this stage, needs analysis and assessment is carried out to determine the scope of the project and the size of the problem. This is also the stage at which knowledge gaps can be identified and made part of the overall assessment of the user's needs. Every project is unique with start and end dates, detailed project plans, budget, schedule, human resources, technology infrastructure, and deliverables, and all these areas have rich knowledge content. The *PMBOK Guide* identifies nine knowledge areas that are important to the success of any project:

1. **Project integration management.** Deals with project knowledge concerning choices of where to concentrate resources during the project. It includes the knowledge of processes and activities to identify, define, combine, coordinate, and integrate the various activities.
2. **Project scope management.** Project knowledge describing the processes involved in ascertaining that the project includes all the work required and only the work required to complete the project successfully. It includes scope planning, scope definition, and work breakdown structure. Knowledge boundaries are defined in clear terms.
3. **Project time management.** Project knowledge describing the processes concerning timely completion of the project. It includes activity definition, activity sequencing, and activity resource estimating. Knowledge of the logical sequence of activities in projects is essential.
4. **Project cost management.** Project knowledge concerning the process to ensure that the project is completed within the approved budget. That will include planning, estimating, budgeting, and controlling costs. While primarily concerned with the cost of resources, it should also consider the effect of project decisions through the project life cycle. Knowledge of budget for each activity should be spelled out, and it should be monitored as the project starts.
5. **Project human resources management.** Project knowledge concerning effective management of the project team and others to accomplish the project objectives. Project knowledge in developing teams and team management for the appropriate knowledge culture is included.
6. **Project quality management.** Project knowledge describing the processes involved in assuring that the project will satisfy the objectives for which it was undertaken. Knowledge includes quality planning and performing quality assurance. Knowledge processes may include planning to identify project roles, acquiring project team members through the life of a project, developing skills

and competencies of project team members, and tracking performance. This is a critical area of knowledge management in projects to ensure that deliverables meet the specifications of the client.

7. **Project communications management.** Project knowledge describing the processes concerning the timely and appropriate generation, collection, dissemination, storage, and ultimate disposition of project information. It includes communication planning, information distribution, and performance reporting. This area of knowledge management is critical for project transparency to add value to both current and future projects.
8. **Project risk management.** Project knowledge describing the processes concerned with risk management in a project. It includes knowledge on risk management planning, risk identification, qualitative risk analysis, risk response planning, and risk mitigation. It is not possible to handle these areas unless project knowledge is captured.
9. **Project procurement management.** Project knowledge describing the processes that purchase or acquire products and services, as well as contract management processes. It includes the plans for purchases, acquisitions, plan contracting, selection of sellers, requests for seller responses, and contract administration. Capturing knowledge in projects in these areas is absolutely necessary for successful implementation.

Knowledge is created and flows through all nine areas of project management and in all phases of the project life cycle. Project managers and staff constantly seek knowledge to address various problems: resources, deadlines, deliverables, goals/objectives, team, planning, communications, and conflicts. Traditionally, the emphasis for project management was on developing tools and techniques such as networks and earned value analysis. Now the project management focus has shifted toward managing the knowledge resources in projects including capturing or transferring implicit knowledge. It is the responsibility of senior management staff in organizations to ensure that they create an environment in which projects can and will succeed. By managing knowledge in projects, projects can be successfully completed on time, on budget, and with quality deliverables to satisfy customers. Project teams in organizations need to learn to manage more effectively the knowledge that they acquire and accumulate from their projects so that other projects in organizations can benefit.

Knowledge gained by learning from project failures or successes is vital for long-term sustainability and to compete in the business environment. Projects do not have organizational memory like organizations have, as projects are temporary in nature. Knowledge types in projects may include sector knowledge, technical knowledge, and organization knowledge. Knowledge management helps in all these areas and also helps staff to have a shared vision of the project.

The phenomenon that projects do not have an organic organizational memory in the same sense as organizations and that knowledge from one project can be critical to the success or failure of a later project is a compelling reason for the importance of KM in project management. Organizations are organic; they are "incorporated" bodies in order to give them longevity as people come and go. Their knowledge has longevity. Projects die when they are finished. To "incorporate" their knowledge in the organization is the role of KM. One can argue, therefore, that KM is nowhere more important than in project management.

KM INFLUENCE ON PROJECTS

The knowledge environment in projects is mainly influenced by the culture of the organization, formal and informal organizational policies, staff behavior toward knowledge capture and sharing, knowledge architecture, business processes, and overall strategy. Critical knowledge in projects resides with people. They need to understand the value of knowledge and the value of sharing that knowledge. In this context, Kliem (1999) outlines several positive effects of knowledge management on projects:

- Dealing with "gray" situations with greater confidence
- Encouraging greater collaboration among employees
- Identifying best practices
- Improving the capacity for product and processing innovation
- Increasing the competencies of existing employees
- Minimizing the negative impacts of employee turnover
- Responding cost effectively to rapidly changing environments

In every project, individuals, whether on the project management side or the customer side, carry tacit knowledge that would be valuable to the project. Experienced project managers carry with them the knowledge of many projects, and likewise, members of a project team have implicit knowledge from their own experience. Koskinen (2004) describes knowledge management as a necessity in project management for harnessing the implicit knowledge of all involved in the project. Because project team members share project knowledge, making their communication more effective is the best way to further develop project knowledge. Koskinen goes on to describe four environments in which knowledge management influences project management.

The mechanical project management environment relies primarily on explicit knowledge through a series of clearly defined instructions, tasks, and interpretations. This environment is very likely to use information technology, which is certainly a particularly good model for a project involving geographically dispersed teams.

The organic project management environment is more likely to rely on implicit knowledge. Information is ambiguous, tasks are inconsistent, and change is constant, so nonlinear problem solving surfaces. In this environment, information technology does not facilitate communication as effectively; rather, knowledge is typically transferred through face-to-face interaction, making this environment less suited to projects involving geographically dispersed teams.

Semimechanical and semiorganic environments are the last two and occur more commonly than the first two. Communication takes place both face to face and through information technology. Knowledge creation, transfer, and use are weighted more toward information technology in a semimechanical environment, while a semiorganic environment relies more on face-to-face interaction.

It would seem that the two hybrids would be more effective than the purely mechanical or organic ones. Using information technology to codify knowledge can help a project team decide what implicit knowledge is applicable to the project. Where project specifications are highly refined, the use of information technology is extremely valuable, whereas in projects that rely heavily on creative processes, face-to-face time and tacit knowledge are more critical. However, the recording of tacit knowledge can be very much facilitated by using technology.

The benefits of knowledge management in projects extend to strategic advantage (planning), sharing best practices, promoting innovation, and retaining the knowledge of experienced employees without having to recreate or pay again for that knowledge. Therefore, knowledge management in projects has become an invaluable tool and a fundamental necessity for the success of projects and for the sustainability and growth of organizations.

Specifically, the following benefits can be listed as shown below. This involves knowledge management in all the areas discussed in the *PMBOK Guide*, and it involves archiving knowledge for future reference and use. The major benefits of KM in projects are deliverables on schedule, cost savings, time savings, and improved quality, but in addition, KM in PM:

- Avoids reinventing the wheel
- Enables the tapping of existing knowledge in the current project environment to be applied toward future projects
- Provides a strategic advantage to the organization
- Helps to avoid waste, duplication, and some mistakes
- Captures lessons learned
- Learns from the problems or issues encountered and solutions devised in past projects and applies them to current projects
- Helps share best practices
- Uses collaborative tools
- Allows the project team to share knowledge through collaborative tools such as ERP
- Promotes successful innovation and enables teams to make better and faster decisions
- Provides better customer service functions
- Streamlines customer service through better responses, products, and services
- Enhances the retention of key employees
- Avoids having to recreate or pay again to acquire knowledge that the organization once had or still has in a silo
- Avoids costly mistakes
- Increases the rate of return in projects
- Promotes collaboration, collective wisdom, and experience
- Assists in evaluating contents in documents (as most documents are sanitized) by noting undesirable aspects of a project through debriefing and capturing implicit knowledge

We don't know what we know and what we don't know. In projects there is often no dearth of knowledge, but the problem is that the team members aren't sure what they know and what they don't know. This unawareness becomes a bottleneck in utilizing resources and knowledge efficiently and cost effectively in projects. The classic problem is that knowledge and information are generally not organized and not easily accessible. If knowledge is captured and managed properly, then the project:

- Provides faster access to knowledge and/or information to project members, leading to new ideas and creativity. In virtual project management KM becomes essential as it helps in sharing the same knowledge and information easily at all locations. This leads to less confusion among team members at distributed locations.
- Helps in improving productivity and providing better customer relations and satisfaction.
- Improves the decision-making process in terms of quality and time if knowledge is shared efficiently.
- Helps in improving the quality of training and reducing the training time for trainees in projects.
- Improves collaboration and coordination, as teams look at the same knowledge base. In short, it helps in creating a collaborative environment.
- Reflects intellectual capital through the collective wisdom and experience of human capital assets. This helps in improving performance in the project and the quality of project work.
- Helps to avoid waste and duplication by encouraging knowledge reuse, thus reducing cost and time.
- Identifies risk by addressing the various risks existing in a project and its related tasks.
- Mitigates risk. It improves the flow of knowledge in all directions, integrating processes.

Managing knowledge properly in projects helps to increase rate of return for the project by capturing, organizing, and storing knowledge and experiences from the organization's human capital and making this knowledge available to others. In essence, it enhances quality and consistency, increases knowledge sharing and transfer, improves productivity, avoids "reinventing the wheel," and saves cost and time. All these contribute to an increased rate of return on projects.

One of the main advantages of KM is the notion of the big picture and the connectedness of the system. It is the ability to see the big picture and the dependency of various components of the project on one another. Knowledge in some knowledge areas is obvious, and knowledge in other areas needs to be evaluated to determine whether the knowledge is critical for the project. When a project manager applies KM to develop the project team, the manager is transforming implicit knowledge into explicit knowledge. Once such knowledge is collected, a profile can be generated with a core set of information knowledge for each project using descriptors, metadata, and a taxonomy. Once this is done, detailed knowledge of the project can be captured, which will enable users to access knowledge in those projects with context in mind.

The profiles for projects can appear in a wide variety of formal and informal document sources. The project proposal or RFP is the typical good starting point. This will give relevant information on project planning such as project name, goals and objectives, sector, client, budget, schedule, primary components of the project, project subcomponents, related projects with clients, project benefits, project constraints/risks and lessons learned in similar projects, expected project outcome, the operational plan to complete the project, and often details of implementation. Once the project is ongoing, knowledge can be recorded on problems or challenges faced by the project, problems or challenges solved by the project, questions answered, efficacy of the answers, knowledge required at each stage or phase, knowledge sharing tools utilized, unexpected outcomes of the project, factors affecting outcomes, innovations, products, and other outcomes or transferables created by the project, and amount of knowledge captured on the project.

Team members' recollection of details regarding the project should elicit important aspects of the project and can add value. Human feedback is able to provide details about project work that are more granular than those reported in documents. It is a known fact that most documents are sanitized and do not include or discuss the undesirable aspects of project implementation, yet those are precisely the details that yield knowledge likely to have immense value in the design of future projects. Although documents provide the general detail, the depth is always provided by human interviews. To maximize knowledge capture from projects, a mechanism has to be created to debrief project team members periodically. This enables the recording of successes, failures, issues, and other qualitative information/knowledge aspects that are relevant. The output of this process can then be used as project knowledge leading to application in other areas. This requires an ongoing process. Information and knowledge slips away if it is not gathered promptly.

A CODA

KM has been accused of being a fad, and its death (quite premature, as Mark Twain would comment) has been announced on several occasions, most notably perhaps by David Snowden in his presentations at the KM World Conferences in 2007 and 2008, but KM is not a fad.

The late twentieth century was indeed characterized by a parade of business enthusiasms, many of them fads, and it is not surprising that many people expected KM to be just another car on that train, but KM is quite unlike any of the rest. It is quite literally now in a class by itself.

A few years ago, we could begin to recognize that difference. Building on previous work by Abrahamson (1999), Ponzi and Koenig (2002) demonstrated that KM was already behaving in a fashion quite unlike previous business fads of the late twentieth century. KM was clearly something new, or at least an unusually broad-shouldered business enthusiasm. Previous fads had all shown a boom and bust pattern of approximately five years of dramatic growth and then a precipitous decline that was almost as rapid. Figures 1.2 and 1.3 are representative graphs for "quality

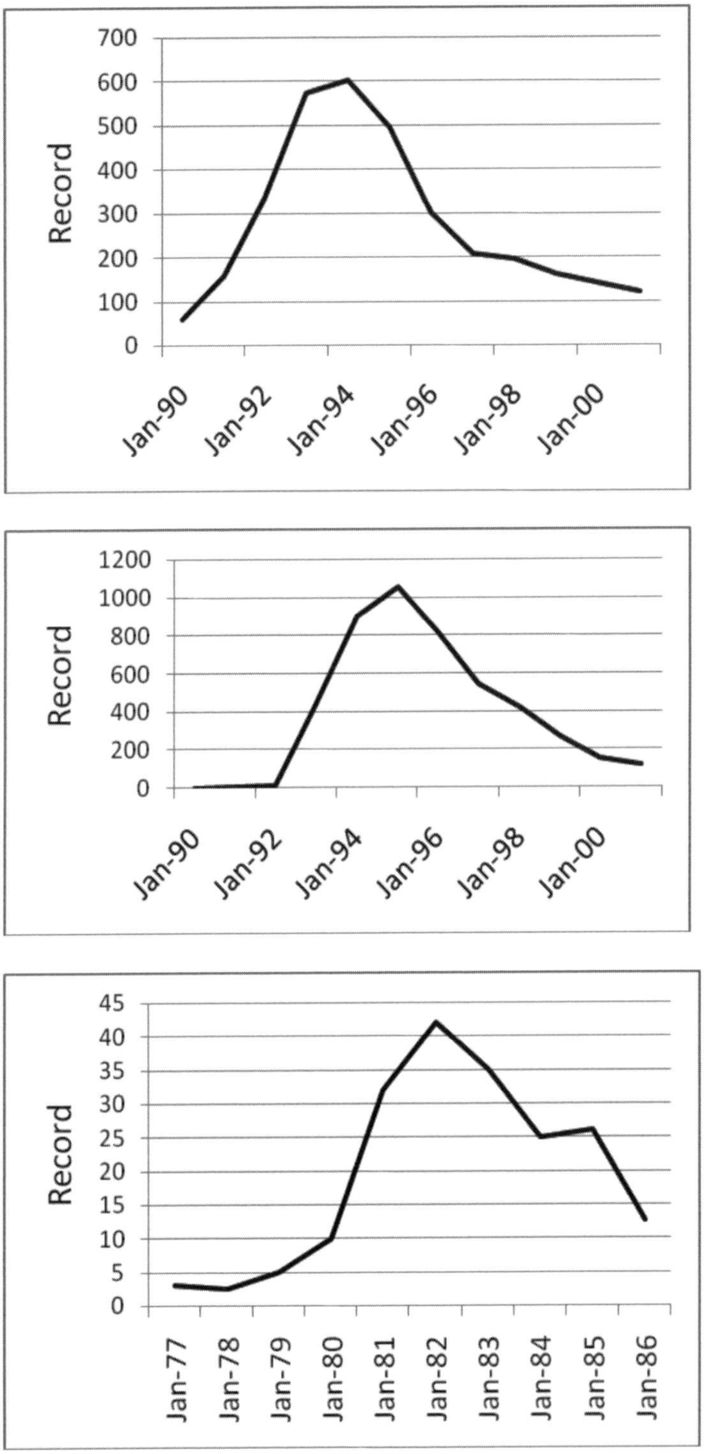

Figure 1.2. Representative Graphs of "Qualitative Circles," "TQM," and "Business Process Reengineering"

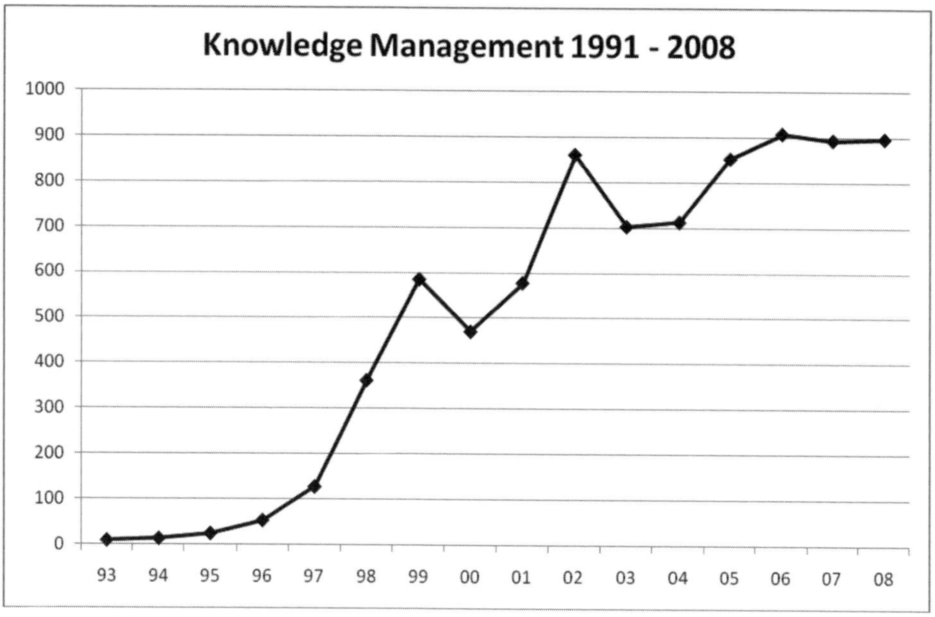

Figure 1.3. Graph Similar to Those Shown in Fig. 1.2 but Markedly Different Due to the Influence of KM

circles," "TQM," and "business process reengineering." Notice the similarity of the patterns in figure 1.2, almost as though they came from the same mold. Now look at figure 1.3. It is fundamentally and dramatically different. KM is here to stay to help projects succeed through managing knowledge.

REFERENCES

Abrahamson, E., & Fairchild, G. (1999). Management fashion: Lifecycles, triggers, and collective learning processes. *Administrative Science Quarterly, 44*, 708–740.

Al-Hawamdeh, S. (2003). *Knowledge management: Cultivating knowledge professionals*. Oxford: Chandos Publishing.

Beckman, T. (1999). The current state of knowledge management. In J. Liebowitz (Eds.), *Knowledge Management Handbook*. Boca Raton, FL: CRC Press.

Davenport, T. H., & Prusak, L. (2000). *Working knowledge: How organizations manage what they know*. Boston, MA: Harvard Business School Press.

Drucker, P. (2008). *Management* (rev. ed.). New York: HarperBusiness.

Drucker, P. (2000). Knowledge work. *Executive Excellence, 17*(4), 11–12.

Drucker, P. (January–February 1988). The coming of the New Organization. *Harvard Business Review*, 45–53.

Duffy, J. (1999). *Harvesting experience: Reaping the benefits of knowledge. ARMA* International.

Horibes, F. (1999). *Managing knowledge workers*. New York: Wiley.

Kliem, R.L. (1999). *The role of project management in knowledge management*. Retrieved April 4, 2007, from www.brint.com/members/online/20100210/ projectkm/.

Koskinen, K. U. (2004). Knowledge management to improve project communication and implementation." *Project Management Journal, 35*(2), 13–19.

Long, D. D. (1997). Building the knowledge-based organisation: How culture drives knowledge behaviours (Centre for Business Innovation, Ernst & Young working paper). Retrieved from http://www.cbi.cgey.com/pub/docs/CultureDrivesBehavior.PDF 10/08/02.

McDermott, R., & O'Dell, C. (2001). Overcoming cultural barriers to sharing knowledge. *Journal of Knowledge Management, 5*(1), 76–85.

Nonaka, I., & Takeuchi, H. (1995). *The knowledge-creating company*. New York: Oxford University Press.

Ponzi, Leonard J., & Koenig, Michael E. D. (2002). Knowledge management: Another management fad? *Information Research, 8*(1) Retrieved from http://informationr.net/ir/8-1/paper145.html.

Project Management Institute. (2004). *A guide to the project management body of knowledge: PMBOK guide* (3rd ed.). Newtown Square, PA: Author.

Senge, P. (1990). *The fifth discipline*. New York: Doubleday.

Wenger, E., McDermott, R., & Snyder, W. M. (2002). *Cultivating communities of practice*. Boston: Harvard Business School Press.

II

Deployment Issues

2

Gatekeepers, Boundary Spanners, and Social Network Analysis

Creating the Project Team

Michael E. D. Koenig

Beginning with T. J. Allen's seminal work in the late 1960s and 1970s, an important corpus of work has developed highlighting the importance of "gatekeepers," as Allen described them, or "information stars" within successful project teams. Several important corollaries relating to successful project management descend directly from this work and its successors. Furthermore, with:

- The increased importance of digital communications to project teams, and
- The consequent ability to create geographically dispersed project teams, and the increasing utilization of such project teams (see Chapter 17 by Srikantaiah, "Knowledge Management at Infosys: An Assessment," for a good example of this phenomenon), and
- The increased capability of social network analysis, SNA, to identify and recognize such information stars, this work and those corollaries take on increased salience and importance.

The combination of the recognition of information stars and the use of SNA results in a very important KM-related project management tool.

THE BACKGROUND

Commencing in the late 1960s, Thomas J. Allen of MIT (Allen and Cohen, 1969; Allen 1977) conducted seminal research on communications relating to technical matters that is particularly salient to the current interest in KM in the context of project management. He conducted a number of studies relating to information flow in industrial and corporate R&D laboratories. Although he conducted a number of different studies, his most ingenious contribution to the field was to seize upon the phenomenon that in many cases in the context of military R&D and procurement, a contract is awarded to two different organizations to achieve the same end. At first glance, this appears extravagantly wasteful, but if a subproject or component is crucial to the development of a larger project or system, it may well be penny-wise and pound-foolish to put all the eggs in one basket, as it were. Duplicative development contracts may well be worthwhile insurance for key components of a system. Allen's realization was that this provided an ideal test bed to look at communication flow. For each project there would be a winner and a loser, or at least one party more successful than the other, and differences between the more and the less successful could be examined. This provided a wonderfully robust context in which to examine information flows and what distinguished the information flows in the more successful projects from those in the less successful.

Furthermore, in most of the studies that Allen conducted, the emphasis in those R&D labs was upon not the R, research, but upon the D, development. In other words, the context in which Allen studied information flows was in many respects very similar to the context of project management; indeed, in many cases it could quite accurately be described as project management.

Allen coined the term *gatekeeper* to describe his information flow stars, the heavily connected nodes in the information flow pattern. The reason that he chose that term was that much of the development and project work that he investigated was classified military work, where there seemed to be something of a paradox—how was a team to be successful if it didn't effectively connect with the world of information outside the organization? But how did it do that in a classified and communication-restricted environment? What Allen discovered was that the information stars, the sociometric stars, were the answer to that paradox; they were the information channels through which external information reached the project team. That role was so crucial in the contexts that Allen typically investigated that he termed his sociometric stars "gatekeepers"—they manned and guarded the gates through which external information reached the projects. Indeed, in a very real sense they were not just the gatekeepers, they were the gates themselves.

The terminology is understandable given that context, but a bit misleading and rather too narrow, for the gatekeepers did much more—they were also the channels for information sharing and exchange within the organization and within the project. Allen himself, in fact, in developing and explicating the role of gatekeepers, introduces and explains his gatekeepers with the term *sociometric stars* and then steps on past. "Information stars," a term emerging later (Tushman & Scanlan, 1981a, 1981b), is however perhaps a more apt description, one that brings to mind more of the multiple roles and functions that such persons perform.

DISCUSSION AND RESULTS

Allen found that the more productive teams were particularly characterized by having had more diverse information contacts outside the project team than did the less productive teams. In particular, he elucidated and illuminated the rich informal communication networks typically quite independent of the formal organizational structure but characteristic of the more successful companies and management's relative unawareness of either the importance of, and in many cases even the existence of, those networks.

In relation to project management, however, the most salient and compelling result of Allen's work was the discovery and the highlighting of the importance of "gatekeepers" or information stars to the successful completion of development projects. What defined these stars for Allen was the frequency with which other persons communicated with them and the frequency with which information and advice was sought from them. They were central to information flow both within the organization at large and within their project or projects. What characterized these stars in addition was:

- Extensive communication with their field outside of the organization
- Greater perusal of information sources, journals, and so on—they were information mavens
- A high degree of connectedness with other information stars (one can infer that their utility was not just having more information at their fingertips but knowing whom to turn to within the organization for further information)
- A higher-than-average, compared with their project teammates, degree of formal education

These characteristics of information stars were further corroborated by Mondschein (1990) in a study of R&D activities across several industries.

One of the more intriguing findings, given the context and the nature of security restrictions, was that the more successful teams made less use of external consultants. At first glance, this seems surprising. Wouldn't external consultants help bring in that external information that would be helpful? The answer seems to be that the more successful teams had better gatekeepers. The teams with better gatekeepers needed external consultants less and used them less.

Another of Allen's findings was that management was surprisingly unaware of the nature of the information flow within their organizations, including being unaware of the importance of their information stars.

The emergence of social network analysis, discussed below, and the ability to algorithmically identify information stars, has, one hopes, recently made management more aware in this regard. But this is still likely to be a problem. The awareness of social network analysis and its capabilities still seems to be largely within the domain of the academic world and now increasingly within the KM world.

Another finding was that the information flow structure was not particularly related to the formal organizational structure and that the information stars did not map onto any consistent pattern of organizational placement or level. The relationship between formal organizational structure and the information flow structure also seems to be in part a function of the larger corporate culture. For example, Frost and Whitley (1971) adopted Allen's techniques to examine information flow in R&D labs in the United Kingdom and found a somewhat higher overlap between formal organizational structure and the information flow structure than Allen had found in the United States. The suggestion here is that the more rigid the organizational hierarchy, the more the information flow structure is constrained to adapt itself to the formal organizational structure.

This is consistent with a substantial body of work studying research productivity. Koenig (1992), for example, in the context of the U.S. pharmaceutical industry, studied the relationship between research productivity and the information environment in which that research was conducted. Pharmaceutical research is simply the sum of multiple simultaneous projects. The productivity measure was at base simply the number of approved new drugs (NDAs, new drug applications) per millions of dollars of R&D budget. This measure, however, was refined by weighting the NDAs in regard to (1) whether or not the FDA (Food and Drug Administration) judged the drug to be an "important therapeutic advance," (2) the chemical novelty of the drug, and (3) the filing company's patent position in regard to the drug, an indicator of where the bulk of the research was done. The study is compelling because of the high face validity of the measure of success, the successful introduction of new pharmaceutical agents, since that is what pharmaceutical companies are about after all, and because of the statistical robustness of the results, a consequence of the fact that the more successful companies were found to be not just 20 or 30 percent more productive than the not-so-successful companies, they were 200 or 300 percent more productive. The more productive companies were characterized by:

- A relatively egalitarian managerial structure with unobtrusive status indicators in the R&D environment
- Less concern with protecting proprietary information
- Greater openness to outside information—specifically, greater attendance by employees at professional meetings
- Greater use of their libraries and information centers
- Greater information systems development effort
- Greater end-user use of information systems, more encouragement of browsing and serendipity, and more time spent browsing and keeping abreast
- Greater technical and subject sophistication of the information services staff

Note the relationship with research/project success and a corporate culture that is relatively egalitarian and enjoys relatively unobtrusive status indicators. Also most interesting is that the correlation with concern for protecting the confidentiality of proprietary information was negative, and it also had the strongest single correlation with research project success, with an unassailably high statistical significance.

Michael Tushman (Tushman, 1977; Tushman & Scanlan, 1981a, 1981b) further extended the Allen tradition. He examined development activities, both at the departmental level and at the project level, at a medical instruments company and strongly confirmed Allen's conclusions. He introduced and added the concept of "boundary spanning" to describe much the same phenomenon that Allen described as gatekeeping. He extended Allen's work by distinguishing between two types of communication stars, "internal communication stars" and "external communication stars," and defining boundary spanners as those who were both internal and external communication stars. His emphasis is clearly directed to projects and project management, and his theme is that boundary spanners should be recognized, utilized, and nurtured for facilitating project success. Tushman's work is worth reviewing at this juncture as SNA developments have made recognition and subsequent utilization and nurturing of boundary spanners/information stars that he recommends far more feasible and practical than they were when his work appeared. SNA provides the level of detail to clearly and easily identify internal communication stars, external communication stars, and boundary spanners.

The Allen and Tushman tradition has not been lost, but it does need to be reexamined, resuscitated, and reinvigorated. Between when the Allen tradition work appeared, from the late 1960s through the early 1980s, and the appearance of KM in the early 1990s (Koenig & Neveroski, 2008), there appears to have been something of a loss of corporate memory in the management literature.

Two books in recent years in effect continue that tradition. They are excellent commentaries and offer valuable insights on information flow and information use in a modern organizational environment: Davenport and Prusak's (1998) *Working Knowledge*, which cites both Allen and Tushman, and Brown and Duguid's (2000a) *The Social Life of Information*. The emphasis and the examples in both books center on the for-profit corporate domain, but their significance is far broader than that. Davenport and Prusak focus more on project management, but the relevance of both books is obvious. For example, Brown and Duguid's work (2000b) analyzing the work and communication structure of Xerox field reps will resonate with anyone involved in project management. Anyone concerned with information flow within projects and with the effectiveness of project teams is well advised to read both books.

LACK OF RECOGNITION OF THESE FINDINGS IN THE BUSINESS COMMUNITY

Unfortunately, in the business community there is a surprising lack of recognition of these findings about the importance of information stars. This is in fact a subset of an even larger problem—the lack of recognition in general in the business community of the importance of information and information-related managerial actions.

A large body of investigative and research work on research and project work reaches conclusions that are very consistent and that are therefore robust to a surprising degree in what is basically a fairly soft research area (Koenig, 1990; 2009). The central conclusion to all these studies is that richness and openness in communication flow and in access to information are very highly correlated with research success, project success, and productivity, a conclusion that is totally congruent with the central tenets of KM.

The business community and within it the systems development community are often unaware and even obtuse in perceiving and acting on the consistency of these findings.

For example, one major study that reviewed a large corpus of work on R&D innovation (Goldhar, Bragaw, & Schwartz, 1976) concluded that there are six characteristics of environments that are conducive to technological innovations. The three most important characteristics are all related to the information environment and information flow—specifically (1) easy access to information by individuals, (2) free flow of information both into and out of the organizations, and (3) rewards for sharing, seeking, and using "new" externally developed information sources. Note the "flow in and out" and the "sharing, seeking, and using." The sixth characteristic is also information environment related, the encouragement of mobility and interpersonal contacts. Yet in a remarkable oversight, the studies' authors never remarked on the dramatic win, place, and show finish of information and knowledge factors.

Another similarly rigorous study (Orpen, 1985) examined productivity in R&D intensive electronics/instrumentation organizations. It analyzed various aspects of the behavior of research project managers as perceived by their staff and team members and found that in the more productive organizations (as defined by rates of growth and return on assets) the managers were perceived to be significantly more characterized by three aspects of their behavior, all information related: (1) they routed literature and references to scientific and technical staff; (2) they directed their staff to use scientific and technical information (STI) and to purchase STI services; and (3) they encouraged publication of results and supported professional meeting attendance and continuing education. Particularly striking was the finding that not only did information-related management behavior tend strongly to discriminate between "high-performance" and "low-performance" companies, but also that none of the non-information-related management behaviors measured had any discriminatory value. Here, given the inability to find any significance for other managerial factors, the failure to remark upon the importance of information and knowledge factors can be described as truly remarkable.

OVERALL CONCLUSIONS

The conclusions are based on Allen, Tushman, Koenig, and others.

- Communication flow patterns are often quite different from what management believes them to be.
- A few key people, the information stars, those Allen termed "gatekeepers" and Tushman termed "boundary spanners," are critical to good information flow within the project.
- Those same gatekeepers or boundary spanners are also critical to getting information to the project team from outside the project.
- Communication flows in development efforts and in projects are only loosely linked with the formal organizational structure. They can be congruent, orthogonal, or anywhere in between.
- In assessing likely information flows it is necessary to understand the corporate culture, both the corporate culture of the larger organization and the corporate culture that is likely to evolve within the project team.

SOCIAL NETWORK ANALYSIS

Allen's work was an early example of sociometric analysis and the use of sociograms, the technique that since it has become automated has now come to be called social network analysis, SNA. When person-to-person communication maps, sociograms, had to be drawn manually, as Allen had to do, the technique was simply called sociometric analysis, but when digital e-mail communications resulted in easily trackable person-to-person communications within and outside the organization and software was created to recast that data into easily apprehensible graphic form, the result was such an "Aha, that's neat" breakthrough that a new name needed to be coined, and that new name was SNA, social network analysis.

The connection between the importance of information stars and the ability to easily identify those stars within your organization, without having to go through the labor-intensive techniques that Allen or Tushman had to use, so that those stars can be connected to or assigned to key projects is obvious. Or it should be obvious. Again, though, like the overall lack of recognition of the importance of information mentioned above, there is still rather less recognition of the importance of SNA than there should be in the business and systems communities. A quick Google search of "social network analysis" (as of June 2009) results in about 3,120,000 hits, an impressively large number. But a quick perusal of those hits shows comparatively little in the domain of business or systems, despite the popularity of SNA in the academic world, particularly in the field of sociology.

That is not to say that there has not been some important work in the area of business. Perhaps the most central and most often cited piece is that by Cross, Borgatti, and Parker (2002) on using SNA to support strategic collaboration. Their work emphasizes the importance of informal networks within the organization and stresses that with increasingly delayered and geographically dispersed organizations, those informal communication networks are becoming more important and more vital. While their focus is top-down on strategically important groups such as top leadership networks and strategic business units, rather than a more bottom-up focus on projects, they do use "new product development teams" as an example of where SNA can be applied. Its publication in a prominent management journal, the *California Management Review*, has helped bring SNA to the attention of the management community. Specifically in the area of project management, Mead (2001) introduces SNA and describes using SNA to analyze communications within a project team.

The point that this piece is attempting to make is that the greatest utility of SNA in project management is not after the fact, but before the fact, as a key tool with which to design and assemble a project team. Table 2.1 lists some social network analysis tools.

THE LESSONS LEARNED

- All project teams should have an information star, a gatekeeper/boundary spanner as a key component of the team.
- Project teams should be put together keeping very consciously in mind that a known information star should be part of the team.
- Identify your information stars (gatekeepers and boundary spanners).
- An organization should be consciously applying social network analysis to identify those information stars.
- When you have identified your information stars, give them extra attention and extra support. Those stars have a leveraging effect. Support for them not only enhances their performance, it enhances the performance of the project team.

Table 2.1. Social Network Analysis Tools

Tool	*Website*
UCINET	www.analytictech.com
PAJEK	tutorial: http://iv.slis.indiana.edu/lm/lm-pajek.html: downloadable from http://vlado.fmf.uni-lj.si/pub/networks/pajek/
NEGOPY	www.sfu.ca/~richards/Pages/negopy.htm

- Project teams with gatekeeper/boundary spanner members are more likely to be successful.
- Project teams with gatekeeper/boundary spanner members are less likely to need to use external (and expensive) consultants.

REFERENCES

Allen, Thomas J. (1977). *Managing the flow of technology: Technology transfer and the dissemination of technological information within the R&D organization*. Cambridge, MA: MIT Press.

Allen, Thomas J., & Cohen, Stephen I. (1969). Information flow in research and development laboratories. *Administrative Science Quarterly, 14* (1), 12–19.

Brown, John Seely, & Duguid, Paul. (2000a). *The social life of information*. Boston, MA: Harvard Business School Press.

Brown, John Seely, & Duguid, Paul. (2000b). Balancing act: How to capture knowledge without killing it. *Harvard Business Review, 78*(3), 73-80.

Cross, Rob, Borgatti, Stephen P., & Parker, Andrew. (2002). Making invisible work visible: Using social network analysis to support strategic collaboration. *California Management Review, 44*(2), 25–46.

Davenport, Thomas H., & Prusak, Laurence. (1998). *Working knowledge: How organizations manage what they know*. Boston, MA: Harvard Business School Press.

Frost, Penelope A., & Whitley, Richard. (1971). Communication patterns in a research laboratory. *R & D Management, 1*(2), 71–79.

Goldhar, Joel D., Bragaw, Louis K., & Schwartz, Jules J. (1976). Information flows, management styles, and technological innovation. *IEEE Transactions on Engineering Management, EM-23*(1), 51–61.

Koenig, Michael E. D. (1990). Information services and downstream productivity. In Martha E. Williams (Ed.), *Annual review of information science and technology, volume 25* (pp. 55–56). New York: Elseview Science Publishers for the American Society for Information Science.

Koenig, Michael E. D. (1992). The information environment and the productivity of research. In H. Collier Ed.), *Recent advances in chemical information* (pp. 133–143). London: Royal Society of Chemistry.

Koenig, Michael E. D. (2009). Productivity impacts of libraries and information services. In Marcia Bates & Mary Niles Maack (Eds.), *Encyclopedia of Library and Information Sciences* (3rd ed.). Boca Raton, FL: CRC Press.

Koenig, Michael E. D., & Neveroski, Kenneth. (2008). The origins and development of knowledge management. *Journal of Information and Knowledge Management, 7*(4), 243–254.

Mead, Stephen P. (2001). Using social network analysis to visualize project teams. *Project Management Journal, 32*(4), 32–38.

Mondschein, Lawrence G. (1990). SDI use and productivity in the corporate research environment. *Special Libraries, 81*(4) (Fall), 265–279.

Orpen, Christopher, 1985. The effect of managerial distribution of scientific and technical information on company performance. *R&D Management, 15*(4), 305–308.

Tushman, Michael L. (1977). Special boundary roles in the innovation process. *Administrative Science Quarterly, 22*(4), 587–606.

Tushman, Michael L., & Scanlan, Thomas J. (1981a). Characteristics and external orientations of boundary spanning individuals. *Academy of Management Journal, 24*(1), 83–98.

Tushman, Michael L., & Scanlan, Thomas J. (1981b). Boundary spanning individuals: Their role in information transfer and their antecedents. *Academy of Management Journal, 24*(2), 289–305.

3

The Role of Knowledge Management in Requirements Management

Stephanie M. White

ABSTRACT

Since the 1960s developers of software-intensive systems have had problems delivering systems within cost and on schedule, and many of the delivered systems do not do what users really want. Inadequate requirements management (also called requirements engineering) is a major contributor to these problems. This chapter discusses the requirements management process and informs managers and practitioners how they can use information management and knowledge management to improve requirements management.

INTRODUCTION

"A requirement is something that the product must do or a quality that the product must have. A requirement exists either because the type of product demands certain functions or qualities, or the client wants that requirement to be part of the delivered product" (Robertson & Robertson, 1999, p. 5).

Requirements management covers "all the activities involved in discovering, documenting, and maintaining a set of requirements for a computer-based system" (Kotonya & Sommerville, 1998, p. 8).

Requirements management (RM) applies to the development of all software-intensive systems. RM entails capturing a significant amount of knowledge and frequently involves people from different disciplines. RM requires maintenance of a large amount of information during a period when that information is rapidly changing. RM necessitates modeling the functional design—a task that requires modelers to think analytically. RM is even more complex when several organizations collaborate to develop the system. Collaboration, communication, and knowledge management problems result in subsystem interface errors and unrecognized interdependencies. To make matters worse, requirements errors and omissions are not normally found until the system is operational, when they are very expensive to fix.

To provide a basis for understanding requirements management, the requirements process is described, including requirements elicitation, capture, and verification. Recommendations are made for (1) eliciting and sharing knowledge, (2) organizing perceptions concerning the problem the project is trying to solve, (3) using language terms and structure to capture requirements, and (4) modeling the requirements. Finally, a number of problems are identified with the current practice in requirements management, and suggestions are made as to how the practice can be improved through knowledge management. Before discussing the requirements process in detail, it is useful to have a high-level concept of the requirements process and its purpose.

OVERVIEW OF THE REQUIREMENTS PROCESS

Requirements are written for several reasons: to identify what an organization must deliver, to obtain consensus from users, and to provide detailed specifications to designers. Transforming a real-world system into a list of requirements and constraints and a computational model is the task of requirements management, which includes requirements elicitation, definition, capture, analysis, modeling (logical design), traceability, and verification. Software projects have been capturing and modeling requirements since the early 1980s, when methods for modeling the system functionality (called functional requirements or logical design) were first developed and databases for capturing requirements and related information were built by universities and the Department of Defense. In the late 1970s and early 1980s, problem statement language/problem statement analyzer (PSL/PSA) was built by the University of Michigan (Teichroew, 1980), and the systems requirements engineering methodology (SYSREM)/requirements engineering methodology (SREM) was built by TRW for the Army (Alford, 1985).

In July 2009, a survey performed by the Tools Database Working Group of the International Council on Systems Engineering (INCOSE, 2009) was documented at www.paper-review.com/tools/rms/read.php. The INCOSE survey evaluates requirements management tools against a set of features. Important features include (1) capturing requirements, (2) classifying requirements, (3) producing documentation according to specification standards, (4) bidirectional linking of requirements to system elements, (5) capture of allocation issues and rationale, (6) history of requirement changes, (7) requirement progress/status reporting, (8) support of concurrent review, (9) executable requirements, and (10) support for user groups. Many features are those that you would want in a knowledge management system. From examining the tool features listed in the survey, one can see that requirements management today is heavily dependent on information management and has been for over a decade. Tools often used in industry include Doors, Core, Requisite Pro, Statemate, and Rhapsody.

Some requirements documents are written at a high level of abstraction. For example, writers of contractual documents omit details so that they do not have to rewrite the documents as requirements mature. In general, requirements documents do not start with details. They support human cognition by first providing high-level information and then providing details. The high-level information could be deemed ambiguous if it had to stand on its own, as, for example, the requirement, "the system will provide the operators with a clear integrated picture." The words *clear* and *integrated* are ambiguous at this level but provide a concept that can be further defined in later paragraphs or negotiated and agreed upon at a later time.

Incompleteness and ambiguity are necessary at some levels of specification, but this need for ambiguity has not been adequately addressed in methods research. This issue is identified in a mid-1990s paper (Edwards & White, 1994) and is still true. A project can require that ambiguities be specifically labeled as TBD (to be determined), but sometimes it is not obvious that a requirement is vague, and it is not easy to create a nonambiguous form that has the intended meaning. Incompleteness is necessary at high levels of abstraction, but precision is necessary at detailed levels, as designers create a system to meet the requirements in the specification.

Current procurement practice normally requires delivery of natural language requirements documents. Therefore, a project that generates natural language documents from the requirements structure is efficient. Such requirements may exist in a database and/or other digital media (e.g., images, documents, models, and repositories). The generated documents should provide high-level statements of need to support understanding and gradually add details so that readers can absorb a large amount of complex information. The tools mentioned above generate documents from their requirements database.

REQUIREMENTS METHODS AND MODELS

Requirements engineers use different views to visualize and capture system requirements. A number of methods distinguished by the inclusion of temporal as well as function and data relationships have been proposed for modeling real-time requirements. Temporal relationships, which are necessary to support the modeling of system reaction to external events, are described in most methods using a structure similar to a finite state machine. In methods that incorporate both function and state decomposition, functions, data, and states can be decomposed to relate decomposition of control to decomposition of function.

Methods must include a set of specific elements such as events and states and a formal mathematical basis such as input-to-output mapping and function composition. Models must be easy to comprehend and to construct; separation of stakeholder concerns helps in this regard. Models developed during the requirements phase must not include design decisions, as they make the specification harder for customers to understand and limit designer options. They must be design independent to provide a basis for a number of potential designs and give designers the flexibility they need. Nevertheless, many requirements modeling methods show the transformation from input to output and thus include design decisions.

Modeling methods must allow for decomposition and stepwise refinement as systems of systems are too large to model as a single layer. Modeling methods must also provide the ability to associate nonfunctional requirements (e.g., performance, and security) with the functional model and provide support for design tradeoff analysis, test identification, specifying TBDs, and model verification and reuse. Models should also include both stochastic and probabilistic aspects to support prediction of effects.

FOUR DIMENSIONS OF REQUIREMENTS DEFINITION

In *Organizing Knowledge and Organizational Effectiveness*, Lambe (2007) discusses four dimensions of knowledge management, which he calls logos, sophos, pathos, and ethos (see figure 3.1). Logos represents information management at the individual level. Sophos represents what an individual has learned over time through experience (tacit knowledge). Pathos represents personal collaboration with others about a current situation and the distribution of that knowledge socially. Ethos represents the culture, history, and knowledge of the organization.

In requirements definition, logos relates to requirements capture by a requirements analyst or engineer. Sophos relates to the knowledgeable expert providing his or her tacit knowledge to the requirements engineer. It is much more difficult to capture tacit knowledge and expertise than to capture information. Requirements engineers create use cases to capture what users do in the normal case and what they do if something exceptional occurs. For requirements definition, pathos relates to facilitated meetings with a group of stakeholders to obtain information about how the system currently works and the problems with the current system. Pathos also relates to teams of requirements analysts sharing knowledge to improve requirements and to make sure requirements are consistent and complete. Organizations should use expertise directories and social network maps to show where knowledge resides and who shares knowledge with whom.

For requirements definition, ethos relates to sharing knowledge with other people in the organization through communities of practice, apprenticeship, and integrated product teams. With a team (or a knowledgeable community), one person doesn't have to know everything; each team member plays his or her part; and junior members learn from more senior members on the team. Ethos also relates to the development of product lines. Corporations are recognizing the value of domain engineering—developing product lines or product families instead of single products. For example, Hughes recognized that the functionality it developed for the air defense domain was very similar to that of air traffic control. Hughes bid on and won a contract in the air traffic control domain and developed an architecture and domain assets that could be used for both air defense and air traffic control, promoting reuse and significant cost savings (White & Edwards, 1996).

THE REQUIREMENTS PROCESS

The requirements process, as in knowledge management, consists of elicitation (knowledge pull), acquisition and capture, and the creation of information and

Knowledge gained over time	**Sophos**	**Ethos**
Knowledge about current situation	**Logos**	**Pathos**
	Individual knowledge	Group knowledge

Figure 3.1. Four Dimensions of Knowledge Management according to Lambe

documentation for other users and uses (knowledge push). Team members analyze requirements for consistency, completeness, and correctness (the right functionality, dependability, maintainability, integrity, and so on). The "right functionality" is the functionality that customers require. One should not build more or less. If more functionality is provided, the customers are paying for more than they need. Some practitioners call this "gold-plating."

THE STATE OF PRACTICE

During the 1970s, the standard software development process was called the "waterfall." All requirements were defined before the start of design. There wasn't any feedback from customers or users until the project was complete, at which time much work had to be redone at great cost, monetarily and architecturally. This was true even for projects of medium size. In the 1980s, a technical team was still likely to create the system requirements without getting feedback from all stakeholders. There were many failures because of this. The Melbourne and London ambulance systems failed, in part, because of lack of communication with stakeholders (Dalcher, 2001; Flowers, 1996).

The typical requirements process today iterates between requirements elicitation and system representation. A multiview system model provides the vehicle for communication between developer and customer, presenting system facts and system demonstration in an organized form that a customer can understand. The same model provides views of function and capability to the implementer at a more precise level. One of the primary methods for analyzing requirements is the creation of functional models, which may be executable. Static textual representations of a system depicting hierarchical sets of functions are insufficient. Executable modeling tools such as Core (Moulding & Smith, 1992), Statemate (Harel & Politi, 1998), and Rhapsody (Efroni, Harel, & Cohen, 2005) provide dramatic advances over static modeling methods. The requirements team traces requirements to their source (a document or a person) so that others will know where to go for additional knowledge. They also trace requirements to other system elements (design and test cases) so that if requirements change, developers will know which part of the design and which test cases must be changed. The design is traced to physical parts and software packages and classes.

Project managers recognize the need to capture stakeholder knowledge. Unfortunately, this is a difficult process, as people have a problem transferring tacit knowledge. One of the methods used in the systems and software disciplines is documentation of use cases (Cockburn, 2001). Use cases are similar to operational scenarios. Another method for capturing knowledge is prototyping the user interface and obtaining user feedback. A third is using joint application development (JAD) sessions, where future system users and others, including a JAD facilitator, work together to identify needs, workflow, and how they want the new system to work.

Requirements are normally identified as belonging to one of two types: functional and nonfunctional. Functional requirements express the need for capabilities, while nonfunctional requirements express how well these capabilities shall be performed (how fast, how reliable, how secure, and so on). Types of nonfunctional

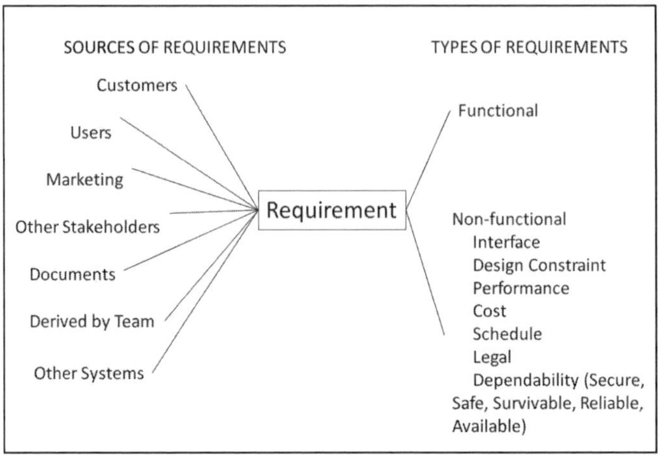

Figure 3.2. Requirement Sources and Types

requirements are listed in figure 3.2. Nonfunctional requirements include performance, dependability, maintainability, usability, and operational requirements. They also include documentation, legal, and cost and schedule requirements and constraints on the interface and on design (for example, requiring a specific software programming language). Requirements analysts must consult many sources to obtain these requirements. A number of requirements sources are shown in figure 3.2.

REQUIREMENTS ELICITATION

Requirements are sometimes discovered and sometimes created. That depends on the project. Requirements can come from marketing, from a customer, from users, from a higher-level specification (software requirements are derived from a system specification), or be created by a visionary manager or team of engineers/developers.

If requirements come from users, the first major task is to elicit and define requirements. Figure 3.3 provides an overview of major tasks when eliciting and defining requirements and associated information flows. Requirements knowledge is elicited through (1) interviews with managers, users, customers, maintainers, developers, and others; (2) facilitated brainstorming sessions with groups of these stakeholders; (3) feedback on prototypes; (4) surveys; (5) document review; (6) examination of input forms and reports; and (7) examination of previous and similar systems (even previous manual versions and competitor systems). The project should review corporate knowledge related to the system the corporation is planning to build. It is advantageous to have knowledge concerning the development and use of similar projects, including captured knowledge about project requirements, architecture, design knowledge and experience, decisions, risks, cost, schedule, and lessons learned. Also, corporate communities of practice and social networks that support the needed knowledge areas are quite useful.

There will be changes to the requirements as development proceeds. Understanding of requirements will be affected by individual and team expertise, team cohesion, organizational support for questioning and learning, and working conditions,

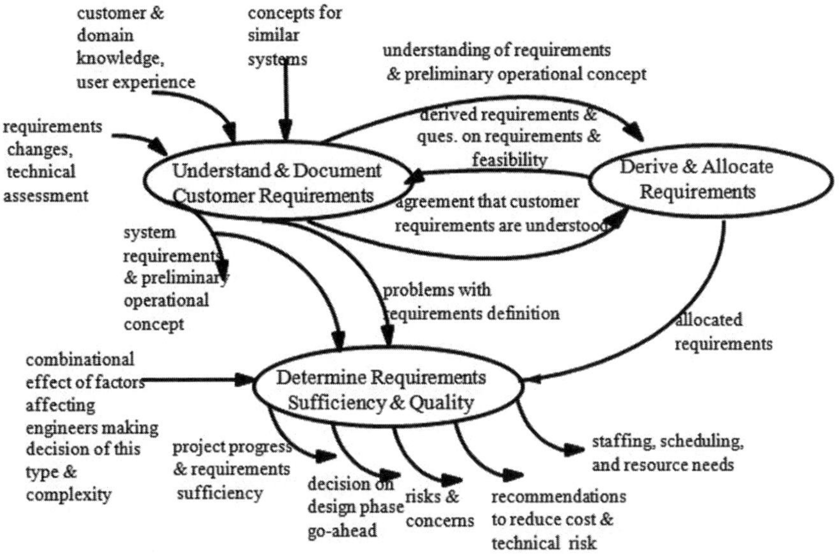

Figure 3.3. Dataflow Diagram of the Task to Elicit and Define Requirements

for example, the stress of tight schedules. When the team agrees that it understands customer requirements, it produces a preliminary system requirements specification and a preliminary operational concept, and it documents any problems that still exist in the requirements definition. It allocates requirements to subcontractors and subsystems and derives additional requirements for interfaces between these subsystems. As this is performed, questions concerning the requirements and feasibility are addressed. The team must make a decision as to requirements sufficiency and technical, economic, and operational feasibility. The team determines whether it has the knowledge resources to build the system, whether the system will provide sufficient return on investment, and whether users will adopt it. The team continuously evaluates the quality of the requirements with respect to consistency, correctness, and completeness. It determines whether to continue defining requirements or proceed more extensively with design. Proceeding will depend on whether the requirements are sufficiently defined and whether cost, schedule, required staffing, and risk are feasible. The assessment to proceed will document risks and concerns and include staffing and resource needs and a recommended schedule.

USE CASES

Practitioners, who have knowledge concerning the tasks the new system is expected to support, are interviewed as to how they performed their tasks in the past and how they want the new system to work. From these interviews, use cases are created. A use case is defined for each task that an "agent" (person or system) performs. The use case specifies the normal operational scenario and what might happen if exceptions occur. Table 3.1 shows a use case in which a university faculty member searches a university website for information about a specific faculty committee.

Table 3.1.

Actor	*System*
1. Faculty Member enters Employee ID and password.	2. Website system accepts ID and password, recognizes visitor, and launches faculty information page.
3. Visitor selects a link from the list of faculty committee links on the faculty information page.	4. A new page appears that shows information on the chosen faculty committee, including any links.
Alternate Scenario	In step 2, if the system does not recognize the Employee ID or password, the actor cannot access the site.
	In step 3, if the link is broken, the system provides a message to that effect and an e-mail address for a contact.

The actor is the person performing the task in the use case. The preconditions must hold prior to use case execution. Postconditions hold after the use case executes. The analyst asks the knowledge expert to explain what happens if everything goes well and documents this in a "normal scenario." The analyst then goes through each step in the normal scenario and asks the knowledge expert what could go wrong in that step. At the end of the normal scenario, exceptions are documented. Exceptions are placed at the end as interrupting the normal scenario with many exceptions would make use cases too difficult to follow. Use cases can be helpful in all knowledge acquisition that relates to process; they are not specific to requirements.

CAPTURING/RECORDING REQUIREMENTS

A structured approach to requirements capture identifies what information is to be captured and provides a technical language to do so. Multiple views are provided to alleviate communication problems. These views map the structured language to terminology that is familiar to the various groups and disciplines. A good requirements framework permits temporary inconsistency, allowing stakeholders to negotiate conflicting goals and needs. The framework provides a context for capturing requirements and helps personnel avoid assumptions. A structured approach improves communication and provides analysts with needed capabilities, including support for requirements model development, analysis for consistency and completeness, traceability, and impact analysis.

Numerous analyses can be performed once a requirements structure is in place. A template for entering requirements helps project personnel determine whether they have omitted information. Different views can be generated from the structure, helping personnel see the information in different forms that support understanding and human analysis. Automated analysis can be performed in certain cases; examples include reliability, timing, and checking the consistency of interface specifications.

FACETED CLASSIFICATION VERSUS PREDEFINED TAXONOMY

Taxonomic designation is needed in system requirements definition, but there is a problem as new information is constantly emerging. For example, users may realize they want a new capability; analysts derive new requirements from those existing; and developers realize they have overlooked a constraint. A predefined taxonomy doesn't work well when new information is rapidly appearing, as analysts using such taxonomy have to identify a single correct predefined position in the taxonomy for the new information. Instead, a number of researchers in requirements engineering recommend a faceted taxonomy (Bouillet et al., 2008; Opdahl & Sindre, 1995; Lee & Kuo, 1998).

Patrick Lambe (2007) discusses the value of facets for organizing emerging knowledge. Facets do not have to be predefined. Since a facet is a dimension in which information can be specified, new facets can easily be added. Faceted classification schemes do not work well when you have to order the information so that you can find a physical item, but they work very well for digital information, where locating information and documents can be accomplished by tagging or indexing. Analysts must make sure that facets are mutually exclusive to avoid ambiguity.

Recommended Facets for Capturing Requirements

The following facets, which are normally captured when managing requirements, are documented in White and Edwards, 1995. The highest level of the taxonomy includes the operational environment, system capabilities, system constraints, development requirements, and specification for growth and change. At a more detailed level, the operational environment (the environment in which the system operates) includes the natural environment, external man-made systems, and human aspects. For developing a new automobile, the operational environment would include wind, weather, road conditions, and human reaction speed. The operational view also includes operating requirements: operational plans, goals, strategies, missions, policies, operational profiles, operational limits, and operating conditions.

System capabilities define and measure the system's ability to achieve objectives. System capabilities are described by information (inputs, outputs), physical items on which the system operates, functions, and behavior, and by nonfunctional system measures such as performance, dependability, and security.

System constraints are restrictions that affect capability, architecture, process, and resources. Technical restrictions result from previous architectural decisions; existing policies, operations, or systems; and the need for commonality to reduce procurement, training, or maintenance costs. These restrictions include the use of certain facilities, hardware, or software; requirements to interact with existing systems; and requirements to use specific languages (French, Japanese). Cost and schedule constraints and the requirement to conform to certain policies and procedures impose limits on what can be built. For example, the requirement to use specific computer resources could affect cost, schedule, and capability.

Development requirements include requirements relating to organization and staffing, planning and management, audit and control, quality assurance, configuration management, requirements elicitation and analysis, designing, implementing, maintenance, documentation, reviews, delivery, and operation.

Verification and validation (V&V) requirements include requirements for test equipment and requirements for support software that stimulates the system, simulates the external environment, and analyzes test results. V&V requirements also include product functionality to support tests, such as functions that access system data.

Specification for growth and change is an important aspect of requirements definition. Complex systems normally have a long life, and technology advancements and need for new capabilities drive system evolution. Occasionally, future change has been defined. More normally, specific changes have not been defined, but knowledgeable personnel can predict what might change based on previous experience. Knowing this information in advance allows designers to develop architectures that can accommodate expected change.

A number of issues must be considered to create a useful requirements structure. These include the need to support (1) different types of stakeholders, (2) different levels of abstraction, and (3) natural language generation.

VERIFYING REQUIREMENTS

Users, customers, management, domain specialists, systems engineers, software specialists, hardware specialists, psychologists, maintainers, and reliability, safety, security, logistics, and manufacturing engineers are all involved in developing requirements. They negotiate system requirements, and each has different goals and objectives. For example, a system engineer might impose a requirement on manufacturing that is too costly. A reliability engineer must negotiate availability with a safety engineer who would prefer to shut down the system rather than risk a critical failure. Each of these disciplines has its own language, notations, methods, and tools. A requirements structure must support the team in negotiating among conflicting requirements. After the negotiation, management has to have agreement that the requirements are consistent, complete, and correct.

Lambe recommends concept mapping as a useful technique for checking for coherence and completeness. Entity-relationship diagrams are concept maps that have been used in requirements modeling since the 1980s. Figure 3.4 shows an example of a concept diagram for evacuation in case of a hurricane. In hurricane evacuation, it is important to know which areas won't be flooded (dry areas), where people can stay (shelters), which routes to take (evacuation routes), and where food is stockpiled for emergencies (a food source). Relationships connect the entities. For example, evacuation route "needs" food source.

PROBLEM SOLVING AND ORGANIZING PERCEPTIONS

Requirements definition is about solving a problem, improving a business, helping humanity, or satisfying a user group. People recognize, remember, and use both general principles and specific facts in solving problems and building systems. Both principles and facts must be recorded.

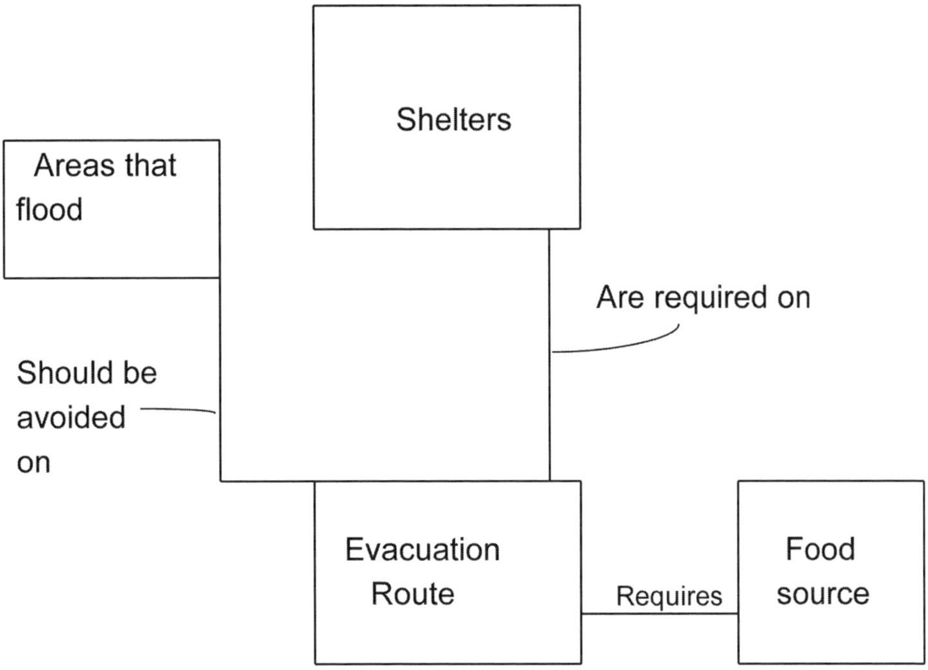

Figure 3.4. Concept Diagram for Evacuation, Based on Entity-Relationship Notation

Schema, Frames, Concept Graphs, and Semantic Networks

A number of philosophers have theorized about problem solving. Immanuel Kant used the word *schema* for a rule that organizes perceptions (Kant, 1781/1966). The German psychologist Otto Selz used the word *schema* to specify a network of concepts and relations that guide the way a person thinks (Selz, 1922). Based on Selz's ideas, Minsky (1975) developed the concept of "frame." He wrote:

> When one encounters a new situation (or makes a substantial change in one's view of the present problem) one selects from memory a structure called a Frame. This is a remembered framework to be adapted to fit reality by changing details as necessary. A frame is a data-structure for representing a stereotyped situation, like being in a certain kind of living room, or going to a child's birthday party. Attached to each frame are several kinds of information. Some of this information is about how to use the frame. Some is about what one can expect to happen next. Some is about what to do if these expectations are not confirmed. We can think of a frame as a network of nodes and relations.

John Sowa (1983) used conceptual graphs and semantic networks in a manner similar to Minsky's frame: "The model has two components: a sensory part formed from a mosaic of percepts, each of which matches some aspect of the input; and a more abstract part called a conceptual graph, which describes how the percepts fit together to form the mosaic" (p. 69). In conceptual graphs, there are two types of nodes. Concept nodes represent entities, attributes, states, and events, and relation nodes show how the concepts are interconnected. "The collection of all the relationships that concepts have to other concepts, to percepts, to procedures, and to motor mechanisms is called the semantic network" (p. 76). The semantic network may include words and grammar rules of language, rules for assembling percepts, a hierarchy of concept types together with type definitions, the context for a conceptual graph, and emotional overtones associated with the context or episode to which the conceptual graph is linked.

Figure 3.5 shows a conceptual graph of evacuation in case of hurricane in Sowa's notation. The relation NOT LOC stands for "is not located in,", and REQ stands for "requires."

SOFT SYSTEMS METHODOLOGY

Peter Checkland (1999) developed soft systems ethodology (SSM) to model human activity situations in which problems exist that might be solved by building a system. The basis for SSM was the realization that all real-world situations are characterized by humans wanting to take purposeful action. This is the first step in requirements engineering—understanding the environment of a potential to-be-built system. The "rich pictures" developed by Checkland do not represent everyone's view of the world but form a basis for discussion and argument.

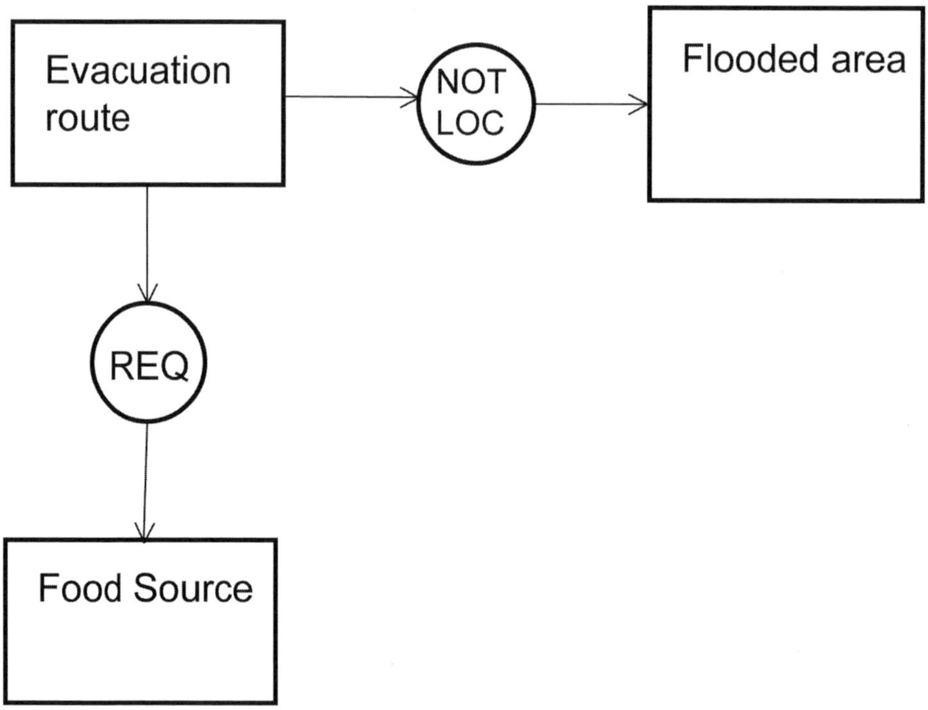

Figure 3.5. Conceptual Graph for Evacuation, Based on Sowa's Notation

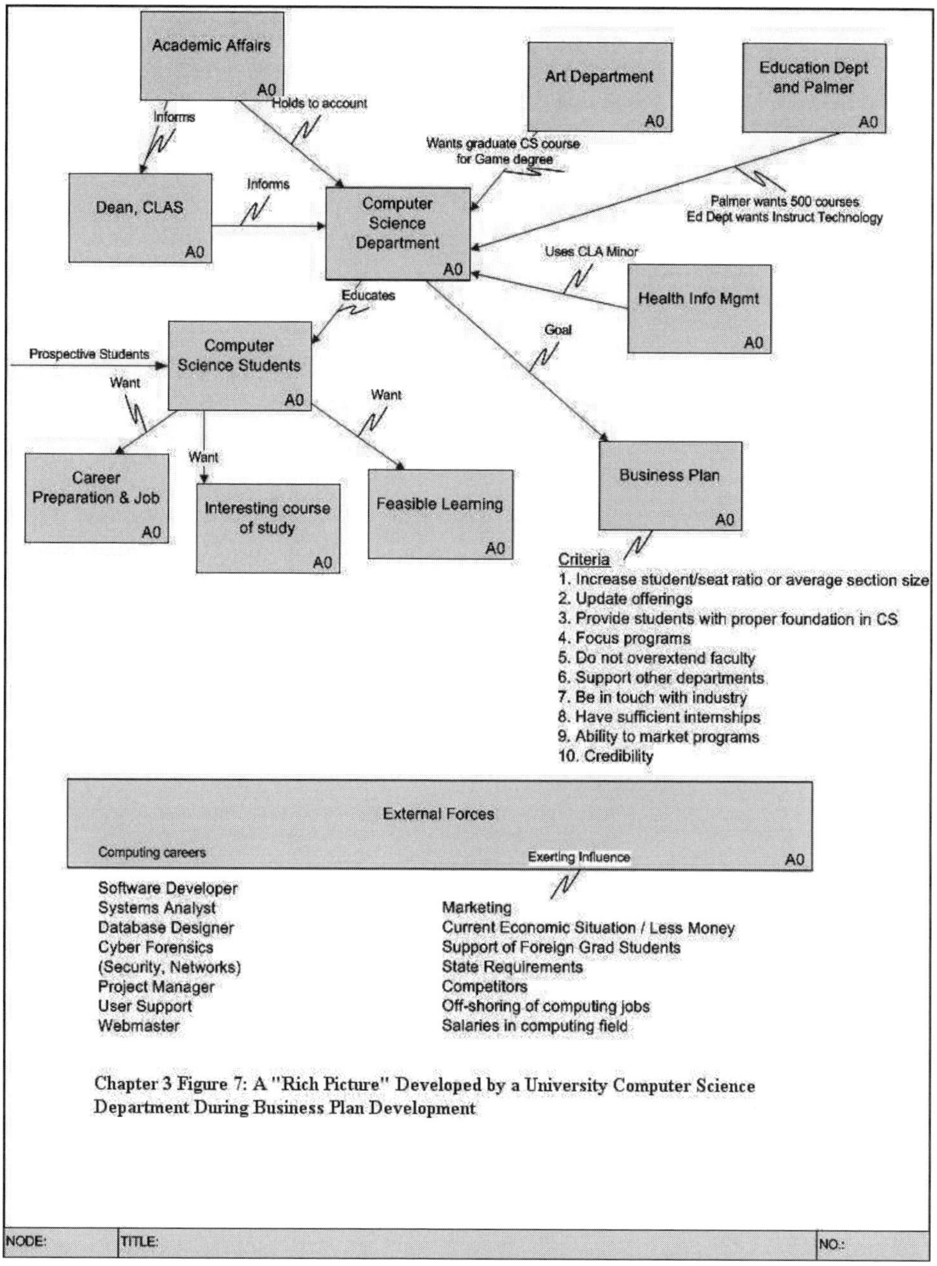

Figure 3.6. A "Rich Picture" Developed by a University Computer Science Department during Business Plan Development

Figure 3.6 is a rich picture developed by a university computer science department during business plan development. The picture encourages discussion and knowledge sharing in the organization. In the picture, Academic Affairs works through the dean of the College of Liberal Arts and Science to inform the Computer Science

Department of desired outcomes but directly measures the success of the department with respect to identified criteria. Various departments request minors in computer science and/or graduate courses for their students. The students look for courses that satisfy their needs, including career preparation, interesting course of study, and material that they have the ability and prerequisites to learn. The rich picture includes potential computing careers that course work might address and criteria that the academic vice president will use to evaluate the plan. External forces such as marketing, the current economic situation, and the availability of computing jobs will affect the outcome.

ERA MODELS AND ONTOLOGY

Sowa's concept graphs are similar to Chen's entity-relationship-attribute (ERA) model, which he developed for designing databases (Chen, 1976). Table 3.2 specifies the entities and attributes for a business that searches for and sells rare books. Figure 3.7 shows the relationships among entities in the business. Both ontology and ERA models are used in development of requirements knowledge bases. Ontology has been defined by Gruber with respect to information systems development as "a formal, explicit specification of a shared conceptualization" (Gruber, 1993). Ontology for a domain includes a vocabulary of terms and a specification of meaning for the terms, ideally grounded in logic. Both an ERA model and ontology have

- Elements (called entities in an entity-relationship model and classes or concepts in a class model and ontology)
- Relationships (called relationships in an entity-relationship and class model and relations or properties in an ontology)
- Element attributes (called attributes in an entity-relationship and class model and properties, slots, or roles in an ontology)

Figure 3.8 compares development based on ERA models with development based on ontology. In entity-relationship modeling, entities, relationships, and attributes are used to create a relational model from which a relational database is produced. Using ontology, the concepts, relations, and properties are transformed into an XML schema. XML is a standard developed by the World Wide Web Consortium (W3C) that defines data formats and data structures and is used to create structured computer documents and share data on the Web.

Table 3.2. Entities and Related Attributes for a Business That Searches for and Sells Rare Books

Entities/Classes	*Attributes*
Client	clientID, name, address, phone
Order	orderDate, orderNumber, subtotal, total
Book	bookID, bookAuthor, bookTitle, pubPlace, pubDate, edition, binding, condition, currentPrice, purchasePrice, dateOfArrival, shippingDate
BookSearch	initiationDate, terminationDate, searchStatus, resultAtTermination
SearchProgress	date, workPerformed, outcome
Charge	chargeType, chargeAmount

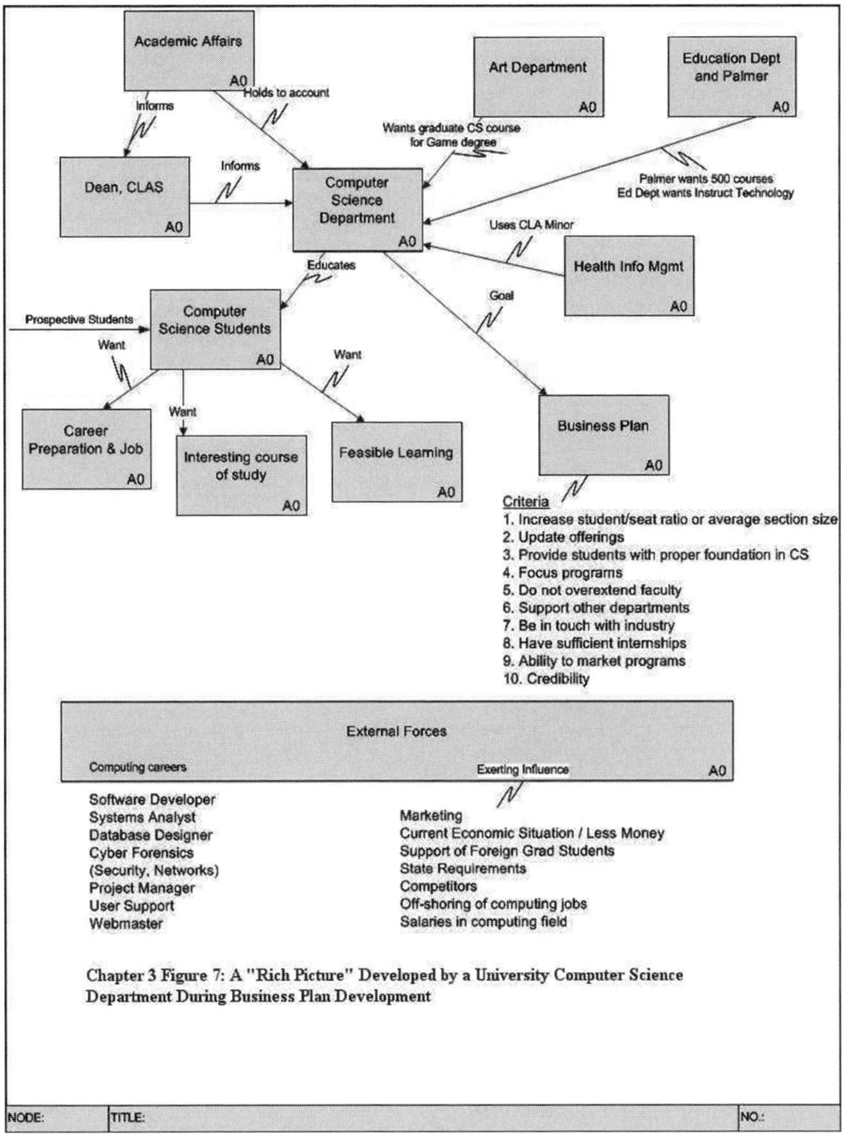

Figure 3.7. Simplified Entry-Relationship Model for the Rare Book Business

Building an ontology supports the development of knowledge bases and automated reasoning in artificial intelligence (AI), and much of the terminology comes from the AI domain. The specification of an ontology is usually encoded in a formal logic-based language, which prevents ambiguity and supports inference of additional information from the specification. Inference is also used to check ontology consistency. The set of classes or concepts in the ontology are normally arranged as a taxonomy or lattice. Ontology models use constraints in a manner that is different from the way ERA models use these concepts. The purpose of constraints in ontology is to support automated reasoning, while the purpose of constraints in a

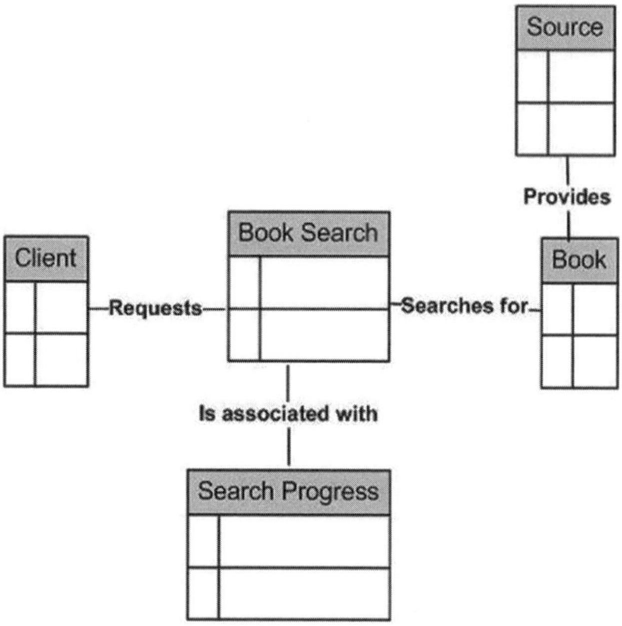

Figure 3.8. From Design to Implementation, Entity-Relationship Model versus Ontology

database schema is to ensure data integrity. Constraint enforcement for database schema is expensive, so many constraints identified during analysis are not defined.

REQUIREMENTS MODELING TERMINOLOGY

White provides a synthesis of the terminology used in requirements models (White, 1987; 1994; 2009). Figure 3.9 is a model of the types of entities and relationships required to model behavior for a system of systems. For example, to describe behavior, an analyst has to identify functions and the data a given function sets and uses. The model in figure 3.10 is useful, as it identifies the elements analysts must include in their models. It includes both environment functions and system functions. The model also decomposes state, function, event, and data. Current methods normally decompose either event or state, but not both. Decomposition of both state and event would provide more power for describing systems of systems and for tracing system requirements to software requirements. In the illustration, rectangles represent objects, circular nodes represent relationships, and the nodes are numbered for identification. The relationship holds in both directions.

A system of systems contains systems (see figure 3.9). Both the environment and system contain functions. A function is performed in certain states, causes and is triggered by events, is a refinement of a more abstract function, and uses and sets data. States can have subparts and are contained in a state-machine-abstraction, which can be a refinement (detailed definition) of a more abstract state. Events contain and affect states. Events are decomposed, and the levels of event refinement relate to the levels of data refinement. Events contain events, and an event at

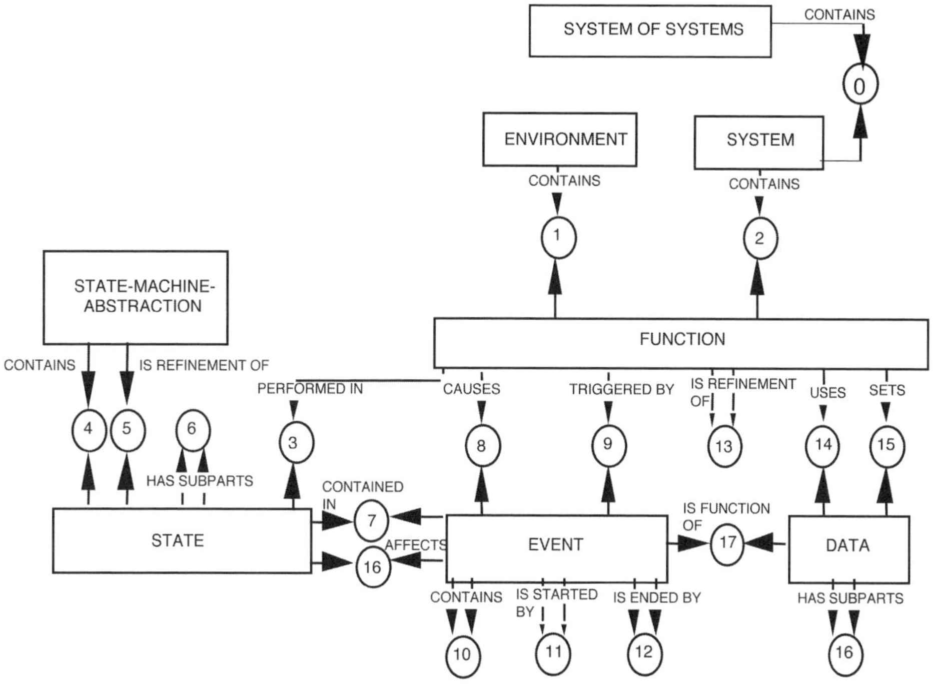

Figure 3.9. Basic Terminology Needed When Modeling System Functionality

an abstract level is started and ended by events at a more detailed level. Events are a function of data, which is also decomposed.

This figure appears deceptively simple, as the intrasystem relationships are explicit, but the effects of one system on another are implicit. That is, a function may use (see node 14 in figure 3.9) data that is initially set (15) by a function in a different system. An event that occurs in one system may eventually trigger (9) a function that occurs in another system. Similarly, an event in one system may eventually affect (16) a state in a different system. As more systems are added to a system of systems, the complexity increases exponentially.

ADDRESSING PROBLEMS WITH REQUIREMENTS MANAGEMENT PRACTICE

Most practitioners agree that requirements management is a difficult task. If not done properly, requirements definition has significant cost impact as problems are not found until the system is operational, when it is very expensive to fix them (Boehm, 1981). The following paragraphs address problems that projects incur in performing requirements management. These problems can be alleviated or solved using knowledge management methods and techniques.

Addressing Problems Due to the Interdisciplinary and Distributed Nature of Projects

Most projects are interdisciplinary. For enterprise systems, the disciplines include those of the business domain (e.g., accounting, finance, and procurement), computing, and security. For physical systems, the number of disciplines increases. For example, to build an aircraft, in addition to communications, control, human factors, hardware, software, reliability, and security, the project needs engineers who are knowledgeable about safety, navigation, federal aviation administration policies, vehicle flight characteristics and performance, avionics systems, pilot controls and interfaces, and logistics, including training and maintenance. Frequently, organizations that are specialists in building subsystems (for example, navigation, digital flight control, pilot controls, and communication) are geographically and even internationally dispersed. With outsourcing, projects may have teams all over the world.

Engineers and information system personnel do not have the same educational background and do not understand each other's terminology, processes, and challenges. Engineers from different disciplines also have problems in understanding each other's area of expertise. When the team is distributed geographically or there are cultural differences, it is even more difficult to clarify technical, language, and communication issues. Because the requirements process is interdisciplinary and dependent on the joint understanding of all members of the team, this is a problem that must be recognized and addressed. Communities of practice, integrated product teams, and joint training provide reasonable support.

Natural language such as English is the standard practice for expressing business and system requirements, while software developers use model-driven development usually based on UML and produce documents from the models. Information provided by business and systems analysts to practitioners in other disciplines must be understandable by the recipients. To achieve this, the analysts must use that discipline's methodology and notation, as the use of inconsistent description languages by different disciplines increases communication and traceability problems. Unfortunately, business analysts and systems engineers may not be familiar with another discipline's terminology and methodology. Some system analysts are starting to use requirements models, for example, SysML, which was developed to provide consistency between system and software requirements models (OMG, 2008). Training programs on projects must take a more interdisciplinary view, providing courses that are shared across disciplines. Projects must work toward the development of a common set of semantics.

A team of practitioners collaborates to identify requirements for a typical project. The team members elicit business needs, evaluate feasibility, identify trades, and negotiate priorities. As identified in Edwards and White, 1994:

> They hope to capture the 'true' requirements of a system, which are those that satisfy the needs of stakeholders (users, customers, management, and others). There are several reasons why the set of specified requirements is not normally equivalent to the set of 'true' requirements, including:
>
> - Natural language is imprecise.
> - Different disciplines use inconsistent terminology.

- Conflicts are not readily recognized and therefore not properly negotiated.
- Assumptions are not clearly documented.

Also, practitioners

> . . . use different representation schemes, even within a single discipline (drawings, tables, natural language, and semi-formal models), leading to inconsistencies and ambiguities that are not likely to be discovered until the system is operational. Different system users and sponsors often have different needs, which may be in conflict. Negotiation is frequently required so that the system is satisfactory to all. Without a clear statement of each stakeholder's 'true' requirements, proper negotiation does not occur and some stakeholders are not satisfied.

Joint development sessions where stakeholders can discuss their goals, rationale, and grievances would help.

Requirements definition is a complex cognitive task involving negotiation among stakeholders with different and sometimes opposing goals (e.g., insurer and insured with respect to an insurance claim). Requirements identification involves assessment of numerous factors and features that are often interdependent (e.g., time of surgery and prescription dosage for a patient in a hospital). Requirements are frequently defined at varying levels: system, subsystem, software/hardware/human, which makes the task more complex as consistency among levels must be maintained. Team and project leaders have to negotiate among team members to prioritize goals (e.g., which is more important, security or information access?). Capturing goals for each stakeholder and evaluating the relationship of these goals to one another and to organizational objectives would support prioritization and trade-off analysis. Tracing goals to the design would help in the determination as to whether goals will be met.

Practitioners specifying requirements frequently do not document their assumptions. This may occur because there isn't a policy for such documentation. However, it is commonly unintentional. As noted by Edwards and White (1994), it often occurs because "users, sponsors, and others become so accustomed to a method of doing business, a previous system's operation, or a system concept that they do not realize that assumptions are unstated. Other practitioners, who do not understand these assumptions, misinterpret requirements." Recognition of these problems and the use of facilitated group sessions to discuss requirements might help to alleviate these problems.

Thus, techniques recommended in both requirements management and knowledge management literature can alleviate some of the problems associated with identifying, capturing, and validating requirements.

Addressing Problems Due to System Complexity

To compound the above issues, most systems today include a very large amount of software. Consider, for example, that it takes dozens of microprocessors running one hundred million lines of code to get a premium car out of the driveway, and this software is only going to get more complex (Charette, 2009). Developing high-complexity systems can cost billions of dollars (low-complexity systems may cost less than a million), and system size and complexity is growing. The asynchronous event-driven nature of software greatly increases system complexity (the system has to respond to a human or other system performing an event, e.g., putting a car in gear). The large number of interdependencies among system parts is also a complexity factor. Because software can be changed, customers and marketing departments request many more requirements changes for software than hardware. The inherent complexity and the changes in requirements and scope add to the difficulty in managing software requirements.

To reduce complexity, requirements analysts need many views of the requirements; each should address a single question. Since understanding interdependencies is important, these views must not only address system parts, but must also include threads through the system (stimulus-response) and behavioral views. Practitioners also need useful paradigms that promote reuse of information in existing requirements specifications and other documents and reuse of previously developed architectures, models, and components. They need a repository together with descriptions that not only identify the parts but also describe where to use them.

The following methods for addressing system complexity were identified in White et al., 1993. Practitioners need models for generating a wide range of operational scenarios, including many with low probability. They need these scenarios to make an early determination whether requirements are consistent and adequate. Without these scenarios, engineers must wait until the system is operational to determine whether the system works properly within its environment. Checklists are also needed, for example, of the various trade-offs that could arise and ways of resolving them. Analysis for completeness, consistency, and correctness is primitive. Methods and tools should apply logic, temporal analysis, and domain understanding to the analysis problem.

In too many cases, systems engineers and business analysts do not understand what information is to be provided to implementers. They provide information in the wrong sequence and with insufficient detail. These problems can be solved by defining a dialogue structure. For example, projects can define the correct level of information needed to determine feasibility versus the correct level needed for design.

When requirements change, system and software analysts evaluate design decisions to determine whether they are still valid. To support this evaluation, decisions must be well defined, and documentation must include the decision rationale. Systems engineers and business analysts make "high-level," "architectural," or "systemwide" design decisions. These are policy decisions that inform and constrain subsequent design and management decisions relating to various subsystems. It is unclear how to present and propagate these key decisions. For example, practitioners do not know how to monitor subsystem design decisions to ensure that they are not in conflict with system-level design decisions. In addition, many high-level (business- or system-level) decisions result in major consequences to the software system. Often, practitioners do not understand the consequences when making high-level decisions. Corporations must keep track of the types of decisions in their domain that have major consequences and the ramifications of those decisions. They need a policy as to how such decisions are to be made and monitored.

Because work done by one contractor affects another at the interface, definitive interface specification is important. Sometimes requirements and design are not well defined at the time that subsystem interfaces must be specified. This can be due to an overly optimistic schedule or inadequate knowledge of the domain, or it may be unavoidable due to the uniqueness of the project. When it is not possible to fully define an interface, it is important to track and report changes to the interface as soon as problems are identified, as changes become more expensive later in the life cycle. Encapsulation of interface software prevents widespread change to software and documentation in many cases.

COGNITIVE THEORIES, KNOWLEDGE, AND REQUIREMENTS MANAGEMENT

As individuals, teams, and organizations (together, agents) need a common operational picture to work together effectively, they have to turn information into knowledge. They do so by constructing a mental model of the situation. According to researchers who study individual and team cognition, such mental models allow agents to work together effectively and predict outcomes of potential action (Rouse, Cannon-Bowers, & Salas, 1992). A system that supports the mental models of each team member and shows where an individual's mental model is inconsistent supports team cognition. Creating (1) system models with multiple views and (2) executable prototypes supports consistent mental models if the views are defined at different levels of abstraction, are sufficiently precise, and are consistent.

Three Cognitive Theories Applied to Requirements Management

Three cognitive theories provide insight into team communication and problem solving: (1) situated action (Zsambok & Klein, 1996), (2) activity theory (Kaptelinin & Nardi, 2006; Leont'ev, 1978; Nardi, 1996), and (3) distributed cognition (Hollan, Hutchins, & Kirsh, 2000; Hutchins, 1994; Salas & Fiore, 2004). Situated action research has analyzed teams working on time-critical tasks to understand and improve training and team performance. Investigators have found that people with sufficient training and experience act without hesitating to plan their actions. They appear to know what to do without a great deal of thought about the process. Thus, organizations could benefit from knowledge management systems that help individuals and teams learn and practice the tasks they have to perform. Examples of support for requirements elicitation include sample lists of interview questions, techniques for writing good requirements, lessons learned from previous projects, and practice on small projects prior to working on more complex ones.

Activity theory is based on the work of Leont'ev (1978), who describes an activity as composed of subject, objective (called object of the activity), actions, and operations. Actions are similar to tasks and require more thought than operations. For example, driving a car is an action, whereas shifting gears in a car is routine (for a driver with standard transmission) and is considered an operation. The ideal requirements management system performs that which is routine (operations) and aids people in more complex tasks (actions). For example, requirements management tools capture requirements, their source, and interdependencies (operations) and support a team member in discussions about a requirement with others (action).

When a person performs a new, difficult, or high-risk task, the person internalizes the task and "simulates" in his or her mind what could possibly happen and what he or she would do. People also internalize what they learn in virtual communities (Peddibhotla & Subramani, 2008). The level of internalization depends on the degree to which knowledge seeking and learning is a characteristic of the individual. This indicates that workers who have an interest in seeking out knowledge may excel over others in requirements management.

Activity theory recognizes that tools embody the experience of the people who built the tool to make a task easier or more productive and that tools affect the way people interact with their environment. Therefore, the next generation requirements management system should capture what people learn when performing a task and use that information to help others. A tool should also act as a mentor, helping a person learn how to perform a new task or connecting the developer with those in the company or elsewhere with the needed expertise. Nardi, a notable proponent of activity theory, who has authored a considerable number of articles and two books on the subject, writes that a team cannot have cognition or consciousness, only an individual can (Nardi, 1998). A tool that supports the mental models of each team member and shows where individual mental models are inconsistent would support team cognition. Multiview models and executable prototypes do this, but they are time consuming and costly to build.

Although research in team cognition is still in its adolescence, research on team effectiveness has produced valuable results, including an improved understanding of how the skills, roles, awareness, and communication of team members result in team coordination (Hutchins, 1994; Salas & Fiore, 2004). A system is needed that helps organize a team's work, coordinates work and information, and updates information as situations change. Metrics and measurement must be used to help teams evaluate process progress and problems. One such metric is "earned value," which helps teams understand whether they are meeting their schedule. The system must also aid team members in locating people with specific knowledge and locating information in artifacts (documents, images, models, and prototypes). The system must use computer support where appropriate to off-load work, including communication tasks, from overloaded personnel.

Teams and organizations share a joint understanding or *context*. Such contexts are hierarchical and overlapping, as shown in figure 3.10. Examples of contexts for teams building an emergency room support system are (1) the team building the subsystem supporting emergency room activities, (2) the team building the subsystem supporting patient medical histories, and (3) the team building the subsystem matching physicians with specific cases. When the emergency room support system records an entering patient's data (name, address, physician, symptoms, criticality), the patient medical history is consulted to determine overall health issues and prescriptions, and the physician matching system is consulted to find the identified physician and other physicians whose skills may be needed.

Cognitive Theory Applied to Information Integration

The phrase *joint context* infers that people, teams, and organizations have a common mental model (all are referred to in this chapter as agents). The mental models

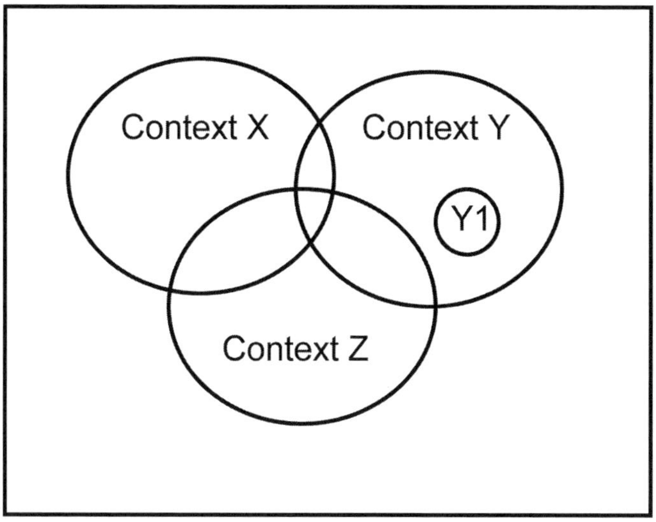

Figure 3.10. Overlapping Contexts

of different individuals may approach commonality but never be exactly the same, as people come from different environments and have different histories. If existing systems are being integrated, it is likely that information was captured by different organizations that do not necessarily share common mental models. The models and schema could be quite different and even conflicting. People work together optimally when they share common mental models; if not, the team can incur serious problems (Hutchins, 1994). The situation is even worse if the schema or ontology in automated systems are different, in which case the systems may not even be able to communicate. The problem with different schema or ontology is so pervasive that the Department of Defense (DoD) created high-level architecture (HLA) so that DoD simulations would work together (Dahmann, Fujimoto, & Weatberly, 1997).

Semantic heterogeneity is one of the key challenges in integrating and sharing data across disparate sources (Doan et al., 2004). Web services and XML do not solve the problem. Web services are focused on physical connectivity and do not consider the semantics of exchanged data. While XML does consider semantics, it does not solve integration problems, as people use terms differently and translation is not a simple problem. Standards for domain terminology would help, such as that under development for postsecondary education. While heterogeneity can arise at the schema and data level, this chapter addresses only the schema level.

At the schema level, systems can differ in names, relations, level of detail, normalization, and coverage of the domain. Matching (mapping) between schemas from different sources remains a difficult problem, despite the amount of research and experimentation in this area (Doan et al., 2004). For example, suppose two systems include maps of an area. One system is used by ambulances to find a location. The other is used by a central call center for emergencies, such as 911. Suppose we want to integrate these two systems and in the ambulance system, routes are identified by number while in the call center, routes are identified by street/road name where available. Since a route number can be associated with several street names, depending on location, and a street name can be associated with several routes, integrating the two systems would be difficult. Techniques that support automated schema matching include using heuristics to identify similarities in the schema, using a domain ontology or analogous structure to support matching, and using multiple matchers and combining their findings for greater confidence in the results (Bergamaschi et al., 1999; Embly, 2004; Motro, 2004).

CONCLUSIONS

In the past projects have transformed knowledge into information to support requirements management, and this is important. Communication of knowledge is just as important. For a corporation to be effective, each individual, team, project, and organization must act as a resource to others and in turn must obtain knowledge from others. Many people working on projects have a myopic view of the system they are building. They understand their part of the system but do not see the larger picture. Others have an understanding of the system at a high level but do not understand the details, yet the details can have a significant impact on how the overall system operates. These team members must share their knowledge for a project to work effectively. "Rich pictures" provide the team with a basis for discussing the problem. Multiview models and executable prototypes provide the team with a basis for discussing the proposed system.

At the corporate level, knowledge experts must be identified and available, and the corporation must have a knowledge-sharing culture. Communities of practice, integrated product teams, and joint training help in addressing communication problems. Joint development sessions where stakeholders discuss their goals, rationale, and grievances are worth the time and effort. Capturing assumptions and decisions provides the basis for the team to discuss whether the assumptions are correct and the decisions are satisfactory. Capturing lessons learned allows the corporation to learn from its successes and mistakes.

REFERENCES

Alford, M. (1985). SREM at the age of eight: The distributed computing design system. *IEEE Computer, 18*(4), 36–46.

Bergamaschi, S., et al. (1999). Semantic integration of semistructured and structured data sources. *ACM SIGMOD Record, 28*(1).

Boehm, B. W. (1981). *Software engineering economics*. Upper Saddle River, NJ: Prentice-Hall.

Bouillet, E., Feblowitz, M., Liu, Z., Ranganathan, A., and Riabov, A. (2008). A faceted requirements-driven approach to service design and composition. *Proceedings of the 2008 IEEE International Conference on Web Services*, 369–376.

Cannon-Bowers, J. A., Salas, E., and Pruitt, J. S. (1996). Establishing the boundaries of a paradigm for decision-making research. *Human Factors, 38*(2), 193–205.

Charette, R. N. (2009). This car runs on code. *IEEE Spectrum* (February).

Checkland, P. (1999). *Systems thinking, systems practice*. Chichester, England: John Wiley & Sons.

Chen, P. P. (1976). The entity-relationship model: Toward a unified view of data. *ACM TODS 1*(1). Republished in Stonebraker, M. (Ed.). (1988). *Readings in database systems*. San Mateo, CA: Morgan Kaufman.

Cockburn, A. (2001). *Writing effective use cases.* Boston: Addison-Wesley.

Dahmann, J. S., Fujimoto, R. M., and Weatberly, R. M. (1997). The Department of Defense high level architecture. Retrieved from 1997 Winter Simulation Conference, http://www.wintersim.org/prog97.htm

Dalcher, D. (April 2001). "Ambulance Dispatch Systems: The Melbourne Story," IEEE Engineering of Computer Based Systems Symposium (ECBS01), Washington DC, Los Alamitos: IEEE Press, 337–342.

Darren, D. (2001). Ambulance Despatch Systems: The Melbourne Story. *Proceedings of the Eighth Annual IEEE International Conference and Workshop on the Engineering of Computer Based Systems.*

Doan, A., et al. (2004). Introduction to the special issue on semantic integration. *ACM SIGMOD Record, 33*(4).

Edwards, M., & White, S. (1994). RE-views: A requirements structure and views. *Proceedings of the fourth annual international symposium of the National Council on Systems Engineering.*

Efroni, S., Harel, D., and Cohen, I. R. (2005). Reactive animation: Realistic modeling of complex dynamic systems. *IEEE Computer, 38*(1), 38–47.

Embly, D. W. (2004). Automatic direct and indirect schema mapping: Experiences and lessons learned. ACM *SIGMOD Record, 33*(4).

Flowers, S. (1996). *Software failure: Management failure.* Chichester, England: John Wiley & Sons.

Gruber, T. (1993). A translation approach to portable ontology specification. *Knowledge Acquisition,* 5.

Harel, D., & Politi, M. (1998). *Modeling reactive systems with statecharts: The Statemate approach.* Columbus, OH: McGraw-Hill.

Hollan, J., Hutchins, E., & Kirsh, D. (2000). Distributed cognition: Toward a new foundation for human-computer interaction research. *ACM Transactions on Computer-Human Interaction (TOCHI), 7*(2).

Hutchins, E. (1994). *Cognition in the wild.* Cambridge, MA: MIT Press.

INCOSE Tools Database Working Group. (2009). INCOSE Requirements Management Tools Survey. Retrieved from: http://www.paper-review.com/tools/rms/read.php

Kant, I. (1966). *Critique of pure reason* (F. Max Muller, Trans.). Garden City, NY: Anchor Books. (Original work published 1781)

Kaptelinin, V., & Nardi, B. A. (2006). *Acting with technology: Activity theory and interaction design.* Cambridge, MA: MIT Press.

Kotonya, G., & Sommerville, I. (1998). *Requirements engineering.* Chichester, UK: John Wiley & Sons.

Lambe, P. (2007). *Organizing knowledge and organizational effectiveness.* Oxford, England: Chandos Publishing.

Lee, J., & Kuo, J. Y. (1998). New approach to requirements trade-off analysis for complex systems. *IEEE Transactions on Knowledge and Data Engineering, 10*(4), 551–562.

Leont'ev, A. (1978). *Activity, consciousness, and personality.* Englewood Cliffs, NJ: Prentice-Hall.

Minsky, M. (1975). A framework for representing knowledge. In P. Winston (Ed.), *The psychology of computer vision.* New York: McGraw-Hill. Retrieved from: http://web.media.mit.edu/~minsky/papers/Frames/frames.html

Motro, A. (2004). Multiplex, fusionplex and autoplex: Three generations of information integration. *ACM SIGMOD Record, 33*(4).

Moulding, M. R., & Smith, L. C. (1992). Formalizing a CORE requirements model in the air traffic control domain. *The Future—IEE Colloquium on Software in Air Traffic Control Systems.*

Nardi, B. A. (Ed.). (1996). *Context and consciousness: Activity theory and human-computer interaction.* Cambridge, MA: MIT Press.

Nardi, B. A. (1998). Concepts of cognition and consciousness: Four voices. *Journal of Computer Documentation, 22*(1).

OMG Systems Engineering DSIG. (2008). *OMG systems modeling language (SysML) specification*, ver. 1.1. Retrieved November 2008: http://www.omg.org/spec/SysML/1.1/changebar/PDF

Opdahl, A. L., & Sindre, G. (1995). Facet models for problem analysis. *Advanced Information Systems Engineering, Springer Lecture Notes in Computer Science*, 54–67.

Peddibhotla, N.B., & Subramani, M. R. (2008). Managing knowledge in virtual communities within organizations. In I. Becerra-Fernandez & D. Leidner (Eds.), *Knowledge management: An evolutionary view. Advances in Management Information Systems Series* 12. Armonk, NY: M. E. Sharpe.

Robertson, S., & Robertson, J. (1999). *Mastering the requirements process*. New York: ACM Press.

Rouse, W. B., Cannon-Bowers, J. A., and Salas, E. (1992). The role of mental models in team performance in complex systems. *IEEE Transactions on Systems, Man, and Cybernetics, 22*(6).

Salas E., & Fiore, S. M. (Eds.). (2004). *Team cognition: Understanding the factors that drive process and performance*. Washington, DC: American Psychological Association.

Selz, O. (1922). *Zur psychologie des produktiven denkens und des irrtums*. Bonn, Germany: Friedrich Cohen.

Sowa, J. F. (1983). *Conceptual structures: Information processing in mind and machine*. Reading, MA: Addison-Wesley.

Teichroew, D., Macasovic, P., Hershey III, E.A., & Yamamoto, Y. (1980). Application of entity-relationship approach to information processing systems modeling. In P. Chen (Ed.), *Entity-relationship approach to systems analysis and design* (pp. 15–34). Amsterdam: North-Holland.

White, S. M. (1987). *A pragmatic formal method for computer system definition* (Doctoral dissertation). Polytechnic University, New York.

White, S. M. (1994). Comparative analysis of embedded computer system requirements methods. *Proceedings of the IEEE Conference on Requirements Engineering.*

White, S. M. (2006). Requirements for distributed mission-critical decision support systems. *Proceedings of the 13th Annual IEEE International Symposium and Workshop on Engineering of Computer Based Systems.*

White, S. M. (2009). Modeling a system of systems to analyze requirements. *Proceedings of the 2nd IEEE Systems Conference.*

White, S. M., et al. (1993). Systems engineering of computer-based systems. *IEEE Computer, 26*(11), 54–65.

White, S. M., & Edwards, M. (1995). A requirements taxonomy for specifying complex systems. *Proceedings of the First IEEE International Conference on Engineering of Complex Computer Systems.*

White, S. M., & Edwards, M. (1996). Domain engineering: The challenge, status, and trends. *Proceedings of the IEEE Symposium and Workshop on Engineering of Computer Based Systems.*

White, S., Pallack, P., Dorchak, S., Keane, J., Sztipanovits, J., Davis, J., Rozenblit, J., & Owens, J. (1998). *A process centered environment for complex system development that emphasizes situation assessment and decision making*. SBIR Report for Naval Surface Warfare Center, Contract No. C-N00178-97-C-3017.

Zsambok, C. E., & Klein, G. A. (Eds.). (1996). *Naturalistic decision making*. Mahwah, NJ: Lawrence Erlbaum Associates.

4

The Use of KM Tools and Techniques to Reduce Coordination Problems in Project Management

Miguel A. Morales-Arroyo, Yun-ke Chang, and Gabriel de las Nievas Sánchez-Guerro

Lack of coordination usually delays and increases the costs of a project. In this chapter, we present the effects of lack of coordination in project management and what KM techniques can be used in each stage to reduce it. First we identify common causes of most project failure. Second, the types of interdependences among individuals and teams and their connection with coordination mechanisms are defined. Third, we describe the effects of interdependence derived from the organizational structure of a project on the coordination of activities. Fourth, we present the links among KM processes, coordination, and interdependences. Finally, we suggest a set of tools that can be used to reduce coordination problems in project management.

PROJECT MANAGEMENT FAILURES

A project is a short-term effort carried out to generate an exclusive service or product. Consequently, project management can be understood as applying expertise, techniques, and a body of knowledge to project activities in order to accomplish project requirements. Project management has specific processes: definition of goals, planning, executing, monitoring and controlling, closing, and evaluation (Project Management Institute, 2008).

Traditionally, the concepts of planning, scheduling, and control techniques have been related to project management (Dinsmore, 1984). This body of knowledge was originated by the engineering profession—largely from civil engineering. Although these principles, practices, tools, and techniques have been a great utility to reduce chaos in managing engineering projects, some adjustments are needed to manage information technology (IT) and business projects in which complexity is a constant situation (Kapur, 1999). Table 4.1 lists a set of main differences between conventional and unconventional projects. Building projects are the examples of the traditional type; unconventional types include most IT projects and those whose technology and effects have not been totally tested (e.g., carbon capture and sequestration [CCS]).

Table 4.1. Key Differences between Traditional and IT Projects

Traditional Projects	*Unconventional Projects*
Intended purpose is well defined through models, exact drawings and specifications previous to any production effort initiates.	The intended goals are vague on a regular basis
Most are with linear project phases.	Phases may overlap, and sometimes there are escalation of phases.
Projects usually have well-defined boundaries.	The limits may be undefined.
Usually, the project involves the use of predesigned or pretested components.	Oftentimes, needed components need to be developed from scratch.
Most deliverables are defined in precise terms.	Deliverables are defined vaguely and are open to interpretation by the stakeholders.
Cost estimation is facilitated by the extensive information broadly available in databases.	Cost estimation is based on team members' best guesses.
There are well-defined roles and responsibilities of team members.	An individual's role and responsibilities may evolve over time.
Standard nomenclature and symbols are used.	Each stakeholder may use ad hoc nomenclature and symbols developed by himself.

Source: Kapur (1999).

Some factors have been identified as causes of project failure, such as having unrealistic deadlines, assigning underskilled project managers to highly complex projects without solid support from top management (Standish Group, 1999), not considering competing demands from other projects (Garner, 1997), failing to understand the role of the project within the parent organization, and failing to handle the complexity of distributed environments (Standish Group, 1999). Some of the failures in projects could also derive from the fact that unconventional projects require more specific definitions of goals, limits, stages, deliverables, processes, and terms used.

The definition of requirements affects the project scope, the objectives to achieve, and the specific project processes (Garner, 1997; Standish Group, 1999; Brandel, 2006). Lack of definition has been reported to have great impact on many areas of the project. On the other hand, high complexity in a project may be the result of failing to break a project into smaller manageable units for achieving specific goals.

The reduction in scope has a direct effect on project success (Brandel, 2006; Marchewka, 2006; Melymuka, 1998). The implications of downsizing a project into smaller ones are the reductions on the number of required team members involved, time, and cost. The Standish Group studied more than twenty-three thousand IT projects since 1994, and it reported that project success is inversely proportional to the project size; in other words, the smaller the project, the more likely it is to succeed.

COORDINATION

The study of coordination is highly relevant in project management since many setbacks will manifest themselves directly or indirectly as the result of lack of coordination; for example, resources needed are not allocated to the correct unit, or milestones are not delivered on time. Another reason for better understanding coordination is the need of cross-functioning between different departments or teams, both across and up the line. Coordination is also fundamental when there is interrelation of business units, which demands communication at the horizontal level. Essentially, coordination is the integration of all project activities to facilitate its development and its success. Coordination includes (a) defining priorities, the correct amount of resources and time, and their impact on the project scope; (b) deciding the order and precedence of activities in a progression that best match the project requirements; (c) the adjustment of alternatives available to achieve the objectives; (d) monitoring the project to keep it continuously attuned to circumstances; (e) keeping expenditures under budget; (f) maintaining the use of resources under control; and (g) adapting tools for their use in the project (Fayol, 1984; Graham, 1995). In other words, coordination is a need when actions of interdependent actors have to be integrated to achieve common goals.

TYPES OF INTERDEPENDENCES

Individuals and teams need to share their resources, skills, and knowledge to achieve complex tasks. In other words, individuals and teams are interdependent. There are four types of interdependences: social, pooled, sequential, and reciprocal (Blau, 1964; Brown, 1995; Kumar & Dissel, 1996; Thompson, 2003). Social interdependence is based on social exchange, in which individuals have expectations of obtaining rewards. They exchange favors and resources as long as the interchanges are considered fair and rewarding. However, the value of some recompenses and obligations derived from the exchange cannot be specified in advance, which makes the interchange practice an evolving process (Blau, 1964). In figure 4.1, social interdependence is represented with a dotted line with the intention to show a loosely bonded interdependence. The exchanges between actors A and B create future obligations, but these obligations cannot be enforced by the actors. Obligations that derive from exchanges are enforced by the rule of reciprocity and social norms, and the expectation of obligations fulfillment is based on trust. In a project context, social interdependence occurs in informal exchanges, sometimes in simple exchange of information.

Pooled interdependence is that in which each party contributes to the totality, and the totality sustains each party when all parties belong to the same organization (Thompson, 2003). In this situation, staff members contribute to achieve the common good, and the organization will provide the resources for each of them to achieve their particular objectives. Although individual members may have diverse goals, all of them have to contribute to the common good. Obligations are enforced by a central authority. In the case where parties belong to different firms, they use common resources but are independent in other aspects (Kumar & Dissel, 1996).

Figure 4.1. Social Interdependence

Figure 4.2. Pooled Interdependence

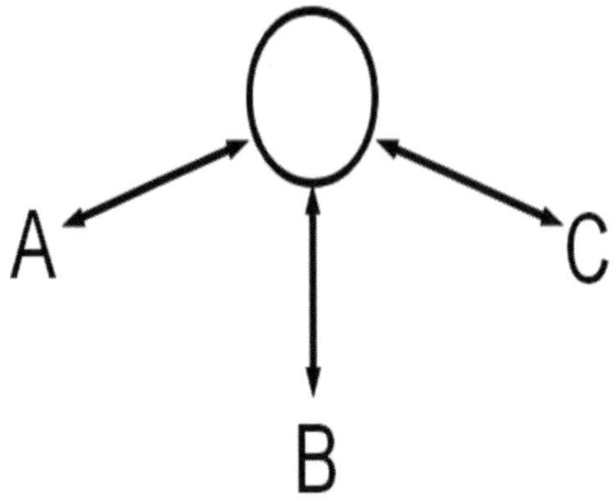

Usually in this situation, these organizations have different objectives. Obligations are enforced by a standard agreement that is followed by all participating organizations, and the interaction among firms is minimal. Pooled interdependence is illustrated in figure 4.2.

Sequential interdependence is a consecutive arrangement; the outcomes of one party are the raw materials for another. When sequential interdependence is present, pooled interdependence is present, too. Obligations are enforced by a central authority. A typical example of sequential interdependence happens in a process when the output of actor "A" is used by actor "B" and the output of "B" is used by "C," which is illustrated in figure 4.3.

Reciprocal interdependence occurs when parts interchange resources and services reciprocally. The more interdependence there is among partners, the more difficult it is to coordinate activities among them. The level of contingency increases when the level of coordination and interdependence is high (Kumar & Dissel, 1996; Thompson, 2003). This type of interdependence is shown in figure 4.4.

Mechanism of Coordination

For each type of interdependence, there is a mechanism for coordination. Social interdependence is coordinated by social conventions. A convention is a standardized behavior that most members assume to unravel a particular trouble. Conventions are uniformity in behavior, supported by the need for coordination and the hope that others will fulfill their obligation (Lewis, 1969). Therefore, social convention promotes routines and voluntary behaviors among population members, which facilitates the coordination of their actions to provide fair and satisfactory results but not necessarily an optimal solution to the problem. Moreover, accepting the outcome does not mean that population members prefer those specific results (Brown, 1995).

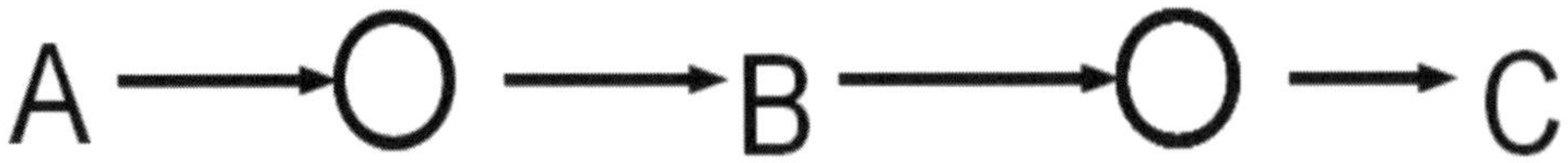

Figure 4.3. Sequential Interdependence

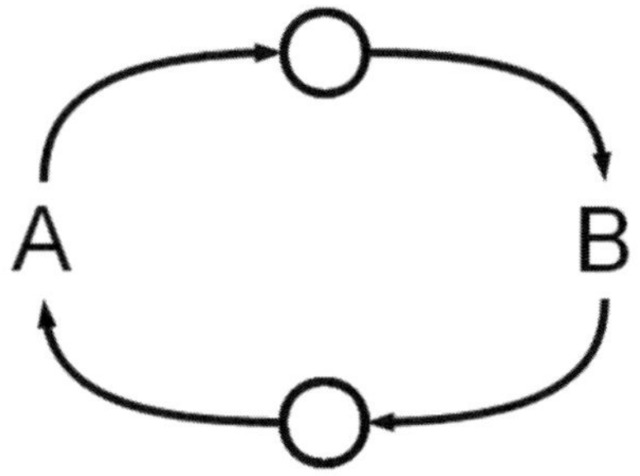

Figure 4.4. Reciprocal Interdependence

Conventions are hard to bring into being. When they are robust, almost no one remembers how they were created, and trying to change them is complicated. In order to adopt conventions, a certain number of participants is required; the quantity also depends on environmental aspects and the type of problem to solve. When a convention is successful in solving the problem, people involved usually express things such as, "Here, things work in this way," while nobody remembers how or when the convention was initiated. These types of behaviors are associated with the organizational culture. Similarly, conventions are developed among the members of a community (Brown, 1995).

With pooled interdependence, coordination is achieved by standardization. This includes the creation of rules or routines that restrict the actions of each party into channels coherent with those used by other participants. The arrangement of routines or rules must have inner consistency, and the conditions in which they are relevant must be fairly steady and recurrent. The number of routines and rules should be small in order to allow appropriately matching them with those conditions, which is a supposition for coordination by standardization (Thompson, 2003).

With sequential interdependence, coordination is achieved by plan. Coordination by plan includes the creation of schedules and the use of control techniques so that the behaviors of interdependent parts can be managed. Coordination by plan is more suitable for more dynamic conditions.

With reciprocal interdependence, coordination is achieved by mutual adjustment. Coordination by mutual adjustment involves the transmission of new information during the process of action. The more erratic and irregular are the conditions, the larger the dependency on this type of coordination will be (Thompson, 2003). Figure 4.5 synthesizes interdependence with the mechanisms of coordination, and it shows how as coordination of mechanisms gets more complex, the costs, decision-making process, and communication increase in difficulty.

Social conventions are usually hidden; they are based on trust and are difficult to change (Brown, 1995). The loads of communication and decision-making process progress intensively as the type of coordination moves from the social convention to standardization, to plan, to mutual adjustment. In other words, coordination by mutual adjustment requires more communication and decision actions than does coordination by plan, and coordination by plan needs more communication and decision actions than does standardization. There are absolutely actual costs and time implicated in coordination of activities (Thompson, 2003).

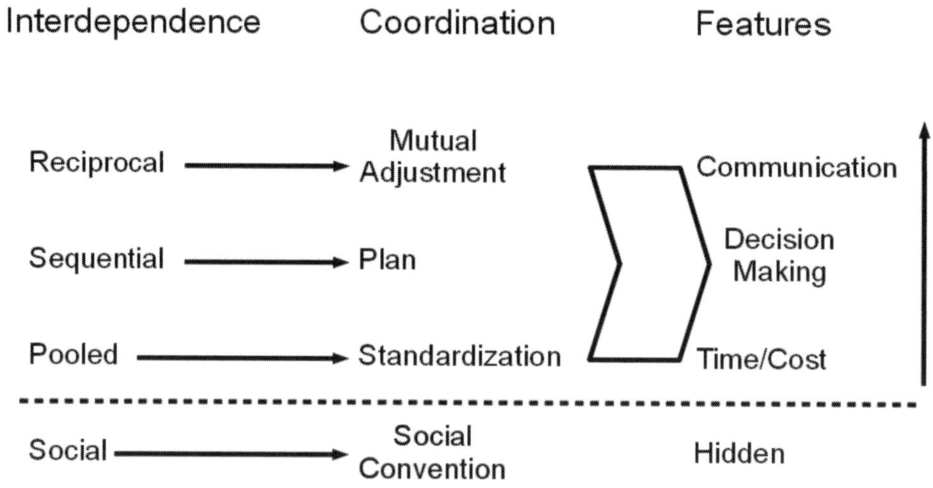

Figure 4.5. Relationship between Interdependence and Coordination Mechanisms

ORGANIZATIONAL STRUCTURES

Coordination requires a structure that allows the provision of resources in time (Chisholm, 1989; Kumar & Dissel, 1996). A structure is the way in which tasks are shared among teams or individuals in a project. Each team has its particular roles, and coordination should be accomplished among those roles. In other words, structure is the degree of definition of responsibilities, rights, functions, processes, and information flows (Kumar & Dissel, 1996). The higher the initial degree of definition of coordination factors, the better the original structure in the organization of the project will be (Kumar & Dissel, 1996).

Chisholm (1989) describes two types of coordination in terms of organizational structures: formal coordination with a hierarchical structure and central authority, and informal coordination with informal horizontal links and no central authority. Formal coordination derives from the formal design of the project structure. Informal coordination derives from the everyday agreements, needs, and interactions, and it compensates for the failures resulting from inadequate adaptation of the formal agreements to particular conditions.

The nature of formal coordination is time consuming. Other disadvantages of formal coordination include that it may have an incomplete design and be incapable of providing sufficient resources, for there could be ambiguity about the responsibility for problems not delineated in the original plan, and fast obsolescence of the conditions for which the formal structure was originated.

Informal structure emanates from everyday trial and error and adjustments to particular goals and promotes compromises in situations with divergence and dissent. Also, roles are constantly delineated by experience, and definition of tasks is decided by negotiations, but not by any central authority. In addition, informal structures act in response to the consequences of problems in sight. They may be composed of elements of similar level, and they are flexible and adaptable, problem oriented, pragmatic, based on trial-and-error experiences, self-organizing, and innovative. In spite of all these advantages, informal structures require formal structures to subsist and to decentralize activities, which benefit horizontal relationships (Chisholm, 1989). The disadvantages of informal coordination also include the fact that managers do not have formal control over it, and obscurity makes it difficult to examine and understand. Information coordination may be at risk of being used for antiethical activities.

In the context of project management, coordination by convention is part of the informal structure, and coordination by standardization, by plan, is a component of the formal structure. Coordination by mutual adjustment has both formal and informal components. Traditionally in project management, three formal structures have been used: functional, matrix, and project based (Marchewka, 2006). These formal organizations have advantages and disadvantages, but they are beyond the scope of our topic.

KM PROCESSES IN THE CONTEXT OF PROJECT MANAGEMENT

An organization's know-how makes it possible to blend and utilize resources, which results in the delivery of products and services. This knowledge is rooted in and sustained by numerous elements, involving organizational identity and culture, practices, organizational conventions, guiding principles, work procedures, documents, and staff members. The use and creation of organizational knowledge is more important than the amount of knowledge possessed by organizations at any given time (Alavi & Leidner, 2001). In the context of project management, the relevance of KM is how to better make use of and be able to find new solutions. In particular, we focus on the relationship among project phases and KM processes and what tools and techniques can be used to facilitate the project development.

Knowledge creation is the heart of innovation (Ichijō & Nonaka, 2007). It implies making novel ideas available in two modalities: tacit and explicit knowledge. With the help of social exchanges and collaborative actions in addition to a person's cognitive processes, knowledge is generated, shared, expanded incrementally, and validated in organizational environments (Alavi & Leidner, 2001). Efficient knowledge creation relies on facilitating circumstances, such as the freedom to make mistakes (Krogh et al., 2000). As there is social interdependence among knowledge creators during knowledge creation, the coordination process is mainly informal and requires informal exchanges among creators.

KNOWLEDGE STORAGE/RETRIEVAL

Organizations generate and assimilate knowledge, but they as well host their organizational memory. Thus, the storage, organization, and retrieval of organizational knowledge constitute an important aspect of effective organizational knowledge management. Organizational knowledge storage, also known as knowledge retention, includes written documentation, organized data saved in computer databases, systematized human knowledge saved in expert systems, written organizational processes and procedures, and tacit knowledge obtained through individuals and social networks (Alavi & Leidner, 2001). In knowledge storage/retrieval, the interdependence among stakeholders is pooled. This process can be broken into two elements: (a) identifying critical knowledge and (b) gathering critical knowledge according to the type of knowledge (Fruchter & Demian, 2002). The coordination of activities requires the development of standard procedures for retrieval of relevant information and knowledge.

KNOWLEDGE TRANSFER

Information flows and communication practices deliver knowledge transfer in organizational settings. Knowledge transfer is a process in which content is passed on among individuals, teams, and business units by both formal and informal mechanisms. It takes place at different levels: transfer of knowledge between individuals, from individuals to explicit sources, from individuals to groups, between groups, across groups, and from groups to the organization. In order for knowledge to be used, the identification of knowledge sources, types of knowledge need, and potential users are a necessity. Organizations often are not sure of what they know, and they usually have weak systems for identifying sources and retrieving knowledge that exists in them. As a result, knowledge transfer is a complicated process.

Knowledge transfer and sharing may have three types of interdependence—social, pooled, and sequential—depending on the type of knowledge that is transferred or shared. For example, sharing tacit knowledge usually is achieved by the use of social conventions through informal exchanges. Transfer of explicit knowledge could be carried out by creating repositories of organized knowledge, which facilitates retrieval of relevant knowledge. In other words, the stakeholders are pooled-interdependent in their relationship and use standards to create the repository. Sequential interdependence may occur when a sequence of structured courses or workshops are delivered.

Before implementation of KM in organizational settings, and specifically in project management, it is important to find out the organizational readiness. Duffy (1999) suggested the use of three dimensions to assess the readiness of organizations to implement KM strategies: technology environment, business environment, and organizational environment. In particular, the issues that require more attention are infrastructure, organizational culture, knowledge needs, and technology requirements. Table 4.2 summarizes the major knowledge processes and their relationship with main project management phases.

In order to select tools that reduce coordination problems in project management context and foster learning and exploit owned and created knowledge, we will follow the sequence of project stages. We start by identifying and defining objectives and requirements needed for the project. Later, the planning stage includes the analysis of alternatives, identification of risks, and definition of budget, schedule, milestones, and quality criteria. In this stage, breakdown structure, PERT/CPM, Gantt diagram, and knowledge strategy have to be defined. Execution and monitoring involves report generation, dealing with the human issues of the project, confronting conflict, and sometimes organizational change. The lessons learned and best practices are developed in the closing and evaluation stages. Other tools do

Table 4.2. KM Processes and Project Phases

	Definition of Goals	*Planning*	*Execution and Monitoring*	*Closing*	*Evaluation*
Knowledge creation	•	•	•		
Knowledge capture	•	•	•	•	•
Knowledge transfer—sharing	•	•	•		
Knowledge reuse	•	•	•		•

Source: Adapted from Owen (2005).

not apply directly to the knowledge processes, but they are required by the project. These tools are included in the last row of table 4.3, named "Project development."

The objective of table 4.3 is to provide a quick reference that allows project managers to define what techniques are available to them to reduce problems in each stage of the project, specifically defining goals, limits, stages, deliverables, processes, costs, and terms used, among other issues. Most of the tools do not require further information, but others are not well known. For this reason, we define some of the techniques in appendix 1.

There are two limitations of this work: we do not provide techniques for conflict resolution, and we do not provide detail about the use of each tool since overcoming those limitations would require going beyond the intended scope of this chapter.

CONCLUSION

In management theory, the classic thinkers dedicated great parts of their writing to understanding coordination. After them, relatively few scholars have paid rigorous attention to the coordination problem. Some of the components of coordination are deeply rooted in social practices; the same occurs with some of the KM processes that involve social aspects that have not been properly defined. We addressed this issue by bringing in the ideas developed on social exchange theories. However, more work is needed in this area, both at the conceptual and empirical levels.

Social convention, a coordination mechanism, is complex since team members and some of the rules are hidden. Its development, structure, and the exchanges among the members are difficult to control by formal organizational structures. All the relationships are based on trust, and when some members leave the informal network, there could be negative effects in the flows of information.

Coordination by standardization and coordination by plan are formal mechanisms of coordination. One of the frequent recommendations made to project

Table 4.3. Selecting KM Tools for Project Management

	Definition of Goals	*Planning*	*Execution and Monitoring*	*Closing*	*Evaluation*
Knowledge creation	• Conceptual models • Brainstorming • Assumption busting	• Conceptual models • CATWOE			• Lessons learned • Best practices
Knowledge capture	• Document management systems	• Document management systems	• Document management systems • Inf. retrieval systems	• Document management systems • Inf. retrieval systems	• Document management systems • Inf. retrieval systems
Knowledge transfer—sharing	• Social network analysis • Groupware and communication technologies	• Social network analysis • Groupware and communication technologies	• Groupware and communication technologies		• Groupware and communication technologies
Knowledge reuse	• Lessons learned • Best practices	• Knowledge repositories • Inf. retrieval systems • Experts systems • Business intelligence	• Knowledge repositories • Inf. retrieval systems		
Project development	• Project management Software	• Project management software • TKJ • SWOT analysis • Ideal redesign • TGN • *Morphological analysis*	• Project management software • WBS • PERT • Gantt diagram • ZOPP	• Project management software	• Project management software

managers is to standardize as much as they can that will reduce the coordination of activities. Planning is the most frequent mechanism of coordination in project management. However, when the definition of objectives, requirements, and others fail, the consequences are increased project delays, costs, the number of decisions that have to be made, and the saturation of communication channels. In other words, when there is a problem in any of the stages of the project, it will have an impact on the coordination of activities.

APPENDIX 1: DEFINITION OF TOOLS

CATWOE analysis, originated in systems thinking, is a tool useful in describing a human activity system when diagnosing a problematic situation. *C* stands for customers of the system—those who directly benefit or suffer the consequences of a problematic situation. *A* represents the actors (persons, groups, organizations, institutions, and/or agencies) performing the required activities. *T* means transformation; in other words, it is the processes or changes that are going to take place. *W* denotes the weltanschauung (worldview) of the stakeholders, for each of them may have different perceptions and priorities about the problematic situation. *O* corresponds to the system owner(s) who are in charge of the human activity system. Finally, *E* embodies the environmental restrictions that may include tendencies, events, technological requirements, political, legal, economic, social, and ethical issues and demographic and competitive forces around the problematic situation (Checkland, 1981; Wilson, 1984).

Ideal design starts by identifying the project vision, the justification for considering a specific project. The second step is the identification of the mission, the rationale to justify building the project. For example, it could be a justification (vision) to send a human in spaceflight to Mars, but not a practical justification (mission) to send someone there (cost and technical restrictions could be a limitation). Once the vision and the mission have been identified, the next step is to identify the specifications and properties requirement in the project. The last step is to define how to obtain specification and properties identified previously (Ackoff, 1974).

The Ishikawa diagram, called a cause-and-effect or fish bone diagram, is a graphic tool used to explore and display potential causes and effects that contribute most significantly to the problematic situations being examined. It is an extension of the black-box model, where the potential causes of problem are drawn at the left of the diagram of the black box, and the consequences are entered at the right of the diagram at the end of the main "bone." The idea is to identify from three to six main categories that encompass all possible influences for causes and consequences. Each category represents a "bone" that connects to the main bone. Brainstorming is typically carried out to add potential causes and effects to the main axis (bone) and more specific causes and effects to each category. This subdivision process continues as long as the problem areas can be further subdivided. The practical number of subdivision goes from three to six levels. After the diagram is fully constructed, we obtain a quite complete picture of all the possibilities about what could be at the root of the problem under study (Ishikawa, 1985).

Morphological analysis is a method for dealing with all the potential solutions to a difficult multidimensional problem that is not easy to quantify. The objective of this technique is to contrast the basic elements in a matrix in order to find new relationships among those elements and identify solutions or alternatives. This is achieved by decomposing a system into functions or process to the required level and contrasting one function with others in a matrix arrangement according to the analysis needs. This technique was developed by Fritz Zwicky, and it is used, when exploring new and different ideas, to help unblock the creative potential when people are stuck and to force a different way of thinking (Gerardin, 1973; Zwicky, 1969).

Social network analysis is used to identify and measure relationships and information flows between people and/or groups in organizations. The nodes in the network are the people, while the links show relationships or flows between the nodes. The analysis provides a visual representation of social structures in terms of network theory about nodes. These networks are made of individuals who are joined by one or more specific types of interdependencies (Brightman, Elrod, & Ramakrishna, 1988; Cleveland, 1996).

Nominal group technique (NGT) is an extremely structured group process that supplies a methodical mechanism for gathering qualitative information from groups who are intimately related to the problems at hand. NGT is also a decision-making method that takes into account all opinions among groups who want to make a quick decision. The decision does not come from the majority group, as in direct vote. In the first step, every member of the group proposes his or her solution(s), with a short explanation. At the second stage, identical solutions are removed from the list of potential alternatives, and the participants rank the proposed solutions. The solution with the highest rank is chosen as the final decision (Delbecq, Vande-Ven, & Gustafson, 1975).

The "use of solution for problem identification" is based on the fact that people are more inclined to suggest solutions than identify problems; in order to avoid conflicts within the hierarchical structure, people do not give their real opinions. The technique uses four steps, and the first is a question that asks something like this: if you do not have any kind of limitation, what changes do you suggest? Second, it is gathering and information analysis. Third, it consists of identification of problems, and finally, the problems are addressed (Graham, 1976).

TKJ (Team Kawakita Jiro) was developed to discover meaningful categories of ideas within a raw list created by a group of participants. It is vital to allow the groupings to appear naturally, using the right side of the brain, instead of using categories previously defined. This technique is used to refine brainstorming results into something that could make better sense and be more manageable. Essentially, it is to assist finding connections between proposed ideas, synthesizing large amounts of information, and reducing information overload (Kawakita, 1991).

SWOT analysis is a strategic planning method used to evaluate the strengths, weaknesses, opportunities, and threats involved in a project. Strengths are personal, team, or organizational attributes that are helpful in achieving a specific objective. Weaknesses are deficiencies of the entity that damage or hinder the development of objectives. Opportunities are external conditions that contribute to achieving the project objectives. Threats are the environmental restrictions that could limit the achievement of objectives. SWOT analysis has four stages—the first two are identification of strengths and weaknesses, followed by the identification of opportunities and threats. The third stage is the situational analysis (synthesis process), and the fourth stage is the definition of strategies (Dyson, 1990).

ZOPP stands for *Ziel Orientierte Projekt Planung* (project planning based on objective). It is a participative technique in which stakeholders deliberate and discuss potential solutions to the problem at hand that require stakeholders' commitment. This technique has three main stages—analysis of the problematic situation, integration, and planning the implementation process (GTZ, 1990).

REFERENCES

Ackoff, R. L. (1974). *Redesigning the future*. New York: Wiley.

Alavi, M., & Leidner, D. E. (2001). *Knowledge management and knowledge management systems: Conceptual foundations and research issues. MIS Quarterly, 25*(1): 107–136.

Blau, P. M. (1964). *Exchange and power in social life*. New York: Wiley.

Brandel, M. (2006). What's next in 2006: Project management, five biggest project challenges for 2006. *Computerworld, 40*, 2.

Brightman, H., Elrod, R., & Ramakrishna, H. (1988). Matching problem diagnostic tools to managers' decision styles: a contingency approach, *Omega, 16*(1), 1–9.

Brown, D. W. (1995). *When strangers cooperate: Using social conventions to govern ourselves*. New York: Free Press.

Checkland, P. (1981). *Systems thinking, systems practice*. Chichester, England: John Wiley & Sons.

Chisholm, D. W. (1989). *Coordination without hierarchy: Informal structures in multiorganizational systems*. Berkeley and Los Angeles: University of California Press.

Cleveland, D. (1996). *Strategic management of teams*. New York: Wiley.

Delbecq, A. L., VandeVen, A. H., & Gustafson, D. H. (1975). *Group techniques for program planners*. Glenview, IL: Scott Foresman.

Dinsmore, P. C. (1984). *Human factors in project management*. New York: American Management Association.

Duffy, Jan. (1999). *Harvesting Experience: Reaping the Benefits of Knowledge*. ARMA International.

Dyson, R. (1990). *Strategic planning: models and analytical techniques*. New York: Wiley.

Fayol, H. (1984). *General and industrial management*. New York: IEEE Press.

Fruchter, R., and Demian, P. 2002). *Knowledge management for reuse*. Paper presented at the CIB W78 conference 2002, Distributing Knowledge in Building, International Council for Research and Innovation in Building and Construction, Aarhus School of Architecture, Denmark.

Garner, R. (1997). Captain of crunch. *Computerworld, 31*(40), 81–82.

Gerardin, L. (1973). Morphological analysis: A method for creativity. In J. R. Bright & M. E. F. Schoeman (Eds.), *A guide to practical technological forecasting* (pp. 422–457). Englewood Cliffs, NJ: Prentice-Hall.

Graham, P. (Ed.). (1995). *Mary Parker Follett—prophet of management: A celebration of writings from the 1920s*. Boston: Harvard Business School Press.

Graham, R. (1976). The use of solutions for problem identification. *Interfaces, 7*(1): 63–65.

GTZ. (1990). *ZOPP*. Frankfurt: Deutsch Gesellschaft für Technische Zusammenarbeit.

Hoffman, T. (2008). Building an IT project pipeline: Long-range planning helps a Hess Corporation IT unit to partner more effectively with its businesses. *Computerworld, 42*: 2.

Ichijō, K., & Nonaka, I. (2007). *Knowledge creation and management: New challenges for managers*. New York: Oxford University Press.

Ishikawa, K. (1985). *TQC to wa nani ka, Nihon-teki hinshitsu kanri. (What is total quality control? The Japanese way)* (David J. Lu, Trans.). Englewood Cliffs, NJ: Prentice-Hall.

Kapur, G. K. (1999). Why IT project management is so hard to grasp. *Computerworld, 33*, 1.

Kawakita, J. (1991). *The original KJ method* (Rev. ed.). Tokyo: Kawakita Research Institute.

Krogh, G. V., et al. (2000). *Enabling knowledge creation: How to unlock the mystery of tacit knowledge and release the power of innovation*. New York: Oxford University Press.

Kumar, K., & Dissel, H. G. v. (1996). *Sustainable collaboration: Managing conflict and cooperation in interorganizational systems. MIS Quarterly, 20*(3), 279–300.

Lewis, D. K. (1969). *Convention: A philosophical study*. Cambridge, MA: Harvard University Press.

Marchewka, J. T. (2006). *Information technology project management: Providing measurable organizational value*. Hoboken, NJ: Wiley.

Melymuka, K. (1998). Keep that project simple. *Computerworld, 32*: 1.

Owen, J., and Burstein, F. (2005). "Where Knowledge Management Resides within Project Management," Murray E. Jennex (Ed.), *Case Studies in Knowledge Management*. Idea Group Inc., IRM Press, Chapter 9, 138–153.

Project Management Institute. (2008). *A guide to the project management body of knowledge*. Newtown Square, PA: Author.

Standish Group. (1999). *Chaos: A recipe for success*. Boston: Author.

Thompson, J. D. (2003). *Organizations in action: Social science bases of administrative theory*. New Brunswick, NJ: Transaction.

Wilson, B. (1984). *Systems: Concepts, methodologies and applications*. Chichester, England: John Wiley & Sons.

Zwicky, F. (1969). *Discovery, invention, research—through the morphological approach*. Toronto: Macmillan.

5

Success Factors for Knowledge Management in a Strategy Project

Siegfried Neubauer and Franz Barachini

ABSTRACT

The German company ABS, with fifteen thousand employees worldwide and active in more than forty countries, started a strategy development project in the year 2007. The company had been very successful in the past. The motivation to start a strategy project was twofold. Management wanted to secure existing success potential on one hand, and they wanted to identify new potential for success on the other. Additionally, it was important to order and organize more than one hundred business segments and to concentrate power. The moment was properly selected since at this point there was no financial or economic crisis on the horizon. Another goal was to implant a coherent strategy process for the whole company and to educate a critical mass of managers in strategic management issues.

ABS is the property of a family who is part of the supervisory board. According to German law, the boards of management were separated in two separate governance boards—the supervisory board, representing the owners, and the management board, representing management. The project was initiated by the supervisory board, and the chair of the management board (CEO) was asked to start the project. He himself was not motivated to start such a project because from his point of view, there was no reason for the project—the company was successful anyway. Therefore, at the beginning there was not too much support from the board manager for this project.

The project lasted about one and a half years and was supported by an external consulting company. This company contributed methodologies in knowledge identification, knowledge creation, and process management. Expertise about markets, customers, trends, and specialized expert knowledge was to a great extent available in the ABS company itself. The main challenge for the consulting team was to gain access to the available implicit knowledge and to make this knowledge explicit so that the strategy project could possibly be successful.

ORGANIZATIONAL STRUCTURE AND KNOWLEDGE FLOW BETWEEN GROUPS

In order to select the correct organizational project structure, the consultant tried to identify cultural dimensions. A so-called cultural due diligence yielded a hierarchical management behavior accompanied by more masculine than feminine properties, although there were differences in different subsidiaries in different countries. The company and its fifteen thousand employees followed a rigid "bottom-line" management offering space for innovation as well. It was crucial to establish a proper organizational structure. Three different levels and five different "teams" were defined, as shown in figure 5.1:

1. Core team "strategy and knowledge"
2. Team management board
3. Strategy team of the supervisory board
4. Supervisory board
5. Steering board

1. Core Team "Strategy and Knowledge"

This team worked on strategy questions, and it consisted of key employees from the mother company and the big and powerful subsidiaries. The team was highly

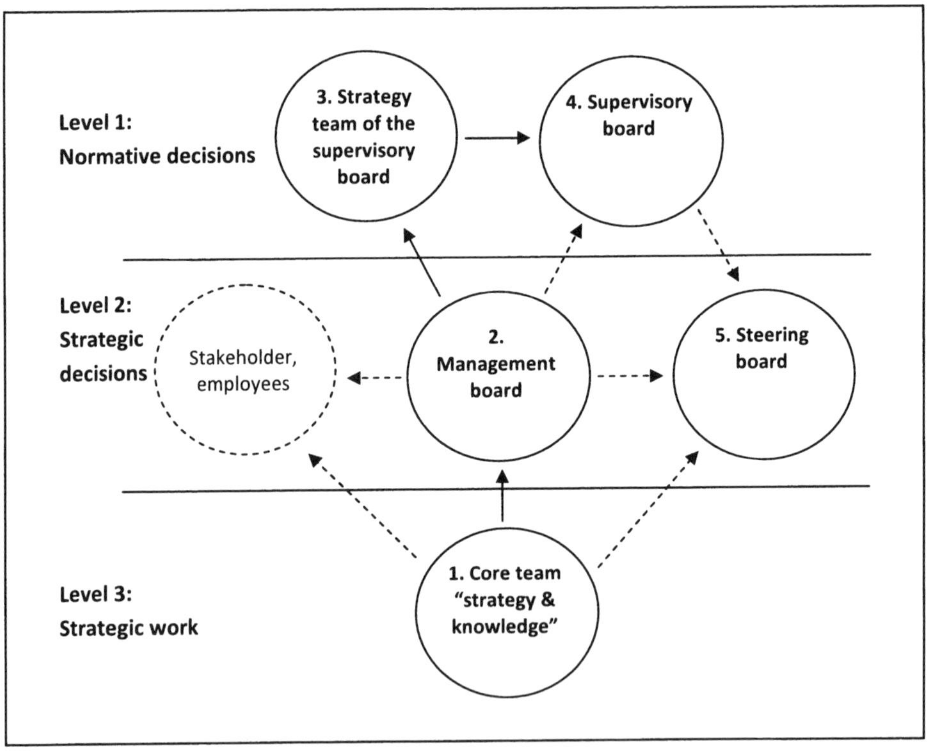

Figure 5.1. Levels and Structures of Teams

heterogeneous regarding regions and countries, levels of management, age, and experience. It included twenty persons consisting of engineers, product managers, business field leaders, and marketing experts from five continents. The team was determined by the CEO, the internal project leader, and the consultant. At the beginning, the team had to handle the following problems:

- Members had to become acquainted with one another; they stemmed from different cultures
- Members had to learn about "other" products and ways to run a business
- Cultural sense of the company was hierarchical

The heterogeneous team was selected because the project sponsors believed that different knowledge and different views could result in new insights and a high commitment right from the start. Also, these people had the best knowledge concerning markets and customers. A CEO has no such knowledge because normally he (or she) is not working at the operational level.

The task of the core team was to traverse the different phases of the newly defined strategy process, to discuss common strategic issues, and to prepare decision criteria. Each month the team met for four days and worked on the new strategy definition process. It was not the task of the core team to make decisions for the company. A regular knowledge exchange process was defined between the core team "strategy and knowledge" and the management board.

2. Team Management Board

The CEO was the project originator, and he and the whole management board were not involved in the operative strategy work. The management board was responsible for the fields of finance, research and development, manufacturing, and sales.

The management board was regularly informed by the project leader about the progress of the project. The complete management board got an update, in so-called board sessions once per month after the meetings of the core team. The management board discussed these results, made decisions, and steered through its decisions the work done at the operational level in the core team "strategy and knowledge." In addition, the management board discussed strategic issues with the strategy team of the supervisory board once per month.

3. Strategy Team of the Supervisory Board

The representative of the owner was interested in influencing the strategy process as well. Therefore, a working group consisting of supervisory board members was established. This group influenced the decisions of the management board. It also met once per month "after" the board sessions. During these meetings members were informed about the progress of the project by the CEO, who was supported by the project leader. The decisions were further improved and matched with the visions of the owners.

4. Supervisory Board

At the end of each phase of the strategy development process, the complete supervisory board and the management board were briefed about the project progress. The strategy team supervisory board reported "officially" to the complete supervisory board and was supported by the CEO. The company owner participated in these meetings, and he had the chance to directly intervene if necessary.

5. Steering Board

For the implementation of the new strategy and of strategic thinking throughout the whole company, the commitment of the first management level is a critical issue. The first management level represents the regions (regional presidents) with much power but less responsibility than the business field leaders and functional leaders of the second management level. Just to recall, the core team "strategy and knowledge" directly reported to the management board. Therefore, the first-level management was informed about project status in steering board meetings from the team "management board" and from selected team members of the core team "strategy and knowledge" after the board sessions. This board had an informational character only.

All five groups were connected through an internal hierarchical database with special access rights using socialware and an e-mail communication facility. The project leader was part of team 1 and was supported by two database managers who were responsible for taking care of content and proper database handling. However, the project originator (CEO) insisted that the above described meetings were held face to face despite high expenses. This was important to foster the new strategy process.

PROCESS PHASES

The project needed careful planning to handle the complexity regarding the number of strategic business fields, the number and heterogeneity of project groups, the duration of the project, challenges and strategic issues, and cultural aspects. Knowledge should be identified and propagated as soon as possible and as deeply as possible. The project itself consisted of the following phases, as shown in figure 5.2:

1. As-is analysis
2. Option discussion on strategic business field level
3. Details/product/market strategy on strategic business field level; strategy on company level and functional issues
4. Implementation/strategic controlling

1. As-Is Analysis

In this phase, a corporate policy needed to be developed and the status of the initial situation needed to be elaborated. That meant that in the first step, there

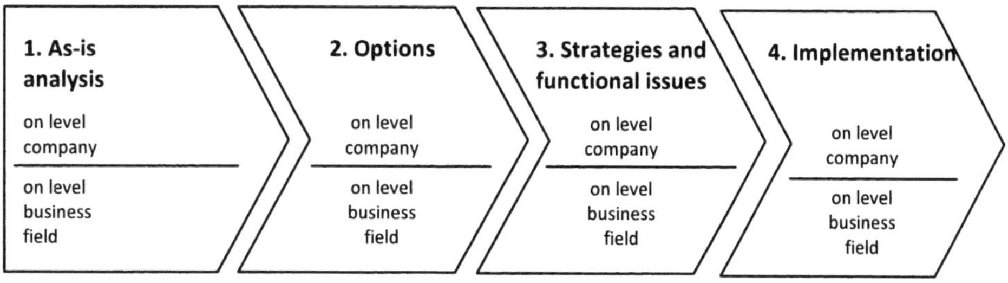

Figure 5.2. Phases of the Strategy Development Project

was the development of normative values and beliefs, the development of mission and vision statements, and the identification of corporate identity. The results were propagated to all employees in a top-down, bottom-up approach. On this basis, in a second step an environment analysis (Stöger, 2007), a competition analysis (Porter, 1983), and a SWOT (Lombriser, 2005) were established. From about one hundred business segments, thirty strategic business fields were derived and analyzed from their strategic potential and customer value point of view.

2. Option Discussion on Strategic Business Field Level

In the second phase, a portfolio discussion (Gälweiler, 2005) at the strategic field level was performed. A goal position per strategic field was defined. Using the Ansoff matrix (Eschenbach, 2003), options for products and markets were defined, and the goal position relative to the competitors was justified. Consequently, variants of the portfolio were discussed along the following dimensions:

- Consolidating strategy with organic growth ® focused strategic direction
- Growth strategy with full investment support ® focused strategic direction
- Semifull liner strategy with organic growth ® conservative strategic direction
- Extensive growth strategy with massive acquisition ® offensive strategic direction

By means of a decision support system and by comparing to normative elements of the company, a goal portfolio was developed. This goal portfolio was the basis for further work.

3. Details/Product/Market Strategy

The strategic business fields belonging to the goal portfolio were now further detailed. The qualitative and quantitative goals for each business field needed to be developed, and actions and resources needed to be defined. Also, requirements per strategic business field to the organizational functions needed to be defined. This knowledge had to be elaborated and then transferred into the organization. The reason is that the operative units and functions had to realize this strategy and reach the goal position in the portfolio. A check with the SWOT developed in phase 1 would guarantee that competitive advantages in each business field were exploited. Finally, the strategy of each strategic business field was checked for robustness using a kind of a scenario analysis (Simon & von der Gathen, 2002).

At the company level a consolidation of all business field strategies took place. All goals, requirements, and resources needed were consolidated, redundancies eliminated, and priorities fixed. Requirements to company functions were further refined. The output consisted of "internal" functional strategies that supported the implementation of "external" product/market strategies of the strategic business fields.

4. Implementation/Strategic Controlling

Only implemented strategies can support the economic viability of companies. In order to guarantee implementation of a strategy, a rigorous controlling of measures, a controlling of relevant market position goals, and an early warning system were needed, and it was crucial to apply them permanently. To maintain the strategic knowledge flow, strategy reviews and strategy circles were held every three to four months at the regional level. In this way strategic know-how was propagated on a worldwide basis.

Know-How Detection and Transfer in the Core Team

The core team consisted of twenty people stemming from different cultures, different countries, and different management levels and met every month for a four-day workshop. The concept of the face-to-face workshops was motivated by the following aspects:

- The core team should concentrate its work on content. Formal work and support should not be done by the team.
- The output of the core team should be timely and transparent to all members on a worldwide basis.
- Workshops should be prepared using socialware (wikis and CoPs), which are technically supported by a separate team reporting to the project manager.

This setup was developed according to the three main goals of this project: first, for each business field, a strategy had to be developed. Secondly, a process for strategic planning had also to be developed and integrated into the process landscape of ABS. Finally, a critical mass of managers had to be educated in strategic management issues.

The core team meetings followed an effective learning model called elm (see fig. 5.3). It is a reference model designed by the consulting company ACM-Quadrat Ltd. and helps to understand learning in projects and organizations. This model incorporates circular learning. According to this principle, education can be modeled meeting requirements of employees and managers. The core team used the reference model throughout the project.

In his book *The Fifth Discipline*, Peter M. Senge (2006) points out that both flexibility and the ability to change are dependent on the ability and willingness to

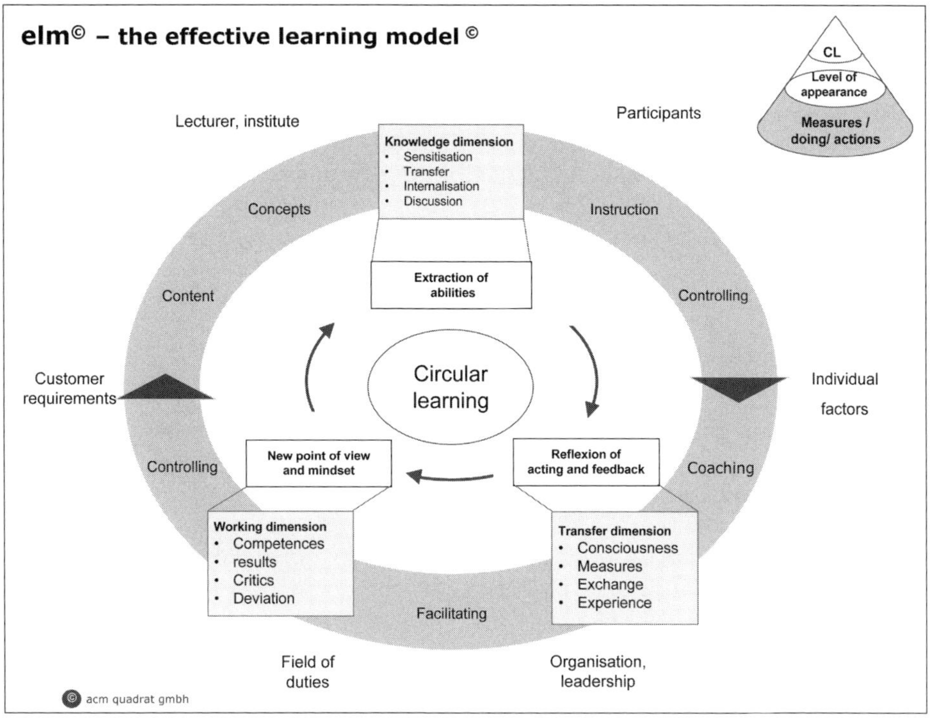

Figure 5.3.

learn. Therefore, "knowledge" was the starting point of elm, and in each education part of the project, strategic knowledge needed to be distributed. The education phase was also intensively supported by the consulting company.

Knowledge Dimension

The first approach was to detect and extend the knowledge of strategic thinking. The challenge at this stage was to equip the core team with the right knowledge in an effective way. That means core team members were not only listening but also active and totally integrated. The key element for success is the approach: "sense—input—discussion prepare for transfer." This approach guarantees the necessary involvement of the group members. After conveying knowledge, many education programs unfortunately stop. But after gaining, for example, more strategy know-how, there is still a long way to go in order to reach the goals on internalized acting level.

Transfer Dimension

The new knowledge about strategy deployment needed a sustainable mental anchor. Consciousness and thinking patterns were changed during discussions and reflections about the situation of the ABS Company. Feedback loops with experts were installed for reflection. In addition, experts stemming from other consulting groups were asked for their expertise. In this way, the new knowledge was being tested and challenged in several loops and from different points of view. The strategy development project served as a learning project for the whole company. In this way, the new knowledge about strategy had a real chance to become "productive."

In this stage, the professional attitude of the core team members and the clear commitment of the board members were critical success factors as well as the professional support of the consultants who contributed strategic and methodological know-how.

Working Dimension

New insights were immediately tested and transferred in practice so that results were measurable. The experiences from the knowledge dimension and the transfer dimension were implemented in strategies of the business fields of ABS. In this way, new knowledge was contributing to productivity and thus adding value to the company.

A very important part of this stage was to permanently challenge each finding with practicability and to detect deviations between experience and theory. Together with external changes, new demands for knowledge emerge, and the circle starts again (refer back to fig. 5.3).

KNOWLEDGE MANAGEMENT TOOLS USED

Each workshop was intensively prepared with a detailed sequence plan, forms, and didactically proper elements. The working groups were supported by facilitators who documented the results in real time and made them visible for each member of the working group. A very important point was the hierarchic access control to the electronic documents, which were saved on a central drive. Only the project leader and the consultants were entitled to modify these documents. It was necessary to ensure a high quality of content, a consistent layout, and a waterproofed version of the documents.

Another very successful tool was the Q & A session. Apart from the working sessions in these question-and-answer sessions, all other questions concerning fear, critics, and concerns regarding the project were discussed. These sessions helped management to understand the fears of uninvolved employees and to build a bridge between those involved and those not involved. Emerging disharmonies, bad sentiments, and misunderstandings within the core team were solved. It also helped the project leader and the consultants to understand the "hidden rules."

Another element for learning was the invitation of special guests into the meetings. They reported about their experience in other organizations using similar methodologies. Some special guests stem from internal organizations, for example, members of the management board, and some stem from external companies the consulters were able to organize.

The employees knew that their bosses were working on a new strategy process. To inform these employees correctly and consistently on a worldwide basis, so-called communication charts were designed. During the working sessions, the consultants had already made suggestions for these communication charts. At the end of each working session, the core team discussed the basis of these charts—what and how communication should be done. After the core team meetings, these communication charts were put on an electronic blackboard so that they could be read by all employees worldwide and explained by the managers. The communication charts served as an information source for the openly held Q & A sessions.

A very effective way of knowledge distribution was the "marketplace." The marketplace operates similar to a knowledge coffee (kaffeeklatsch). The core team normally worked in different groups on different subjects. At the end of the day, a consolidated agreement of the complete group was needed. For this reason, the partial results of the group results were visualized on pin boards. In a "silent process," the participants in the other groups commented on the results and made notes. After that silent process, a facilitator went through the results and notes, and the participants were allowed to ask questions. After a ninety-minute discussion, twenty people had a global view and a consensus about the overall result of the whole group.

An interesting instrument for cross-linking of knowledge was the "relevance filter" (Beer, 1994), which was used to identify options. The relevance filter normally is used when many ideas of a large group have to be considered in order to get few but relevant statements. The starting point is the "big starting question," which opens the brain of the participants but focuses enough to gain the right content. In this process, after the first silent step about four hundred ideas were visualized with cards as results on pin boards by using brain writing (von Werder, 2002). All participants were invited to read the cards of the others in order to know their ideas and thoughts. Subsequently, in the second step knowledge was cross-linked. The group members had to "sell" mentally bundled ideas as an option condensed out of the four hundred on eight flipcharts to colleagues—similar to a "bazaar." Everyone could have the role of a buyer or seller. The currency for buying an option was the "signature." The selling process ensured that the option was discussed in front of the flipchart by at least three to five participants and that knowledge was cross-linked again. After gathering at least five signatures, the option was in the next round. In the third and last step, the options were accepted, consolidated, and tested against redundancy. After about three hours, twenty people developed about four hundred ideas, discussed them, and consolidated them into approximately thirty-five fundamental strategic options.

Another very useful idea was that everybody on the core team could select a peer from the company. In this way, a "shadow" group, not being part of the official project, contributed as well. These persons were people who had special relations to the core team members. They acted as mentors. These people were involved in case of psychological problems or problems where the consulting company was not trusted enough. We don't know how often these bilateral meetings took place and exactly what the purpose of these meetings was. The core group mentioned that indeed it helped them to overcome personal dissonances among group members, and in some cases solutions to concrete practical problems were discussed.

In all the meetings the consulting company tried to create an inspiring environment. Nonaka (Nonaka & Takeuchi, 1995) called this place the "Ba" in the learning cycle. Beneath optimal facilities and the inspiring location of the meeting room, cultural and sports events were celebrated regularly.

LESSONS LEARNED

The cornerstone for success in a big industrial project is typically dependent on more than one factor. Very important for a strategy project is a proper project structure with efficient communication channels, the "right" people in the working groups, and diversity in its composition. The latter is necessary so that new ideas will emerge, as F. Johansson (2006) describes in his book. In group meetings it should be respected that knowledge can be traded like goods (Barachini, 2009) and that knowledge has value.

Most important from our point of view is that the consulting company be able to offer the "right" method and the "right" tool in due time. The consulter should also be able to create a "learning" environment so that employees feel that they are respected—consequently, they will contribute more openly to company goals and they will disclose their weaknesses and fears. In such an open atmosphere of trust it is easier for the consulter contributing the "necessary" complementary know-how to the project. The consultant should act as supporter rather than as executor.

A strong project leader and a quality group supporting all kinds of layouts, documents, and electronic means as, for example, moderation of communities of practice and wikis, are also important. Finally, as in all projects, an investment plan, risk assessment, and availability of planned budget are preconditions for success.

RESOURCES

Barachini, Franz. (2009). Cultural and social issues for knowledge sharing. *Journal of Knowledge Management, 13*(1), 98–110.

Beer, Stafford. (2002).*Beyond dispute: The invention of team syntegrity*. New York: Wiley.

Eschenbach, Rolf. (2003).*Strategische Konzepte. Management-Ansätze von Ansoff bis Ulrich* (4th ed.). Stuttgart: Schaefer-Pöschl.

Gälweiler, Aloys. (2005). *Strategische Unternehmensführung* (3rd ed.). Frankfurt: Campus Publisher.

Johansson, Frans. (2006). *The Medici effect*. Cambridge, MA: Harvard Business School Press.

Lombriser, Roman. (2005). *Strategisches Management* (4th ed.). Zürich: Versus.

Nonaka, I., & Takeuchi, H. (1995). *The knowledge-creating company*. New York: Oxford University Press.

Porter, Michael E. (1983). *Wettbewerbsstrategie*. Frankfurt: Campus.

Senge, Peter M. (1990). *The fifth discipline*. New York: Doubleday/Currency.

Simon, H., & von der Gathen, A. (2002). *Das große Handbuch der Strategieinstrumente*. Frankfurt: Campus.

Stöger, Roman. (2007). *Strategieentwicklung für die Praxis*. Stuttgart: Schäffer-Poeschl.

von Werder, Lutz. (2002). *Brainwriting und Co*. Berlin: Schibri.

6

Project-Based Knowledge Management

Improving Productivity for Knowledge Professionals on Single-Time Efforts

Charles A. Tryon and Suliman Hawamdeh

For many years, organizations have recognized a growing gap between what they need to know and the knowledge they possess. The emerging discipline of knowledge management has transformed this conceptual challenge into an active discussion for executives charged with plotting the future of their organizations. But while most organizations recognize the value and importance of knowledge management, senior management is still reluctant to invest significant funds and time in knowledge management activities. They want to see direct, tangible benefit for their investment.

Some of the most significant knowledge management activities within an organization are actually being overlooked. Knowledge is the natural by-product of a special type of organizational project best known as single-time efforts.

Claude Burrill and Leon Ellsworth (1981), two IBM fellows, were the first to officially recognize the significance of single-time efforts in their book *Modern Project Management*. This project type, however, is as old as innovation. As organizations focused on stable, repetitive, continuous efforts to mass-produce products and services, single-time efforts were often viewed as unpredictable and, therefore, unmanageable research and development activities.

Today, we know single-time efforts as the primary mechanism for organizations to introduce innovation, new thought, and new products or to launch major change. Some have relegated this project type to information technology initiatives, but these facilitators of innovation and change reach across all business units and demand large quantities of organizational resources in the search for new value. Resultant products and services are commonly completely new or significantly different from anything the organization has in place. Single-time efforts facilitate transformational thought. Single-time efforts are surrounded by organizational knowledge, knowledge that is often stored in obscure archives and never viewed again. Simply, single-time efforts are the lifeblood to any thriving organization.

PROJECT-BASED KNOWLEDGE MANAGEMENT

Project-based knowledge management leverages the natural processes and by-products of two prominent project-oriented disciplines, requirements management and project management. These two established disciplines hold the keys to a fresh and natural perspective on knowledge management. And they already exist in most modern organizations.

Limited organizational vision and confusing, contradictory priorities often compromise formal attempts at requirements management and project management so severely that the knowledge they can offer never materializes. The rush to meet arbitrary, unreasonable schedules renders any potential project knowledge ignored and unreliable. It is time for that to change.

REQUIREMENTS MANAGEMENT

Requirements management is a formal strategy to store and transition a well-defined statement of needs into some type of solution . . . while maintaining the ability to trace from the statement of needs to the solution or from the solution to the need.

Requirements take on many forms, including written documents, engineering drawings, technical schematics, specifications, test criteria, and even physical products. Any organizational process that begins with an abstract concept and terminates with a tangible solution is a candidate for requirements management.

The success of projects charged with building new products or services is dependent on requirements management. Bad requirements gathering will ultimately produce a bad final outcome. Garbage in, garbage out. Without a valid understanding of needs, the best an organization can hope for is a brilliant solution to the wrong problem.

Because of this reality, most projects begin with some form of requirements work. Using names such as architectural engineering, research, business analysis, systems analysis, conceptual design, engineering study, discovery, or requirements gathering, early project activities focus on learning about organizational needs and then transforming those needs into a workable solution.

The reality of these efforts, however, often falls short of the intended goal. Requirements gathering is frequently considered optional by senior management and curtailed long before the process is complete.

Yet these requirements are the very heart of organizational knowledge. The failure to fully define requirements means that vital knowledge remains undiscovered and undocumented. Projects offer the ideal time and place to capture the data, information, and decision criteria needed to support critical business functions.

Even when requirements are discovered during a project, most are not captured in any meaningful way. They may be placed in a three-ring binder of documentation, rolled up and stored on a shelf, or retained somewhere on a shared drive. Too frequently, this critical knowledge asset is put away on a dusty physical or electronic shelf.

Organizational knowledge is dynamic. It is active and constantly changing. As a result, all forms of requirements should be detailed, captured, and then regularly updated.

Formal product repositories must be created to capture a variety of information related to an organization's products and services. All relevant knowledge components should be carefully recorded in these repositories and maintained over the life of the products and services.

This organizational knowledge will enable rapid response to future market or technology shifts without having to "rediscover" existing or previous information. These product repositories should capture the "knowing that" and "knowing how" information so critical to the total enterprise.

For this to happen, an enterprise-level knowledge inventory should identify the types of knowledge-bearing requirements that should be kept by all projects. Failure to set this standard will result in incomplete and inconsistent by-products from active projects.

PROJECT MANAGEMENT

No topic has captured the attention of corporate leaders over the past few years more than project management. Yet few are realizing the true benefit this discipline offers.

Modern project management is the corporate act of planning, leading, organizing, and controlling the work required to accomplish the objectives of a single-time effort. This significant project type is performed only once within a reasonable period of time. Single-time efforts are the organizational vehicle to create something new, one time. If a similar project is launched by an organization, even if only a few months or years later, so much will have changed that it will again be a single-time effort.

Project management defines how an organization chooses to conduct project work. That, in itself, is organizational knowledge. Test yourself. Can you, this moment, locate a document that describes to a new employee or customer how you will manage your projects? Does this information explain a repeatable project life cycle that is independent from any specific product development strategy? Does it explain the roles and responsibilities that are crucial to the success of your projects? Does it identify the tactical planning techniques that will be used to create meaningful schedules? Are the simple steps required to create a defendable project plan included in this information? Are templates for project deliverables available, or will each project manager reinvent them on each project?

Positive answers to these critical questions yields a project management framework. This information should be a core resource for every project performed by your organization. In addition to reducing the effort of performing a project, this organizational knowledge will also produce new organizational knowledge from each project.

A project repository should contain project charters that clearly explain the goals, objectives, scope, and intent of each project. All of the project plan components should be kept along with status reports, issues logs, and change requests.

An even more significant contribution from project management comes at the end of each effort. Project postmortems provide a forum to identify things that were done well and pitfalls to avoid in the future. This collection of lessons learned and best practices must be captured and then shared across the organization. Failure to do so results in lost opportunities and repeating old mistakes.

While a project repository may not have the same long-term value as the product repository, it provides a central location for project information that may be accessed by any project participant. This is vital when transitioning roles on the project when the project organization changes. It also provides examples that future projects may use to guide their own efforts.

An enterprise-level knowledge inventory should identify the types of knowledge every project must contribute to the project repository. Templates for these components will promote greater consistency in the by-products used to manage a project.

KNOWLEDGE WORKERS

As organizations become more dependent on single-time efforts to create new value, they tend to incorrectly apply industrial-era practices to accomplish work by applying people management processes that worked well when operating factories and general staff. These measures, however, do not fit modern knowledge workers. The result is that limited resources are being overcommitted on far too many projects. While this may "look" productive to high-level observers, it is failing miserably. Projects are taking too long to complete, project planning is largely ignored, and knowledge professionals are being blamed and compromised in the process. As a result, morale is low in many project organizations.

For most modern organizations, entry into the knowledge age brings significant, and sometimes uncomfortable, change. Shifts in technology and the demands of fickle consumers force these organizations out of their comfort zone of routine operations and mass production into a world dominated by single-time efforts.

Of all the shifts brought about by this transition to single-time efforts, the most significant and challenging is the role of the knowledge worker. Yesterday's task-based employee, the human engine of industrial, repetitive processes, has been replaced by teams of highly educated professionals who commonly apply multiple skills on numerous, simultaneous projects.

Managing this new generation of knowledge professionals is forcing organizations to rethink outdated resource assumptions. Using industrial-age management processes for knowledge professionals is dampening productivity, generating low morale, and causing project delays and failure.

While many writers anticipated changes in a postindustrial era, it was John Naisbitt (1982) who popularized the formal shift into an information age with his business classic *Megatrends*. In this best seller, Naisbitt predicted that the shift from the assumptions that had guided the Industrial Revolution would soon be replaced with a new set of realities.

Futurist Alvin Toffler (1980) described this transition in terms of waves of social change. "A new civilization is emerging in our lifetimes," he said, "and blind men everywhere are trying to suppress it." He adds, "The dawn of this new civilization is the single most explosive fact of our lifetimes."

But it was Peter Drucker (1999) who best recognized the realities of the emerging knowledge worker and the productivity challenges that would come with this shift.

"The most important and indeed the truly unique, contribution of management in the 20th-century was the fifty-fold increase in the productivity of the manual worker in manufacturing," he writes. "The most important contribution management needs to make in the 21st-century is similarly to increase the productivity of knowledge work and knowledge workers. The most valuable assets of the 20th-Century Company was its production equipment. The most valuable asset of the 21st-century institution (whether business or non-business) will be its knowledge workers and their productivity."

While Drucker (1993) clearly articulated the reality of the knowledge worker and the need for dramatic productivity improvements, he focused most of his attention on how this new worker would shape world economies. Business consultants Tom DeMarco and Timothy Lister (1987) used their knowledge of information technology projects and teams to identify organizational patterns, physical environments, and processes that limit the production capability of highly creative knowledge workers assigned to major projects.

IMPROVING PRODUCTIVITY

Creating a productive environment for single-time efforts should be a top priority for organizations wishing to foster creativity and innovation. Failure to do so will result in wasting millions of dollars, loss in productivity, and lost opportunities. Once squandered, it can never be regained. Most importantly, failure to address productivity demoralizes knowledge professionals and leads to even lower productivity.

A study of productivity issues was conducted with people directly associated with single-time efforts. A focus group of thirty-two professionals was created using an online discussion board. The participants represented the medical, transportation, shipping, communications, energy, military, law enforcement, software services, and IT consulting industries. Their titles ranged from CEOs to CIOs, directors, department managers, project managers, business analysts, and software engineers. Participants signed in to a website where they were presented with nine questions. They could choose to respond with a new topic or reply to an earlier response.

While distinct from face-to-face discussion groups, online discussion boards are becoming increasingly recognized as a valid method for focus groups. Lim and Tan (2001) conclude, "Online discussion is convenient in that it links participants across time and space, reducing the hassle of scheduling. Its asynchronous nature affords more time for participants to reflect and react and for the interviewer to manage and facilitate the discussion and resolve conflict. Further," they add, "the lack of social cues reduces social dominance and the possibility of 'group think.'" Hansen and Hansen (2006) report, "Using an asynchronous discussion board for online focus groups shows promise as a tool to gather qualitative data, especially when participants are geographically dispersed."

The participation in the discussion was voluntary, and no compensation was offered. The discussion generated more than a hundred responses that were analyzed and classified. Once the data was coded, a process of summarizing, comparing, and elaborating took place (Bloor 2001; Krueger and Casey 2000).

NEGATIVE PRODUCTIVITY INFLUENCES

There are many reasons for negative impacts on productivity in projectized organizations. Based on evaluation of the focus group's responses, relevant literature, and personal observations, the most common are:

- Excessive simultaneous project assignments

In general staff assignments, it is common for an employee to work on a number of simultaneous activities. In a specialty arena, this employee may perform the same basic activities for many clients. This form of employee utilization is a by-product of the industrial standardize, specialize, and synchronize philosophy. It yields strong economies of scale. The assumption of this strategy is that the basic work is the same, and only the target is different.

Project organizations attempt to use this approach without the benefit of these assumptions. Knowledge workers are frequently assigned to four or more simultaneous single-time efforts, often playing very different roles. Not only does this make it difficult to determine when someone will be available to work on a team assignment, deployment to multiple projects also ignores the productivity loss when these people must regain the focus required for the deep thought required on single-time efforts.

When asked how many simultaneous project assignments knowledge workers should maintain, focus group participants observed that there can be no absolute limit, as their roles can range from oversight or advisory to total participation. Project size and complexity were also listed as significant contributing factors. The participants also recognized that some people are more adept at multitasking. However, most concluded that the maximum number of simultaneous assignments should be limited to three. If the project is large and complex, this limit may drop to one.

Overdeployment of project resources to multiple project assignments results from a breakdown in total organizational resource management. Each project is staffed independently, often with people working on other single-time efforts. The net result is rushed projects, pressured professionals, and delayed deliverables.

- Limited time for creative thinking

One casualty in overdeploying people to projects is that critical thinking time is eliminated. Project management author and consultant Tom DeMarco (2002) decries the decline of people slack. "Slack," says DeMarco, "is the time when reinvention happens. It is time when you are not 100 percent busy doing the operational business of your firm. Slack is the time when you are 0 percent busy. Slack at all levels is necessary to make the organization work effectively and to grow. It is the lubricant of change."

This limited thinking time is exacerbated by the information overload from too many project assignments. "Information anxiety," says author Richard Saul Wurman (1989), "is produced by the ever-widening gap between what we understand and what we think we should understand. It is the black hole between data and knowledge, and it happens when information doesn't tell us what we want or need to know."

As knowledge professionals are required to balance more mental balls, their productivity drops, and frustration rises.

- Interruptions due to support roles

Participating in single-time efforts requires time and focus. Unwanted interruptions break thought patterns that deliver breakthroughs. Many organizations not only fail to prevent interruptions, but encourage them. They assign knowledge professionals to projects and then give them support responsibilities as well. Client or product support is the emergency response to problems in the operation. When internal or external customers have a problem, they call support. If a product fails, support is contacted.

Client and product support are vital to day-to-day operations for organizations. Demand for this service can come at any time and can range from simple activities to complex, time consuming issues. No matter how important, however, it is impractical to overlay this role on project assignments. Project work is forced aside, and thinking is fragmented.

Focus group responses were unanimous on this topic. They cited the inefficiency of this blended role due to the inability to accurately estimate support roles, lack of rest needed for creative project work, and the negative impact on time-critical project activities. One CIO stated that he found it ineffective to ask people with the greater visionary perspectives to be pulled down into the "weeds of on-call" duties.

- Failure to utilize available skills

In the confusion from staffing projects, organizations tend to fall into familiar patterns. In the process, people are easily stereotyped. Knowledge professionals are recognized for a limited number of specific skills.

With the wide range of training and experience many of these resources possess, significant skills go unrecognized and underutilized. People then feel unappreciated. Worse is when an organization brings in outsiders to perform high-end work that falls within the skills capabilities of internal staff. This form of outsourcing leads to significant employee dissatisfaction and a loss of organizational knowledge.

According to the focus group responses, the participants capped the use of their capabilities at no more than 50 percent. One participant decried the attempts by organizations to force all employees into a "one size fits all" mold, an industrial view of task-based workers. Another respondent, who holds multiple postgraduate degrees and teaches for a major university, believes organizational politics limits access to jobs that more fully suit her full capabilities.

To thrive in the knowledge age, organizations must break free from the "interchangeable cog" view of industrial workers.

- Limited time for training

In the knowledge economy, organizations can no longer own their most valuable assets. Traditional business strategies assumed that key revenue producers, such as raw materials, buildings, and land, belonged to the organizational entity. Now that knowledge professionals comprise the most significant element of an organization's worth, former assumptions no longer apply.

Noted author and MIT professor Lester Thurow (1999) states, "But if we are now moving to a world dominated by the knowledge industry, the key assets become the brainpower of individuals and you cannot own individual human beings—that will change what we mean by capitalism. What will capitalism mean when you cannot own key assets?"

To operate at peak efficiency, knowledge professionals need to work with other high-performing people. Refining people requires constant education. This education may come in the form of trade journals, professional societies, books, and formal education. When knowledge professionals feel overwhelmed with their job schedules, they have little time for such luxuries.

When organizations encounter the smallest financial hurdle, one of the first items removed from the budget is training. Without constant educational opportunities, knowledge professionals become staid. They lose the competitive edge that made them an asset. Their value becomes based more on what they know about previous activities than on what they can help an organization create in the future. As a result, creative thinkers producing something new are overlooked as the organization places emphasis on people who have been in the organization for extended periods.

Many knowledge professionals see training as a reward. They desire the opportunity to step away from project pressures to explore topics they find interesting, even if they cannot utilize those skills immediately.

When asked about the importance of training for the knowledge worker, respondents used words like "crucial" and "vital." One participant said, "Training is an important part of keeping pace in this fast-paced world. Ideally training sessions will provide opportunities to stop the frenzy, broaden horizons, and focus on personal development and skill enhancement." A senior executive described his training dilemma with, "Employers typically know that they have to provide training, but they are worried about that trained expert leaving to find employment somewhere else. In the end, they have to figure this into the cost of doing business and provide what is needed to make their employees the best they can be. This will attract new knowledge workers and will act as a retention tool."

Instead of recognizing the need to constantly update the skills of knowledge professionals, organizations often fall into the trap of "just-in-time" training used for industrial, task-based workers. They wait until some specialized knowledge is required and then attempt to train project team members. This response is as illogical as an emergency room doctor asking a sick patient to wait while the doctor attends training on the patient's condition.

- Employee frustration

As knowledge assets cannot be owned by their employers, they also have the right to leave at any time. Employee departure takes on several forms. The most dramatic is unforced resignations. Less noticeable but equally harmful to an organization's creative capabilities is when knowledge assets transfer into operational activities to escape the unreasonable stress of projects. Most damaging to an organization is when knowledge professionals lose their motivation to succeed. These "quit and stays" become nonproductive, pessimistic, cynical burdens on their organization. In addition to the loss of productivity these people represent, they also tend to demoralize people around them. Having these types of people on a project devastates productivity.

PROPOSED STRATEGIES

Just as there is no single cause for the loss of productivity among knowledge professionals, there is no single cure. In fact, it may take implementing a wide range of strategies to achieve peak performance. These strategies include the following:

- Separate project-specific resources

While there are many elements to promoting the productivity of the knowledge professional, the most significant is to ensure the availability of staff to assigned single-time efforts. This is most easily accomplished by dividing knowledge assets into two distinct units. One group is responsible for ongoing support of products and clients. These units may be responsible for activities such as marketing, customer relations, help desk, and software maintenance. They may also fulfill shared services roles demanded by the total organization such as technology support, training, legal review, and corporate finances.

Distinct from these support organizations should be the knowledge assets who will work on projects. Project resources should remain fully dedicated to project activities. While project-specific professionals may at times transition into support roles, this should be considered a formal transfer, not a part-time assignment. On the other hand, projects may need to reach into the support pool for short-term assistance or expertise. It is common to need subject matter expert assistance during discovery activities on a project. During the time these assets are assigned to a project, they should not be called on for client or product support.

- Reassign reporting relationships

Separating knowledge professionals who are dedicated to single-time efforts from support staff will require a new way of managing these assets. Functional assignments for each project team member will come from a project manager. Project managers typically have neither the time nor the expertise to properly guide these people outside their project assignments.

To provide proper support for project-dedicated knowledge assets, organizations should identify a resource manager who provides administrative duties such as career counseling, salary administration, educational planning, and employee evaluation. The resource manager has no functional authority over these knowledge assets but makes sure each person is fully deployed to projects. Should there be a conflict with project assignments, the resource manager resolves the matter with the appropriate project managers. When a project manager needs a specific skill set for a designated period of time, he or she makes the request to the resource manager.

As a resource manager focuses totally on the administrative needs of knowledge professionals, it is common to place a large number of people under this manager. This also ensures that common services are provided to all knowledge professionals and that each receives consistent information.

- Index project staff to organizational goals

To ensure that a proper number of knowledge professionals are available for single-time efforts, an organization should create a formula that associates staffing in this pool with one or more goals of the total organization.

One measure that could influence this formula is the amount of market growth or revenues an organization forecasts due to current markets, current products, and current services in comparison to new markets, new products, and new services. If future growth is dependent on new business offerings, a proportionate investment must be made in project-dedicated staff.

When contemplating organizational needs for project staffing, it is vital to consider all of the skills needed for future single-time efforts. As these projects often cross organizational boundaries, nontraditional development skills are an integral part of a project team. People with operational expertise, for instance, become critical subject matter experts early in a project.

- Implement valid processes for project identification

A very tangible source for predicting the needs for future project staffing occurs during project identification. This component of a project's life cycle begins when a project concept is first recognized by an organization. Most organizations entertain discussions of future projects during their annual budget meetings. True project needs are often overlooked, however, as unrealistic, high-level cost numbers are proposed.

Project identification should be refined into a holistic and meaningful process that includes (1) full definition of candidate projects, (2) a ranking of these candidate projects based on due dates, size, complexity, risk, and value to the organization, (3) the skills and quantities of people needed for project success, and (4) an evaluation of resources and skills available to work on projects.

Without sound processes for project identification, an organization falls into the trap of approving more projects than it can possibly staff. Even if dedicated to project work, knowledge resources become spread too thin, and productivity falls.

- Maintain skills inventory

Equally important to project identification and ongoing assignment of staff to single-time efforts is the role of a current skills inventory. A skills inventory should be maintained for each knowledge professional available for project assignment. Each person should be evaluated for competency against each of the skills that the organization believes is valuable and useful for project work. This inventory should also encompass individual skills that extend beyond organizational expectations.

The resource manager coordinates the evaluation of each project staff member before placing that staff member into the available pool. Stable criteria for the listed skills and competency levels should be utilized by the resource manager.

The result should be a searchable, consistent repository of resources available to projects. As assignments are made from this inventory, the skills remain listed, but the availability changes. This becomes a vital resource for project managers seeking specific skills for target periods of time. This repository also provides knowledge professionals with a formal statement of the skills important to their organization. It can be used as the foundation for performance evaluation and a baseline for personal educational plans.

- Validate weekly project assignments

A time-honored practice of formal project management is resource leveling. The technique is applied to maintain a consistent quantity of task-based workers to assignments on the assembly line across various shifts. The concept is also applied to organizations with scheduling peaks (restaurants) and variable shift operations (call centers, hospitals) where specified staff numbers are required for general operations.

Due to the dynamics of project assignments, consistent staff levels are rarely needed. Instead, staff continuity is the greater challenge for resource leveling. Once project team assignments are made by the resource manager to specific projects, it is imperative that all project managers present the resource manager with their staff plan on a weekly basis. This provides the resource manager and affected project managers a short-interval validation that project staff will be properly utilized.

If any person has been deployed beyond his or her 100 percent availability, changes must be made. If, due to project schedule changes, a team member is not needed as planned and that employee's skill set is now available, he or she may be offered in the interim to other projects in need of those skills.

- Implement realistic employee evaluations

With the separation of project resources, the addition of a resource manager and a current skills inventory, project assignments will be far more dependable and less problematic. It is important to add a realistic process for employee performance evaluation.

In a traditional staff structure, an employee reports to a manager who provides both administrative and functional support. In this industrial model, a manager is well equipped to evaluate the direct staff and provide career counseling and salary administration.

In a matrix management environment, where an employee reports to one person for administrative assistance and to one or more other people for functional assignments, no one person has the total insight to evaluate performance on all of the project assignments. Further complicating the process is that many project assignments are performed by multiple team members, making individual contributions hard to evaluate.

A more project-sensitive employee evaluation process is required to ensure consistency, accuracy, and fairness. These processes will require:

- Project-level employee evaluations
- Documented roles and responsibilities to a project
- Formally defined skills sets from the skills inventory

- Team member participation in the evaluation process
- Team member evaluations for project managers
- Administration by the resource manager

Accompanying this process should be a salary administration system that rewards employees based on real and current contribution, not number of years of employment. "Time-in-grade" pay scales are based on industrial-era, task-based skill improvements that usually occur with years of experience. When salary administration fails to reward knowledge workers based on current contribution, knowledge workers are forced to leave an organization to be more fairly compensated for their skills and performance.

ENABLING CREATIVE THINKING

The focus group made it clear that time of day has little to do with high levels of personal productivity. When asked about their most productive times of the day, they covered most of the twenty-four hours on a clock. Some mentioned early morning, while others opted for late night. They rapidly shifted the discussion, however, to what allows them to be highly creative and, more importantly, what prevents this mode of thinking. This question generated more responses and more views than any other question in the discussion. Among the factors they listed that allowed them to be more productive were:

- Fewer interruptions
- Solitude
- A peaceful, calm, quiet environment
- The ability to concentrate
- Staying on a single task
- Freedom from distractions

Without prompting, these respondents went on to identify factors that prevented them from reaching a productive state. They listed:

- E-mails
- Phone calls
- Instant messages
- Meetings
- Personnel issues
- Operational problems

None of these considerations can be a surprise to anyone engaged in knowledge work. The problem is universal and serious. It is robbing organizations of the very brainpower they hired people to provide. Yet so little is being done to correct this problem.

DeMarco and Lister (1987) describe getting into the "flow," a notion they borrowed from psychology. It is a condition of "deep, nearly meditative involvement." This mental state allows focus, concentration, and creative results. For those asked to perform highly creative work, getting into the flow is a vital mental requirement. DeMarco and Lister explain that getting into the state of flow requires "a slow descent into the subject, requiring fifteen minutes or more of concentration before the state is locked in. During this immersion period, you are particularly sensitive to noise and interruption. A disruptive environment can make it difficult or impossible to attain flow."

Modern knowledge workers have become too interruptible. We work in offices with desk phones that ring at the request of the sender and public address announcements that pay little heed to individual work activities. We are called to attend endless meetings where little is resolved. Knowledge workers complicate the matter by strapping to their heads, wrists, ears, and waists every imaginable type of technology that is capable of interrupting their concentration at any time. And we wonder why we accomplish so little in a given day.

Until organizations are willing, as Drucker suggests, to examine the productivity factors of knowledge workers with a diligence equal to the efforts of our industrial-era thinkers, productivity will remain an elusive notion. This factor alone, we believe, is the most significant productivity factor facing any modern organization that is dependent on knowledge workers to create new products and services or make major enhancements to current products and services.

REDESIGNING THE PROJECT ENVIRONMENT

As a backdrop to all of these issues is the work environment for project teams. Project assignments generally require intense periods of collaboration with other team members followed by focused individual or small-group effort.

Many of today's office facilities actually damage the productivity levels of knowledge professionals when engaged with project assignments. The most common office setup for knowledge professionals is modular offices, more commonly known as "cubes." Low walls and open doorways allow constant distractions from surrounding people and equipment. Space is so limited that there is often no room to meet with other team members.

In an effort to create an environment that stimulates creativity and promotes productivity, facilities planners suggest creating a future center concept (Lugt, Janssen, Kuperus, and de Lange 2007). These researchers describe the future center at the Dutch tax and customs administration as "a physical instantiation of the organization's efforts to foster intellectual capital."

A proven suggestion for a project work environment incorporates a project suite featuring a common "war room" for collaborative efforts. Individual professionals may then move to more personalized "caves" to focus on personal assignments. All equipment needed by the project team should be included in its project suite.

To facilitate teamwork, it is vital that all team members have access to common technology and software products. Wrestling with incompatible technology or different software versions wastes time that should be spent on the project. As team members are often called to contribute to the same end deliverable, collaboration software is a vital need. Discussion threads are far superior to endless e-mails that may or may not reach all of the intended audiences.

As important as what should be included in the project environment is what should not be included. Quiet zones should be free of cell phones and any other devices that can disrupt the thought process. Executive management must assume the responsibility as productivity "gatekeepers" who limit access to an engaged project team. This may include requiring that all requests that would interrupt the dynamics of a project team be approved by the executive before they reach the individual on a project.

BENEFITS AND CALL FOR ACTION

Addressing the productivity needs of knowledge workers should be a top priority for any organization dependent on the results of single-time efforts. Creating processes and environments that promote productivity for knowledge professionals assigned to single-time efforts will benefit both the employee and the employer. Knowledge professionals benefit from:

- The ability to focus on project assignments
- Realistic work schedules
- Assignments that match their skills
- An opportunity to pursue new skills that are needed on future projects
- A fair and balanced employee evaluation process
- Respect for all of their skills and capabilities

The employer benefits from:

- More productive work and higher-quality results
- More dependable project schedules
- Greater resource utilization
- Less need to bring in outside expertise
- More consistency in the administration of employees
- Higher employee morale
- Lower turnover rates

According to Drucker (1999), "Making knowledge workers more productive requires changes in basic attitude, whereas making the manual worker more productive only required telling the worker how to do the job. Furthermore, making knowledge workers more productive requires changes in the attitude not only on the part of the individual knowledge worker, but on the part of the whole organization."

Wonderful examples of effective knowledge management may be found in most successful organizations. These examples, however, are often fragmented and isolated within the corporate structure. When new leadership takes office, these efforts are easily ignored and soon forgotten.

While requirements management and project management will not address all aspects of knowledge management, they contribute tangible, valuable, and visible elements. To gain full value from these project disciplines, it is critical that their contributions not be decided by the whims of a specific subcomponent or era of leadership in the organization.

It is time for modern organizations to either launch a new knowledge management initiative or enhance one that is already underway. To do so, they should:

- Create an enterprise-level knowledge inventory that serves to coordinate KM activities within the organization and its projects.
- Establish knowledge management as a corporate strategy actively supported by senior executives.
- Standardize deliverables that contain valued organizational knowledge.
- Create an accountability structure to nurture knowledge management efforts and hold accountable those who choose to ignore it.
- Commit to creating and maintaining both product and project repositories.
- Facilitate and promote knowledge sharing activities within the organization.

An effective project-based knowledge management strategy will allow intelligent organizations to retain and expand their base of knowledge. Only then can an organization truly thrive in the knowledge age.

REFERENCES

Bloor, M. 2001. *Focus group in social research.* London: Sage.

Burrill, Claude W., and Leon W. Ellsworth. 1980. *Modern project management: Foundations for quality and productivity.* New Jersey: BEA.

DeMarco, Tom. 2002. *Slack: Getting past burnout, busywork, and the myth of total efficiency.* New York: Broadway Books.

DeMarco, Tom, and Timothy Lister. 1987. *Peopleware: Productive projects and teams.* New York: Dorsett House.

Drucker, Peter F. 1993. *Post-capitalist society.* New York: HarperCollins.

Drucker, Peter F. 1999. Knowledge worker productivity: The biggest challenge. *California Management Review* 41(2): 79–94.

Hansen, Katharine, and Randall S. Hansen. 2006. Using an asynchronous discussion board for online focus groups: A protocol and lessons learned. Presentation for the 2006 College Teaching & Learning Conference, Orlando, Florida.

Krueger, R. A., and M. A. Casey. 2000. *Focus groups: A practical guide for applied research* 3rd ed. Thousand Oaks, CA: Sage.

Lim, Cher Ping, and Seng Chee Tan. 2001. Online discussion boards for focus group interviews: An exploratory study. *Journal of Educational Enquiry* 2(1): 50–60.

Lugt, Remko van der, Sebastiaan Janssen, Sjoukje Kuperus, and Ernst de Lange. 2007. Future center "The Shipyard": Learning from planning, developing, using and refining a creative facility. *Creativity and Innovation Management* 16(1): 66–79.

Naisbitt, John. 1982. *Megatrends: Ten new directions transformingour lives.* New York: Warner Books.

Thurow, Lester. 1999. The future of capitalism. *Leadership & Organization Development Journal* 18(2): 93–98.

Toffler, Alvin. 1980. *The third wave.* New York: Bantam Books.

Wurman, Richard Saul. 1989. *Information anxiety.* New York: Doubleday.

7

A Time-Based Model of Collaboration for Knowledge Management and Project Management

Deborah E. Swain

ABSTRACT

Collaboration can structure teamwork. Knowledge management (KM) systems for information sharing have been built to support collaboration. Often engineers and project managers using traditional processes and milestones have dismissed the need to collaborate. The research reported on here was undertaken to analyze time-dimension patterns in collaboration during information systems project development and to determine whether the timing and format of information sharing affected project progress. The researcher noticed that the timing of information sharing impacted project success during a pilot study. The pilot study assumed that collaboration positively influenced software engineering projects. As a result of the pilot study, follow-up research was conducted to investigate specifically how collaboration impacted deadlines. With a collaboration process model, knowledge management could help projects meet dates and goals. The research described in this chapter used cognitive analysis to verify a pattern of behavior and to propose a model of collaboration for a group, not the individual, completing tasks. Qualitative data on information sharing were collected about four project teams using two different collection methods and were analyzed in terms of knowledge and time. The projects represented both business and academic environments. The research results revealed a pattern of cognitive modes of activity over time and suggested a KM model of collaboration for project management (PM). The model included development phases and feedback loops that closed information gaps. The study also documented how knowledge-generating activities resolve issues and may promote faster collaboration within a project. The summary mode during the presentation phase particularly seems to provide a useful PM communications process.

INTRODUCTION

Whether building a highway, reorganizing companies, or designing an information system, development projects require collaboration for teams to share information and make decisions. How does communication during projects provide insight into collaboration that affects management? When is collaboration needed? Knowledge management (KM) supports the appropriate exchange or dissemination of information to facilitate the sharing of knowledge (Alter, 2002). Collaboration is defined as working on a goal and being open to sharing knowledge (Iivonen & Sonnenwald, 2000; Mattessich & Monsey, 1992; Schrage, 1995), both explicit and tacit. Operational definitions and research terms about collaboration and policy (Bruner, Kunish, & Knuth, 1992) provide a vocabulary for analysis and for developing a practical model of collaboration as an integral part of project schedules and resource allocation.

The research described in this chapter tried to answer questions about how collaboration works from a KM perspective that project managers would appreciate. Studies of four different teams validated a pattern of communication during collaboration by using a methodology that applied qualitative research tools and a conceptual framework. The resulting model is based on evidence from identifying and analyzing cognitive modes of collective intelligence. A cognitive mode (Smith, 1994) is a way of thinking used for a task or purpose. To really collaborate, participants must move through each mode sequentially or iteratively and complete knowledge-construction tasks (Smith, 1994, 88–89). The cognitive modes cover three basic "processing sequences" (Smith, 1994, 30): discussion, presentation, and delegation. Unlike some models, cognitive stages can represent the dimension of time during collaboration.

THEORETICAL AND PRACTICAL MODELS

Early cognitive models connected humans and machines. Historically, conceptual models for thinking machines (computers) reflected or imitated human processing; for example, the model human processor (Card, Moran, & Newell, 1987) characterized computer architecture based on how humans process information, and the GOMS (goals, operators, methods, and selection) model predicted how users behave doing computer-based tasks. Computer design models of human-computer interaction (HCI) applied short-term memory and long-term recall to reduce the amount of time it takes to perform an action (Card, Moran, & Newell, 1983).

By expanding the psychological model of cognitive tasks performed by individuals to a team perspective, the model views collaboration as a single collective intelligence. Looking at the dimension of time, "if we are to understand how groups develop large, complex artifacts over long durations, we must first identify the basic process sequences they habitually use" (Smith, 1994, 30). So the research summarized in this chapter produced a time-based model of collaboration for KM and PM. The cognitive modes supplied the framework to describe behaviors that took place in meetings and events where intangible, tacit knowledge was developed. During projects, to resolve issues the team were observed going through the three stages sequentially, or in a "spiral" if activities occurred out of order, and members had to loop back and go through the phases in order: discussion, presentation, delegation.

As a field of study, KM explores theoretical models about the role of human intellectual capital or knowledge. Knowledge is considered a fundamental factor and major enabler of performance in an enterprise, and knowledge managers try to understand how people's behaviors, including computer-based activities, are affected by what they know and when. Some enterprises apply KM to manage knowledge systematically and deliberately, and thus apply intellectual capital to improve project performance. Others deploy "'enhanced' knowledge management models in contemporary organizations" (Wiig, 2004, 48) to go beyond traditional models. Researchers have included creative chaos (Srinkantaiah & Koenig, 2000) to study learning organizations where the systematic and deliberate creation and application of knowledge occurs (Wiig, 2004). Knowledge managers have used models of knowledge flow to resolve conflicts and to prescribe collaboration during development projects (Citera, McNeese, Brown, Selvaraj, Zaff, & Whitaker, 1995). In one ontology of KM in the business setting (Holsapple & Joshi, 2004), collaboration was an important part of the development process.

The writing process can also be considered an analogy for team collaboration. Information science researchers have used cognitive processes as a framework when interviewing information seekers. College students assigned to write a term paper, for example, have been studied using a university library (Swain, 1996). In addition to collecting logs and observing students in the library, structured interviews to validate findings were conducted using the sense-making method (Dervin, 1977). The research verified Carol Kuhlthau's (1988) search-process model, which had been developed based on searching done by high-school writing students.

The research described here supports applying collaboration to avoid unnecessary rework and project delays. The resulting model of collaboration indicates when information sharing can be used to promote collaboration, positively influence team performance, and provide knowledge for decision-making activities. Using the dimension of time in the KM model of collaboration, knowledge and project managers can track collaboration activities and identify communication gaps inhibiting knowledge discovery and the resolution of issues.

CASE STUDIES OF COLLABORATION AND COMMUNICATION

The four case studies show the KM model of collaboration applied on project teams who wrote documentation and software code collaboratively. Cognitive activities performed by groups illustrate collaboration when there was dialoguing (Groff & Jones, 2003) and knowledge development during sense making or bridging of information gaps (Dervin, 1992). Showing the relationship between collaboration and KM among software project teams in academia and business, the three cognitive modes provide time and process dimensions against which data about communication, information sharing, and knowledge development can be analyzed by project managers.

Data from the team activities of four business and academic projects (studies A, B, C, and D) showed the use of communication and collaboration to resolve issues and develop knowledge. Researching both past and ongoing software teams, several examples of information sharing to resolve conflicts and knowledge management to improve products were found. Engineers on one case study team were heard by the researcher complaining about wasting time at meetings. Teams work very hard to meet deadlines. When a 9:00 a.m. meeting, which the researcher was going to observe, had to be postponed until the afternoon, it was because several project members had worked very late—until 5:00 a.m. But meetings were necessary, as one design engineer noted in a personal communication log: "A daily 15-minute discussion is usually enough to stay 'synchronized,' and on the same priority list with project management. Also, I learn [the] political situation and head off issues early before they become bigger problems" (study B).

By definition, communication and information exchange among team members and other teams is required for designers, programmers, testers, users, and others to develop a software system. Plus, collaboration can uncover tacit knowledge. "Collaboration is not about debate or discussion—it is about dialogue. The paradox of collaboration is that through the process of interacting with others, individuals discover more of themselves. This occurs because collaboration often uncovers ideas that we find alien or threatening. These ideas are often the very ideas we have denied or repressed within ourselves" (Groff & Jones, 2003, 57).

Because of the Internet and advances in telecommunications, collaborations can involve virtual meetings and seem less intrusive. The use of wireless connections, phone landlines, and/or cable networks makes locations that are widespread and global feel more local. This research suggests that regardless of specific medium, mediating devices, and geographical distances, collaborative teams participate in cognitive activities in order to resolve conflicts, solve problems, and share information. The three cognitive modes provide a time-based model of collaboration:

1. Discussion
2. Presentation
3. Delegation

The modes are grounded in Herbert Simon's (1977) problem-solving process that required three cognitive subprocesses: (1) intelligence, (2) design, and (3) choice. Looking at observable, externalized tasks and group behavior, decision-making models and tools, such as Kepner and Tregoe's (1965), map to Simon's problem-solving model. Eventually Simon added a fourth phase of implementation for systematic decision making. However, once a choice is made and work is delegated, collaboration, by definition, is complete, so a fourth phase is more about "recommending" than implementing. Plus, according to Turban, Aronson, and Liang (2005), the process might include monitoring or feedback as a fifth phase.

The case studies presented here look at aspects of collaboration that occur before the work of implementing or, if problems arise, before rework is done. Because implementation of a decision is not a thought process, models of collaboration, problem solving, and decision making stop before the work phase. The three models can be compared as shown in table 7.1. In the left column, the KM model of collaboration's submodes for discussion (discussion, conflict resolution, and brainstorming) and presentation (presentation, summary, and demo) are in parentheses.

CONFLICT RESOLUTION AND SPIRALS

Project team observations showed that the collaboration process seemed to "spiral" around conflicts during research and analysis. For example, a group in study

Table 7.1. Comparison of Related Collaboration Models

Cognitive Modes	*Problem Solving*	*Decision Making*
Discussion (discussion, (conflict resolution, brainstorming)	Intelligence	Intelligence
Presentation (presentation, summary, demo)	Design	Design
Delegation	Choice	Choice Implementation or recommendation

C was documented going through modes (and submodes) in this order: *Discussion* (brainstorm) ® *Discussion* (discussion) ® *Presentation* (presentation) ® *Delegation* ® *Discussion* (conflict resolution) ® *Presentation* (demo) ® *Presentation* (summary) ® *Delegation*. The content of the final delegation for work to be done was significantly altered after additional collaboration from the first delegation. However, as a participant in study C noted about the project, "[the] UNC-W team slowed down when Eduprise was not ready yet, so they started without them since they could not sit around and had to show something done [to the granting agency]. Later it was hard to catch up on the schedule when we had to redo and dovetail work."

RESEARCH METHODS

Both historical case study and field study methods of research were applied to the four case studies, methods grounded in the qualitative paradigm of naturalistic study from the human sciences (L. Smith, 1992). Qualitative research involves the discovery of chronological flow and the identification of events that lead to specific consequences. In a subject domain, for example, software engineering, the team or teams of people work for a common goal and collaborate. From word-based data, qualitative research results are word-based concepts or models and can be as useful as numerical data, as explained in the following quotation:

> Words, especially organized into incidents or stories, have a concrete, vivid, meaningful flavor that often proves more convincing to a reader—another researcher, a policymaker, a practitioner—than pages of summarized numbers. (Miles & Huberman, 1994, 1)

COLLECTING QUALITATIVE DATA FOR KM

In a historical study, current or historical documents, e-mails, and meeting observations are collected for qualitative analysis. Because all types of information, including ephemeral, tangible, and intangible, can be shared as knowledge is generated, personal logs and interviews are also analyzed. Logs and interviews also provide triangulation of data for study. Research suggests that memories about communication problems and conflicts remain particularly vivid (Reynolds & Flagg, 1983).

During interviews, interviewees use personal notes and documents to refresh their memories.

Thus, qualitative data collection requires different approaches to acquire various types of information. Software engineers work alone to write code but, by necessity, work with others to create systems that meet human and computer requirements. In the beginning of a project, the concept or design may vary in method of distribution, as well as media, display format, and documentation style. For example, early code designs are often developed in front of other team members and drawn on whiteboards. For such ephemeral information, KM can use Internet discussions, whiteboards, interviews, or observation. In comparison, software engineering specifications for a system are usually documented and maintained as tangible information so that all stakeholders can access them throughout a project. This explicit knowledge can be managed in knowledge management systems or collected as artifacts for information research. However, other ideas about a product or process are intangible information carried in the heads of individuals and become tacit knowledge, which is understood and applied unconsciously (Alter, 2002). After analyzing data from documented artifacts, notes, and meeting records, follow-up interviews provide information about cultural experience and social interactions in a specific environment.

ANALYTICAL TOOLS

Qualitative data analysis as used in the social sciences involves a structured, replicable process and tools for the collection and iterative analysis of data. Data can be collected for analysis in "three concurrent flows of activity: data reduction, data display, and conclusion drawing/verification" (Miles & Huberman, 1994, 10).

For the case studies presented here, iterative processes were followed in both historical and field studies. The following were generated inductively as the data was collected and analyzed:

1. Initial project timeline (updated during research)
2. Interviews documented in contact summary forms (revised if new issues are identified)
3. Tables to track event sequences from identified sources (for researcher's use)
4. Case dynamic matrices to identify issues that cause contested collaboration
5. Causal network diagrams to analyze influences (high, medium, low) on results
6. Table to map events by issue into cognitive modes

Summarizing these researcher's tools, project and knowledge managers can use the KM model of collaboration for tracking collaboration and resolving issues.

ANALYSIS PROCESS—USE OF THE TOOLS

Initial timelines based on collected documents and first interviews provided start-end parameters for defining the project and team(s) in each case study. The timeline was also used during interviews to orient the interviewee. (See the sample below.) Applying semistructured interview methods or "sense-making" (Dervin, 1977), the interviewer asked participants to identify events or activities that illustrate gaps in information or issues that needed to be resolved. Interview notes and recordings were summarized in contact summary forms (see appendix A for a template) and could be revised after additional interviews and analysis.

Sample Timeline from Study C (academic grant project)

1998: Bill and Dick share ideas informally
1999: Write grant proposal ; receive review comments; revise and resubmit to NSF
2000: Grant awarded; kickoff meeting for full project team (6/20–21)
2001: Begin weekly team meetings at UNC-W (1/01); present LOM (1/4); status summarized and paper/article drafted (2/1); all-hands meeting to review design and delegate work (2/2–3); end user types defined (4/12); specifications drafted (4/19); meeting to review and resolve differences about: process, vocabularies, database, criteria (4/26); taxonomy revisions presented (8/6); initial public release of iLumina Digital Library (8/10); Dave McArthur analysis presented (8/30); NSDL meeting attended (9/19–21); Marty presents SQL server and metadata proposal (9/20); task list on revisions and media types e-mailed (9/26–27); project meeting discusses status and prioritizes task list (10/3–4)
2002: External slides for SMEC meeting prepared (1/30); Math Association of America (MAA) meeting can brainstorm standards and present iLumina (2/15–16); propose DL sustained by Randall Library at UNC-W (3/1); pilot of automation and evaluation distributed (3/21); NSDL portal communicated to team (4/12); virtual NSDL discussion led by Sarah (4/30); prioritization of tasks requested by Dick, PI (5/17); usability iIssues discussed; Marty reassigned tasks (5/30); Dublin Core (DC) metadata elements distributed (12/11)
2003: Project meeting on status of materials collected; discuss NSDL grants; project meeting minutes archived (3/19); chart comparing LOM and DublinCore updated (7/23); second grant awarded for maintenance and process.

Collected data were used to construct event sequence tables for tracking information flow, listing significant team events, and discovering examples of the cognitive modes used during group gatherings. Then the major issues of conflict or examples of "contested collaboration" (Sonnenwald, 1996) were identified from the comments of team members about the need for collaboration.

Case dynamic matrices were constructed to analyze these conflicts in terms of assumptions, organizational responses, and end results. The matrices documented the primary issues that needed resolution. An example is shown from case study of business projects in table 7.2.

Analyzing the significance (high, medium, or low) of what impacts decisions requires evaluation of perspectives, concerns, and personal issues of subjects who are interviewed. Tools such as the causal network provide graphical documentation of internal knowledge or viewpoints, which influence group decisions (Miles & Huber-

Table 7.2. Sample Case Dynamic Matrix for Study B (Business Project)

Date	Event	Comments
9/97	New product and managers introduced to lab	Meeting observed as it occurred. New director and new direction for the lab.
10/27/97	Kickoff meeting	New team first assembled: staff moving from other projects at the lab and from other labs.
1/9/98	Test team meeting	Testing planned before architecture design.
2/2/98	Review design doc	Early design from other organization; created outside lab.
3/25/98	Managers' work session	Meet to align project managers and staff resources; design organization.
4/98	Process rollout	New process using Web developed at the lab for any team in new company; time savings.
4/98	Project A starts	Staff interviewed for details and possible study selection.
5/5/98	Retrospective on test project	Retrospective scheduled on early test-only project.
6/98	Project B learning and developing	Other organization presented background and communication concerns; schedule cites development milestones.
7/8/98	Review meeting for project model	Preparing for test phase. Note: concurrency of phases.
8/98	Project B product delivered	Delivery announced; also demo at conference shared as news.
10/12/98	Retrospective for project B	New key learnings forms used to conduct postmortem on project.

man, 1994). Specifically, in this research such networks could be used to compare data with the model's process and pattern.

Therefore, for additional qualitative analysis of cause and effect, causal networks were used to identify and prioritize (levels) the organizational influences (boxes) and the flow (arrows) toward results or resolution (see figure 7.1 for an example). During research the flow or level of influence when drawing conclusions about issue resolution and collaboration was recorded in causal networks. These graphical tools provided triangulation to inferences from a model. Overall, the iterative process supported deductive analysis but also provided inductive analysis of qualitative data to validate or prove an *a priori* theory of cause as in this research. The final table in each case study was a synthesis of the data analysis: a KM model of collaboration.

RESULTS: A KM MODEL OF COLLABORATION

As defined for research (Schrage, 1995), collaboration depends on the dissemination of information and the creation of shared knowledge. Knowledge managers and project managers can apply a model of collaboration to distribute information

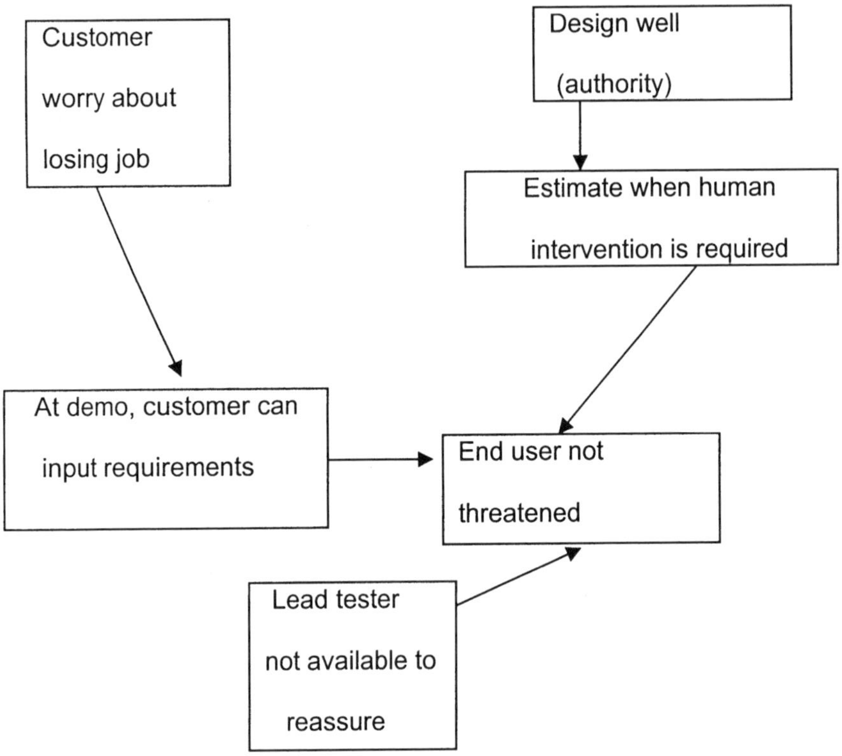

Figure 7.1. Sample Causal Network with Levels of Influence in Case Study A (Business System)

effectively during a systems development project. Systems analysts, computer architects, product designers, and software engineers can use a KM model of what they do. Similar to all the tables, matrices, and diagrams used in the research described here, communication data on a team project can be illustrated in an updated KM model of collaboration. Status on communication, issues resolution, and collaboration is reduced, visualized, and displayed for overall status. By beginning with the first cognitive mode—discussion—issues that require information exchange can be proactively resolved, repeating the presentation and delegation mode if necessary. Thus, the flow of knowledge during collaboration can be tracked, and projects can move forward more rapidly with issues resolved and cognitive understanding shared by the team.

Descriptive models of project and flow were inductively synthesized into a single, more prescriptive KM model of collaboration. Proposed for use in KM and project management, the sample shown in table 7.3 was derived using the descriptive models of collective cognition from the software projects studied. Although a deductive process of "conceptual" analysis was used during research, the resulting model of collaboration outlines cognitive stages of activity, which a knowledge manager can use to track knowledge issues and to promote collaboration during a software development project.

Table 7.3. Sample KM Model of Collaboration Showing Events (E) over Time

Discussion	E1			E10	
Conflict Resolution			E6		
Brainstorming		E1	E9		E13
Presentation		E3			
Summary	E2	E4	E11	E14	E14
Demonstration		E5			E15
Delegation	E5	E7	E8 E12	E16	
Issues	1	2	3	4	5

The proposed KM model of collaboration is illustrated in table 7.3 and includes columns for different issues from a sample project. The table can be a tracking tool for the modes of collaboration (vertical axis) and is based on data from the four case studies. Communication events, such as meetings, telephone conferences, and Internet presentations are shown in chronological order E1–E16; however, they are recorded according to the issue they affect, so they are in different columns because the five issues are on the horizontal axis. Some events may impact more than one issue (E14) or involve more than one submode (E1). The model indicates when and how collaboration occurs.

Most of the events supported collaboration in a sequential order; however, issue 3 shows how a team may require a spiral or iterative process. After discussing E6 conflict resolution for issue 3, it jumped to delegation or action E8. However, it returned to the first mode E9 to brainstorm and then followed the sequence with summary E12 and a second decision meeting to delegate E12. Applying modes to knowledge sharing over time, collaboration can remove bottlenecks in a development process. Using the model directs group KM over time so that a team goes through modes to collectively make intelligent decisions and to complete a project.

CASE STUDIES

The case studies researched to develop the KM model of collaboration research were software systems projects from a business environment and a grant team in an academic setting (with business contractors). The projects involved a lab producing international telecommunications software and a digital library involving multiple universities and disciplines. The researcher was in each environment over two years collecting artifacts, interviewing participants, observing meetings, and analyzing qualitative data. The case studies supported a cognitive-based model of collaboration although data were congruent and incongruent concerning KM.

The business projects (case studies A and B) involved global development teams working for an advanced software lab owned by a large U.S. corporation. The lab collaboratively developed software for international telecommunications companies. To sell profitable commercial software, the business managers had to meet market sales opportunities or risk losing revenue and so were driven to meet project dates. Later the company issued a successful initial public offering (IPO) of stock and experienced a period of increased pressure to force collaboration among divisions, labs, sites, and newly acquired companies. The researcher studied information-sharing and project management in the field while the IPO stock became "hot" and teams collaborated.

Case Study A

In this historical study, a seven-year-old project to develop an expert system to monitor and maintain telephone switches with communication artifacts from four years of design and development was researched. From the archived files of two project participants, 292 documents were analyzed. From a list of nine major participants, five interviewees were selected to respond to questions about the past project. Three were no longer employees of the telecommunications software lab, but they were willing to spend time with the researcher. The interviewees ranged in age from twenty-nine to fifty-six, had up to twenty-five years of experience, and had college degrees in computer science, business, or engineering. Participants remembered the expert system project because it gave them a unique opportunity to work on "leading-edge" technology and with a new team at the lab. To clarify recollections, copies of the collected artifacts were shared with all interview subjects. An iterative process of data collection and data analysis was used to establish a project timeline, to identify conflicts/issues affecting collaboration, and to document knowledge-sharing events.

A key staff member, who had worked on the project the whole time, validated and revised the timeline. Later subjects were asked to fill in details about the events listed, and the timeline was revised accordingly. After summarizing notes and tape recordings from interviews, event sequence tables were constructed, and the contact forms and the tables were updated iteratively after more interviewing, documenting, and analyzing. After being analyzed for information flow, the final sequence of events with the source identifiers were used for verification. Also, significant issues causing conflict among team members were defined during event analysis. Six were selected for conflict analysis based on interviewees' emphasis and providing a broad view across corporate organizations:

1. Early estimation of resources needed to develop the expert system product
2. Estimation of resources for follow-on expert system product
3. Architecture determination
4. How to resolve communication link failure
5. On-site testing to meet delivery deadline
6. Assuring customers that expert systems won't replace people

A case dynamic matrix was developed on each issue, and an end result was analyzed. Next, causal networks with boxes and arrows were drawn to represent organizational influences on conflicts. As an iterative process, new networks were created and networks were combined to represent the issues as an additional interview was conducted and more documents were analyzed during the study. The refined causal networks reflected the social culture (Miles & Huberman, 1994). Evidence of "modes of collective thinking" verified the model of collaboration (table 7.2). Communication and conflict data were mapped onto the framework of cognitive modes (see appendix B, "Cognitive Modes in Case Study A"). Group activities that represented collaborative events concerning the issues were mapped to models of the three modes (discussion, presentation, and delegation) and submodes (conflict resolution, brainstorming, and summary). Cognitive modes applied over time for the architecture (#3) and customer view (#6) issues were spiral, looping back to phases over time. For example, preliminary discussion was held to prepare for the architecture. Later, a brainstorming session, called an "architecture discovery" meeting, was set up. Architects were flown to the lab from sites across the United States so that development team members could discuss the proposed architecture. Then a presentation was given at a formal "architecture review" to approve the collaboration-driven plans. Design and development work based on the architecture was delegated to the team, and tasks were assigned in a presentation to the lab (next-to-last row). Noticeably, there was no specific data to indicate a summary presentation. The sequence of events then showed a loss of productivity and time. As one subject noted about the lack of summary and understanding: "This split the center. Some said, 'This isn't going to work.' Later we started weekly team meetings to summarize status, design, and plans."

Case Study B

A field study involves collecting and analyzing data as events occur. In any ethnographic study, researchers go through repeated interactions between data collection and analysis while making observations. Case study B was a field study involving observations of the natural environment for the project and prolonged contact with participants. Tables and flowcharts were developed as well as event sequences, case dynamic matrices, and causal networks. The timeline was documented in real time as the events occurred and while interviews and meetings were being summarized. Issue threads from meetings, interviews, and documents were tracked and validated using later meetings, additional interviews, and data queries to identify the significant issues that needed resolution. In addition, personal communication logs of sense-making events were requested, collected, and analyzed.

Compared with case study A seven years earlier, KM had evolved technologically as users relied less on hard-copy documents and more on computer-mediated documents and Web-based e-mail. In case study B, 355 specific hard-copy artifacts were collected, including internal and external printed documents and memoranda; e-mails; personal and technical notes (typed and handwritten); flowcharts and screen captures shared by the team; meeting notices, agendas, and notes; code printouts; faxes; overhead transparencies; and printed forms.

During the field study, team members used e-mail extensively, and the researcher collected e-mail by subscribing to the product development List-serv. During twelve months of research, 324 project e-mails were collected and analyzed. Threads in the e-mail were tracked on a spreadsheet. Some issue threads traced brainstorming efforts to resolve communication problems, such as shortening or splitting lists to reduce e-mail clutter. Also, hypertext links to Web pages (over forty-five specific links) were cited in the e-mails. The Web pages contained displays of facts, links to document files, and interactive forms to fill out. Compared with case study A, fewer people archived their printed documents because most project documents were accessible through an intranet.

Recent organizational changes and new processes were noted. The company owning the lab participated in a lucrative IPO of stock, and the staff at the lab almost doubled, from 95 to 180 during one year. Products were planned for fast delivery to a growing market full of changing customer interests. Intelligent network features, such as phone cards, wireless devices, and portable phone numbers, were developed at the software lab where case study B was done. At the beginning of the study, a specific project for an intelligent network feature was selected while in its initial architecture phase. When that project was canceled, a second team was found for the case study. Both projects were part of a lab effort to develop intelligent network telecommunications.

The researcher had the opportunity to investigate meetings as a participant observer and to determine constraints, mediating devices, and any impact on collaboration from gaps in communication. The first meeting observed was a kickoff meeting for the whole team at the lab; the discussion mode was verified. At subsequent meetings and interviews, handwritten notes were taken. Seven meetings were also tape-recorded. The researcher identified on contact sheet forms the communication events, issues, and cognitive modes from meetings and interviews.

To look deeper into the ethnography of the software engineering environment and the behavior of individuals, personal communication logs were also collected. Daily log forms were distributed to ten volunteers. Each agreed to keep a log or journal of communication events for about three months. After the logs were completed, participants were interviewed about their experience. The interviews and communication logs provided additional data about tacit knowledge and thoughts as team members shared information and collaborated.

As related events were defined in an event sequence table, the project was tracked for more than a year.

A case dynamic matrix was used to analyze each of the significant issues recorded in interviews and observed at meetings. See table 7.3 for an example. For triangulation of communication data, the documents and personal logs were reviewed to corroborate issues and determine the most influential conflicts. Eleven major issues were documented:

1. Define a new, simpler, and faster process
2. Define new management and organizational structure
3. For "path forward," investigate other site directories; sleuthing
4. Meet date in schedule for delivery
5. Work with customer to define requirements
6. Staff a project team with resources transferred or hired
7. Share lab resources; develop effective lab scheduling
8. Train new and transferred staff on a steep learning curve
9. Reduce use of e-mail unnecessarily distributed to many
10. Provide a rapid development process for other company labs to use
11. Gain International Standards Organization (ISO) quality certification

Combining and comparing the case studies, both differences and similarities are evident in behavior related to communication and strategies. A long-term planning strategy to reduce the time to market for lab products became a crucial tactical goal for the IPO to achieve market share as early as possible. A comparison of collaboration at the lab before and after the company went through an IPO was made based on the different causal networks. During case study B, the marketing organization shared information only with executive management. Thus, communication flow patterns changed as the corporation and lab were restructured, and positions of influence switched after the IPO. During case study A, the information flow was more back and forth, and the executive managers sent directions to an "open" development team; for example, a brainstorming architecture discovery meeting included architects flown to the lab from sites across the United States. Thus, the development team was able to collaborate with architects on the expert system's design. Specific knowledge-sharing problems occurred concerning the product platform during case study A; however, sharing information led executive managers to identify the need for an open environment to improve product quality and reduce development time.

In contrast, external auditing and quality assessment, such as standards certification, became a major focus of the lab during case study B. Process planners replaced process designers. During interviews, experienced subjects noted the change between the case studies from an authoritative approach dictating new processes to a more investigative approach collecting process data and deriving processes from observations and requirements. As one who was a subject in both studies said, "We used to be a year ahead and would apply technology to the next project we proposed. They [executives] came to see us."

During case study B, the team supported activities related to saving time; for example, in order to take new employees over a steep learning curve and into development sooner, their training and orientation was reduced from six to four weeks. In order to complete testing faster, testers used machines at another lab after midnight when labs operating in other time zones did not have priority. Saving time was crucial in case study B, giving knowledge managers more reasons to support fast, effective information sharing.

Case Study C

Previous information science research has analyzed scientific collaboration on academic teams (Hara, Solomon, Kim, & Sonnenwald, 2003) and developed a framework for forms of collaboration among scientists based on associated factors, such as personal compatibility and incentives. Another collaboration study chronicled the use of acknowledgments among authors in scientific chemistry publications and built on similar studies in the humanities and social sciences (Cronin, Shaw, & LaBarre, 2004). Thus, the focus in previous research has been on the spread of intellectual knowledge, and researchers have found evidence of the importance of collaboration for research discovery. For case study C, an academic environment was chosen; the focus of the project team was creating a new digital library and meeting grant deadlines.

The iLumina Digital Library system is comparable to the software products in the business studies. The software teams collaborated over six years meeting requirements for two grants issued by the National Science Foundation (NSF). Under grant no. IIS-0002935, first the team developed the iLumina electronic, Web-based library as a collection of undergraduate math and science teaching materials. The project objectives included (1) producing an accessible repository of electronic resources (see http://ilumina-dlib.org/), (2) investigating cost benefits of IEEE Learning Object Metadata (LOM) specifications, and (3) testing the effectiveness of digital libraries (Heath et.al., 2005). Case study C examined the history of collaboration under the original NSFgrant. A follow-up grant from the NSF (grant no. 0333628) in 2003 investigated maintenance and procedural development for digital libraries. Note: Case study D documented observations from the field about collaboration under the second grant.

Six partner organizations participated in the first grant, but a student-faculty team at the University of North Carolina at Wilmington (UNC-W) did the primary development work. However, the development team did collaborate with programmers and technical experts from Eduprise, Inc. (Geisler et.al., 2002). Academic partners were from Virginia Tech, Georgia State University, the College of New Jersey, and Grand Valley State University. Organizations contributing materials to iLumina included the Computer Science Teaching Center (CSTC; www.cstc.org), the ACM SIGGRAPH Education Committee's Digital Library (SECDL; www.education.siggraph.org); and UNC-W (aa.uncwil.edu/dl).

For the case study, six months were spent examining documentation and conducting interviews with primary participants who had actually developed software or digital material for the iLumina Digital Library. The project manager had archived documents; she provided access to electronic documents as well as hard-copy files of papers. A total of 106 documents were analyzed. In addition, fourteen interviews were held: three with members of a nonprofit research institute, Eduprise, and eleven with members of the team at UNC-W. Except for two undergraduate student volunteers, all UNC-W interviewees had PhDs. Two of the Eduprise employees had PhDs, and one had a master's degree. Interviewees ranged in age from nineteen to fifty-eight years. Notes and tape recordings were taken during interviews, and contact summary forms (see appendix A) were developed and updated as needed. Color keying as a tool for analysis was used to track issues discovered in notes from interviews and meetings.

The timeline did not list all weekly meetings; however, as records indicated, the team consistently met each week for four years. Using semistructured, sense-making interview techniques, the gaps in information suggested issues that illustrate contested collaboration. The event sequence table showed that collaboration among the major participants sometimes involved resolving issues or different views between UNC-W and Eduprise team members.

The following five issues were selected as major:

1. Choice of metadata specifications—investigate IEEE Learning Object Metadata (LOM) and compare with Dublin Core (DC) and the IMS Global Learning Consortium learning resource metadata information model
2. Development and reuse of taxonomies for the specific disciplines (for example, mathematics and chemistry)
3. Database design and architecture to be based on either entity relationship diagram (ERD) modeling or application of eXtensible-Markup Language (XML) tagging for the Web

4. Usability issues for contributor and user, including types of search features
5. Sustainability and maintenance of digital library as an accessible collection after grant

The choice of metadata was a core issue (1) for the iLumina project team during its five-year effort to implement metadata standards for learning objects stored in a digital library (Heath et.al., 2005). The causal network for issue 4 showed how the design of iLumina features was affected by different social variables. Both the database design and the database management groups had influence. Although software developers from both UNC-W and Eduprise worked on Web-based interfaces, agreement within the whole team was required for final system approval. Such an approval had lower influence on collaboration and resolving the issue because it was only the institutionalization of final approval. However, the project members had higher influence as they verified usability testing personally or through students using the system. Note: Additional delegation and collaboration occurred on the iLumina project after the 2003 grant was awarded. These events were part of a field study conducted for case study D.

Case Study D

The primary partner organizations within the second grant's team were the Randall Library at UNC-W and most of the UNC-W team of scientists from the first grant. The project team included:

- Ten scientists from chemistry, computer science, mathematics, and biology and the grant evaluator (knowledge manager for the project)
- Eight librarians, including the special formats cataloguer responsible for the iLumina Library at the end of the project
- Four technical support staff and programming students (fluctuating by semester)

The objectives of the grant were to establish a sustainable home for iLumina and to document procedures that other libraries and academic teams could use when building a digital library for university-level users. The library accepted maintenance responsibility for the iLumina collection, and its staff involvement increased to include a software engineer and a special formats cataloguer. For this fourth case study, the research process involved numerous cycles of collecting data as events occurred in the field and analyzing issues of collaboration in the office, before collecting more data. Just as with the previous studies, the analysis required use of timelines, tables, and flowcharts to develop event sequences, case dynamic matrices, and causal networks.

Using ethnographic data collection techniques, the researcher attended two meetings as a nonparticipant observer and conducted seven sense-making interviews with participants. The knowledge manager had been the media lab/office manager for the first grant. She provided access to meetings, copies of handouts, and online access to any meeting agendas, notes, and notices; a total of a dozen documents were analyzed.

Although e-mail was used for communication by the team, the members primarily shared information in person at weekly meetings, specifically updates about the status of data transfer, ongoing publicity for iLumina, and software for new interfaces. Most project team collaborations occurred at two-hour meetings presided over by the principal investigator (PI). As with the business part of this research, there were organizational changes on the academic team after the historical study. In fact, roles and responsibilities were an issue compared with the first grant as the team changed to allow more leadership from the library. A librarian served as one of the co-principal investigators, and the library staff had controlling responsibility for digital artifacts.

During meetings the constraints and mediating devices included a computer-driven LCD projector, laser keyboard and pointing devices, and Smartboard interactive and recording resources. A minimal timeline based on e-mail, meeting observations, and interviews was constructed during the field study to define the start and end of the project. The full team regularly met each week on campus near the PI's office for two years, including summers (but not holidays). There was no geographic barrier to face-to-face meetings on campus. Attendance at extraorganizational, professional meetings was encouraged to support marketing.

The event sequence table illustrated gaps in information and examples of contested collaborations, and it showed evidence of changing roles, which impacted collaboration, as iLumina became a Randall Library resource. Behavior at the meetings clarified how team members were clearly divided over certain important issues. Six major issues were selected after analysis of interviewees' comments and meeting observations and used for collaboration analysis:

1. Converting to metadata specifications and WorldCat requirements: subjects for browsing, required fields, and use of Library of Congress (LOC) MARC tags for contributed artifacts
2. Publicity and marketing for iLumina, including attending professional conferences and doing demos, having a brand or logo, and determining paths and portals for access
3. Make the transition of iLumina materials and collecting new artifacts automatic (computer based) in contrast to manual submissions and/or computer-based aids for librarians
4. Usability issues, such as a Pocket PC option, and human-computer interaction (HCI) features
5. Process and procedures for users, contributors, librarians, and technical support in an academic environment as a goal of the grant
6. Roles to be played by the team for the sustainability and maintenance of the iLumina digital library

Influences from different organizations especially affected the roles to be played in preparing the iLumina Digital Library for maintenance by Randall Library and to be part of WorldCat. The influences are observed in interviews and primarily during meeting interactions. Observation provided by field studies enhances understanding of the social influences on each issue and provides triangulation for issue identification. Cognitive mode analysis of collaboration showed that sometimes the modes were followed in order over time but were repeated; early delegation led to restarts.

Academic projects must be managed similarly to business projects when they have grant monies, deadlines, and constraints on resources and finances. During case study C, approval itself was not a turbulent group task because it was a formal step of low influence. However, results from usability testing were high in terms of social influence. Overall, the project in case study D seemed more organized and to have a shared business plan, perhaps because of the team's experience during the first grant project. Interestingly, more issues per event were observed during the field study than reported for the historical project. The difference could be due to the research methodology employed and a chance to observe full meetings. The need to have the library "perpetualized," as some on the team referred to it, led to the support of an external process (WorldCat) and pressured team members from the first grant to revise classifications. The team united around the goal of university library ownership for iLumina to survive.

Both grant teams had natural divisions that contributed to contested collaborations. On the first grant, the roles and responsibilities of the nonprofit organization, Eduprise, shifted over time, while the academic team members at UNC-W changed very little. On the second grant, the scientists had a different background and perspective on digital libraries compared with the professional librarians at the Randall Library. It was found that such differences can lead to contested collaborations.

RESULTS OF RESEARCH

In terms of cognitive modes, there were frequent "restarts" to resolve different aspects of issues, both in the business environment and during the academic projects. Case study A provided no evidence of the summary mode. Although there might have been informal summaries or one-on-one discussions outside a team meeting, the lack of formal summary presentations seemed to contribute to a gap in knowledge and to lead to the need to repeat the architectural definition process. As a result there were product delays. In comparison, during case study B summaries were given to the team covering technical information as well as market product analysis, such as a summary of an executive's view that a certain customer's product delivery was critical. The absence of the cognitive mode suggests that summary presentations may be required to ensure that everyone on a team receives the same message and to promote effective collaboration.

In case study D, the order of events for issue 3 (automate collection) showed a tendency to delegate as soon as possible. This push may have been due to concern about student programmers providing technical support when limited by their class schedules; nevertheless, there is a lack of presentation events. Several scientists expressed in interviews and meetings feelings of "déjà vu" and dissatisfaction about rewriting software from the first grant. As one team member expressed in a meeting, "It worries the hell out of me [to be changing things]. Why, we did our taxonomy in one afternoon [on first grant], and no one has complained." Nevertheless, Randall Library representatives needed updated tools and had to develop procedures for inclusion in OCLC's WorldCat, so programming and in-house tools were needed.

A biologist on the project expressed frustration about redoing classifications, but he said his main concern was automating the submission process without reducing the quality of digitized photos. He wanted about 2,800 pictures added to the iLumina digital library, including slides from the microscopy lab (such as tissue samples for histology), three hundred flowers photographed by a retiring botanist (including rare orchids native to North Carolina), and genus-species-seed pictures from other botanists. The biologist wanted an automated, faster method and also wanted assurance about color quality and high resolution, especially if pictures were digitized from film/analog photographs. The librarians wanted to meet professional quality standards for WorldCat objects. In the end, although scientists and librarians had different backgrounds and training, they chose to collaborate to prepare a high-quality digital library for professional maintenance. If cognitive modes, such as brainstorming, conflict resolution, or summary, have to be added or repeated during a development project, the research on the academic teams shows that it takes time to go back to a mode in order to collaborate and resolve an issue. In summarizing results, the theoretical framework of group modes showed how KM might positively influence project schedules and resource management during collaboration. The research proved that information can be gathered about collaboration in different environments using two valid methodologies: the historical study and real-time, field study.

A COLLABORATION MODEL

Collaboration need not mean face-to-face meetings and travel. The case studies' participants were documented taking advantage of meetings to resolve several issues and to cover cognitive modes of collective intelligence that had not been experienced. Cognitive modes seem to be a useful framework for KM and knowledge discovery in any type of collaboration. The KM model of collaboration presented in table 7.3 is a synthesis of results from all four case studies of software projects. The case studies showed that time spent on project issues and problems can be reduced if knowledge is shared. With the model, a project manager can check for any missing activities that indicate a gap in collective, cognitive behavior. Although collaboration does not have to restart with discussion or repeat a mode that has not been covered, the case studies suggest that issues are resolved when all three modes are covered. Thus, when conflicts are defined or communication breakdowns become apparent during a project, it may be useful to consider whether or not any cognitive modes have been skipped. Thus, using a collaboration model in real time may be the better approach.

DISCUSSION

In all four case studies, the cognitive modes framework was applied inductively to analyze qualitative data collected from the software engineers. Overall, results suggest that a KM model of collaboration is appropriate for software engineering and perhaps other development environments. Social roles and life experiences often affect an individual's view of and access to information. Collaboration mode activities seem to have social influences that can affect the transfer of information. These influences show up in social networking and Web-based communication among team members that impact the project schedule. The Internet and telecommunications allow project teams to work from different geographic sites. The importance of this research on collaboration is that the model can be used for teams who meet around the water cooler as well as for global teams that never meet face to face. It is the challenge of knowledge management to provide data in a format that informs and leads to decision making.

For example, in case study B, an individual tester needed to fill knowledge gaps when trying to schedule test labs. To reach all sites, including Italy and England, communication was done by both phone and e-mail. Based on his communication logs of gaps, the tester still had problems, worked late at night, and then "I requested a specific machine with 8 links, but I only got 4 links." To resolve such problems around schedules, a test system administrator created a Web page to communicate with parties at all levels of social influence and to deliver presentations. She used e-mail exchanges to send all team members and managers updates with a Web link to the page. It contained a form-based tool for sharing lab time and helped resolve the issue about sharing test machines. The issue required several cognitive modes for a new process to be approved and accepted: discussion, conflict resolution and brainstorming activities before presentation, and then summary communication before the delegation of tasks. Thus, Internet-based social activities enhance but do not alter the matrix structure of the KM model of collaboration.

Despite technological improvements based on the Internet during case study B, software engineers could have enhanced collaboration with customers during the project. Users have choices, and there are many ways to apply technology to collaboration. For example, information technology played an important part in resolving the internal business issue of lab scheduling (7). The Internet also supported collaboration to resolve communication problems around keeping development processes consistent and achieving quality audit certification (issues 10 and 11). A new process was introduced into software labs at multiple sites in various countries for global development of products. The shared development process was presented on an intranet Web page with hypertext links to supporting documentation, and a process checklist was displayed on another Web page so that projects and executives knew the status of all work products internationally.

Furthermore, knowledge managers were seen to take advantage of telecommunications and the Internet in case studies. For example, in the late 1990s team members at the lab started providing hypertext links to documents or Web pages within e-mails. In case study D, demos were conducted at meetings using specific websites. Also, participants shared links and addresses so that usability testing and reviewing could continue outside meetings. Thus, advanced communication technology supports the ability to distribute information before or after a meeting, as well as during it when discussion, presentation, or delegation modes are experienced firsthand. So technological developments in Web-based knowledge management may reinforce communication and enhance access to information, but they have not been shown to replace the need for systematic conflict resolution and collaboration based on cognitive modes.

Did a higher level of social familiarity over eighteen years among academic team members make it easier for the academic teams to talk openly and to collaborate? Collaboration may have been achieved more easily in case studies C and D because many on the team participated on both grant projects for a total of six years together. In fact, several of the scientists had been doing projects together at the university for over fifteen years. (Note: They were pleased to volunteer that additional information about collaboration during interviews.) Such long-term collaborating was not as evident in the business environment, although one study participant from the historical project also participated in the field study, representing eight years at the lab. However, he did not work with the same project teams over that time. Of all the teams researched, the project team for case study D was most experienced with working together. After four years on the first NSF grant, many participants seemed to make time at each meeting to discuss all the issues that concerned them.

During the research, it was observed that knowledge was developed based on information sharing regardless of technology. Moreover, the need to discuss, present, and then delegate remained the same over the years and across the studies. Particularly, there seemed to be a need for further discussion to resolve conflicts if the presentation or summary cognitive mode was skipped. Knowledge managers may be able to assist collaboration when conflicts or issues arise if they become aware of cognitive modes and whether or not they have been applied by the team.

CONCLUSION

Project managers traditionally track dependencies and due dates. The research supports knowledge managers and project managers using the KM model of collaboration and cognitive processes as information tools to track conflict resolution and to support collaboration as well as project management over the dimension of time. The case studies proved that collaborative cognitive mode activities cover more than one development cycle and cross geographical boundaries. Because the KM model of collaboration presented here (table 7.3) is based on qualitative research that examined only software project teams, in the future information scientists and researchers might look at other domains to test the model.

Overall, this chapter describes research on how collaboration occurs on projects. The primary goal of the research was to adjust a KM model inductively from data collection and analysis. The original assumption was that knowledge managers can apply a time-based model of collaboration activities to project events in order to enhance the delivery of information and decision making. A cognitive model could be used during or after a project to track collaborative team activities and/or the absence of modes or steps in the group collaboration process.

Thus, the KM model of collaboration template in table 7.3 can be used as a checklist to promote collaboration in different cognitive situations. The project context can be any organization, corporation, or institution where individuals work through issues and form a collaborative team. Issues can be listed to match defined projects. Collaboration is seldom seamless, and conflicts are expected. The model is designed to be flexible and context driven so that it can be used to track issues over time in various situations. Defined issues are listed numerically in the bottom row header, and events are labeled in the order in which they occur, such as "E1," "E2," and so on, for event 1, event 2, and so forth. Then the coded abbreviation for each event is mapped to a square based on mode (defined by rows) and issue (define by column).

Managing knowledge for a project and reducing communication problems can mean ensuring that the cognitive activities shown in the rows of the KM model of collaboration occur. Such activity might imply that gatekeeper roles be assigned to track cognitive activities by the team as a whole, but it can also mean simply analyzing the level of collaboration as issues occur within a team. This author hopes that knowledge managers, as well as project managers, systems analysts, computer architects, product designers, software engineers, and anyone on a project will be able to track the absence of collaboration in order to resolve issues more quickly. Understanding the cognitive modes of collective intelligence may help knowledge management provide a time-saving, effective solution to problems on a project. Realizing the contribution of modes, for example, how the summary mode during the presentation phase provides a time for cross-team communication, might positively impact schedules and support effective collaboration.

APPENDIX A: CONTACT SUMMARY FORM (TEMPLATE)

Contact Type: __________ Date: _______ Name and Role: ________________

_____ Interview mm/mm/yy ____________________________

_____ Document ____________________________

_____ Meeting

Cognitive Mode Information:

1. What were the main issues or themes that arose from this contact?

2. Summarize information (or lack of information) on the target areas:

   A. Timeline

   B. Communication Boundary Organizations

   C. General Communication Roles

   D. Sensemaking/Gaps

   E. Contested Collaboration (CC)

   F. Cognitive Modes
   DISCUSSION:
   PRESENTATION:
   DELEGATION:

   G. Determining Factors (meet schedule dates)
   1. Goals:
   2. Products:
   3. Processes:
   4. Constraints (mediating devices):

3. Anything else that seemed salient, interesting, illuminating, or important.
4. What new (or additional) target areas or concepts to explore with other, future contacts?

APPENDIX B: COGNITIVE MODES IN CASE STUDY A

Table 7.4.

Examples of Modes	*Goal*	*Product*	*Process*	*Constraint*	*Situation and Mediating Device*
Discussion: *Architecture preparation (preliminary)*	• Externalize information	• Group-level awareness of information	• Dialog • Analysis	• Take turns talking	• Whiteboard used
Conflict Resolution: *Determine. source of communication link*	• Externalize information	• Group-level awareness of information • Resolving a conflict: *Go forward to get assistance from original designer*	• Dialog • Analysis	• Take turns talking • One topic addressed • Subset of group involved: *Front end engineers sure of architecture error* • Different opinions encouraged	• Informal exchange
Brainstorm: *Architecture discovery*	• Externalize information	• Group-level awareness of information • Generating ideas	• Dialog • Analysis	• Take turns talking	• Whiteboard conference room; attendees flown in from other sites (same time)

Brainstorm: *Customer insecure about jobs*	• Externalize information	• Group-level awareness of information tester work with marketing • Generating ideas	• Dialog • Analysis: *Must convey reality of systems limitation and built-in requirement for human intervention*	• Take turns talking	• Informal exchange
Presentation: *Architecture presented to center*	• Assign task	• Understanding of work responsibility	• Delegate and explain • Listen and evaluate	• Senior member delegates to *Tech Mgr 1 and 2*	• Whiteboard and viewgraphs used; e-mail and documents distributed
Presentation: *Formal architecture review*	• Introduce information	• Group-level understanding of information	• Teach and inform • Listen, learn, question, evaluate	• One individual controls: *Tech Manager 1*	• Whiteboard and viewgraphs used in conference room
Demo: *Show customers expert system beta*	• Introduce information	• Group-level understanding of information	• Teach and • Listen, learn, question, evaluate	• One individual controls	• Computer system used for on-site user-group meeting
Delegation: *Architecture presented to center*	• Assign tasks	• Understanding of work responsibility	• Delegate and explain • Listen and evaluate	• Senior member only delegates to Tech Mgr 1 and 2	• Whiteboard • Viewgraphs • E-mail • Documents

REFERENCES

Alter, S. (2002). *Information systems: Foundation of e-business.* Upper Saddle River, NJ: Prentice-Hall.

Blakeley, K. (1990). The application of modes of activity to group meetings: A case study (Tech. Report No. TR90-045). Chapel Hill, NC: University of North Carolina, Department of Computer Science.

Boehm, B. (1988). A spiral model of software development and enhancement. *IEEE Computer, 21,* 61–72.

Brooks, F. (1986). No silver bullet: Essence and accident of software engineering (Tech. Report No. TR86-020). Chapel Hill, NC: University of North Carolina, Department of Computer Science.

Bruner, C., Kunish, L., & Knuth, R. (1992). What does research say about interagency collaboration? *North Central Regional Educational Laboratory.* Retrieved August 2004: www.mcre;/prg/sdrs/areas/stw_esys/8agcycol.htm

Card, S., Moran, T., & Newell, A. (1983). *The psychology of human-computer interaction.* Hillsdale, NJ: Erlbaum.

Card, S., Moran, T., & Newell, A. (1987). Computer text-editing: An information processing analysis of a routine cognitive skill. In R. Baecker & W. Buxton (Eds.), *Readings in human-computer interaction* (pp. 219-40). Los Altos, CA: Morgan Kaufmann.

Citera, M., McNeese, M., Brown, C., Selvaraj, J., Zaff, B., & Whitaker, R. (1995). Fitting information systems to collaborating design teams. *Journal of the American Society for Information Science, 46*(7), 551–559.

Coulter, N., Monarch, I., & Konda, S. (1998). Software engineering as seen through its research literature: A study in co-word analysis. *Journal of the American Society for Information Science, 49*(13), 1206–1223.

Cronin, B., Shaw, D., & LaBarre, K. (2004). Visible, less visible, and invisible work: Patterns of collaboration in 20th century chemistry. *Journal of the American Society for Information Science and Technology, 55*(2), 149–159.

Dervin, B. (1977). Useful theory for librarianship: Communication, not information. *Drexel Library Quarterly, 13,* 16–32.

Dervin, B. (1992). From the mind's eye of the user: The sense-making qualitative-quantitative methodology. In J. Glazier, J. & R. Powell (Eds.), *Qualitative research in information management* (pp. 61–84). Columbia, MO: Libraries Unlimited.

Geisler, G., Giersch, S., McArthur, D., & McClelland, M. (2002). NSDL: Creating virtual collections in digital libraries: Benefit and implementation issues. In *Proceedings of the 2nd ACM/IEEE-CS joint conference on digital libraries,* July 2002.

Goetz, J., & Compte, M. (1984). *Ethnography and qualitative design in educational research.* Orlando, FL: Academic Press.

Groff, T., & Jones, T. (2003). *Introduction to knowledge management.* London: Butterworth-Heinemann.

Hara, N., Solomon, P., Kim, S., & Sonnenwald, D. (2003). An emerging view of scientific collaboration: Scientists' perspectives on collaboration and factors that impact collaboration. *Journal of the American Society for Information Science and Technology, 54*(10), 952–965.

Hayes, J., & Flower, L. (1980). Identifying the organization of writing processes. In L. Gregg, & E. Steinberg (Eds.), *Cognitive processes in writing* (pp. 3–30). Hillsdale, NJ: Erlbaum.

Heath, B., McArthur, D., McClelland, M., & Vetter, R. (2005). Metadata lessons from the iLumina Digital Library. *Communications of the Association of Computing Machinery (ACM), 48*(7), 68–74.

Holsapple, C., & Joshi, K. (2004). A formal knowledge management ontology: Conduct, activities, resources, and influences. *Journal of the American Society for Information Science and Technology, 55*(7), 593–612.

Iivonen, M., & Sonnenwald, D. (2000).The use of technology in international collaboration: Two case studies. In *Proceedings of 63rd ASIST Annual Conference* (pp.78-92). Medford, New Jersey: Information Today.

Kepner, C., & Tregoe, D. (1965). *The rational manager.* New York: McGraw-Hill.

Kuhlthau, C. (1988, Winter). Developing a model of the library search process: Cognitive and affective aspects. *RQ,* 234–242.

Mattessich, P., & Monsey, B. (1992). *Collaboration: What makes it work.* St. Paul, MN: Amherst H. Wilder Foundation.

Merriam, S. (1988). *Case study research in education: A qualitative approach.* San Francisco, CA: Jossey-Bass.

Miles, M., & Huberman, A. (1994). *Qualitative data analysis: An expanded sourcebook.* Thousand Oaks, CA: SAGE.

Reynolds, A., & Flagg, P. (1983). *Cognitive psychology.* Boston: Houghton Mifflin.

Schrage, M. (1995). *No more teams: Mastering the dynamics of creative collaboration.* New York: Currency/Doubleday.

Simon, H. (1977). *The new science of management decisions.* Englewood Cliffs, NJ: Prentice-Hall.

Smith, J. (1994). *Collective intelligence in computer-based collaboration.* Hillsdale, NJ: Erlbaum.

Smith, L. (1992). Ethnography. In *Encyclopedia of educational research* (6th ed.) (Vol. 2, pp.458–462). New York: Macmillan.

Solomon, P. (1997a). Discovering information behavior in sense making: I. Time and timing. *Journal of the American Society for Information Science, 48*(12), 1097–1108.

Solomon, P. (1997b). Discovering information behavior in sense making: II. The social. *Journal of the American Society for Information Science, 48*(12), 1109–1126.

Solomon, P. (1997c). Discovering information behavior in sense making: III. The person. *Journal of the American Society for Information Science, 48*(12), 1127–1138.

Sonnenwald, D. (1993). *Communication in design.* Unpublished doctoral dissertation. Rutgers, The State University of New Jersey.

Sonnenwald, D. (1996). *Communication roles that support collaboration during the design process.* London: Design Studies.

Srinkantaiah, K., & Koenig, M. (2000). *Knowledge management for the information professional.* Medford, NJ: Information Today.

Swain, D. (1996). Information search process model: How freshmen begin research. In *Proceedings of ASIS '96: The 59th ASIS annual meeting: Global complexity: Information, chaos, and control* (pp. 95–99). Medford, NJ: Information Today.

Swain, D. (1999). *A communication model for a software engineering environment.* Unpublished doctoral dissertation, University of North Carolina, Chapel Hill.

Turban, E., Aronson, J., & Liang, T. (2005). *Decision support systems and intelligent systems.* Upper Saddle River, NJ: Pearson Education.

Wiig, K. (2004). *People-focused knowledge management.* Oxford: Elsevier-Butterworth-Heinemann.

8

Preliminary Research Context for Investigating the Use of Wikis as Knowledge Management Tools to Project Management–Based Initiatives

Michael J. D. Sutton

ABSTRACT

The goal of this chapter is to set the stage for future research on the use of a wiki within the context of a project management (PM)–based knowledge management system (KMS). There is a critical need to study the impact of wiki use on performance, efficiency, and effectiveness. I first describe how wikis are emerging within project-based, team-oriented initiatives as a predominant KMS of choice. I then establish a connection between project-based wiki use and PM-based activities. Finally, I propose a research context for embarking upon numerous investigations that could establish the business value proposition and efficacy for more widespread adoption of wikis. I will propose additional suggestions in terms of next steps.

INTRODUCTION

Organizations are increasingly leveraging their knowledge assets with wikis. Wikis provide a virtual workspace for authoring and distributing material for both local and geographically dispersed employees. The wiki platform furnishes executives, professionals, staff, and stakeholders external to the organization with a repository for knowledge sharing and dynamic team communications. Wikis have emerged during the past five years as a new type of knowledge management system (KMS). Very few quantitative or qualitative researchers have studied the impact of wiki use on performance, efficiency, and effectiveness. Anecdotally, many knowledge management (KM) professionals have noted that one of the common applications for the wiki has been project-based, team-oriented initiatives.

Project management (PM) initiatives match the profile of project-based, team-oriented initiatives. Yet there are few reported instances of information systems innovations within PM-related initiatives since the introduction of project charting and scheduling tools in the 1970s. Moreover, enterprises are continuing to shift from hierarchical work breakdown to matrix and teamcentric problem solving. New wiki KMS applications may hold a significant business value proposition for firms looking to increase performance, efficiency, and effectiveness in PM-based initiatives. Virtual projectcentric communities are recognized as significant contributors to individual and organizational performance (Peddibhotla & Subramani, 2008).

A need exists to stimulate research that would investigate sense making, knowledge creation and sharing, and decision-making effectiveness in structurally diverse distributed project team environments. Wiki use (in terms of a KMS tool) could benefit from deeper analysis. This chapter describes how wikis are emerging within project-based, team-oriented initiatives as a predominant KMS of choice. A connection will be established between project-based wiki use and PM-based activities. Finally, a research context will be proposed for embarking upon numerous investigations that could establish the business value proposition and efficacy for more widespread adoption of wikis. Suggestions for next steps are also proposed. Based upon the anecdotal evidence amassing in trade and academic sources, it is my belief that wikis will emerge as a critical KMS tool for knowledge asset and business process management.

WIKI—A KM TOOL?

Short Background and Description of Wikis

Although wikis have been around since 1995, they have recently emerged as social collaboration and classification platforms for collecting, linking, and editing documents (Klobas, 2006; Mader, 2006, 2008). As a Web-based authoring tool accessed via an Internet browser, the outcome of wiki software is essentially an editable website. The unique trait of a wiki is the collaborative nature of its interface, that is, an ability to draw together a group of viewers, contributors, and gatekeepers who can create, acquire, modify, manage, secure, distribute, and archive information. Wikis are the archetype of Berners-Lee's original vision of the Web: where "people can communicate . . . by sharing their knowledge in a pool . . . putting their ideas in, as well as taking them out" (as cited in Carvin, 2005). Moreover, wikis operationalize the new open source content goals sweeping the practices in business education (Friedman, 2005).

Historically, the origin of the wiki has been proposed as Ward Cunningham's first wiki, the WikiWikiweb, http://c2.com/cgi/wiki?WelcomeVisitors (Mader, 2008). This platform was constructed to store software design modules and permit their modification by team members. Cunningham (2005) chose the Hawaiian term *wiki* (quick) because it expressed a concept that emerged from his personal experience with a Wiki Wiki bus ride at the Honolulu International Airport. Passengers came and went from the airport, riding the bus for short or long distances between terminals. Likewise, wiki members use the software for short or long edits of material, coming and going as they please.

Hierarchical work design based upon Taylor's scientific management, as witnessed in the famous opening description of a pin maker in Smith (1937), has been the cornerstone of traditional business operations and economics, even into the twenty-first century. Regretfully, this technique continues as the dominant paradigm of business and manufacturing. Even supposed white-collar work, as highlighted in the original study of *The Organization Man* by Whyte (2002), continues to see significant evidence of the rationalization and the application of scientific method in business process management, Six Sigma, and lean design. However, in the past two to three decades, evidence has accumulated supporting the business value proposition of team-based collaboration and problem solving for the success of a modern organization (Weber, 2004).

Relationship of a Wiki to KM Tools

So how are wikis in any way connected with knowledge management, and how could they possibly serve as an emerging stealth tool in the proliferation of knowledge management? Wikis have grown from primitive authoring and social spaces for collecting information in 1995 to robust authoring and delivery platforms (Allen, 2004; Klobas, 2006; Mader, 2006, 2008; Richardson, 2009). Finally, wikis have taken a substantial foothold in business, education, government, and nonprofit-sector organizations as a knowledge creation, distribution, sharing, and management tool (Klobas, 2006; Mader, 2006, 2008; Paquet, 2006). Although the following list is not exhaustive, the application of the wiki platforms includes a wide spectrum of applications in all types of organizations:

- Back-office templates
- Business processes documentation
- Blogging
- Collaborative academic writing projects
- Conference speaking information and schedules of events
- Community newsgroups
- Corporate policies and procedures
- Course and learning management systems (CMSs and LMSs)
- Educational internships
- E-mail archive
- Employee contact information, expertise directory, and personal blogs
- Employee resettlement resources
- Event planning
- Football team biographies and club history
- Forms repository
- Functional business teams, user groups, and special interest groups
- Information dashboards
- Learning objects repositories
- Meeting agenda and notes
- Multisemester and international collaboration research projects
- Organizational charts repository
- Personal Web spaces
- Photographic library
- Project management and control
- Source for helps systems, FAQs, and product support
- Technical documentation, marketing, and competitive information
- Tenders and request for proposal repositories
- Website navigational frameworks

RELATIONSHIP OF A WIKI TO PROJECT MANAGEMENT

Regardless of variety of wiki applications, this chapter is interested in proposing the need for deeper research on the emergent use of wikis as a KM tool within PM (including classroom and course management). Mader (2006, 2008) and Paquet (2006) presented a range of PM-related cases of wiki applications, from corporate projects in enterprises to learning management in educational organizations. The cases suggest a breadth of KM-related activities that need further analysis to validate the impact of the KM tool. Cases discussed in detail included:

- Corporate enterprises:
  - Atlassian
  - Dresdner Kleinwort Wasserstein
  - Informative, Inc.
  - JavaPolis
  - LeapFrog.com
  - McGraw Hill
  - Michelin China
  - Red Ant
  - Sun Microsystems
  - Ziff Davis Media
- Educational organizations:
  - University of Arizona
  - University of British Columbia-Education
  - Case Western Reserve University-Weatherhead School of Management
  - Center for Scholarly Technology
  - Dublin Core Education Working Group
  - George Mason University
  - University of Illinois
  - Johns Hopkins University
  - National Science Digital Library
  - OpenWetWare
  - Queensland University of Technology
  - Seattle Pacific University
  - University of Southern California
  - SUNY
  - Westwood Schools

Mader has emerged as a wiki evangelist within the educational community, especially in terms of PM as it relates to learning management (classes and courses) and research collaboration. Many others (Augar, Raitman, & Zhou, 2004; Goodwin-Jones, 2003; James, 2004; Lange & Patterson, 2005; Raman, Ryan, & Olfmam, 2005) have begun to describe the value and utility of wiki platforms in teaching and learning, which is very often project related.

With the increased visibility of reported PM-related cases, an imperative is emerging to embark upon a number of well-focused research initiatives. These investigations could furnish credibility, authenticity, and validity for the use of wiki KM tools in PM-based environments. Such research could herald a new period when, at last, evidence could support the efficiency and effectiveness of practical KM tools in the organization. Consequently, the need to teach KM and learn more about how KM is taught (Baghdadabad, 2008; Sutton, 2007) could be increasingly justified in educational institutions that have either curtailed or sidetracked KM educational programs because the value of KM has not been easily proven.

PROJECT MANAGEMENT PRACTICES AND APPROACHES TO KMSS

Over three decades ago the field of PM matured to a professional practice. The visibility and professional respect the field commands resulted from the establishment of the Project Management Institute and the acceptance of its pragmatic body of knowledge—PMBOK (PMI, 2000). Wysocki (2007) documented his research that established the existence of five common phases within a PM life cycle, which corresponded to and preceded the adoption of the PMBOK (p.35):

1. Define the problem
2. Develop detailed plan
3. Launch the plan
4. Monitor/control the plan
5. Close out the project

Each phase encapsulated a number of common activities that must be successfully completed in order to manage a project. Wysocki spent the remainder of that text describing different configurations of these phases in terms of three different PM approaches he felt could be adopted for a project, depending upon the purpose, goal, and objectives of the initiative. The underlying infrastructure described by Wysocki encompassing the PM life cycle is permeated by artifacts and processes that capture project information and knowledge associated with:

- Assumptions and constraints
- Audits
- Budgets
- Charts and graphs
- Deliverables
- Forms
- Manuals
- Organizational charts
- Meeting agenda and notes
- Plans
- Proposals
- Requirements
- Reporting documents
- Roles and responsibilities descriptions (governance scheme)
- Standards, conventions, and common vocabulary (glossary)
- Schedules
- Team communications

- Technical specifications
- Testing results
- Work breakdown structures

These artifacts and their underlying processes structure the individual and team-based flow of PM data, information, and knowledge as it moves through all the roles within the project team and community of stakeholders. My purpose in suggesting richer research around the use of wikis in PM practices is to find a means to articulate the actual business value of this KM tool on knowledge asset and business process management. But since the goal of a project manager is to deliver not only a single project, but successive projects that result in successful outcomes for the organization (Kotnour, 1999, 2000; Kotnour & Hjelm, 2002), how could the impact of this KM tool be measured on the project manager, team leaders and members, and stakeholders?

Fong (2008) described how projects seldom start "new," and, in fact, there is generally a reuse of lessons learned and previous project knowledge when a project is launched. He suggested that the interproject and intraproject foci of PM predicated the need for project knowledge management and that numerous project practices have critical parallels to knowledge management methods: after action reviews, best practices, communities of practice, lessons learned, peer assist, project debriefings, project review/audits, and storytelling. His imperative for project knowledge management was supported by Kasvi et al. (2003), Lundin and Midler (1998), and Crawford (2000), since "the project in itself cannot and has not been created to memorize and store what has been learnt" (Fong, 2008, p. 212).

Such connections infer the creation and sustainability of learning organizations (Senge, 2002) from project management teams and the stakeholders (Coakes et al., 2005; Owen & Burstein, 2005). Could a wiki be the basis for establishing, designing the architecture for, and maintaining organizational interproject and intraproject learning and learning histories (Bartezzaghi et al., 1997)? Could the application of a wiki platform improve project performance, efficiency, and effectiveness through the creation of a long-term project knowledge repository (Jeffries et al., 2005)?

A number of case studies have been reported on the use of Internet-based knowledge bases in PM (de Kretser & Wilkinson, 2005; Smyth, 2005; Jewell & Walker, 2005; Orange et al., 2005; and Whelton et al., 2005). Two qualitative research studies reported challenges associated with interorganizational collaboration tools (Hardy et al., 2005; Majchrzak et al., 2005). Stein and Zwass (1995) proposed an organizational memory information management framework (OMIMF) for studying collaborative technology. In this framework, Stein and Zwass outlined three support requirements for project teams:

1. Intelligently, continuously, and easily acquire and encode knowledge from information producers;
2. Maintain the integrity of knowledge over time; and
3. Implement pattern matching during search and retrieval.

The goals of these features are to keep team members focused and informed about all project life cycle activities. Majchrzak and colleagues (2008) integrated their dynamic team memory system for studying the use of virtual workspaces within teams with the framework of Stein and Zwass. Team members were asked to rate eighteen specific virtual workspace features. The researchers reported that the use of dynamic team memory systems showed higher levels of knowledge-sharing effectiveness. Finally, Peddibhotla and Subramani (2008) surveyed and reported on a wide range of different research streams that had studied virtual communities, including project-based teams. However, none of these studies appeared to study the specific application of a wiki to performance, efficiency, and effectiveness. Next, I discuss a contextual framework that could serve as a foundation for numerous research studies of wikis in PM-based initiatives.

RESEARCH CONTEXT

Discovering a Conceptual Framework within a Contextual Paradigm

The KM field has produced a large volume of conceptual frameworks for looking at knowledge and "knowledge about knowledge" (metaknowledge). Other related business, management, and library science disciplines have also proposed numerous conceptual frameworks from which to choose. When I began my dissertation proposal in 2002 the volume of KM frameworks was probably less than 25 percent of its number today, which I would estimate to be about two hundred. Although a conservative estimate, this figure has been affirmed by others such as Dalkir (2005), Koenig and Srikantaiah (2004), Srikantaiah and Koenig (2000), and Holsapple and Joshi (2003).

In my study of KM educational programs (Sutton, 2007) I surveyed numerous frameworks that would suit the study of the phenomenon of KM based upon their prominence in the literature, and this section is excerpted and adapted from that study. I identified a framework that could, subsequently, situate the study of the use of a wiki within the context of a PM-based KMS. The study could comprise an historical examination of the chronological sense-making, knowledge creation, and decision-making experiences of the managers, leaders, and team members of a project. A syncretic theoretical framework would be useful to relate all three elements in a balanced fashion. As I surveyed models and frameworks I discovered Dr. Chun Wei Choo's knowing cycle (CKC) conceptual framework (see figure 8.1), which was described in his book *The Knowing Organization: How Organizations Use Information to Construct Meaning, Create Knowledge and Make Decisions* (1998). Choo's model suggested a practical yet theoretically rich formalized conceptual framework.

The contextual paradigm I located could provide a theoretical foundation for data collection, analysis, and eventual interpretation of the findings. This contextual paradigm suggested an exploratory and, to some extent, explanatory study. Exploratory studies are deemed essential when unexplored territory is being investigated, and such studies usually result in original insights about what is going on that may advance theory associated with a new subject or raise new questions. Use of a wiki within a PM-based KMS environment is certainly an unexplained territory, and original research could advance the knowledge associated with the emerging area of investigation into the use of a wiki as a KMS.

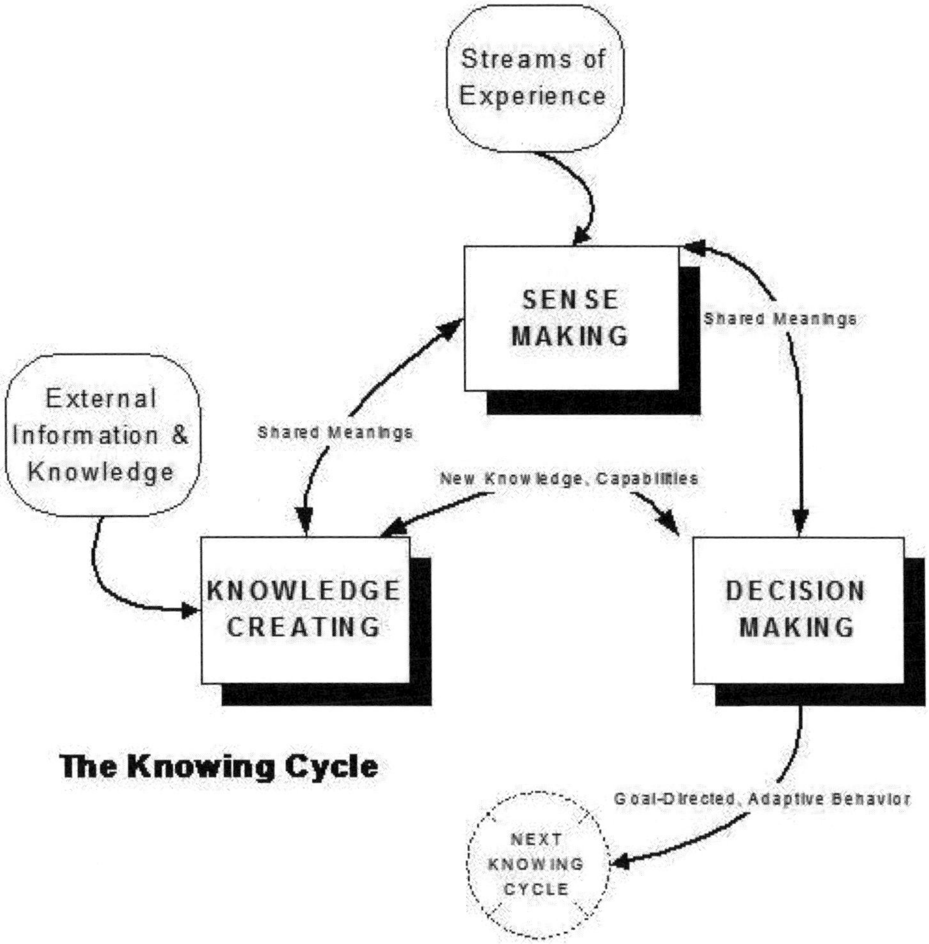

Figure 8.1. The Knowing Cycle
Source: Adapted from Choo, 1998, p. 18.

An original study would need to explore and explain the sense-making processes, decision-making processes, and new knowledge constructed by the wiki participants. An explanatory study would seek to explain the "how" questions behind the individuals, group, and organizational behavior underlying the use of a wiki within the context of a PM-based KMS. It would be impossible to control or manipulate the events that took place from an empirical perspective; I propose to concentrate on the historical record through systematic interviewing and a review of the artifacts available, as suggested in Yin (1994). The use of the case method would permit a researcher to examine contemporary events associated with the use of a wiki within a PM-based KMS environment.

A researcher might consider locating a "budding" PM-based wiki deployment and document its progress with ethnographic methods. However, because of the competitive nature of many wiki deployments, locating a new project-based wiki deployment where an ethnographic study might be undertaken could prove problematic. Hermeneutics and phenomenology could also be used; but many researchers feel uncomfortable with presenting potential results with these methods because they are seldom used in business, management, or library and information science research. Thus, the syncretic unification of Choo's conceptual framework with case and grounded theory analysis could create a robust foundation for a research methodology and design.

Conceptual Framework

The knowing cycle conceptual framework (Choo, 1998, p. 18) suggested the use of models that were premised on individual or group (team) construction of reality, that is, sense-making theory, knowledge creation, and decision making. In order to scope a study into a manageable investigation, the emphasis could be on any one of the three components. Choo's knowing cycle presents a model for discerning the information elements and processes that could feed into the organizational action resulting from the use of a wiki as a PM-based KMS. Organizational action within the knowing organization could be achieved through three information processes:

- Sense making
- Knowledge creation
- Decision making

Action could result from the concentration and absorption of information from the external environment through each successive mode of information use. First, meaning would be socially constructed as information and filtered through the sense-making process. The sense-making stage could facilitate "making sense" of the information streaming from the external environment. Common interpretation could be constructed by the individuals from the exchange and negotiation of information fragments and artifacts that could be combined with the participants' previous experiences and knowledge. Second, the individual participants could create new knowledge about the external world through the transformation of their individual knowledge into shareable information and knowledge. Dialogue, discourse, sharing, storytelling, and codification of personal information and knowledge among the individuals would characterize the knowledge creation stage.

Third, a threshold could be reached at some specific point when the organization as a whole may be prepared to act in a rational manner and choose a decision alternative based upon the organization's inherent goals, objectives, and strategy. The decision-making stage could rely upon rational decision-making models to identify and evaluate alternatives by processing the information and knowledge collected. A subsequent cycle could be spawned when the action chosen changed the external environment and influenced ongoing decisions related to an original choice. Finally, the three organizational information processes would create the architecture for the knowing organization, as posited by Choo. The information processes would rely upon specific techniques and methods to construct, transform, and manage the underlying information and knowledge: sense making, knowledge creation, and decision making.

Sense-Making Theory

Karl Weick (1979), in *The Social Psychology of Organizing* (and subsequently in Weick, 1995, 2001), proposed a microlevel theory called sense making. The theory described how performance could be improved within well-structured and relatively stable organizational environments. Weick suggested methods for tangible metrics to coordinate the actions emerging from chaotic episodes. Weick proposed that chaos could be transformed into sensible and orderly processes through the shared interpretation of the individuals in an organization. In these loosely coupled systems, individuals constructed their own representations of reality. Sense making, like *knowing,* can take place only after the decision or event has transpired. An individual tries to make sense of the situation by comparing the current event with experiences through a retrospective view of the situation.

Weick (1979) described the sense-making process in an organization through four tightly integrated processes within a feedback circuit (see figure 8.2):

- Ecological change
- Enactment
- Selection
- Retention

A change in the environment external to an organization disturbed the flow of information to the participants. The significance of the change triggered an ecological change in the organization. Organizational actors enacted their environment by attempting to scrutinize elements of the environment, for example, "[They] construct, rearrange, single out, and demolish many 'objective' features of their surroundings.

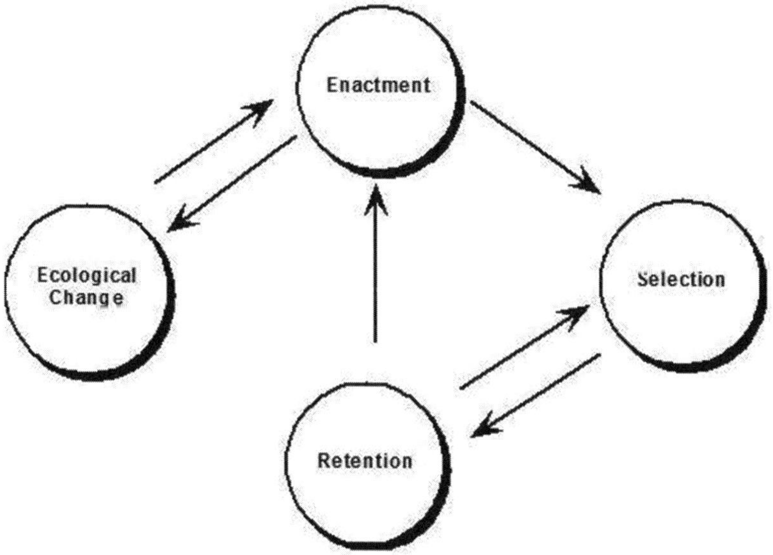

Figure 8.2. Integration of Sense-Making Processes,
Source: adapted from Weick, 1979, p. 132.

. . . They unrandomize variables, insert vestiges of orderliness, and literally create their own constraints" (Weick, 1979, p. 164).

The data resulting from the process of enactment clarified emerging issues for the selection process, where individuals attempted to interpret the rationale for the observed and enacted changes. Finally, the interpretations were retained in personal memories or documented in the retention process, furnishing the organization with a memory of successful and unsuccessful sense-making experiences. Eventually the retained information and knowledge could be reused in future situations to interpret new changes and stabilize individual interpretations into a team-based organizational view of events and actions. The uncertainty associated with ambiguous, unclear, or poorly defined information was reduced through an iterative, common interpretation process until the meaning had been distilled to an agreed-upon unequivocal interpretation or an agreed-upon ambivalence.

Weick (1979) suggested that "sensemaking is largely solitary in the sense that structures contained within individual minds are imposed on streams of individual elapsed experiences that are capable of an infinite number of individual reconstructs" (p. 142). Weick's theory could help frame and interpret the sense-making experiences transpiring within the minds of the PM-based participants using the wiki. Additionally, Weick's theory could help interpret the resulting social construction of metaknowledge about the construction and use of KM artifacts. Sense making would serve a study in a number of critical ways that could assist the investigator to (adapted from Klein, Moon, & Hoffman, 2006, p. 72):

- Comprehend what was going on;
- Improve the plausibility of alternative explanations and explain anomalies;
- Clarify the past events described by the participants;
- Suggest future choices and decision streams for other PM-based organizations considering the architecture of a wiki as a KMS;
- Explore the information collected with the support of a shadow "guide"; and
- Promote the achievement of common ground in understanding the social construction activities, not just the collection of individual perspectives.

The two remaining components of the knowing cycle are described below in order to provide a comprehensive understanding of all the model's components. However, a single investigator may encounter a number of barriers once the study begins, such as lack of available time by participants, lack of comprehensive documentation, poor personal and corporate memories, and lack of recollection of the facts. Knowledge creation and decision making could be addressed at a detailed level if a team undertook a study.

Knowledge Creation Theory

The knowledge creation process could be directed through the shared interpretations defined by the participants during the sense-making process in terms of the use of a wiki within a PM-based KMS. The knowledge creation process could widen the spectrum of potential choices for decision making through the acquisition of new knowledge and competencies. The results would feed the decision-making process with innovative strategies that may extend an organization's capability to make an informed, rational decision.

Choo drew upon the knowledge creation theory of Nonaka and Takeuchi (1995), where case studies of successful knowledge creation described the integration and relationship in the organization between tacit and explicit knowledge. Tacit knowledge in the heads of the participants was difficult to formalize and codify. Explicit knowledge was the tacit knowledge that had been codified and transmitted between individuals as well as groups. A complementary relationship existed between these two types of knowledge. The greatest value to the organization was contained in the persistence of the tacit knowledge codified into explicit knowledge. Innovation, according to Nonaka and Takeuchi, was triggered by the transformation and conversion of tacit to explicit knowledge, thus establishing a higher probability of success (and potential profit) for the organization.

The cyclic knowledge conversion process from explicit to tacit knowledge consisted of four stages (see figure 8.3) (Nonaka & Takeuchi, 1995, pp. 62–72):

- Socialization—Tacit knowledge is acquired by sharing personal experiences, resulting in sympathized knowledge.
- Externalization—Metaphors, analogies and models are used to convert tacit knowledge into explicit conceptual knowledge.
- Combination—Explicit knowledge is generated through communication and cross-fertilization of messages from other organizational entities, resulting in systemic knowledge.
- Internalization—Shared mental models and explicit work practices are internalized as tacit knowledge to build new operational knowledge.

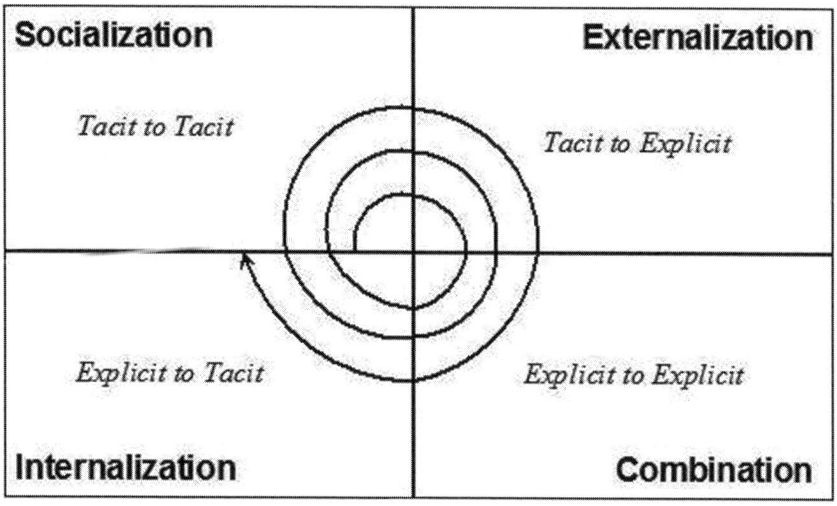

Figure 8.3. Knowledge Conversion Process,
Source: adapted from Nonaka & Takeuchi, 1995, p. 71.

The results from the knowledge creation stage could invigorate the decision-making process with unique innovative approaches to supporting a satisfactory (if not optimal) decision.

Decision-Making Theory

The Carnegie school of organizational decision theory was spawned in the 1940s and 1950s by a number of theorists interested in how organizations came to make particular decisions. This school of thought theorizes that information plays a significant role in decision making and problem solving (Cyert & March, 1963; March, 1988; March & Olsen, 1979; March & Simon, 1958; Simon, 1957). The concept of bounded rationality—limited or constrained rationality—was first proposed by Simon (1957):

> The capacity of the human mind for formulating and solving complex problems is very small compared with the size of the problems whose solution is required for objectively rational behavior in the real world—or even for a reasonable approximation to such objective rationality. (p. 198)

He suggested that the mind has a critical challenge in coping with the complexities of the world and, thus, constructs a simple mental model of reality and tries to work within that model. Even though there may be weaknesses associated with the simple model, the individual who has constructed the model tries to act rationally within it, regardless of ambiguities or contradictions. Simon outlined the ways in which an individual can be bound in a decision-making process (1957, p. 323):

- He or she is limited by his unconscious skills, habits and reflexes.
- He or she is limited by individual values and conception of purpose, which may diverge from the organization goals.
- He or she is limited by the extent of personal knowledge and information.

The organization itself does not constrain the individual decision makers, but instead limits the decision premises that influence the individuals. Neumann explains:

> If the theory of chess were really fully known, there would be nothing left to play. The theory would show which of three possibilities ["white wins," "tie," or "black wins"] actually holds, and accordingly the play would be described before it starts. . . . But our proof, which guarantees the validity of one (and only one) of these three alternatives, gives no practically usable method to determine the true one. (as quoted in Simon, 1957, p. 25)

March and Simon's (1958) book, *Organizations*, described a detailed theory concerned with the management of risk and uncertainty during the decision-making process. March and Simon studied organizations and their decision-making processes in terms of limits with satisficing criteria, that is, the ability to make decisions where available information is constrained but there is enough data to make a good enough or satisficing choice. They proposed that organizations and their managers were bound by their own ability to rationalize and identify satisficing solutions.

Decisions could then be analyzed where constraints imposed on the stakeholders limited the rational basis for the choice. The possibility of nonrational decisions suggested that managers were not always rational and were often irrational. Thus was conceived bounded rationality theory.

The framework of bounded rationality theory is a useful framework when decision makers make a rational choice based upon limited, unclear, or ambiguous criteria. Rationality criteria emerge from the alternatives and the method of choosing alternatives that are in "proper accord" with the preferences, and from beliefs of the individuals or the group involved in the decision. The bounded rationality theory has been accepted in the organizational and management science disciplines as a means of interpreting decision-making behavior under less-than-ideal circumstances (March, 1988).

CONTEXTUAL PARADIGM FOR QUALITATIVE RESEARCH

A paradigm is a "basic set of beliefs that guides action" (Guba, 1990, p. 17). A paradigm is a threefold interpretive framework based upon three assumptions (Denzin & Lincoln, 1998, p. 201):

- Ontological assumption—the ontology of the researcher (the means used to describe the world)
- Epistemological assumption—the epistemology of the researcher (the relationship between subject and object in the world)
- Methodological assumption—the methodology of the researcher (the method used to gain knowledge of the world)

Since the primary element in the chosen conceptual framework is based upon the social construction of meaning (Choo, 2002; Weick, 2001), then the study should be situated within the context of qualitative research. This context implies an emphasis on processes and meanings that are not as precisely examined as quantitative measurements. Qualitative research focuses on the social construction of reality: "[It] seeks answers to questions that stress how the social experience is created and given meaning. In contrast, quantitative studies emphasize the measurements and analysis of causal relationships between variables, not processes . . . within a value-free framework" (Denzin & Lincoln, 1998, p. 8). Thus, a qualitative research context situates the research within a spectrum of four major categories of interpretive social science paradigms—from positivist/postpositivist through constructivist-interpretive, critical, and feminist-poststructuralist paradigms (Bogdan & Biklen, 1998; Denzin & Lincoln, 1998; LeCompte, 1990).

Constructivist Paradigm

The constructivist paradigm places particular emphasis upon individuals participating fully in the social construction of their own reality, that is, reality is an individual construct and such constructs "do not exist outside of the persons who create and hold them" (Guba & Lincoln, 1989, p. 143). By interacting with the world, a constructivist constructs, tests, and refines representations that will help make sense of the world. Denzin and Lincoln (1998) proposed that "the constructivist paradigm assumes a relativist ontology (there are multiple realities), a subjectivist epistemology (knower and subject create understandings), and a naturalistic (in the natural world) set of methodological procedures" (p.27). Findings within a constructivist paradigm are usually presented in terms of the criteria of grounded theory (Strauss & Corbin, 1998).

Lincoln (1990) suggested a very useful description of constructivism that could be used as the contextual paradigm for this study:

> The constructivist paradigm . . . [has] as its central focus not the abstraction (reduction) or the approximation (modeling) of a single reality but the presentation of multiple, holistic, competing, and often conflictual realities of multiple stakeholders and research participants (including the inquirer's). Further, in the presentation of those multiple realities (social constructions), a vicarious déjà vu experience should be created in the reader. This vicarious experience, in addition to providing certain technical help to other researchers (e.g., in the presentation of thick description, which enables judgments regarding transferability to be made), should aid the reader in understanding the nuances and subtleties of conflict and agreement in this place and at this time. Further, the written report should demonstrate the passion, the commitment, and the involvement of the inquirer with his or her co-participants in the inquiry. (p. 73)

Additionally, Confrey (1990) suggested another succinct summary of constructivism that supports my understanding of the paradigm:

> Put into simple terms, constructivism can be described as essentially a theory about the limits of human knowledge, a belief that all knowledge is necessarily a product of our own cognitive acts. We can have no direct or unmediated knowledge of any external or objective reality. We construct our understanding through our experiences, and the character of our experience is influenced profoundly by our cognitive lens. (p. 108)

Since any resulting theory from this research should be posited within a social science paradigm, the proposed contextual paradigm of constructivism will:

1. Provide an overarching social science framework for exploring and interpreting the use of a wiki within a PM-based KMS.
2. Reflect the categories and assumptions of the particular worldview.
3. Establish the macrotheoretical means to interpret and analyze the research problem.
4. Furnish suggested perspectives for interpreting the study's findings, explanations, and conclusions.

Numerous flavors of constructivism have emerged, including radical, social, physical, evolutionary, postmodern, social constructionism, and information-processing constructivism (Ernest, 1995, p. 459). Heylighen's (1993) explanation of social constructivism was that it "sees consensus between different subjects as ultimate criterion to judge knowledge. 'Truth' or 'reality' will be accorded only to those constructions on which most people of a social group agree" (para. 8). Social constructivism declares that truth and reality are partially constructed within a social context and are thus malleable, depending upon the particular social context. Social constructivists have two key foci:

1. The examination of social networks of meaning that underlie a construction, and
2. The place of social relations in constructing truth and reality.

I recommend that a researcher construct an interpretation of the use of a wiki as PM-based KMS within this social constructivist paradigm. The investigator could collect perceptions of the sense-making processes that transpired among the participants involved in the use of a wiki as PM-based KMS. Of course, effort to construct meaning may appear incomplete, since the investigator will not directly participate in the experience of sense making. However, the attempt to understand, represent, explain, and describe the sense-making process could generate new interpretations.

NEXT STEPS

A study by Dennis, Ko, and Clay (2008) outlined a useful survey methodology for collecting qualitative data from field service representatives after a KMS had been operational for over a year. This study could be the basis for constructing a structured questionnaire as a data collection instrument. Whelton and colleagues (2005) described critical details in the collaborative approach to developing a project definition and a needs/requirements document for a PM initiative. This would be an obvious stage to focus a proposed study, since there would be a high volume of sense making, decision making, and knowledge creation within this phase of a project.

De Kretser and Wilkinson (2005) outlined three types of knowledge bases created during a PM initiative. These could be the basis for categorizing much of the material posted into a wiki during the knowledge creation process. Mader (2008) identified an evolving matrix of people patterns and antipatterns as well as adoption patterns and antipatterns that emerge when wikis are adopted by an organization. This could also form a very good perspective for qualitative analysis within a PM-based initiative. Any of these studies could support the scoping of a research initiative into a manageable team-based investigation or individual dissertation.

My hope is that a researcher looking for a context for his or her initiative may stumble across this chapter. If so, I would be satisfied knowing that I have been able to contribute a context that was previously proven in Sutton (2007) and that might now be specifically applied to study the use of a wiki in a PM-based KMS.

REFERENCES

Allen, C. (2004). *Tracing the evolution of social software.* Retrieved May 31, 2009, from the Life with Alacrity website, http://www.lifewithalacrity.com/2004/10/tracing_the_evo.html.

Augar, N., Raitman, R., & Zhou, W. (2004). Teaching and learning online with wikis. In *Beyond the comfort zone: Proceedings of the 21st Annual Conference of the Australasian Society for*

Computers in Learning in Tertiary Education (ASCILITE) (pp. 95–104). Retrieved on May 31, 2009, from http://ascilite.org.au/conferences/perth04/procs/augar.html

Baghdadabad, A. H. (2008). *The implications of knowledge management for library and information science education: A mixed method investigation*. Unpublished doctoral dissertation, RMIT University, Melbourne, Australia.

Bartezzaghi, E., Coros, M., & Verganti, R. (1997). Continuous improvement and inter-project learning in new product development. *International Journal of Technology Management, 14*(1), 116–138.

Benkler, Y. (2006). *The wealth of networks*. New Haven, CT: Yale University Press.

Bogdan, R. C., & Biklen, K. B. (1998). *Qualitative research for education: An introduction to theory and methods*. Boston: Allyn & Bacon.

Carvin, A. (2005, February 1). *Tim Berners-Lee: Weaving a semantic web*. Retrieved May 31, 2009, from http://www.digitaldivide.net/articles/view.php?ArticleID=20

Choo, C. W. (1998). *The knowing organization: How organizations use information to construct meaning, create knowledge and make decisions*. New York: Oxford University Press.

Choo, C. W. (2002). Knowledge in organizations: Sensemaking, knowledge creation, and decision making: Organizational knowing as emergent strategy. In C. W. Choo & N. Bontis (Eds.), *The strategic management of intellectual capital and organizational knowledge* (pp. 79–88). Oxford: Oxford University Press.

Coakes, E., Bradburn, A., & Blake, C. (2005). Knowledge management in a project climate. In A. S. Kazi (Ed.), *Knowledge management in the construction industry: A socio-technical perspective* (pp. 130–137). Hershey, PA: Idea Group Publishing.

Confrey, J. (1990). What constructivism implies for teaching. In R. B. Davis, C. A. Maher, & N. Noddings (Eds.), *Constructivist views on the teaching and learning of mathematics* (Vol. Monograph 4, pp. 107–124). Reston, VA: National Council of Teachers of Mathematics.

Crawford, L. (2000). Profiling the competent project manager. In *Proceedings of PMI Research Conference*, Sylva, NC: Project Management Institute (pp. 3–15).

Cunningham, W. (2005). *Correspondence on the etymology of the wiki*. Retrieved May 31, 2009, from http://c2.com/doc/etymology.html

Cyert, R. M., & March, J. G. (1963). *A behavioral theory of the firm*. Englewood Cliffs, NJ: Prentice-Hall.

Dalkir, K. (2005). *Knowledge management in theory and practice*. Boston: Butterworth-Heinemann.

Dennis, A. R., Ko, D-G, & Clay, P. F. (2008). Building knowledge management systems to improve profits and create loyal customers. In I. Becerra-Fernandez & D. Leidner (Eds.), *Knowledge management: An evolutionary view* (pp. 180–203). Armonk, NY: M. E. Sharpe.

Denzin, N. K., & Lincoln, Y. S. (Eds.). (1998). *The landscape of qualitative research: Theories and issues*. Thousand Oaks, CA: SAGE.

Ernest, P. (1995). The one and the many. In L. Steffe & J. Gale (Eds.), *Constructivism in education* (pp. 459–486). Hillsdale, NJ: Erlbaum.

Fong, P. S. W. (2008). Can we learn from our past? Managing knowledge and learning within and across projects. In I. Becerra-Fernandez & D. Leidner (Eds.), *Knowledge management: An evolutionary view* (pp. 204–226). Armonk, NY: M. E. Sharpe.

Friedman, T. (2005). *The world is flat: A brief history of the twenty-first century*. New York: Farrar, Strauss andGiroux.

Goodwin-Jones, R. (2003). Blogs and wikis: Environments for online collaboration. *Language, Learning and Technology, 7*(2), 12–16. Retrieved on May 31, 2009, from http://llt.msu.edu/vol7num2/emerging/default.html

Guba, E. G. (1990). The alternative paradigm dialog. In E. G. Guba (Ed.), *The paradigm dialogue* (pp. 17–30). Newbury Park, CA: SAGE.

Guba, E. G., & Lincoln, Y. S. (1989). *Fourth generation evaluation*. Newbury Park, CA: SAGE.

Hardy, C., Lawrence, T. B., & Grant, D. (2005). Discourse and collaboration: The role of conversations and collective identity. *Academy of Management Review, 30*(1) 58–77.

Heylighen, F. (1993). *Epistemology, introduction.* Retrieved May 31, 2009, from http://pespmc1.vub.ac.be/EPISTEMI.html

Holsapple, C. W., & Joshi, K. D. (2003). A knowledge management ontology. In C. W. Holsapple (Ed.), *Handbook on knowledge management: Knowledge matters* (Vol. 1, pp. 89–128). Berlin: Springer-Verlag.

James, H. (2004). My brilliant failure: Wikis in classrooms. *Kairosnews.* Retrieved May 31, 2009, from http://kairosnews.org/node/3794

Jeffries, M. C., Eng, C. S., & Zenke, R. (2005). Evaluating an organization's learning culture using learning histories. In A. S. Kazi (Ed.), *Knowledge management in the construction industry: A socio-technical perspective* (pp. 130–137). Hershey, PA: Idea Group Publishing.

Jewell, M., & Walker, D. H. T. (2005). Community of practice software management tools: A UK construction company case study. In M. Jennex (Ed.), *Case studies in knowledge management* (pp. 112–128). Hershey, PA: Idea Group Publishing.

Kasvi, J. J. J., Vartiainen, M., & Hailikari, M. (2003). Managing knowledge and knowledge competencies in projects and project organizations. *International Journal of Project Management, 21*(8), 571–582.

Klein, G., Moon, B., & Hoffman, R. R. (2006, July–August). Making sense of sensemaking 1: Alternative perspectives. *IEEE Intelligent Systems,* (21), 70–73.

Klobas, J. (2006). *Wikis: Tools for information and work collaboration.* Oxford: Chandos Publishing.

Koenig, M. E. D., & Srikantaiah, T. K. (Eds.) (2004). *Knowledge management lessons learned: What works and what doesn't.* Medford, NJ: Information Today.

Kotnour, T. (1999). A learning framework for project management. *Project Management Journal, 30*(2), 32–38.

Kotnour, T. (2000). Organizational learning practices in the project management environment. *International Journal of Quality and Reliability Management, 17*(4/5), 393–406.

Kotnour, T., & Hjelm, M. (2002). Leadership mechanism for enabling learning within project teams. *Proceedings of the 3rd European Conference on Organizational Knowledge, Learning, and Capabilities.* Athens, Greece.

de Kretser, S., & Wilkinson, S. (2005). Strategies for managing project generated knowledge: A New Zealand case study. In M. Jennex (Ed.), *Case studies in knowledge management* (pp. 1–17). Hershey, PA: Idea Group Publishing.

Lange, M., & Patterson, J. (2005). Assignment—Using a wiki for a collaborative essay. In *An introduction to digital learning environments.* Retrieved May 31, 2009, from the University of Edinburgh, http://www.malts.ed.ac.uk/idel/assignment/wiki/000008.html

LeCompte, M. D. (1990). Emergent paradigms: How new? How necessary? In E. G. Guba (Ed.), *The paradigm dialog* (pp. 246–255). London: SAGE.

Lincoln, Y. S. (1990). The making of a constructivist—A remembrance of transformations past. In E. G. Guba (Ed.), *The paradigm dialog* (pp. 67–87). London: SAGE.

Lundin. R. A., & Midler, C. (1998). Emerging convergences or debates. In R. A. Lundin & C. Midler (Eds.), *Projects as arenas for renewal and learning processes* (pp. 231–241). Boston: Kluwer.

Mader, S. (2006). *Using wiki in education.* Retrieved May 31, 2009, from http://www.lulu.com/content/2175253

Mader, S. (2008). *Wikipatterns: A practical guide to improving productivity and collaboration in your organization.* Indianapolis: Wiley.

Majchrzak, A., Malhorta, A., & John, R. (2005). Perceived individual collaboration know-how development through information technology-enabled contextualization: evidence from distributed teams. *Information Systems Research, 16*(1), 9–27.

Majchrzak, A., Malhorta, A., & John, R. (2008). Dynamic team memory systems: Enabling knowledge sharing effectiveness in structurally diverse distributed teams. In I. Becerra-Fernandez & D. Leidner (Eds.), *Knowledge management: An evolutionary view* (pp. 204–226). Armonk, NY: M. E. Sharpe.
March, J. G. (1988). *Decisions and organizations*. Cambridge, MA: Blackwell.
March, J. G., & Olsen, J. P. (1979). *Ambiguity and choice in organizations* (2nd ed.). Bergen, Norway: Universitetsforlaget.
March, J. G., & Simon, H. A. (1958). *Organizations*. New York: John Wiley & Sons.
Nonaka, I., & Takeuchi, H. (1995). *The knowledge-creating company: How Japanese companies create the dynamics of innovation*. New York: Oxford University Press.
Orange, G., Onions, P., Burke, A., & Colledge, B. (2005). Knowledge management: Facilitating organizational learning within the construction industry. In M. Jennex (Ed.), *Case studies in knowledge management* (pp. 130–149). Hershey, PA: Idea Group Publishing.
Owen, J., & Burstein, F. (2005). Where knowledge management resides within project management. In A. S. Kazi (Ed.), *Knowledge management in the construction industry: A socio-technical perspective* (pp. 138–153). Hershey, PA: Idea Group Publishing.
Paquet, S. (2006). Wikis in business. In J. Klobas (Ed.), *Wikis: Tools for information and work collaboration* (pp. 99–117). Oxford: Chandos Publishing.
Peddibhotla, N. B., & Subramani, M. R. (2008). Managing knowledge in virtual communities within organizations. In I. Becerra-Fernandez & D. Leidner (Eds.), *Knowledge management: An evolutionary view* (pp. 229–247). Armonk, NY: M. E. Sharpe.
PMI. (2000). *A guide to the Project Management Body of Knowledge (PMBOK guide)*. Newton Square, PA: Project Management Institute.
Raman, M., Ryan, T., & Olfmam, L. (2005). Designing knowledge management systems for teaching and learning with wiki technology. *Journal of Information Systems Education, 16*(3), 311–320. Retrieved May 31, 2009, from http://findarticles.com/p/articles/mi_qa4041/is_200510/ai_n15715725/pg_12/
Richardson, W. (2009). *Blogs, wikis, podcasts, and other powerful web tool for classrooms* (2nd ed.). Thousand Oaks, CA: Corwin Press.
Senge, P. (2002). *The fifth discipline: The art and practice of the learning organization*. New York: Random House.
Simon, H. A. (1957). *Models of man: Social and rational: Mathematical essays on rational human behavior in a social setting*. New York: John Wiley & Sons.
Smith, A. (1937). *An inquiry into the nature and causes of the wealth of nations*. New York: Random House.
Smyth, H. (2005). Managing the external provision of "knowledge management" services for projects. In M. Jennex (Ed.), *Case studies in knowledge management* (pp. 34–52). Hershey, PA: Idea Group Publishing.
Srikantaiah, T. K., & Koenig, M. E. D. (Eds.). (2000). *Knowledge management for the information professional*. Medford, NJ: Information Today.
Stein, E. W., & Zwass, V. (1995). Actualizing organizational memory and information systems. *Information Systems Research, 6*(2), 85–117.
Strauss, A. L., & Corbin, J. (1998). Grounded theory methodology: An overview. In N. K. Denzin & Y. S. Lincoln (Eds.), *Strategies of qualitative inquiry* (pp. 158–183). Thousand Oaks, CA: SAGE.
Sutton, M. J. D. (2007). *Examination of the historical sensemaking processes representing the development of knowledge management programs in universities: Case studies associated with an emergent discipline*. Unpublished doctoral dissertation, McGill University, Montréal, Canada.
Taylor,F. W. (1911). *The principles of scientific management*. New York: Harper Bros.
Weber, S. (2004). *The success of open source*. Cambridge, MA: Harvard University Press.
Weick, K. E. (1979). *The social psychology of organizing* (2nd ed.). New York: Random House.

Weick, K. E. (1995). *Sensemaking in organizations*. Thousand Oaks, CA: SAGE.
Weick, K. E. (2001). *Making sense of the organization*. Oxford: Blackwell.
Whelton, M., Pennanen, A., & Ballard, G. (2005). Knowledge emergence and adaptive management: An exploration on the co-production of project needs and requirements by client-specialist groups. In M. Jennex (Ed.), *Case studies in knowledge management* (pp. 251–275). Hershey, PA: Idea Group Publishing.
Whyte, W. (2002). *The organization man*. Philadelphia: University of Pennsylvania Press.
Wysocki, R. K (2007). *Effective project management: Traditional, adaptive, extreme* (4th ed.). Indianapolis: Wiley.
Yin, R. K. (1994). *Case study research: Design and methods* (2nd ed., Vol. 5). Beverly Hills, CA: SAGE.

III

STRATEGY ISSUES

9

KM in Projects

Methodology and Experience

A. Latha, J. K. Suresh, and Kavi Mahesh

This chapter is an account of the successful deployment of KM in customer projects at Infosys Technologies. After introducing the organizational and business context in which projects are executed, the specific requirements for KM in projects are brought out. The experience of Infosys in meeting these requirements is illustrated through an exemplary set of practices used in real projects. The benefits of KM in projects are then described through measurements and metrics that have been developed specifically for KM in projects. Apart from being a case in implementing KM in projects, the chapter highlights several strategies for deploying KM in projects that are different from KM strategies in general.

The chapter presents an overview of an approach to effectively socialize knowledge management (KM) practices in the production organization of Infosys Technologies Limited, (www.Infosys.com), where an acclaimed KM function has been in existence over the past decade. The chapter outlines the business context of the organization, its influence on potential choices for KM design and deployment, and several important lessons learned from the practice of KM in projects.

Infosys Technologies Limited is an IT consulting and services organization headquartered in Bangalore, India. Its U.S. headquarters are in Fremont, California. Founded in 1981, the company has grown at a compounded annual rate of nearly 50 percent over the past decade and reported revenues of $4.6 billion for financial year 2008–2009, employing more than 104,000 people worldwide. The company operates globally, primarily servicing Global 1000 clients located in the Americas, Europe, and the Asia-Pacific region. It has thirteen development centers in India and ten across the rest of the world. In addition, it has marketing offices in about thirty other countries.

An emphasis on excellence—in customer engagements and interactions, internal operations, systems and processes, financial practices, and social accountability—has been an integral part of the company's culture right from the beginning. The company pioneered the global delivery model (GDM) for development of customized IT solutions, which is based on the principle of carrying out work where it can be done best, makes the most economic sense, and carries the least acceptable risk.

Since 1994, it has been accorded a number of recognitions in the fields of corporate governance, financial reporting, and human resource and environment management (http://www.infosys.com/about/awards/all-awards.asp). The company has been a winner of the Asian Most Admired Knowledge Enterprise (MAKE) award six times since its inception in 2002 and the Global MAKE award for five years since 2003.

Structurally, the company has adopted a geographically distributed model for corporate functions such as finance, planning, marketing, quality, HR, education and research (E&R) and information systems. The software delivery apparatus of the company is organized by geos (geographical units), IBUs (integrated business units), ECUs (enterprise capability units), and some units that exclusively focus on individual and large global client accounts and are managed through business unit–specific as well as special organizational structures. The IBUs and ECUs constitute the basic business units (BUs) for the organization along with the aforementioned global accounts. Domain specialists in each of the BUs and a central DCG (domain competency group) provide industry-specific knowledge vital for the delivery of solutions that enable customer business. Another unit, called Setlabs (Software Engineering and Technology Labs), addresses the building of competency in horizontal technology areas such as enterprise architecture, infrastructure, performance, and security. The E&R unit is responsible mainly for training and certifying new and experienced employees in software engineering technologies, methodologies, and project management. The company has extensive infrastructure to support education and learning and spends around 5 percent of its revenues on these activities every year.

Quality processes are a major focus area in the organization. A central quality department defines and owns processes for execution of customer engagements. A network of quality managers is charged with deploying these processes in the software delivery units (geos/IBUs/ECUs) and ensuring their effectiveness. A process council consisting of senior managers from delivery, as well as support services, oversees the process definition and deployment activities.

It may be noted that most of the work that the company carries out for customers is executed in project mode. As such, the work is knowledge intensive and accomplished through a wide spectrum of technologies and products for a large variety of industries the world over.

KM AT INFOSYS

With the increasing acceptance of IT outsourcing across the world in the early 1990s, companies such as Infosys that grew their businesses with dizzying speed and scale perforce experienced significant geographic dispersion, technological flux, and functional specialization. One outcome of this was the growing realization within the organization in the late nineties that it would be difficult to sustain competitiveness, high growth, and market leadership in the absence of strong practices to formally manage its knowledge supply chain (Suresh & Mahesh, 2008). Given the belief of the top management of Infosys that KM constitutes a central dimension of learning, the E&R group was the natural choice for owning the responsibility for developing it as a formal corporate initiative.

It is interesting to note that several characteristics of the company made it easier to build and deploy a KM solution, for example, an environment of continuous learning and collaborative knowledge exchange consciously developed over the years by the top management and a willingness to experiment with new ideas as well as a high degree of voluntarism on the part of a large number of young software developers in the organization.

A primary goal for KM at Infosys was to ensure that the productivity, efficiency, and quality of its services were sustained even as the company inducted ever larger numbers of new employees into its fold. New employees had to be enabled with the knowledge and experience of their seniors so that every project benefited from the collective knowledge of the entire company. At the same time, since the company was rapidly becoming so large that informal networks and acquaintances were inadequate for one to know all the experts throughout the company, there was a strong need for a formal, system-driven solution to determine who knew what in the company. To summarize, important objectives for KM at Infosys included:

- To increase reuse of knowledge assets
- To achieve higher functional effectiveness and competitive advantage
- To apply knowledge to reduce defect rates continuously
- To minimize risk to the company's core software services business by capturing higher-end consulting markets through the efficient use of knowledge
- To enhance the brand value of the company

Since inception, KM at Infosys has been regarded as a rigorous change management exercise characterized as a journey rather than an end (Suresh & Mahesh, 2006). This in turn has facilitated the consideration of KM as a staged evolution of knowledge exchange processes in the organization whose health, performance, and business benefits can be assessed through a framework of measurements appropriate to each stage and whose progress can be monitored and steered through a staged maturity model. Accordingly, a five-level maturity model for KM (see fig. 9.1) was developed as an overarching basis for formulating KM strategy, plans, and activities, and to act as a viable structure for assessing the relative maturity of organizational KM practices over time.

NEED FOR KM IN PROJECTS

After the early successes in instilling the culture and practice of KM across the organization (Suresh & Mahesh, 2006), a key question that confronted the function was related to estimating the benefits and returns from KM. At this point in time, in spite of KM having made deep inroads into the organization, it continued to possess the character of an undifferentiated corporate service. This was largely due to the nature of KM in the early years wherein, in responding to its appeal for bridging islands of knowledge across the organization, the natural impulse of employees was to facilitate greater flows of relatively generic and more widely (acceptable and) applicable knowledge than of highly context bound and locally relevant knowledge. While such flows catered to some significant parts of the knowledge needs of employees, the latter types of knowledge were not well developed in the supply chain.

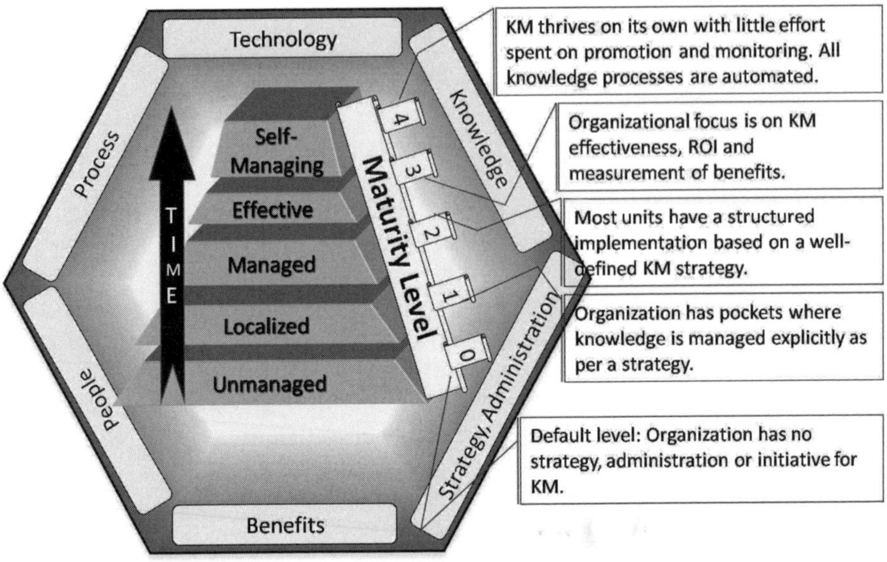

Figure 9.1.

The first step to address this concern was the creation of structures to enable increased elicitation of locally useful knowledge, made possible through tailoring knowledge processes to the specific needs of departments, project teams, and other units and groups of functions. This facilitated the introduction of KM elements in the business processes of units and functions. In addition, it required a resurrection of local knowledge repositories, which in the early years were deprecated in favor of global repositories so as to support the initial agenda of KM in the organization. As a result, KM systems could potentially render knowledge of greater relevance to local requirements through an aggregation of content from global and local repositories.

In addition, KM processes ensured that providing pathways for knowledge needs became easier and helped each unit develop the capability to predict, manage, and produce output that is self-sustaining and measurable. For instance, custom KM processes for software application development and maintenance, a core service area for Infosys, may enforce several KM activities to be undertaken even before a project is begun, such as for acquiring specific skills and knowledge in the domain or technologies that are peculiar to the class of projects being addressed; or for adopting a defined methodology for reusing existing designs, components, code, documents, and the like; or for mandating certain KM activities during the course of execution of the project or after the customer delivery of software; and so forth. In summary, tailoring KM processes for projects provided the means for planned knowledge exchange within the project.

In the following paragraphs, various aspects of this process of structuring and enabling KM in the business units of Infosys are described in detail. The primary organizational unit of discourse here is the business unit (BU), which in general comprises a number of project teams operating in a specific line of service and a few large customer accounts, often involving multiple lines of service. It may be mentioned here that a large account is but a set of projects, usually related to connected business areas, all catering to a single customer organization's needs and therefore identified with it.

CHARACTERISTICS OF PROJECTS

A project typically has four important stages: initiation, planning, execution, and closure. There are many tools, techniques, and practices for managing a project in its different stages (PMBOK, 2008), and they enable the project manager to steer the project through the various stages and deliver the project within budgeted time and cost. A typical set of activities carried out in a project is shown in figure 9.2 and briefly described below.

Initiation: This is the first phase of execution of the project after the basic scope, solution architecture, delivery timelines, and financials of the project are finalized through a contractual process by a team of specialists working closely with the customer. In this phase, the overall approach to the service or solution delivery, the charter, and the governance structure are defined side by side with the structure and protocols for interfacing with an identified group of customer partners.

Planning: In this phase, the deliverables of the project are catalogued, and schedules of various steps involved in the delivery are finalized. In addition, the composition of the project team, its assessment, and plans for skill improvements are drawn up along with risk identification and mitigation measures.

Execution: In this phase, the development, testing, integration, and implementation of the solution for the customer at the customer's location are undertaken. Quality assessment, schedule checks, course corrections, and skill updates are some of the significant management processes involved in this phase.

Closure: Concluding an analysis of plans vis-à-vis actually realized parameters (e.g., effort, time period, quality) and filing of closure reports are two important steps in this phase.

Projects face various challenges during their course in multiple dimensions including changing demands and requirements from the customer, mismatch of the team's skills with the requirements, and geographical distribution of people. These

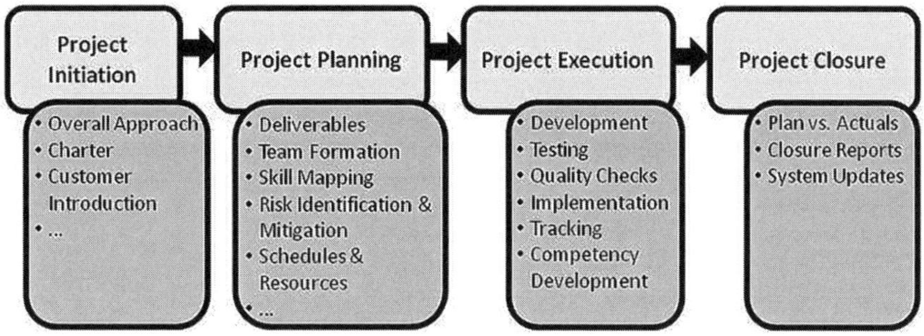

Figure 9.2. Characteristics of Projects

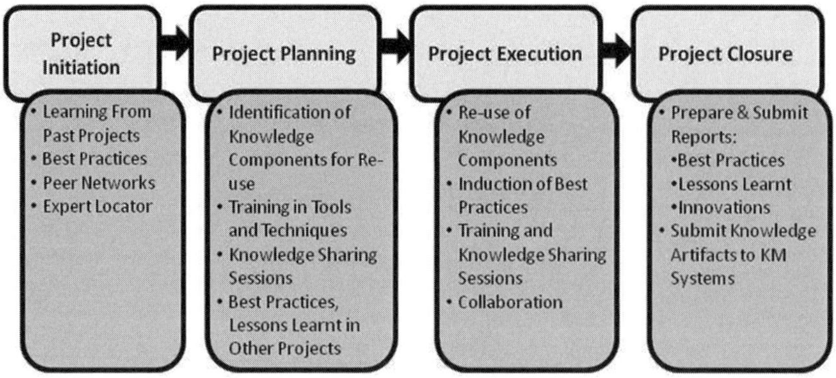

Figure 9.3. Recommended KM Practices at Various Stages of Projects

challenges, coupled with the need to continuously improve quality and productivity parameters, require the project team to be highly enabled and motivated in spite of the complexity of the project and work-life pressures. A deeper analysis of the activities carried out in the projects brings to the fore the important role of KM in projects. Some of the recommended KM practices at various stages of projects are shown in figure 9.3.

CHARACTERISTICS OF KM IN PROJECTS

KM practices are expected to provide significant support and enable projects to achieve their goals. However, experience in projects typically shows that KM systems made available for knowledge sharing across the organization do not address all the KM requirements of projects. Knowledge management in projects, while still sharing the core characteristics of KM in general, has certain special requirements.

A close study of projects brings out the need for separate KM spaces for the teams to deliberate, collaborate, and share knowledge. There are several reasons for this. Confidentiality, intellectual property, or other contractual clauses may require that knowledge of the project be captured, stored, and shared only within the project team. A custom classification scheme may be necessary. It may be desirable to share pitfalls, failures, resolutions, and successes across the team for immediate benefits.

Moreover, KM in projects is necessarily situated in the context of the project whereas KM in general need not be strongly situated in a business context. Being situated in the context of the project has both positive and negative implications for the design of an effective KM solution for projects. Project activities are typically bounded in terms of space, time, and cost. However, project teams are often more effective communities of practice with better familiarity and relationships among their members. Table 9.1 summarizes the key differences between KM in projects and KM in general.

Table 9.1. Key Differences between KM and KM in Projects

Characteristic	*KM in Projects*	*KM in General*
Context	KM as well as mainstream project activities happen in the business context of the project and its customer or sponsor	KM happens in the generic context of the entire organization
Locality	Most members belong to a few well-connected locations	Members are distributed throughout the organization
Time	Typically short timelines with tight deadlines	KM benefits may be realized in the long term
Motivation for Knowledge Sharing	Members are driven by the business and knowledge needs of the project	Members are driven by business needs at times and by long-term career goals at other times
People Network	Informal and close relationships are common among members	Formal and indirect relationships facilitated by systems are essential in large organizations
Type of Knowledge Involved	Tacit and relatively incompletely embodied knowledge can be shared effectively through direct collaboration	Mostly explicit knowledge is shared indirectly through systems; tacit and informal knowledge exchange cannot be directly managed
Measurement	Easier to measure KM parameters and to correlate them with cost, quality, and productivity measures	Measuring KM parameters is difficult; non-KM metrics may not be available to demonstrate KM benefits

ESTABLISHING A KM NETWORK

Among the first steps involved in scoping KM needs for a project or a business unit is the development of an appropriate people network to aid eventual interventions. Since the KM program at Infosys is based upon an approach that encourages practitioner participation not only in useful knowledge exchange but also in the associated management structures, various roles have been created in the business units to help KM address the specific needs of the unit by providing the right combination of infrastructure and practices for the target group. This approach, conceived early in the evolution of KM at Infosys, has been termed a "facilitated, decentralized approach" (Kochikar, Mahesh, & Mahind, 2002) inasmuch as it enforces responsibility and ownership for KM in the business unit while leveraging the experience and expertise of the central KM group and allowing the business context of the unit to determine the quantum of customization of the generic KM framework.

Figure 9.4 provides a pictorial representation of the people network that has been established as a part of the efforts to integrate KM into the activities and processes that are executed in the business units. In the figure, solid lines between the entities (departments or roles) indicate a reporting relationship in the business hierarchy, and dotted lines indicate nonreporting and subsidiary relationships. The dotted arrows, on the other hand, represent the relationship of projects with the quality department, responsible for ensuring conformity with organization-wide quality assurance activities and outcomes. In other words, the goals, targets, and objectives

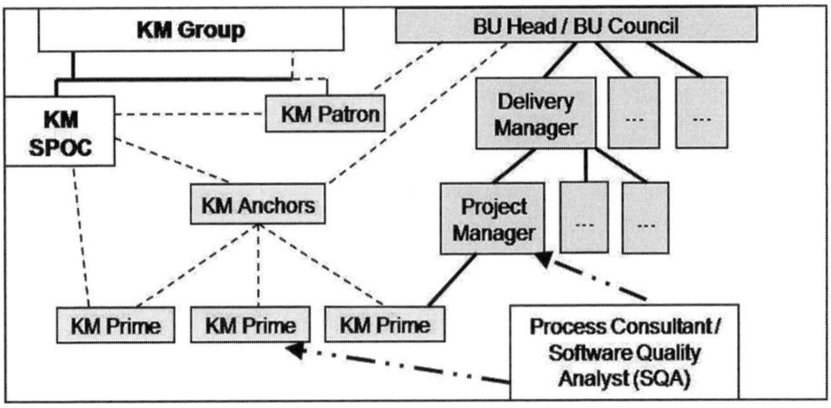

Figure 9.4. Representation of People Network

for business are defined and executed through the first type of relationship and their enablers by the second and third types.

Furthermore, since projects with clearly laid timelines and objectives constitute the bulk of the business for Infosys; the roles themselves have different life spans. For example, the KM prime role terminates at the end of a project, while other roles are not usually tied to project timelines and therefore in theory are more enduring. Yet, given the dynamism of the business itself, the continuous assembly and disassembly of people into teams in the organization has significant influence on the environment and mindsets of employees, as a result of which the longevity of other role players is not high either. This in turn creates important challenges for the central KM group in maintaining people networks and ensuring the effectiveness of KM practice in the many hundreds of projects executed every year in the organization. The constituent roles of the people network responsible for KM in a typical business unit are briefly discussed here:

1. KM SPOC (single point of contact): This is a role derived from the central group for KM in the organization, responsible for the entire life cycle of knowledge usage and its consequences in the unit. Intimately associated with the business unit in deploying, analyzing, and effecting changes in its KM practices, this role shares bottom-line responsibility for the governance and performance of KM in the unit along with the KM patron of the unit. Coordinating the customization of the infrastructure, branding, and promotion activities and measurement for KM programs is an important responsibility for this role.
2. KM patron: The person playing this role, usually a senior BU member with a decade or more of experience in the field, assumes joint ownership—along with the central KM team—for the KM maturity of the business unit and drives the KM program with the help of the network of KM anchors and KM primes.
3. KM anchor: The KM anchor acts as an important link between the KM primes (a project-level role) and the KM patron in that he or she monitors the network of KM primes in the business unit, reviews activities and awareness

measures, and collects and collates unit-level information for the KM patron. This role also partners with the process consultants, the central KM team, and the KM DC champ (the KM champion at the local development center of the company) for KM-related activities (e.g., training in KM for the KM primes).

4. KM prime: This is a mandated role, identified at the time of setting up the project, usually after upstream activities related to finalizing the terms of business engagement with the customer are completed. The project manager (PM) would typically nominate a senior team member as the KM prime for the project. Over time, for projects that run for long periods (more than six months), the role may be rotated among other team members. The role of KM prime is critical to weaving KM into the process fabric of software delivery in the project as an evangelist, enabler, referee, and analyst. Benefits derived by the project from KM as reported by KM metrics through the agency of the KM prime are a key measure of the effectiveness of this role.

The success of KM in the project organization is critically dependent on the people network described above. Appendix 1 provides a comprehensive set of expectations from roles 2 through 4 above.

KM AND BUSINESS REQUIREMENTS

An assessment of the state of practice of KM in a business unit is the second step in developing appropriate solutions to meet its KM requirements for business. In this section, important characteristics of the needs of business are summarized briefly from a KM viewpoint, followed by an outline of an assessment and solution development process to identify and fill gaps in a unit's knowledge management practices.

For a BU, the need to manage and grow its business creates a twofold thrust—toward effectively managing the operational requirements for delivering services to customers through its project engagements and in optimizing the overall performance of the unit as a whole. The project planning and execution processes cater to the first point, as explained in the previous section. However, note that the previous section adequately describes only that type of project that belongs to the development and maintenance (ADM) services offered by the organization (and which account for the largest fraction of its revenues). On the other hand, projects in other services (such as enterprise solutions, system integration, infrastructure, and testing and validation services) offered by the company differ in many respects from the ADM services in terms of both the context and the content of the four phases of projects detailed in the previous section. Even so, the concerns related to KM are significantly similar to those encountered in ADM services and hence, in the following, the impact of such distinctions as may exist between the services on the design and implementation of KM processes can be assumed to be negligible without any loss of generality.

Turning to the second thrust area for a BU, namely, its performance, it is easy to recognize that revenues, margins, and customer and stakeholder satisfaction constitute prime parameters defining the health and benefits of the business. These parameters in turn are outcomes of factors such as productivity, costs, motivation, and competency levels of the employees and the quality of the management processes and the delivered services. Also, the unit's relative performance with respect to the market, competitors, and other units in the organization are important additional considerations that, together with the ones outlined above, provide the means for creating a dynamic agenda for continuous improvements in its strategy and operations, in pursuit of which KM acquires importance.

KM ASSESSMENT

The main goals of a KM assessment are to:

- Identify existing sources of knowledge (e.g., people, processes, repositories, systems) in the BU.
- Categorize prevalent and preferred modes of knowledge exchange in the unit.
- Understand bottlenecks, obstacles, and silos impeding knowledge flows.
- Catalog existing technology infrastructure for content sharing and collaboration.
- Identify knowledge gaps by eliciting knowledge needs to satisfice that no enduring mechanisms currently support.

In line with this, an assessment of the unit may be carried out using an appropriate combination of different methods such as interviews, surveys, polls, and the like across representative parts or the whole of the unit. A typical survey questionnaire is designed to help gauge existing culture, practices, motivation, processes, and systems for knowledge exchange and identify lacunae that need to be filled in order to promote better leverage of knowledge for value realization by the unit (see Appendix 2 for a sample set of questions in a typical KM survey).

Based on an analysis of the responses from various stakeholders, an assessment report is compiled, providing a summary of the state of KM practice in the unit along with a list of knowledge needs and gaps that need to be addressed. This is in turn used to develop the design and plan for KM in the unit.

KM SOLUTION DESIGN

Based on the state of knowledge management practice in the unit, the unit management council, in collaboration with the central KM group, arrives at a statement of objectives for the KM program in the unit based upon the needs of its business. Typical objectives include improvement of effort productivity, quality of software, and customer satisfaction levels, enhancement of competency levels among employees, pervasion of the culture of KM, increased efficiency in handshake processes between teams, and the like.

The scope of the KM program is defined by the composition and structure of the BU as much as it is determined by the gaps discovered in the assessment. For example, if a BU comprises several large accounts and a number of smaller projects, the unit management may choose to exclude the accounts and include only the projects operating in the ambit of the generic KM program, or only include a few accounts, or perhaps use different solutions and implementations in accounts from those used in projects. As a complement, based on generic concerns raised in the gap analysis report, some objectives described above can be identified for action in specified phases of the project, for instance, in selecting the testing and deployment phases as prime areas of focus for KM in order to obtain improved effort productivity or reduced number of defects in the software, perhaps in a scenario where many projects in the unit display unacceptable levels of schedule slippages or cost overruns in these phases.

The next step is to determine the targets to be achieved by the KM program in the unit within the scope defined and the objectives set for it. In this step, operating on an implicit belief that knowledge flows can and do significantly influence outcomes, the objectives of the unit are translated into KM goals so as to enable purposeful actions to begin down the line. Table 9.2 provides sample details of a goal sheet of the KM program for a unit, which provides the basis for tracking the achievement of targets. In practice, the KM patron, SPOC, and anchor, in coordination with the unit leadership, determine the goals for the unit in light of the existing state of the parameters shown in the table. Units are free to choose additional parameters related to productivity and quality based on the state of their KM maturity.

Table 9.2. Parameters for KM Maturity

Parameter
KM Enabling and Planning
% of projects with a KM plan
% of KM primes trained
Competency Building
# of induction programs
# of mentoring programs
# of knowledge transfer sessions across projects
Others
Effective Effort Utilization
# of checklists/guidelines reused
# of code templates/snippets reused
# of person-days of savings reported
# of tools created/reused
Others
KM Infrastructure
# of knowledge portal contributions (authoring and review)
# of instances of usage of knowledge portal
# of documents rated in knowledge portal
# of contributions to collaborative systems
# of instances of usage of collaborative systems
# of knowledge assets shared in project spaces
KM Culture
# of activities, events
Others

While designing the KM solution to cater to the goals that are set for achieving the objectives, a healthy mix of different KM service components, such as infrastructure, branding and promotion techniques, and facilitation can be assembled as required for projects and accounts. For example, in situations characterized by a high degree of need for interactivity within the team, infrastructure for collaboration is likely to be of greater relevance than that for codified content, and hence the solution revolves around identifying appropriate collaborative platforms to be customized for use. Similarly, branding and promotion activities can be chosen in line with the infrastructure and the subcultural context of the unit or the project group.

Another dimension to the design is the special needs of certain business groups. For example, some accounts (usually large ones) function within ring-fenced firewalls where no information flow is possible between other parts of the organization and the account except predefined management information. In such situations, the KM solution acquires an almost completely localized flavor since organizational experiences cannot be easily transferred across the boundaries of the account. Geography poses another design criterion for the KM solution in adapting the infrastructure, process, and branding and promotion to cater to multiple project teams across physical locations while catering to time zone differences, security, and availability concerns.

Once the basic infrastructure, range of operation, and facilitation are designed, corresponding plans for deployment are made considering the needs for promotion, rewards and recognition, enabling, and resource allocation for these activities. Table 9.3 provides a sample summary sheet of the elements of the KM plan for a project.

Table 9.3. Summary Sheet of a KM Plan

Sl. No.	*Plan Element*	*Details*
1	General	This is the KM Plan for PROJECT XYZ.
2	KM goals and metrics	Defines the KM goals for the project. Some items pertain to data that are captured by the central KM group and fed to the KM prime by the KM DC champ/KM group for effective tracking at the project level. Other items are captured and tracked by the KM prime on an ongoing basis.
3	Knowledge acquisition plan	This contains the training needs and the knowledge acquisition plan for the group in domain, technology, processes, or others.
4	Reuse checklist	This contains a checklist as a ready reckoner to locate resources for reuse during different life cycle stages.
5	Sharing plan	This contains the knowledge sharing plan. The group has to share knowledge within as well as outside the project group.
6	Closure analysis	This is typically carried out at the end of the project along with project closure report. If there are logical closures (say, phase 1, phase 2, etc.), they are updated at each closure. Summary of the analysis should become a part of the project closure report.

To illustrate item 2 in table 9.3, KM goals to be met can be chosen by the project in consonance with the unit KM guidelines, for example, in the areas of productivity and quality as shown in table 9.4. Tables 9.5, 9.6, and 9.7 provide sample plans and actions for a project undertaking a KM program. Tables 9.8 and 9.9 provide a sample knowledge-sharing plan.

Table 9.4. Productivity and Quality

KM Goals	*Improvement (%)*
Productivity	5
Cost of quality	5
Defect injection rate	5

Table 9.5. Plans and Actions for a Project

Strategy	*KM Goal Addressed*
Recapitulation of J2EE by team members	Reduction in defect injection rate
Use of Toad as a tool for Oracle	Improvement in productivity
Development and use of coding and documentation standards and checklists	Improvement in productivity and improvement in quality
Group review of code and documents for major release	Reduction in defect injection rate

Table 9.6. Plans and Actions for a Project

Metric	*Target Value at Project Level*	*Strategies Adopted to Achieve Goals*
Knowledge assets accessed	400 per month	Poster campaign Awareness sessions . . .
Knowledge assets used/ reused from the knowledge portal	25 per Month	Promotion campaign Incentives
Subscriptions to knowledge assets by the group	25 per quarter	Contests

Table 9.7. Plans and Actions for a Project

Metric	*Target Value at Project Level*
Knowledge assets submitted by the project team to various repositories	Two per quarter
Technical reports, white papers, publications, etc. created by the project team	Three per quarter
Number of knowledge transfer sessions/ presentations conducted by the project within the group	Seven per quarter
Number of knowledge transfer (KT) sessions/ presentations conducted by the project (for other project teams)	One per quarter
Number of knowledge assets reviewed by the team	One per quarter

Table 9.8. Sample Knowledge-Sharing Plan

Knowledge-Sharing Goals	*Strategies Adopted to Achieve Goals*	*Reasons for Setting the Goals*
Intraproject knowledge sharing application	1. Preparation of system appreciation document	For understanding the existing software
	2. Weekly presentations by team members	Holistic appreciation of the application
	3. Informal knowledge transfer sessions	Impromptu knowledge transfer of important details
	4. Brainstorming sessions	For better understanding of the design of the software application
	5. Preparation of code analysis document	For understanding the existing program code
Interproject knowledge sharing	Presentation on the overall application functionality	Inform other project teams in the department about the project

DEPLOYING KM IN PROJECTS (ROLLOUT PHASE)

We now look at the rollout or actual deployment of KM in a project. As already noted, a network of KM people, including a KM patron, SPOC, one or more KM anchors, and KM primes will have been set up already in the KM assessment phase of the project. The present phase involves setting up KM processes and technology infrastructure and starts promoting KM activities and participation in the project.

Creating KM Awareness

The entire project team needs to be aware of KM objectives, processes, and infrastructure. Creating awareness is the first step in promoting KM in the project. The following actions will help in creating awareness:

- Formally launching the KM program for the project in a well-publicized event
- Carrying out KM awareness initiatives, including virtual and contact sessions and other interactive options
- Inducting the KM network into KM activities and plans by having the KM prime participate in the KM practitioners' guide session conducted by the central KM team
- Promoting the efforts on public forums such as portals, project home pages, and so on

Finally, it is a good idea to measure the impact of the awareness intervention both through systems (e.g., from usage logs of KM systems) and through informal and formal surveys. A good milestone for the awareness phase is a minimum 40 percent coverage in awareness among members of the project team.

Table 9.9. Sample Knowledge-Sharing Plan

Life-Cycle Stage	*Knowledge-Sharing Activity*	*Resource*	*To Be Attended By*	*Planned Date*	*Planned Person-Hours*	*Associated Artifact*
Project kickoff	Project overview given by the project leader	Manish	All team members	13-Sep-08	1 1	Presentation with highlights of domain, technologies, and tools
System appreciation phase	Teleconference with on-site coordinator	Richard, Vasumathi	All team members	20-Sep-2008 to 29-Oct-2008	140	System appreciation document
	Group reviews of the system	Whole team	All team members	20-Sep-2008 to 29-Oct-2008	56	System appreciation document
Development phase	Informal knowledge transfer sessions	Whole team	All team members	20-Sep-2008 to 29-Oct-2008	140 140	Appropriate templates, examples, etc.
	Brainstorming sessions	Whole team	All team members	20-Sep-2008 to 29-Oct-2008	56	System appreciation document
	Presentation given to other project teams of the department	Sebastian	Team in Pune	3-Nov-08	7	Presentation files
Code analysis phase	KT sessions	Whole team	All team members	1-Nov-2008 to 26-Nov-2008	56	KT documents
	Creating code analysis document	Whole team	All team members	1-Nov-2008 to 26-Nov-2008	56	Code analysis documents
	Group review of the code analysis document	Whole team	All team members	1-Nov-2008 to 26-Nov-2008	4	Code analysis documents
Maintenance phase	Weekly meetings	Whole team	All team members	29-Nov-2008 Onward	2 per week	Change request data
	Teleconference with on-site coordinator and on-site senior project manager	Whole team	All team members	29-Nov-2008 Onward	2 per week	List of concerns and changes requested
	Sending e-mails (all mails sent from on-site coordinator to offshore team)	Whole team	All team members	29-Nov-2008 Onward	2 per week	Mails
	Use of Tips Management System	Whole team	All team members	29-Nov-2008 Onward	6 per week	System and content

Setting Up the KM Process Framework

The project management practice prevalent in the organization defines the processes for project initiation, planning, execution, and closure (as outlined, for example, in fig. 9.2). In addition to these, several process tweaks and enhancements may be needed in this phase to enable KM practices to function well with project management processes. For example, a knowledge-sharing plan for the project may be needed. A typical plan was shown in tables 9.8 and 9.9 in the previous section. It can be seen from table 9.9 that the ownership of KM in the project lies with the project team members themselves rather than with the central KM team.

To ensure that the project team meets the targets stipulated in the knowledge-sharing plan by consistently checking with every available knowledge source for various knowledge needs that arise in different stages of a project, a checklist such as the one shown in table 9.10 may be specified. It may be noted here that the success of KM in projects depends critically not only on a well-designed knowledge-sharing plan but also on enhancing the project management processes so that the plan is enforced using checklists or other suitable mechanisms.

Setting Up KM Infrastructure

A variety of KM tools and systems are typically already available at the organization level. Ideally, this infrastructure can also be used for KM at the project level.

Table 9.10. Characteristics of Knowledge Needs

Sr. No.	*Task*	*Typical Knowledge Needs*	*Available Knowledge Resources*
1	Proposal preparation	Similar proposals prepared in the past	Proposal information system on the intranet
		Case studies on Infosys's expertise	Knowledge repositories (main and horizontal capability units)
		Customer interview questionnaire	Customer information database, external websites for advisory services
		Inputs on technology/domain/ culture	
2	Business process modeling/ system appreciation	Technology and domain-related needs	Knowledge portal, domain competency group, process assets, etc.
		Details of past/ongoing projects of similar nature	Project snapshots from knowledge portal
3	Requirements elicitation/ estimation	Comparative study of technology solutions	Knowledge portal for product reviews, event materials, etc.
		Feasibility study of technology solutions	Process assets for leads on estimation parameters for similar projects
		Best practices	Expertise directory for contacting experts
4	Design	Proof of concept, code skeletons, and other reusable artifacts from similar projects	Knowledge portal and process assets for reusable artifacts, tutorials, BoKs, online reference material, etc.

Sr. No.	*Task*	*Typical Knowledge Needs*	*Available Knowledge Resources*
		Utilities and tools	Project snapshots from knowledge portal, process assets, ToolShop site
		Guidance on technology, methodology, architecture, etc.	Expertise directory for experts within Infosys, professional networks and external websites for other experts. Also, SETLabs, domain competency group, and other groups.
		Training needs	E&R course repository
5	Development	Experiential write-ups on tips, tricks, issues, and resolutions faced while using a particular software or hardware	BoKs (body of knowledge entries) in knowledge portal
		Best practices, common mistakes, etc.	Case studies and other contents on knowledge portal and other knowledge repositories
		Tips on performance optimization, product/feature implementation, incorporating security features, etc.	Discussion forum, expertise directory for experts within Infosys, professional networks and external websites for other experts
		Quick help on priority issues	Reusable artifacts from knowledge portal
		Code snippets, error handling routines, in-house utility tools, etc.	
6	Testing	Test strategies, methodologies, automation scripts, and tools	Details from project snapshots, process assets DB, performance testing center
		Comparative study of approaches, tools, etc.	BoKs, best practices, and case studies from knowledge portal and allied repositories
		Best practices, pitfalls	Discussion forum, performance testing center, external advisory sites
		Expert opinion/consulting	
7	Deployment and warranty support/ production support	Deployment strategies, methodologies	Details from project snapshots, process assets DB, and performance testing center
		Warranty support/production support/best practices	BoKs, best practices, and case studies from knowledge portal and allied repositories
		Help desk issues	
		Client/culture-related BoKs	

However, often significant changes and customization may be needed for a particular project. Technical tool infrastructure enables the following functions for KM in projects:

- Knowledge asset contributions (as an author or reviewer)
- Using the knowledge portal to find assets
- Providing feedback or quality rating of assets

Table 9.11. Technical Infrastructure

Systems	*Features*	*Application Areas*
Knowledge Repository/Portal	The knowledge portal that promotes sharing and reuse of knowledge across the organization	For sharing generic knowledge assets across the organization
Search	Search for the required knowledge assets in many different ways	Aids in finding the relevant knowledge resource quickly
Discussion Forum	Online bulletin boards	Helps in resolving issues and technical difficulties of users
Find Experts	An employee "yellow pages" application where users can locate expert resources to help them	Helps in quickly resolving problems
KMail	KMail is an automated e-mail-response system for communities	Helps in developing a dynamically growing knowledge base to promote learning and reuse across the company
Wiki	An intranet wiki portal	Collaborative knowledge asset creation
Blogs	The Intranet blogging platform	A public medium to share, learn, and interact with others on a wide spectrum of topics
Social Networking	Intranet professional networking application	To connect with experts and professionals with similar interests across departments and locations

- Contribution to collaborative systems (K-Mail, wiki, blogs, community blogs, discussion forums)
- Knowledge transfer across projects

In order to support KM in projects, technical infrastructure such as the ones shown in table 9.11 may be needed.

Promoting KM Practices (Developing KM Culture)

Apart from creating awareness of KM infrastructure and processes, promoting KM in a project involves the following steps:

- Facilitation: The organizational KM team typically has ample experience in organizing KM events and in communicating with members of the organization. It is necessary for them to facilitate the conduction of events and communications in projects by helping the KM network in the projects:
- Enable the KM network members to anchor KM sessions and events
- Roll out project-specific KM events on demand
- Roll out communication templates to gather KM best practices from the project
- Recognition: Experience has shown that the most effective way to motivate people to participate in KM is to recognize the efforts and achievements of their own team members related to KM in their projects. Recognition can be provided by:

- Creating a microsite/-section on the project portal to highlight KM efforts and achievements, including audiovisual content and interviews
- Including KM in the project reward and recognition events
- Showcasing exemplary effort and achievement in their projects to the entire organization

In addition, a variety of activities and artifacts could be created to build KM into the culture of the project teams:

- Quizzes on technical, business, or other topics with knowledge or KM as a theme
- Debates on various topics
- Setting up KM kiosks and exhibits during major events in the organization
- Tip-of-the-day contests within projects
- Weekly KM to-do lists for the team
- A "Did You Know" bulletin board for each team where facts about their project are posted onto the board
- A KM telephone directory with all the contact people for KM in different projects

A good first milestone for this phase is a minimum 25 percent of project members participating in KM.

Measuring KM in Projects

Projects typically measure a number of parameters continually. For example, effort estimated versus actual effort spent, productivity, and quality measures are typically tracked even without KM practices. Because of this, projects also offer the possibility of correlating KM metrics with other existing project metrics of cost, quality, and productivity. It is thus easier to measure KM parameters in the context of a project than in the organization as a whole.

Infosys has developed a single aggregate measure of the state of practice of KM in a project (or business unit) called K-Index. K-Index includes all dimensions of KM in projects and maps them to the five key benefits that projects have observed from KM practices:

1. Reduced ramp-up time and transition time: Ramp up time is the time taken for new members of the project team (or for a newly constituted project team) to start productive work in the project; transition time is the time taken for the project work to be transitioned from the customers or their consultants and other contractors to the project team
2. Customer perception of knowledge reuse in projects and the resulting benefits to the customer
3. Better quality and productivity
4. Higher motivation levels
5. Better competency levels

The K-Index is a number in the range from 0 to 100. Values of the K-Index are to be interpreted according to the following indicative ranges:

Green : ≥ 70
Yellow: ≥ 50 & < 70
Red: < 50

The K-Index takes into consideration various dimensions of KM practice as detailed below:

- KM enabling and planning (10 percent weight)
- KM infrastructure (30 percent weight)
- KM culture (30 percent weight)
- Project-level knowledge-sharing activities (30 percent weight)

Table 9.12 shows suggested detailed parameters used to evaluate each of the above components. A sample of KM activities and their scores in computing the K-Index is shown in table 9.13. At the time of writing, Infosys is in the process of measuring the K-Index of a number of ongoing projects in the company.

TYPICAL BENEFITS OF KM IN PROJECTS

A few illustrations from real projects are provided here to show the benefits of KM in projects. Figure 9.5 shows the results of a survey of project teams to collect opinions about the reasons for doing KM in projects as perceived by team members. It is interesting to note that while the majority believe that KM leads directly to higher quality and fewer defects, an even stronger majority says that KM improves teamwork and thereby (indirectly) leads to other benefits for the projects.

Figure 9.6 shows snapshots of quantitative business benefits of KM in projects as measured between 2006 and 2008, based on metrics reported by project teams. Benefits can be seen along all five dimensions of KM benefits (discussed above in the design of the K-Index metric).

LESSONS FROM KM IN PROJECTS AT INFOSYS

Having looked at the methodology used for assessing, designing, deploying, and measuring KM in projects at Infosys Technologies, several strategies can now be inferred from the methodology that led to the success of KM in projects. These strategies, on top of the technical, cultural, and process foundation of the KM practice in the company, enabled projects to customize and adapt KM to their specific needs.

1. KM ownership with the project teams: The success of KM depends on who owns it. It has been an accepted strategy at Infosys that KM in projects should be owned by the project team. KM plans, content, and processes all belong to the project team. The role of the central KM team is to merely provide technology infrastructure and the process and measurement frameworks for the

Table 9.12. Parameters for Evaluation

	General Information	
1	Business unit	
2	Delivery unit	
3	Location	
4	Project code	
5	Project type	
6	Project manager (mail ID)	
7	KM prime (mail ID)	
8	Size of the project	
9	Duration of the project	
10	Effort spent on KM activities (hrs)	
11	Person-days saved due to KM	
A	**KM Enabling and Planning (10%)**	**Weight**
A1	KM-Enabling Activities	
1	Did the KM prime attend KM course?	2
2	Is the project team trained on KM?	1.5
A2	Planning for KM	
1	Is there a KM plan or a tracker for the project?	1.5
2	Are KM activities scheduled in a project plan?	2.5
3	Are KM plans reviewed at every project milestone?	2.5
B	**Project-Level Knowledge-Sharing Activities**	**30%**
1	Is active induction program available?	6
2	Is active mentoring program available?	6
3	No. of knowledge transfer (KT) sessions	3
4	No. of regular knowledge-sharing sessions	3
5	No. of checklists/guidelines created	3
6	No. of code templates/snippets created	3
7	No. of internal tools created	3
8	Others	3
C	**Leverage KM Infrastructure**	**30%**
C1	Knowledge Portal Statistics	
1	No. of artifacts submitted to knowledge portal by the project team	6
2	No. of knowledge artifacts reviewed by the project team	6
3	Usage of knowledge portala1.5	
4	No. of documents rated in knowledge portal	1.5
C2	Collaborative Systems	
1	K-Mail contribution—replies and uploads	1.5
2	K-Mail usage—queries and accesses	1.5
3	Discussion forum contribution—threads	1.5
4	Discussion forum usage—queries	1.5
5	Wiki contribution—updates	1.5
6	Wiki usage—accesses	1.5
7	Other collaborative systems—contribution	1.5
8	Other collaborative systems usage—accesses	1.5
C3	Others	
1	Knowledge assets shared in project space (project portal, local file shares, etc.)	3
D	**KM Culture**	**30%**
1	Quizzes (KM/domain/technology/project related)	2
2	Tips (domain/technology/project related)	2
3	Mailers (domain/technology/project related)	2
4	"Did You Know" bulletin board for posting information	2
5	Expert locator within project	2
6	KM brainstorming session	2
7	Organizing a KM week in the project	2
8	Project newsletter that includes a "KM Corner"	2
9	Conduct KM audits within or across projects	2
10	Rewards and recognition for KM activities	2
11	Best practice sharing session	2
12	Open group discussions and debate	2
13	KM crosswords and other games	2
14	Point-based incentive system to foster participation	2
15	Others	2

Table 9.13. Measuring K-Index

Activity	*Five or More Activities*	*Fewer Than Two*	*None*
Organized knowledge-sharing activities (sessions on domain or technology, best practice sharing, quiz, awareness about tools usage, reuse, rewards and recognition)	40	25	0
Circulate communication related to KM (newsletter, tip of the day/ week/month, KM awareness mailers, KM activities, communication to KM primes)	30	15	0
Contribution to KM case studies (per quarter)	30	15	0
Total Index for Activities	**100**	**55**	**0**

deployment and practice of KM in the projects. In addition, as noted earlier in this chapter, the central team also facilitates the planning and conduction of KM events in projects and business units. The experience at Infosys has clearly shown that project members readily accept KM practices and requirements when it is owned and practiced by their own team members.

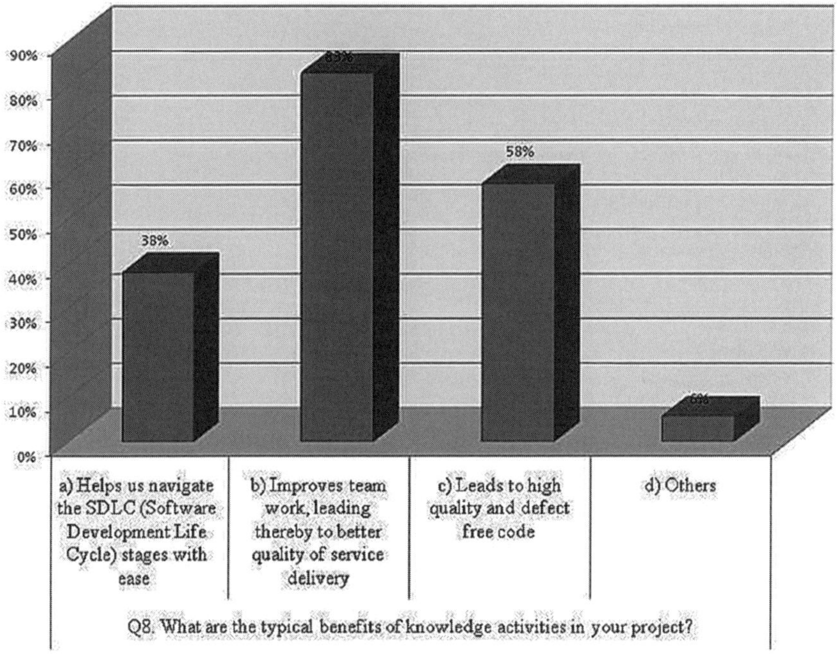

Figure 9.5.

Customer satisfaction: 16% of projects attribute customer appreciation received for project performance improvements to KM practices

Reduction in ramp up time: 32% of projects attribute reduction in ramp up time of fresh team members to KM

Improved quality and productivity metrics: 42% of projects report reduction in defect injection rate from 20 – 80%
54% of projects report a time saved due to KM amounting to a total of over 1800 person days

Competency building: 34% of projects acknowledge the role of KM in building competency of its team members

Knowledge sharing culture: Almost all projects say reward and recognition schemes helped in culture building

Figure 9.6. KM in Projects: Business Benefits (2006–2008)

2. Integration of KM with business process framework: KM in projects is unlikely to be successful if its practice is disconnected from the main business activities of the project. Infosys has strategically integrated KM processes with mainline business processes. This, along with the integration of KM systems with enterprise information systems, has been a key enabler for KM in projects.
3. Focus on special needs: Focusing on the special needs of a project is the only way to make KM successful in projects. In earlier experience, it was found that the biggest obstacle to the ready acceptance of KM practices in projects was the perceived mismatch between the company's generic KM solution and the particular requirements of a project. Many projects are idiosyncratic, and the solution for KM in projects must adapt to the specific requirements of each project.
4. Focus on metrics and measurement: A good framework for measuring KM is essential to (demonstrate) the success of KM in projects. The focus on measuring effort and outcomes of KM activities as well as the analysis that correlates these measures with mainstream measurements of quality and productivity of projects has given the necessary perception of legitimacy to KM in projects at Infosys.

Further work on KM in projects at Infosys has been focusing primarily on the measurement of K-Index values for individual projects as well as entire business units. The near-term objective of this exercise is to relate K-Index measures to a suitable model of KM maturity of the organization.

APPENDIX 1: DETAILS OF KM ROLES AT INFOSYS

1. KM patron has responsibility to:
   a. Own the bottom line for the health of KM in the unit
   b. Ensure the apt utilization of the knowledge capital of the organization and the unit

   c. Encourage growth of the knowledge capital of the unit through submission to content repositories and participation in collaborative platforms
   d. Influence and assess the impact of KM on various performance indices of the unit
   e. Act as a channel through which KM efforts and results are communicated to unit heads, councils, and top management as appropriate
   f. Review KM activities on a monthly basis along with the KM anchors
   g. Be a spokesperson for KM as a unit's chief KM representative in various forums
   h. Act as a single point of contact for providing resources to the KM group or the internal IT systems group
   i. Budget for various KM activities, including for rewards and recognition, travel, KM workshops, and the like
2. KM anchor has responsibility to:
   a. Build a KM network by connecting together the KM primes from all projects within the business unit. The KM anchor will be the default owner of the e-mail distribution lists of all KM primes in the respective delivery units (DUs)
   b. Maintain a plan for improving KM practices in the unit and sustaining the DU-level KM network
   c. Organize KM practitioner courses that provide the necessary techniques for knowledge exchange and measurement practices for all KM primes in the business unit
   d. Act as a knowledge advocate and monitor the health of KM within the business unit by effectively leveraging the KM prime network. In the following, a sample set of activities that need to be carried out by the KM Anchor are provided:
      1. Organize periodic (monthly or quarterly, as the case may be) review meetings of KM primes in the business unit
      2. Circulate monthly newsletter on KM activities in the business unit
      3. Build a competitive environment within projects for knowledge sharing
      4. Organize KM rewards and recognition (R&R) events every quarter in addition to other KM events
      5. Promote best practice sharing across projects
      6. Organize seminars related to various technology, application domains (industry verticals), and applications areas
   e. Identify skills within the business unit that are in high demand and work toward facilitating knowledge sharing in those areas:
      1. By enlisting and enabling employees to submit knowledge artifacts on the subject to content management or collaborative systems
      2. By alerting the central KM team single point of contact (SPOC) about the need for such knowledge
      3. By enabling employees to use various collaborative platforms (e.g., discussion forums) so as to provide speedy visibility to problems and solutions or techniques across the group. This would significantly impact the levels of tacit knowledge sharing.
   f. Participate in organization-level KM activities by way of sharing best practices, improving knowledge sharing through organization-level KM infrastructure

g. Draft a template for reporting monthly activities by KM primes and review of the same on a monthly basis
3. KM prime has responsibility to:
   a. Evangelize KM among project members to facilitate leveraging organizational knowledge through the following means:
      1. Educating project members about the organizational content management systems (e.g., the knowledge portal) and their functions such as those related to:
         - Subscribing to content
         - Reviewing content
         - Submitting content
         - Registering as subject matter experts (SMEs) for knowledge-sharing activities
         - Online rating of content and its translation into usage metrics and incentives such as knowledge currency units (KCUs)
         - Participating in collaborative platforms such as wikis and discussion forums
      2. Subscribing to content on behalf of the project
      3. Creating awareness about various knowledge sources within the company's intranet, such as:
         - Internal and external premier advisory content in the areas of business and technology
         - Intranet sites that promote specialist knowledge content from experts in different departments within the organization who are charged with the responsibility for providing knowledge to projects, e.g., in the areas of industry verticals, software engineering technology, tool groups, and the like
         - The people-knowledge map (PKM), the expertise directory
         - The skills directory of the organization
         - Various research groups, centers of excellence, and competency centers in the company
         - Newsletters and online references
      4. Meeting the knowledge needs of employees in the project by:
         - Helping them to effectively network with other practitioners (primarily through discussion forums, knowledge transfer sessions, etc.)
         - Interfacing with external service providers for paid advisory functions
         - Retrieving knowledge from available sources and providing feeds
         - Interfacing with other project primes to share and gather project best practices
      5. Creating awareness about KM metrics captured as related to content usage and rating, subscription, review, authoring, and expertise registration in the organizational skills directory, and also through enabling conformity to policies for tracking the KM effort, using appropriate codes in weekly time sheets submitted by employees
   b. Be the primary contact point to the project co-coordinator (usually in the customer geography and physically removed from the delivery organization) for his/her knowledge needs. Address queries by searching key

intranet repositories listed above before contacting Infoscions through mailing lists.

c. Develop intellectual property rights (IPR) awareness among members in the project by promoting intranet content on the topic
d. Create and maintain a KM plan for the project so that KM goals are defined and tracked on a periodic basis (monthly, or on achievement of milestones, and at closure)
e. Use business analytics tools available on the knowledge portal (KM kit) to monitor the KM health of the project and make appropriate decisions at suitable points
f. Demonstrate benefits from KM practice
    1. Encourage members to give online feedback on benefits received through use of KM resources. This in turn provides useful KM metrics for the project.
    2. Report to the project manager (PM) on benefits derived at milestones by measuring the involvement of project team in usage, submission, reviews, and so on.
g. Liaise with the process consultant or the project manager for analyzing KM and quality and productivity (Q&P) metrics at milestones
h. Encourage members to opt to register for voluntary knowledge sharing while updating their skills in the central skills repository of the organization
i. Support the central KM group in their surveys on knowledge management and other research initiatives
j. Engage in environmental scanning of trends relevant to the project and disseminate this knowledge projectwide and where applicable, across the business unit and the organization
k. Encourage members to contribute to the organizational knowledge base as authors and as reviewers of the knowledge assets
l. Identify strategic knowledge needs in the project and transmit the information to the research coordinator, if any, of the concerned DU

APPENDIX 2: QUESTIONNAIRE FOR KM STATE OF PRACTICE ASSESSMENT

Section I: Objectives and Scope of KM

1. Which of the following best describes your unit with respect to knowledge management?
    a. Our basic values and purpose emphasize sharing of knowledge.
    b. We think knowledge management is everybody's job, and so everybody has the best of knowledge.
    c. Knowledge management is the task of a few designated people and hence there is no need for knowledge sharing.
    d. We have an open, encouraging, and supportive culture.
2. What are the top four reasons for your unit to consider adapting knowledge management?

3. What are the business goals for this financial year? Which are the areas where you see KM playing a role?

Section II: People, Knowledge Dynamics, and Culture

1. Currently, how do you share knowledge (e-mail, face-to-face meeting, phone calls, etc.) and which among them do you consider the most effective way of knowledge sharing?
   a. Meetings
   b. Phone calls
   c. E-mail
   d. Distribution lists
   e. Collaborative tools
   f. Formal presentations
   g. Documents
   h. Knowledge-sharing events
   i. Training courses
   j. Informal chat
   k. Any other, please specify. __________
2. Please mention the top three among responses for question 1 that you consider most effective.
3. Which of the following best represent cultural barriers one could encounter with respect to KM? (Please choose one or more options from below.)
   a. Lack of willingness to share knowledge
   b. Working in functional silos restricts knowledge sharing
   c. Lack of rewards and recognition to motivate people
   d. Knowledge sharing is not part of the job, hence happens in pockets
   e. Any other, please specify. ___________
4. What are the major challenges faced by you in terms of knowledge availability and sharing? (Please choose one or more options from below.)
   a. Lack of a knowledge-sharing culture
   b. Lack of identified experts
   c. Unavailability of a mechanism to share knowledge
   d. Any other, please specify. ___________
5. How readily and frequently does knowledge sharing happen across accounts?
   a. Very readily and frequently
   b. Readily and not frequently
   c. Not readily
   d. Only in formal presentations
   e. Any other, please specify. ___________
6. What is your primary motive for sharing knowledge with others in your area? (Please choose one or more options from below.)
   a. It increases one's standing as an expert in the unit.
   b. It helps career progression.
   c. I have benefited from others in the past and would like to help others who might find my contribution useful.
   d. Any other, please specify. __________

7. Is knowledge sharing publicly recognized and rewarded in your area?
    a. Yes
    b. No
    c. Sometimes
    d. I don't know
8. What are the factors that will motivate employees to share knowledge? (Please choose one or more options from below.)
    a. Joy of sharing
    b. Rewards
    c. Recognition
    d. Any other, please specify. __________

Section III: Process, Content, and Technology

1. Is there any standardized process for documenting knowledge gained after a project or an engagement is carried out?
    a. Yes
    b. No
    c. I don't know
    d. Any other, please specify. __________
2. How is knowledge stored for reference in your unit? (Please choose one or more options from below.)
    a. BU/account portal
    b. KM portal
    c. LAN
    d. Individual workstations
    e. Any other, please specify. __________
3. What are the types of documents created (e.g., documents, reports, meetings, discussions, etc.)?
4. Are the artifacts classified based on the nature of knowledge (e.g., reports, design documents, best practices, learning, FAQs, installation guides, etc.)?
5. How many hours on average do you spend in a typical work week searching for knowledge relevant to the accomplishment of your task?
    a. 0 to 5
    b. 5 to 10
    c. 10 to 15
    d. More than 15
6. Do other units have access to your unit's knowledge?
    a. Yes
    b. No
    c. Yes, but for select units
7. Which of the following applications (developed by Infosys) have you used for gathering information or query resolution?
    a. . . .
    b. Any other, please specify. __________

8. In continuation of the above, what systems have been implemented in your area for knowledge exchange? (Please choose one or more options from below.)
   a. . . .
   b. Any other, please specify. __________

Section IV: Implementation and Future Directions

1. What may be the challenges, according to you, that a KM initiative in your area may encounter? (Please choose one or more options from below.)
   a. Distributed workforce over multiple locations
   b. Lack of a clear vision, mission, and its communication throughout the organization
   c. Existing culture/attitude toward an initiative
   d. High workload of employee
   e. "Buy in" from field workforce
2. Were similar challenges faced when other initiatives were rolled out?
   a. Yes
   b. No
   c. I don't know
3. What are the best methods of communication, according to you, that could be employed to roll out an initiative in your area? (Please choose one or more options from below.)
   a. Infosys Intranet Home
   b. Mailers
   c. Communication from managers to subordinates
   d. Meetings
   e. Any other, please specify. __________

REFERENCES

Kochikar, V. P., Mahesh, Kavi, & Mahind, C. S. (2002). Knowledge management in action: The experience of Infosys Technologies. In Vlatka Hlupic (Ed.), *Knowledge and business process management*. Hershey, PA: Idea Group.

PMBOK. (2008). *A guide to the project management body of knowledge* (4th ed.). Project Management Institute.

Suresh, J. K., & Mahesh, Kavi. (2006). *Ten steps to maturity in knowledge management: Lessons in economy*. Oxford: Chandos Publishing.

Suresh, J. K., & Mahesh, Kavi. (2008). Managing the knowledge supply chain at Infosys: Ensuring that every project benefits from collective learning. *Knowledge Management Review, 11*(4), 14–19.

10

Knowledge Organization and the Project Management Process

Joseph Kasten

Knowledge organization, as a discipline, is defined as the "organization of information in bibliographical records" (Hjørland 2003). This definition is a bit too narrow for the purposes of project management (PM), but it serves as an effective introduction to the discipline, as well as giving the nonlibrarian and knowledge user (as opposed to knowledge organizer) some insight into the approach taken by those whose task it is to organize the knowledge to be used by an individual, an organization, or, as is our focus in this chapter, a project.

Before discussing the organization of knowledge, we should first address the role of knowledge in a project setting. The *Guide to the Project Management Book of Knowledge* (Project Management Institute, 2004) states clearly that the completion of many important project activities relies upon, among other things, expert knowledge. For example, when developing the work breakdown structure (WBS) for a project, deliverables must be decomposed into smaller, more manageable work packages. The creation of these work packages, including deciding when they are too small or too large, requires "a degree of expert judgment to identify all the work including project management deliverables and those deliverables required by contract" (Project Management Institute, p. 115). This theme is repeated over and over for many of the PM techniques discussed in the PMBOK. It identifies two important knowledge-based issues inherent in project management: (1) projects, even those requiring primarily brute force and muscle to complete, rely heavily upon expert, or domain, knowledge to be completed within the parameters set by contract, and (2) projects require two kinds of knowledge—knowledge of the domain and knowledge of project management processes. Often, these two bodies of knowledge are not colocated in a single person or team. Thus, an important skill to have is to understand the knowledge requirements of the moment and be able to recognize that they are resident not in you or your team, but in another repository or organization that must be accessed.

The typical project, involving compressed schedules, restricted budgets, and sometimes erratic environmental conditions, increases its chances of success when these knowledge repositories are equipped to satisfy knowledge needs quickly, accurately, and efficiently. In order to do this, they must be quickly identifiable, preferably having been identified prior to their need, easily accessible without a great deal of pre-access ceremony or resistance, and efficiently searched. The first two conditions, identity and accessibility, are beyond the scope of this chapter, but the searchability of a knowledge repository is directly related to the manner in which knowledge is organized within it.

The knowledge necessary to the successful completion of a project has a few characteristics that are important to consider prior to the design of a knowledge base conceived to fill these knowledge needs. Project knowledge might include both domain knowledge and project process knowledge, as mentioned earlier. Project knowledge is likely to be dynamic in nature, just as many projects exist within dynamic environments. These dynamics might be driven by changing market conditions, changing customer requirements, changing regulatory requirements, changes in project personnel, or any other variable that forces a project management team to adjust processes or deliverables. Also, project knowledge might be accessed by a wide and ever-changing cast of project personnel, ranging from project management to project employees, outside contractors, external stakeholders, or the customer. These parties will view these knowledge structures differently, bringing their own background, terminologies, prejudices, and applications to bear during the knowledge acquisition process. In order to satisfy each of these legitimate knowledge needs, the knowledge must be organized such that searching can be carried out effectively by each group. This calls for a certain amount of flexibility in the knowledge structure as well as the development of tools to ease the knowledge-searching process.

Much has been written about the postmodern approach to knowledge organization. Mai (2002) and others have discussed the necessity of knowledge searching and finding aids, such as indexes and thesauri, that are tuned such that knowledge seekers from different disciplines and with differing vocabularies can still locate and acquire the knowledge they deem necessary. However appealing this approach to knowledge organization might seem, it is not without its drawbacks. First, any scheme for organizing and locating knowledge that is usable to multiple audiences is bound to be more difficult to build and maintain than one without that aim, and as such might well pose a significant burden, in time and money, to a specific project. In cases where a project team undertakes many projects of the same type and the knowledge fields utilized are relatively stable, as are the various knowledge-seeking groups, then the investment in this more flexible knowledge organization approach will certainly be useful. However, many project environments do not have these luxuries.

We must also remember why we store knowledge for use on a project. One reason is, of course, to operate the project and its processes in as close to an optimal a manner as possible. But we must also remember that the desired outcome of some projects might be, among other things, the creation of new knowledge. Thus, the synthesis of the existing knowledge stores with newly derived knowledge might well play a primary role and, thus, the organization of project knowledge repositories must reflect this. Beghtol (2003) suggests that these two approaches to knowledge organization do not lead to the same classification scheme and that the underlying use of the knowledge base in question must be decided upon prior to the design of the classification system. She also points out that the difference between knowledge organized to optimize retrieval is what professional knowledge organizers consider organized knowledge, while the knowledge organization schemes developed by the users, what she terms "naive" classification, might be more suitable to knowledge discovery. User-created knowledge bases are often constructed based upon how the users interpret the knowledge and its usefulness.

With these insights as a guide, the next section of this chapter is concerned with the various dichotomies inherent in project knowledge and its organization. The section after that examines the role that these knowledge organization issues might have within the project management process, and the final section provides some closing thoughts along with some guidelines to be used when developing project knowledge bases.

KNOWLEDGE CATEGORIZATION

Knowledge can be viewed and classified in as many ways as there are observers and users. However, in each situation, a few significant organizational schemes or dichotomies stand out as dominant. Some of these important organizational issues are discussed in this section. Projects depend upon both project and domain knowledge, and this discussion, begun earlier, is continued in the first subsection. The tacit/explicit dichotomy is addressed in the second subsection, and the organization of knowledge by its format is the topic of the third.

Project and Domain Knowledge

As mentioned earlier, project knowledge deals with project processes, and domain knowledge is that knowledge that addresses and enables the technical aspects of carrying out the project. From a knowledge organization standpoint, it is easy and convenient to simply put project knowledge and domain knowledge on separate shelves (figuratively speaking), create finding aids such as indexes designed for a specific user group (project personnel or product designers, for example), and congratulate ourselves on a knowledge base well organized. However, that would be both an oversimplification as well as a wasted opportunity to create synergies between how a project is managed and what a project does.

Two points regarding these knowledge areas must be understood. First, they are not mutually exclusive. There is no rule that states knowledge of project processes cannot also be used to execute the process. For example, mathematical and statistical tools are certainly useful in managing a project. They are necessary to provide forecasting, scheduling, and resource allocation, among other tasks. However, a project that involves any kind of engineering or design work or that is involved in research and development also has need for extensive mathematical knowledge, thus placing this knowledge area in both the project process and project domain knowledge areas.

A more important point to understand is that these two knowledge areas are not independent. The types of activities undertaken during a project will likely dictate the project management processes utilized on the project. Thus, the understanding of the knowledge areas in use during the execution of the project will help in understanding the knowledge needed to manage the project. For example, a project utilizing the expertise of many disparate organizational entities such as consultants and subcontractors will necessitate more advanced knowledge of contracts and negotiating than would a project being executed solely within an organization's boundaries.

These two points suggest that any knowledge organization scheme put in place must recognize that the knowledge within the system might be used by both project personnel and project management and that these groups will often have different ways of conceptualizing these knowledge areas and will tend to look for, and at, them differently. One group might look at these knowledge areas as tools to be used to complete a particular task, while another might see them as building blocks to be used to create other, more advanced knowledge areas. Thus, any cataloging or categorization process must be flexible enough to allow the more pragmatic user to find knowledge quickly and accurately while allowing more "creative" users the ability to understand the connections between knowledge areas, thereby giving the knowledge synthesis process a head start. Typical approaches to these types of knowledge organization tasks include ontologies and knowledge maps, both of which will display the knowledge areas available and the connections or relationships between and among them.

Tacit and Explicit Knowledge

Most of the knowledge areas referenced in the *PMBOK Guide* are explicit in nature (Reich & Wee, 2006). However, the same cannot be said for that knowledge used within the context of the project team. Much of what professionals do within a project, especially when it comes to value creation, is to utilize their tacit knowledge. Tacit knowledge is why certain employees are sought for projects—they have the experience and understanding to perform their duties beyond the "by the book" approach common in newer team members. However, the effective utilization of this knowledge often depends upon locating it and arranging for its application. This involves some method of managing and organizing tacit knowledge. The organization of tacit knowledge is orders of magnitude more challenging than managing explicit knowledge because it cannot be seen, touched, or accounted for. Tacit knowledge is the result of an inherently unpredictable process (i.e., learning and experience) and does not lend itself to being managed as traditional organizational assets do. Therefore, other approaches must be employed if the project management team is to utilize tacit knowledge.

For tacit knowledge to be leveraged to its fullest potential, it must be identified and applied. The identification of tacit knowledge comes with the ability to understand the qualifications and experience of all key project personnel. This is, of course, the task of the project manager or project office. For tacit knowledge to be applied on a project, it must first be resident there. This can be done either by assigning the most knowledgeable team members to the project or by assigning less-experienced members and trying to increase their stores of tacit knowledge over the course of the project. This is often attempted through mentorship or internship programs, which are very time consuming and do not work well in many project environments. This is why the *PMBOK Guide* stresses the importance of building the project team and why building this team, especially across organizational boundaries, can be so difficult. Team members with the most tacit knowledge are the most valuable and are often in demand by many projects. Thus, access to tacit knowledge places a large burden on the project management team in terms of personnel management and political maneuvering, both of which are beyond the scope of this chapter. The remainder of this discussion will center on the organization of explicit knowledge.

Knowledge Formats

Explicit knowledge is generally considered to be of the written or spoken variety, but it is important to remember that knowledge within a knowledge base might exist in a number of formats, each one presenting its own organizational challenges. Textual documents represent the most straightforward organizational task, although it has been shown that even cataloging books and journal articles is not entirely without difficulties. To be organized in a meaningful way, textual knowledge sources must be analyzed to understand their subject so that they might be grouped with other sources on the same topic. The difficulty here, as any librarian will explain, is that many works are not only on one topic but might cover pieces of many topics. How, then, to group them? More importantly, are these groupings the same for each of the potential user groups mentioned above? In a project to develop a pharmaceutical, will the literature on drug interactions be viewed by the chemist who is working on the project in the same way as the attorney in the project management office? In building a knowledge base, the perspective of the knowledge user must be taken into account from the beginning of the creation process.

Knowledge essential to the project might also be embedded in other types of works. Engineering drawings, sketches, computer software, videos, and music can all be deemed to include some form of knowledge within them. There has been significant research performed dealing with the classification of nontext works, but the core issue is that items like photographs mean different things to different people, and success in organizing these items comes only when the audience is understood. Moreover, the task of understanding nontext knowledge items and their place in the knowledge base is complicated by the type of knowledge they represent. Whyte et al. (2008) suggest that a visual knowledge item, a chart perhaps, include both explicit and tacit knowledge. The explicit knowledge is what is visually represented, and the tacit knowledge is the manner of its interpretation. This suggests that these knowledge items might be viewed differently between groups, just like any other knowledge item, but also differently by members within a group, and possibly differently by the same person at different times. Besides complicating the knowledge organization process, does this also suggest the need for some context to be given by those responsible for knowledge organization in order for the viewer to better understand the item? Again, this brings up challenges of interpretation by the knowledge organizers.

KNOWLEDGE ORGANIZATION WITHIN PROJECT MANAGEMENT

It is most effective to address the manner in which knowledge organization interacts with project management by considering six basic questions: (1) how is knowledge organized on a project, (2) what knowledge is to be organized, (3) when is knowledge organized, (4) where is the organized knowledge kept, (5) who is to organize the knowledge, and (6) why is knowledge organized. We can dispense with the easiest questions first, which are questions 1, 4, and 6.

The question of how to organize knowledge is, of course, not the easiest question to answer. Actually, it is the most difficult, as researchers around the world have learned and continue to learn every day. But to address it in this chapter, without benefit of a specific knowledge domain and project environment to frame the question, all that can be done is to list the factors that will help define an organizational scheme. The process to organize knowledge depends upon the nature of the knowledge (i.e., its breadth and scope), who will use it (i.e., types of users, number of different user groups, and the degree of variation between user groups), what format it is in (i.e., electronic, paper, graphics, etc.), and the time and budget available to perform the process. An understanding of these issues will provide a good start in the determination of an effective and efficient knowledge organization system.

The question of where knowledge is kept was a much more crucial question prior to the digital revolution. In today's project environment, even far-flung locations can access the project database using a variety of connectivity options. The same is true for the project knowledge base, with some possible exceptions. Those knowledge objects that resist digitization either because of technological (e.g., lack of common format) or legal restrictions (e.g., copyright restrictions) might still need to be colocated with their users. Tacit knowledge is also accessible as long as the person holding it is accessible. Again, certain restrictions having to do with connectivity or the reduced amount of clarity sometimes inherent in electronic communications might play a role here.

Why is knowledge to be organized? (Please see the first section of this chapter.)

What knowledge is to be organized? The quick answer is everything that will be needed for the project. The real answer is, of course, much more difficult. The *PMBOK Guide* specifies the knowledge needed for the successful planning and operation of a project. However, domain knowledge is likely to be much more difficult to specify and will often represent a moving target. As discussed above, project domain knowledge can be dynamic, and in fact we often want it to be in order for new knowledge to be synthesized. A discussion with the domain experts will provide a starting point for identifying the knowledge bases and literature to make available from the beginning, but continual oversight is necessary to ensure that the knowledge creation and application processes within the project do not overwhelm the project knowledge base. On the other hand, the control of scope is as important in the growth of a knowledge base as it is in the management of a project. Too much knowledge or knowledge that is irrelevant can be almost as harmful as not having enough. Restraint must be exercised in the acquisition of knowledge. Of course, whatever knowledge organization process is selected must be able to accommodate the continual changes in the knowledge base.

Knowledge should be organized as close to its creation and use as possible. This is both a timing issue and an organizational issue. The timing aspect suggests that knowledge recently created or obtained will be easier to classify because its role in the organizational knowledge base is more clearly understood. Often, knowledge is acquired to fill a specific need, and it is more effective to classify it while that need is still extant. However, flexibility must be built into the system to allow for changes or additions to the role played by a particular knowledge item as it is likely to change as different user groups make use of it and its other uses and applications become apparent.

The organizational aspect of this issue is that knowledge is best understood, at least initially, by those who develop or create it. Therefore, the group or individual who creates or acquires knowledge should be involved in its organization, if for no other reason than the person or group knows best what that organization is. This is not to say that each discipline and individual should be in charge of the organization and classification of any knowledge they develop or acquire. This is a recipe for knowledge anarchy and is a common reason that organizational knowledge bases fail to bring about the rewards for which they were created. There must be some level of consistency and order in a knowledge base, just as in a library. Commonality of nomenclature and organizational philosophy is crucial to allow all users to find what they seek. But there must also be some room for flexibility as knowledge evolves, so a partnership between the knowledge creator/user and the knowledge organizer is a very important contributor to the system's success, thereby addressing the last question.

A KNOWLEDGE ORGANIZATION PLAN

Ideally, a knowledge organization plan should be part of the overall project plan, adhering to the basic tenets of project planning as put forth in the *PMBOK Guide*. However, reality suggests that this plan might emerge as a result of operations rather than be presented in a finished form. In either case, the project management team should be prepared to answer the questions posed in the previous section in terms of its project. At a minimum, the following issues should be considered in the knowledge organization plan.

In the best of circumstances, a person or team trained in knowledge organization techniques should head this effort so that prior knowledge-organizing experience can be brought to bear on the effort; there is no sense in reinventing the wheel when budgets and schedules are already stretched. If people with this background are not available, then subject-matter experts on or associated with the project should be put in charge of the effort. The advantage to this approach is their intimate knowledge of the project, its staff, and the knowledge needs of the people and processes that make up the project. It is important that this person or persons be officially appointed to the task and proper resources allocated. A volunteer effort might start with much vigor, but it will soon evaporate into the fog of other project activities. Moreover, without this official tasking, the person responsible will receive little cooperation in this very time-consuming assignment from other project members. An official seal of approval from management gives the effort weight and a fighting chance for success.

The knowledge to be organized can be identified by examining the needs of current and future project team members as well as other stakeholders, including the customer. Determine whether knowledge developed within the project becomes part of the deliverable package. For example, governmental agencies that order weapons systems from contractors often require that the results from various analyses be included with the other project deliverables. This knowledge must also be included in the knowledge organization effort to improve its value as well as make it easier for analysts to use as a basis for further inquiries.

As noted earlier, knowledge is best organized as it is created or collected. But this is too broad of a description for a specific knowledge organization plan. Knowledge organization activities should find a place on the Gantt chart or whatever scheduling tool is in use. In this manner, the knowledge-organizing activities can be synchronized with the knowledge creation activities. Moreover, this makes knowledge organization activities as visible as any other project activity, and they can be managed in the same manner, especially during resource allocation.

Space must be allocated for knowledge storage. If the knowledge is digital, this will mean designating space on a server or other networked storage device that can be accessed and searched by all appropriate project personnel. However, despite the beliefs of some, all knowledge does not exist in digital form. There may be books, videos, or other entities that make up your project knowledge base. These must be stored properly and in a location where they can be accessed by as many potential users as possible.

Additional knowledge organization activities that should be planned for include training, publicizing the existence of the knowledge organization effort and the knowledge contained in the knowledge base, and a continuation plan. The existence of the organized knowledge might not be apparent to all project members and stakeholders, so some effort must be made to ensure that everyone who might make use of the knowledge knows that it is available. Training should provide an understanding of what knowledge is in the knowledge base and how it is organized, accessed, and searched. Finally, the knowledge base should be organized such that it is useful to not only the current project but subsequent project teams as well, thus leveraging the value of a single knowledge organization effort over many projects.

The creation of a knowledge organization plan can fit into the overall project planning process with little disruption or extra cost. Basic knowledge needs can often be inferred from the project charter or scope statement. Other insights can be gained from project personnel as they are identified and assigned. Prior projects with similar processes, customers, or deliverables can also be consulted if the project management personnel are available or there is extant documentation. These duties should be assigned early on to prevent them from being lost in other project-planning activities.

The communications plan for the project should be devised with the understanding that the information technology employed will have to house the organizational knowledge base. Access and bandwidth requirements should also be designed with these requirements in mind, especially if the project knowledge base contains items that are known to be bandwidth intensive, such as streaming video. Moreover, knowledge bases that deal with tacit knowledge as well as explicit knowledge should provide a means for experts to communicate effectively with those needing knowledge to carry out their tasks. These technologies might include videoconferencing, real-time document sharing and markup, or other tools that are more effective at knowledge sharing than e-mail and telephone.

During the creation of the work breakdown structure (WBS) and activity list, include a discussion of knowledge required and knowledge produced. This will help in identifying which knowledge organization activities should take place. It might be useful to include knowledge as an input for any knowledge-intensive activities defined, just as labor or equipment are often included as inputs to the activities listed. As the planning process proceeds to schedule development, include knowledge organization activities as schedule items. In some cases, knowledge outputs might be represented by their own WBS codes so that they are addressed accordingly. Finally, resource allocations should include the labor and technology required to ensure that project knowledge is available to those who can use it.

Admittedly, including knowledge organization in the project planning process can be difficult, especially if project or organizational culture frowns on the use of resources for activities that appear to be without immediate return. It can be awkward to justify these activities on a financial basis. Often, a qualitative case must be made as to why these resources should be allocated, and the project management team must be able to respond accordingly. This requires the manager to have a clear understanding of the value of this knowledge and how it will be leveraged into project success.

CONCLUSION

Projects depend on their ability to access and utilize knowledge. Some projects depend upon, and exist because of, their ability to create knowledge. In either case, their ability to use knowledge is predicated on their ability to find it, access it, and apply it. The location of knowledge is largely dependent on the manner in which it is organized. In this chapter, a number of issues have been raised that directly affect how knowledge is organized. Some apply to all projects without regard to what the objective of the project is, but many are project-specific and require that they be customized accordingly.

Knowledge organization is most effectively performed by a professional such as a librarian or information scientist. However, the knowledge professional cannot work in a vacuum. Input from project management as well as the people executing the project is crucial to the knowledge organization process, and budget and schedule allowances should be made for these activities. This small investment both in the beginning of the project and throughout its progression will provide substantial dividends in innovation, flexibility, and ultimately a more successful project outcome.

REFERENCES

Beghtol, Clare. (2003). Classification for information retrieval and classification for knowledge discovery: Relationships between "professional" and "naive" classifications. *Knowledge Organization, 30*(2):64–73.

Hjørland, Birger. (2003). Fundamentals of knowledge organization. *Knowledge Organization, 30*(2):87–111.

Mai, Jens-Erik. (2002). A postmodern theory of knowledge organization. In María J. López-Huertas (Ed.), *Challenges in knowledge representation and organization for the 21st century: Integration of knowledge across boundaries. Proceedings of the 7th annual international ISKO conference*. Würzberg: Ergon-Verlag.

Project Management Institute. (2004). *A guide to the project management body of knowledge* (3rd ed.). Newtown Square, PA: Project Management Institute.

Reich, Blaize Horner, & Wee, Siew Yong. (2006). Searching for knowledge in the *PMBOK Guide*. *Project Management Journal, 37*(2):11–27.

Whyte, Jennifer, et al. (2008). Visualizing knowledge in project-based work. *Long Range Planning, 41*, 74–92.

11

Managing Knowledge in Projects

An Overview

T. Kanti Srikantaiah

Managing knowledge in projects is gaining more and more importance because it is useful in carrying out the project efficiently, on time, on budget, and with quality deliverables to satisfy clients.

The World Bank, in its *World Development Report* of 1998–1999, describes knowledge as light, weightless, and intangible. It can easily travel the world, enlightening the levels of people everywhere. At the organization level, knowledge management is about project assets. These assets may include databases, documents, policies, and procedures, as well as previously uncaptured expertise in individual workers. By definition, knowledge management in projects is the systematic process of identifying, capturing, organizing, and disseminating/sharing explicit and tacit knowledge assets that add value to the project(s) and organizations. Knowledge management is a product of the 1990s and is a hot topic in organizations, with many practitioners drawn from different disciplines such as business, engineering, education, epistemology, communication, and information management, among others. This interdisciplinary background of experts has helped projects to treat knowledge as an entity dynamically embedded in networks, processes, repositories, and people. Project processes involved in managing knowledge include storing, transferring, modifying, using, validating and reusing, resulting in billions of dollars in investment worldwide.

Every year hundreds of thousands of projects are done all over the world, both in public sectors and in private sectors. All these projects have one thing in common: knowledge. In the project environment, knowledge economy has replaced the traditional economic models. In any project environment, knowledge is power—but only if it is readily accessible, organized, analyzed, and disseminated to meet the project needs. Knowledge in projects should focus on the proper access and delivery methods for explicit knowledge on the desktop and should also concentrate on tacit knowledge unknown and unavailable to most people in projects. Recently, organizations have begun to realize that capitalizing project knowledge is an effective way to meet organizational goals and objectives.

PROJECTS AND GENERAL MANAGEMENT

Projects have a long history of evolution through the centuries and have a proved dependency on good management.

According to Daft (2008), management philosophies and organizational forms change over time to meet new needs, although some ideas and practices from the past are still relevant and applicable to management today. Today's project managers who ambitiously seek new methods and techniques to gain an edge on the competition and/or make their organizations more effective and efficient are not so different from their predecessors from generations past. Daft further states that social, political, and economic forces have influenced organizations and the practices of management have influenced managing projects. The approach to management has evolved from the schools of scientific management, through various phases and approaches: the bureaucratic organization, administrative principles, humanistic principles and the human relations movement, the behavioral sciences approach, theory x and y, management science perspective, and the systems view, all the way to the learning organizations and e-commerce.

The scientific approach valued standardized jobs, training employees, which worked well for the new industrial economies of the 1800s and 1900s. This approach was beneficial in that it developed and emphasized the ideas of performance-based compensation, scientific and measured study of the work environment, and standardized hiring and training. However, this approach did not pay attention to the individuals, the uniqueness of the workers, and it devalued their input. The bureaucratic organization addressed these shortcomings by standardizing authority, rules and processes, and the structure of the organization. But again, this approach did little for the needs and talents of individual employees. It was then that the humanistic approach, which focused on the needs of the individual, was furthered by the human relations movement. In today's learning organization context, emphasis such as employee empowerment has a strong influence on project management. These schools of thought have influenced managing knowledge in projects during that time.

In the project environment, understanding different perspectives and approaches to management theory helps project managers understand what was done in the past and what is being done now, and offers them ways to think about how to improve management in the future. The workplace and organization structures today are different, and some earlier ideas are still relevant and applicable to management today. Younger workers entering to work on projects today are highly educated and technologically competent, and they have higher career expectations than past generations.

Project managers today are challenged to keep their projects in organizations running efficiently and profitably while simultaneously aligning to change management. Understanding the historical context of past theories can help project managers identify trends and patterns, realize why they occur, and avoid mistakes or capitalize on the successes of other experiences.

PROJECT MANAGEMENT

TheProject Management Institute (PMI) in its *PMBOK* (Project Management Body of Knowledge) *Guide* of 2004 defines a project as a temporary endeavor to create a unique product, service, or result.

Projects are part of organizations. As we all know, organizations are entities designed and structured to meet their goals and objectives. Recently, organizations are focusing on more and more projects to meet their organizational objectives. Organizations and projects are controlled by the internal environment with business plans, strategy, funding, staff, processes, architecture, politics, and culture. Externally, the organizations and projects are influenced by industry and the market, economic, political, social, and technology environments.

When we deal with projects in organizations, project management is different from general management. All projects will have start and end dates, detailed project plans, budgets, schedules, human resources, and deliverables. Every project will be unique in nature and will have a temporary structure. It differs from general management in all these areas.

KNOWLEDGE MANAGEMENT AND PROJECT KNOWLEDGE

At the individual level, all wise men have managed knowledge since the beginning of human civilization. Great thinkers of the world had accumulated a tremendous amount of knowledge in their heads, and when they shared their knowledge, civilizations evolved. In Western society, philosophers like Aristotle and Plato laid strong foundations for knowledge. In science and in literature, individuals have contributed heavily toward knowledge, and the public benefited from those contributions. In the project sense, the same tacit knowledge of individuals plays a big role in the success of any project and in strengthening the organizational knowledge base.

At the organizational and project level, knowledge management is based on organizational and project assets. Over the past few years, knowledge management has emerged explosively through an interdisciplinary approach dealing with all aspects of knowledge in organizations, including knowledge creation, codification, organization, and sharing. KM has become recognized to have a wide application in the project environment. The assets in the project environment may include databases, documents, policies, and procedures, as well as previously uncaptured expertise of individual workers.

Knowledge management addresses the problem of inaccessibility of knowledge in projects and their inadequacy, poor quality, and poor organization. Knowledge management focuses on the proper access and delivery methods for explicit knowledge on the desktop and also concentrates on tacit knowledge that is unknown and unavailable to most people. The knowledge management perspective in projects is to look at assets in a new way at the organizational level, which includes people, customers, databases, documents, products, processes, and services.

The growth of knowledge management is phenomenal. As displayed in table 11.1, the number of hits on knowledge management in Google has grown exponentially. Similarly, WorldCat had approximately nine hundred monographs in

Table 11.1. KM Hits in Google and WorldCat

Source	February 2002	January 2003	September 2004	February 2006	December 2008
Google sites	643,000	1,150,000	10,600,000	32,000,000	69,306,000
WorldCat monographs	912	1,239	6,064	12,765	28,473

the year 2002, which grew to nearly thirty thousand monographs in 2008. Figure 11.1 also displays the the growth of "knowledge management" as a keyword in published titles in graphic form. From 2004 onward, knowledge management in projects has become significant.

The growth of knowledge management in projects can also be attributed to the evolution of technology. In the 1980s, we were dealing with the DOS environment and primitive technology with limited CPU, memory, and so on, which restricted managing knowledge using technology. In the 1990s and beyond, with the increase of CPU and memory, and with the Windows environment, managing knowledge at the individual level has increased. Table 11.2 depicts this point from the individual perspective and laptop/desktop evolution.

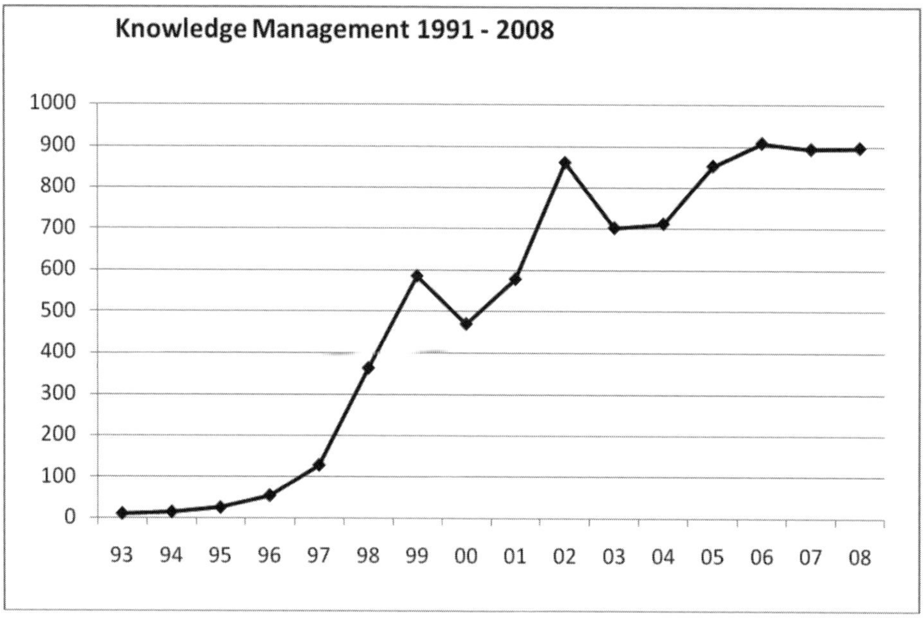

Figure 11.1. Frequency of Occurrence of the Phrase "Knowledge Management" in Journal Article Titles in the Business Literature
Source: Michael E. D. Koenig.

Table 11.2. KM Technology Context

Decade	CPU	Memory	Disk	OS	Cost
1980s	16 MHz 386	2 Mbytes	120 Mbytes	DOS 3.2	$5,000
1990s	33 MHz 486	4 Mbytes	330 Mbytes	DOS 6.2	$4,000
	66 MHz Pent.	16 Mbytes	540 Mbytes	Windows 3.x	
	Pent. II & III	64 Mbytes	1–5 Gbytes	Windows 9/ x2000	$2,000
2000s	1+ GHz Pent.	128+ Mbytes	20+ Gbytes	Windows XP	$1,000

PROJECTS AND KNOWLEDGE MANAGEMENT CONTINUUM

Knowledge is part of project culture. Knowledge is created through processes as we begin communicating with one another in the project environment.

Looking at project knowledge, Davenport's (2000) continuum concept seems relevant. According to him, knowledge management starts with data, which is based on raw facts, figures, or statistics. When these raw facts are contextualized, categorized, calculated, corrected, and condensed, it leads to codification and becomes explicit, or information. When this information is applied by users through comparisons, conversations, connections, and for consequences, it becomes knowledge. In other words, knowledge focuses on experience, on values, and on the context of information applied to a message, and thus it embraces both explicit and tacit knowledge. The last segment of the knowledge management continuum is wisdom, which reflects sound and effective decisions made based on knowledge. Wisdom is a collective application of knowledge in action by wise men and women. In projects, decision making results from data, information, knowledge, and the experience of individuals reflecting on the wisdom of the decision makers, such as project managers.

WHY KNOWLEDGE MANAGEMENT IN PROJECTS NOW?

Why is knowledge management so important to projects now? There are several reasons. First is the advancement of technology. Laptops, the Internet, and cell phones are just a few examples of information technology that has altered our working lifestyle as well as our social lifestyle. The benefits of harnessing this technology to manage knowledge have given an advantage to organizations in managing their assets. In today's work environment, our work life revolves around these technologies.

Second is the exploding nature of online information. Gone are the days where we had all information packages in hard-copy format (on paper). With thousands of websites, search engines, e-mails, and so on, digital information is taking over and replacing hard-copy format in most areas. The volume of digital information is growing each day and has become part of our culture. As the ratio of electronic information versus hard-copy information grows exponentially, knowledge management has become a functional necessity.

Third, organizations have to compete for their survival through projects. These days, organizations get acquired, merged, and fall into bankruptcy if they do not successfully compete with others in the industry. Also, increasingly many projects are operating at the global level, which poses more strategic challenges (see the chapter on KM at Infosys in this book for an example of this phenomenon). In order to stay competitive and survive, organizations are making knowledge management a priority in projects.

Fourth, with the regulatory reforms at the national level and the fast-growing global environment, organizations have realized that the culture of managing projects should change from hoarding to sharing knowledge. The knowledge management systems that are set up in projects are promoting a knowledge-sharing culture. Collaboration among various members of the project team in a synergic way will increase trust and morale, resulting in success of the project. Also, collaboration has the potential to cut costs and fulfill the goals and objectives of the project more effectively. Knowledge management plays a key role in accomplishing these aspects.

Fifth, in the project environment, organizations are influenced by the external economic conditions and internal political conditions (management styles). The current environment requires increasing productivity with fewer resources. In order to do this, knowledge in projects needs to be managed properly. Knowledge management experts are setting up knowledge management systems in projects to accomplish the objective of increasing productivity and collaboration, even with diminishing resources.

KNOWLEDGE MANAGEMENT IN PROJECTS IN ACTION

Knowledge management in projects is a new way of looking at organizational assets—people, customers, databases, documents, products, processes, and services. Knowledge resides with individuals, their conversations, internal records, external publications, data warehouses, internal and external databases, best practices, intranets, and the Internet. Knowledge management deals with both explicit knowledge and tacit knowledge.

Srikantaiah and Koenig (2001) describe the various categories of explicit and tacit knowledge.

Explicit Knowledge in Projects

Explicit knowledge exists in organizations in a wide variety of forms. Explicit knowledge in projects deals with codified knowledge that is documented and is in the domain of structural capital. In projects, it covers a variety of categories, including:

- Print publications (books, periodicals, report literature)
- Internal records (business records, archives)
- Sound recordings, video recordings, graphic material, and so on
- Data warehouses
- E-mail
- Intranet
- Internet

- Internal databases (text, numerical)
- External databases (text, numerical)
- Best practices
- Groupware
- Self-study material
- Newsletters

Tacit Knowledge in Projects

Tacit knowledge refers to the knowledge that resides in an individual's mind and is vital to success of any project. Tacit knowledge, which cannot be codified, is the know-how and experience of the staff member that is vital to projects. Knowledge management practices aim to draw out the tacit knowledge people have, what they carry around with them, what they observe and learn from experience, rather than what is usually explicitly stated. Davenport and Prusak (2000) states that studies have shown that managers get two-thirds of their information and knowledge from face-to-face meetings or phone conversations. Tacit knowledge comprises a variety of categories. These include:

- Formal and informal meetings—face-to-face conversation
- Telephone conversations—formal as well as informal
- Videoconferences and presentations
- Individual knowledge and expertise
- Outside experts
- Mentoring
- Coaching
- Study tours
- Virtual communication and meetings
- Training
- Client knowledge
- Best practices

INTELLECTUAL CAPITAL

Knowledge management in projects centers on the notion of intellectual capital, which became popular in the early and mid-1990s. Intellectual capital represented awareness that, as economists phrased it, information is a factor of production, in the same category as land, labor, capital, and energy. In the early and mid-1990s, there was an increasing awareness in organizations that knowledge was an important organizational resource that needed to be nurtured, sustained, and accounted for. Intellectual capital was characterized as having two major components: knowledge capital and structural capital. Knowledge capital is the organization's knowledge—in our perspective, project knowledge—informal and unstructured as well as formal and structured. Structural capital is the mechanism in place to take advantage of the knowledge capital, as well as mechanisms such as IT that store, retrieve, and communicate that knowledge. The intellectual capital movement gained publicity while demonstrating the importance of valuing and nurturing people who carried knowledge in their heads. Thomas Stewart authored a number of prominently featured articles in *Fortune,* of which the most compelling was "Your Company's Most Valuable Asset: Intellectual Capital" (1994). He also stated that an organization's tangible assets—cash, land, and buildings; plant and equipment; and other balance sheet items—are substantially less valuable than the intangible assets—patents, staff know-how, and so on—not carried on their books. According to Stewart, most important of these intangible assets are the skills, capabilities, expertise, values, and loyalties of staff. In the project sense, all team members connected with the project can enhance knowledge activity by their contributions.

Today, organizations continue to realize that, in addition to tangible assets, intangible assets are a driving force for the project success. The most valuable of these intangible assets are the staffs who work on projects and their skills, expertise, capabilities, and experiences. This recognition has prompted efforts to capture tacit knowledge of staff and the sharing of that knowledge with others in projects to increase productivity, teamwork, collaboration, and effectiveness.

CONVERTING TACIT KNOWLEDGE INTO EXPLICIT FORMAT IN PROJECTS

A survey of professional literature resulted in very few citations dealing with capturing tacit knowledge in projects. Some websites include articles that are ephemeral in nature on capturing tacit knowledge. The American Productivity Quality Center's (APQC) report of 2002, *Retaining Valuable Knowledge: Proactive Strategies to Deal with a Shifting Workforce,* is a useful reference. In this report the following case studies are presented: Best Buy Co., Inc.; Corning Incorporated; Northrop Grumman; Siemens AG; the World Bank; and Xerox Connect. According to APQC, these organizations have made attempts to identify potential knowledge loss, identify the knowledge that needs to be captured and shared, design and implement appropriate approaches, determine the costs associated with these approaches, identify the enablers and barriers to successful implementation, and assess the health and measure the effectiveness of knowledge retention strategies. The professional literature reports that a survey of more than seven hundred U.S. companies shows that only a small portion of corporate knowledge is in shareable form. The majority is in employee's brains and documents not easily shared. Retirement also has a significant impact on knowledge attrition. Rapid growth, turnover, and internal redeployment also create potential knowledge loss or knowledge gaps. Organizations have used one or more of the following approaches to retain knowledge by converting tacit into explicit knowledge:

- Communities of practice (CoPs) and internal networks
- Interviews
- Videotaping
- Subject matter expert (SME) directories ("yellow pages")
- Information/knowledge repositories
- After-action reviews/project milestone reviews

- Mentoring programs
- Knowledge maps
- Recruiting strategies
- Retention strategies

By adopting these measures, organizations have tried to capture valuable knowledge in projects as project staff leave and to build a knowledge-sharing culture in the organization.

In studying the organizations that adopted these approaches, APQC emphasized that learning and sharing tacit knowledge are social activities. As such, culture and people are the keys to allow practices and ideas to flow seamlessly. Accordingly, processes for capturing project knowledge must fit the culture of the organization and the project environment. In projects, people need to be connected who can and are willing to share their tacit knowledge. The key lesson learned about culture is that in projects, one cannot expect people to change the way they work—going from withholding knowledge to sharing it—without a reason to do so. Several principles that typically encourage knowledge sharing include the following:

- People see the connection between sharing knowledge in projects and the business purpose.
- Knowledge sharing is linked to the core cultural values of the organization and is reflected in projects.
- There is strong management influence and peer pressure for people to collaborate and share knowledge in projects.
- Knowledge sharing is integrated with people's work in projects and work processes.
- The rewards and recognition system is aligned with sharing knowledge in projects.

Organizations and projects have discovered three critical elements for successful tacit knowledge transfer in projects. These are senior management support, a central knowledge management support group, and the involvement of different business units or functions in the initiative.

PROJECT KNOWLEDGE: A MODEL

Projects get generated though exploring opportunities generally termed as OTR (opportunity through receipt). Engagement managers and salespeople deal with clients. Once documents are signed, managers produce a code for the project and start planning for the project. However, in most cases there is no mechanism to capture knowledge before RFIs (requests for information) and RFPs (requests for proposals) are produced. This knowledge needs to be captured as it is essential to contribute the core and critical project knowledge.

In an IT consulting organization, as displayed in figure 11.2, we can see how knowledge gets created in a project and how important it is to capture knowledge at all levels for the benefit of the project as well as the institution. The business units in an organization are responsible for handling accounts. These accounts could be a major organization (like American Express, MetLife, Ford, Abbott, United Airlines, etc.), and business units deal with clients with respect to these accounts. Clients may be at the middle management to senior management levels, and the work may deal with HR, finance, operations, marketing, and so on. In other words, within the account it is possible to have different clients. Again, these clients are interested in conducting the project in a specific area addressing one or more issues. Therefore, projects get generated and approved by these clients for the IT consulting firm to do the work. It can be software development projects, training projects, and so on. Knowledge gets generated both within and across the projects. Knowledge of each client and each account becomes very important in capturing knowledge and sharing that knowledge with people who need it. Capturing knowledge helps to understand what is recorded in each RFP, and a good KM implementation should be able to enable the finding of:

- Similar objectives in other projects
- Related outcomes in other projects
- Failures in like projects
- Successes in comparable projects
- Analogous methodologies in projects
- Parallel systems in project areas
- Projects with corresponding types of results
- Approximation of risks in projects
- Lessons learned in like projects
- Similar projects used in the project design

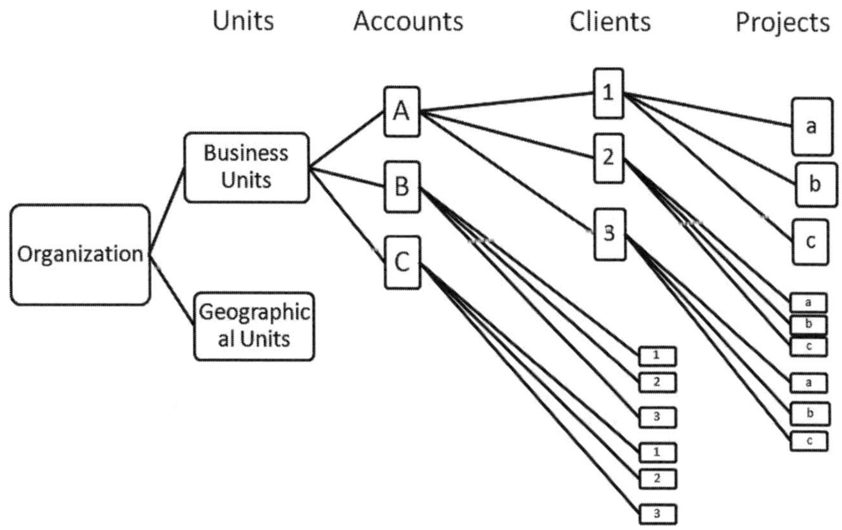

Figure 11.2. Knowledge Capture and Sharing in Projects

AN EXAMPLE: THE WORLD BANK PROJECTS

The World Bank, with its headquarters in Washington, D.C., deals with hundreds of its own development projects every year all over the world.

The World Bank labels knowledge management as "knowledge sharing." This creates an environment that encourages and facilitates the sharing of useful knowledge. The 1996 commitment by the World Bank president resulted in the "knowledge bank," which assumed the role of facilitator, or connector. It includes three broad objectives to cover World Bank activities:

- Improving the bank's efficiency and effectiveness by managing knowledge better and by utilizing modern information technologies
- Offering clients knowledge, training, and advisory services to help the clients' own development agenda, either bundled with lending or as unbundled products
- Building client capacity to create, share, and apply knowledge to help clients take charge of their development and to compete more successfully in the global economy

The World Bank highlights many success stories reflecting on its knowledge management initiatives to capture knowledge in its projects. One such story narrated by Denning (2001) revolves around a Pakistan highways project that was experiencing widespread pavement failure. The project team wanted to try a different technology with an innovative approach. The project team leader (task leader) sent an e-mail from Pakistan to the community of highway specialists and asked for help to be provided within forty-eight hours. Since the knowledge in all projects was captured and managed well, experts and project managers from Jordan, Argentina, South Africa, and New Zealand responded right away with their experiences and suggestions. What would have taken several months of work dealing with meetings, paperwork, and bureaucracy was resolved in a very short time, as knowledge on the projects in those countries was well managed and experts were eager to share their experiences.

DEBRIEFING

Debriefing is part of downloading the tacit knowledge of staff. Debriefing is a systematic process that gives staff the opportunity to reflect on its experiences and identify lessons learned. In turn, this enables staff to share knowledge and helps to create an operational knowledge base for improved quality in project and program design and implementation. Debriefing is done in one-on-one or team interviews after assignments to capture and disseminate lessons learned. Elements include facilitating the interview of the selected debriefee and identifying critical issues to be addressed during missions. It will also help to discuss experiences and identify what worked, what didn't work, and why. It is videotaped and made available to the debriefee for approval and editing before dissemination to users. The video is then edited and made available electronically in its entirety or via shorter clips.

Documents and other resources referred to during the debriefing are relevant to the debriefing and are also provided and highlighted as links. Objectives and activities of the debriefing service include:
Capturing experiences

- Providing time, space, and opportunity for project team members to reflect on issues and achievements
- Helping identify lessons learned
- Capturing important lessons

Sharing lessons learned

- Providing instruments and facilitation for knowledge sharing across teams and networks
- Disseminating important experiences
- Contributing to the knowledge base of good practices
- Providing ground-level feedback on procedures and rules
- Reinforcing values of sharing and learning

Interpreting quality at entry and exit

- Providing pointers to cross-sectoral knowledge sources, good practices, and relevant local knowledge
- Identifying critical issues prior and subsequent to operational missions
- Identifying examples of adapting project design to local institutional and cultural formats

In projects, debriefing is increasingly applied in public and private corporations to capture and share operational experiences. Debriefing can help learning before, during, and after tasks in projects. It can help in sharing critical information about task processes and achievements to aid in planning for future projects and to reduce the risk of future failures in projects. Debriefing increases the knowledge base of good practices and helps to avoid repeating mistakes. Debriefing can point to available knowledge resources and identify knowledge gaps. Debriefing helps us understand what works so that we can improve quality at entry and exit.

The World Bank also captures tacit knowledge by audiotaping individual interviews. The interviewer asks questions such as, "What went well and why?" "What didn't go well and why not?" and "What would or could you have done differently and why?" Experts conduct the audiotaped interviews with project team members. The tape is then transcribed and edited by the interviewee. A hot link is placed in the text whenever a report or document is mentioned, which creates a fully searchable document that incorporates context. The project goal in both videotape and audiotape interviews is to uncover what was not known and not reflected in documents and to gather knowledge in these areas.

The U.S. Army's After Action Review (AAR) is an excellent example of capturing tacit knowledge through debriefing. There are four basic steps in the U.S. Army AAR, which generally takes place as a group discussion moderated by the leaders. Every effort is made to ensure that everyone from the highest rank to the lowest can share his or her opinion. An AAR answers four major questions:

1. What was expected to happen?
2. What actually happened (occurred)?
3. What went well, and why?
4. What can be improved, and how?

The results of AAR are kept as lessons learned so that the next time, in a similar event, the previous actions can be reviewed in order to accentuate the positive and reduce the negative results.

TYPES OF KNOWLEDGE

As stated earlier, knowledge management deals with both explicit and tacit knowledge. Explicit knowledge pertains to codified knowledge that is documented and is in the domain of structural capital. In contrast, tacit knowledge is the know-how and know-what knowledge people hold in their possession, which is the domain of human and customer capital. Knowledge resides with individuals, their conversations, internal records, external publications, data warehouses, internal and external databases, best practices, intranet, and the Internet. Nonaka and Takeuchi in 1995 brought out four basic patterns of explicit and tacit knowledge relevant to project knowledge using the acronym SECI: socialization, externalization, creation, and internalization.

From Tacit to Tacit: When an individual shares tacit knowledge with another face to face or through other modes (socialization)

From Explicit to Explicit: When an individual combines discrete pieces of explicit knowledge and creates a new product (creation)

From Tacit to Explicit: When the organization deals with a knowledge base by codifying experience, insight, and opinion into a form that can be reused by others (externalization)

From Explicit to Tacit: When staff members internalize new or shared explicit knowledge and use it to broaden, extend, and rethink their own tacit knowledge (internalization)

The last two patterns provide a challenge in knowledge management in projects: from tacit to explicit and explicit to tacit. Although it is easier to acknowledge these two areas, how does it actually occur in projects? What conditions encourage such forms of knowledge management in projects?

STAGES OF KNOWLEDGE MANAGEMENT

There are several stages of knowledge management applicable to the project environment. Looking at KM evolution in projects, Koenig and Srikantaiah (2004) noted three established stages in knowledge management and recognized the emergence of the fourth stage in knowledge management. The first stage of KM is "by the Internet out of intellectual capital" and is driven by IT. Organizations, particularly the large international organizations, realized their stock is information and knowledge, that often the left hand, as it were, had no idea what the right hand knew, and that if they could share that knowledge, they would avoid reinventing the wheel and increase profits. This resulted in applying IT to the full extent and concentrating on the intellectual capital and the Internet (including intranets, extranets, and so on). The key phrase here is "best practices," later replaced by "lessons learned." In many projects, knowledge is still managed in this fashion.

The second stage of KM, described simply, added recognition of the human and cultural dimensions. This stage could be described as the "If you build it, they will come is a fallacy" stage; that is, the recognition "If you build it, they will come" is a recipe that can easily lead to quick and embarrassing failure if human factors are not sufficiently taken into account. With this, two major themes from the business literature were brought into the KM fold. The first work was by Senge (1990) on the learning organization. The second was the work by Nonaka (1995) and others on tacit knowledge and how to discover and cultivate it. They were also concerned with knowledge creation and sharing and communication. The hallmark of this stage is "communities of practice." This stage has impacted the project environment to a great extent.

The third stage is the awareness of the importance of content, and in particular, awareness of the importance of the retrievability and therefore of the importance of arrangement, description, and structure of the content. A good alternate description is the "It's no good if they can't find it" stage. The hallmarks of this stage are content management and taxonomy. More and more knowledge management systems in projects are applying these tools.

Srikantaiah (2008) indicated that a fourth stage of KM is emerging, which expands the KM application in the areas of CI, project management, environmental scanning, and knowledge audit. Koenig and Srikantaiah (2004) confirms by saying that there is an emphasis on extending KM systems beyond the parent organization to include, for example, vendors and suppliers, customers, users, alumni, and so on.

PROJECT LIFE CYCLE

There are several phases to a project life cycle. According to the *PMBOK Guide*, projects can be divided into phases to provide better management control. Collectively, these phases become the project life cycle. Many organizations identify a specific set of life cycles for use in their projects. However, all project life cycles will connect the beginning of a project to its end. There is no single best way to define the ideal project life cycle. Some organizations have established policies that standardize all projects with a single life cycle, while others allow the project management team to choose the most appropriate life cycle for the team's project. Project life cycles generally cover technical work needed to be completed in each phase, what deliverables are to be generated in each phase and how each deliverable is reviewed, verified, and validated, the people involved in each phase, and a plan to control and approve each phase.

Project life cycle descriptions can be very general or very detailed. Most project life cycles are generally sequential and are usually defined by some form of technical information transfer or technical component handoff. Cost and staffing levels are low at the start, peak during the intermediate phases, and drop rapidly as the project draws to a conclusion. The first phase involves identification of a problem or need. The second phase involves the development of a proposed solution to the problem or need. The third phase is actually doing the project, utilizing resources, and meeting the stated objectives. The fourth stage involves terminating the project. All projects progress neatly through all four phases of the project life cycle. However, projects vary in duration and complexity.

Every project is unique with start and end dates, detailed project plan, budget, schedule, human resources, technology infrastructure, and deliverables, and all these areas have a high volume of rich knowledge. In terms of nine knowledge areas identified by the *PMBOK Guide*, knowledge is created in all those areas, and knowledge flows through the project as well as managing that knowledge are absolutely necessary for the success of the project. These nine areas include:

1. **Project integration management.** Deals with project knowledge concerning making choices about where to concentrate resources during the project. It includes the knowledge of processes and activities to identify, define, combine, coordinate, and integrate the various activities.
2. **Project scope management.** Project knowledge describing the processes involved in ascertaining that the project includes all the work required, and only the work required, to complete the project successfully. It includes scope planning and scope definition and work breakdown structure. Knowledge boundaries are defined in clear terms.
3. **Project time management.** Project knowledge describing the processes concerning the timely completion of the project. It includes the activity definition, activity sequencing, and activity resource estimating. Knowledge of the logical sequence of activities in projects is essential.
4. **Project cost management.** Project knowledge concerning the process to ensure that the project is completed within the approved budget and will include planning, estimating, budgeting, and controlling costs. While primarily concerned with the cost of resources, it should also consider the effect of project decisions through the project life cycle. Knowledge of the budget for each activity should be spelled out and monitored as the project starts.
5. **Project human resources management.** Project knowledge concerning effective management of the project team and others to accomplish the project objectives. Project knowledge in developing teams and team management for the appropriate knowledge culture are included.
6. **Project quality management.** Project knowledge describing the processes involved in assuring that the project will satisfy the objectives for which it was undertaken. Knowledge includes quality planning and performing quality assurance. Knowledge processes may include planning to identify project roles, acquiring project team members through the life of a project, developing skills and competencies of project team members, and tracking performance. This is a critical area of knowledge management in projects to ensure that deliverables meet the specifications of the client.

7. Project communications management. Project knowledge that describes the processes concerning the timely and appropriate generation, collection, dissemination, storage, and ultimate disposition of project information. It includes communication planning, information distribution, and performance reporting. This area of knowledge management is critical for project transparency to add value to projects.

8. Project risk management. Project knowledge describing the processes concerned with risk management on a project. It includes knowledge on risk management planning, risk identification, qualitative risk analysis, risk response planning, and risk mitigation. It is not possible to handle these areas unless project knowledge is captured.

9. Project procurement management. Project knowledge describing the processes that purchase or acquire products and services as a result as well as contract management processes. It includes the plans for purchases, acquisitions, plan contracting, selecting sellers, requesting seller responses, and contract administration. Capturing knowledge in projects in these areas is absolutely necessary for successful implementation.

Although some projects do not have all of these nine areas described, most will, to some degree, include knowledge. In terms of knowledge management, knowledge capture, transfer, and dissemination become the most important issues.

Knowledge is created and flows through all nine areas of project management and in all phases of the project life cycle. Project managers and staff constantly seek knowledge to address various problems: resources, deadlines, deliverables, goals/objectives, team, planning, communications, and conflicts.

Earlier, the emphasis for project management was on developing tools and techniques such as networks and earned value analysis. Now project management has shifted its focus to capturing tacit knowledge and success-based criteria. It is the responsibility of senior management in organizations to ensure that it creates an environment in which projects will succeed. By managing knowledge in projects, projects can be successfully completed on time, on budget, and with quality deliverables to satisfy customers. Projects in organizations need to learn to manage more effectively the knowledge that they acquire and accumulate from their projects so that other projects in the organization can benefit.

Knowledge can then be embedded within individuals, groups, and organizational and interorganizational processes. Knowledge gained by learning from failures or successes of the project is vital for long-term sustainability and to compete in the business environment. Projects do not have organizational memory as organizations do (or certainly should), since projects are temporary in nature. Knowledge types in projects may include sector knowledge, technical knowledge, and organization knowledge. Knowledge management helps in all these areas and also helps staff to have a shared vision of the project.

CRITERIA AND ROLE OF KNOWLEDGE MANAGEMENT IN PROJECTS

The knowledge environment in projects is mainly influenced by the culture of the organization, formal and informal policies, staff behavior toward knowledge capture and sharing, knowledge architecture, business processes, and the overall strategy.

Critical knowledge in projects resides with people. They need to understand the value of knowledge and share that knowledge. In this background, Kliem (1999) outlines several positive effects of knowledge management on projects:

- Dealing with "gray" situations with greater confidence
- Encouraging greater collaboration among employees
- Identifying best practices
- Improving the capacity for product and processing innovation
- Increasing the competencies of existing employees
- Minimizing the negative impacts of employee turnover
- Responding cost-effectively to rapidly changing environments

In every project, individuals, whether on the project management side or the customer side, carry tacit knowledge that would be valuable to the project. Experienced project managers carry with them the knowledge of many projects, and likewise, members of a project team have tacit knowledge from their own experience. Koskinen (2004) describes knowledge management as a necessity in project management for harnessing the tacit knowledge of all involved in the project. Because project team members share project knowledge, their effective communication is the best way to further develop project knowledge. Koskinen goes on to describe four environments in which knowledge management influences project management:

Mechanical project management environment. This primarily relies on explicit knowledge through a series of clearly defined instructions, tasks, and interpretations. This environment is very likely to use information technology, which is certainly a good model for a project involving geographically dispersed teams.

Organic project management environment. This is more likely to rely on tacit knowledge. Information is ambiguous, tasks are inconsistent, and change is constant, so nonlinear problem solving surfaces. In this environment, information technology does not facilitate communication effectively; rather, knowledge is transferred through face-to-face interaction, making this environment less suited to projects involving geographically dispersed teams.

Semimechanical and semiorganic environments. These are the last two and occur more commonly than the first two. Communication takes place both face to face and through information technology. Knowledge creation, transfer, and use are weighted more toward information technology in a semimechanical environment, while a semiorganic environment relies more on face-to-face interaction. It would seem that the two hybrids would be more effective than the purely mechanical or organic ones. Using information technology to codify knowledge can help a project team decide what tacit knowledge is applicable to the project. Where project specifications are highly refined, the use of information technology is extremely valuable, and where a project relies heavily on the creative process, face-to-face conversations—tacit knowledge—becomes more critical. However, the recording of tacit knowledge can be facilitated by using technology.

BENEFITS FROM KNOWLEDGE MANAGEMENT IN PROJECTS

In this dynamically changing project environment, while managers are expected to deliver more with less, one of the most challenging things an organization must do is to protect its knowledge assets. Therefore, managing knowledge, both explicit and tacit, is an important function in project management. For example, the tacit knowledge of project managers, project team knowledge captured from another project, and explicit knowledge of lessons learned from other projects, can all provide insight on a current project. The benefits of knowledge management in projects also extends to strategic advantage (planning), sharing best practices, promoting innovation, and retaining the knowledge of experienced employees without having to pay for that knowledge. Therefore, knowledge management in projects has become an invaluable tool and a fundamental necessity for the success of projects and for the sustainability and growth of organizations. Specifically, the following benefits can be described, as shown below:

Major Benefits

- The major benefits of KM in projects are deliverables on schedule, cost savings, time savings, and quality.

Avoid Reinventing the Wheel

- KM enables the tapping of existing knowledge in the current project environment to be applied toward future projects.
- Managing knowledge in projects provides a strategic advantage to the organization.
- KM helps to avoid waste, duplication, and some mistakes.

Capture Lessons Learned

- Learn from the problems or issues encountered and solutions devised in past projects and apply them to current projects.
- Managing knowledge in projects helps share best practices.

Use Collaborative Tools

- Collaborative tools such as enterprise resource planning (ERP) allow the project team to share knowledge.
- Use of these tools promotes successful innovation and enables the team to make better and faster decisions.

Customer Services Function

- KM streamlines customer service through response, products, and services.

Managing Knowledge in Projects Enhances Retention

- Without effective mechanisms in place to capture knowledge of experienced employees, project teams may be making costly mistakes or have to pay again for knowledge they once had.

Other

- KM increases the rate of return in projects.
- It promotes collaboration, collective wisdom, and experience.
- It assists in evaluating contents in documents (as most documents are sanitized) by noting undesirable aspects of a project through debriefing and capturing tacit knowledge.

WE DON'T KNOW WHAT WE KNOW

In projects there is no dearth of knowledge, but the problem is that team members don't know what they know. This unawareness becomes a bottleneck in utilizing resources and knowledge efficiently and cost-effectively in projects. The main problem is that knowledge and information are generally not organized and not easily accessible. If knowledge were to be captured and managed properly, then the project would:

- Provide faster access to knowledge/information to project members, leading to new ideas and creativity. In virtual project management it becomes very useful as it helps in sharing the same knowledge/information easily at all locations. This may lead to less confusion among team members at distributed locations.
- Help in improving the productivity and providing better customer relations and satisfaction.
- Improve the decision-making process in terms of quality and time if knowledge is shared efficiently.
- Help in improving the quality of training and reducing the training time for trainees in projects.
- Improve in collaboration and coordination by teams looking at the same knowledge base. In short, it helps in creating a collaborative environment.
- Reflect intellectual capital through collective wisdom and experience of humans.
- Contribute to capital assets. This helps in improving performance of the project and the quality of project work.
- Help to avoid waste and duplication by encouraging knowledge reuse, thus reducing cost and time.
- Help in mitigating the risk. It would improve the flow of knowledge in all directions and in integrating processes.
- Identify risk by addressing the various risks existing in a project and its related tasks. If risk is not known at the proper time, then risk management becomes a costly affair, and its effects on projects may be severe.

RATE OF RETURN

Managing knowledge properly in projects helps to increase rate of return for the project by capturing, organizing, and storing knowledge and experiences from the organization's human capital and making this knowledge available to others. In essence, it enhances quality and consistency, increases knowledge sharing and transfer, improves productivity, avoids "reinventing the wheel," and saves costs and time. All these contribute to an increased rate of return on projects.

THE BUSINESS CASE TO MANAGE KNOWLEDGE IN PROJECTS

The following areas can be considered in developing a business case to capture knowledge, manage knowledge, and transfer knowledge in projects.

- The first priority is to understand the total design of the project and to analyze and understand the nine knowledge areas discussed in the *PMBOK Guide*. Knowledge in some knowledge areas is obvious, and knowledge in other areas needs to be evaluated to determine whether the knowledge is critical for the project. When a project manager applies KM to develop the project team, the manager is transforming tacit knowledge into explicit knowledge. Once such knowledge is collected, a profile can be generated with a core set of information knowledge for each project. This includes using descriptors, metadata, and taxonomy for all salient project information/knowledge such as its name, start and end dates, project plan, and so on. Once this is done, detailed knowledge of the project can be captured, which will enable users to access knowledge in those projects with context in mind.
- The profiles for projects can appear in a wide variety of formal and informal document sources. The project proposal, or RFP, would be a good starting point. This will give relevant information on project planning such as project name, goals and objectives, sector, client, budget, schedule, primary components of the project, project subcomponents, related projects with clients, project benefits, project constraints/risks, lessons learned in similar projects, expected project outcome, operational plan to complete the project, and often implementation dates.
- Once the project is ongoing, knowledge can be recorded on problems or challenges faced by the project; problems or challenges solved by the project; questions answered; efficacy of the answer; knowledge required at each stage or phase; knowledge-sharing tools utilized; unexpected outcomes of the project; factors affecting outcomes; innovations; products and other things created by the project; and the amount of knowledge captured on the project.
- The information contained in documents needs to be compared with people involved in the project through interviews, mainly with the project leader and with team members who carry relevant tacit knowledge. The assumption is that the best source for high-quality information/knowledge will be with the project team members. Team members' recollections of details regarding the project should elicit important aspects of the project and can add value. Human feedback is able to provide details about project work that are more granular than that reported in documents. It is a known fact that most documents are sanitized and do not include or discuss the project's undesirable aspects, which

have immense value in the design of future projects. Although documents provide the general detail, the depth is always provided by human interviews.
- To maximize knowledge capture from projects, a mechanism has to be created to debrief project team members periodically. This enables the recording of successes, failures, issues, and other qualitative information/knowledge that is relevant. The output of this process can then be used as project knowledge leading to application in other areas.

FINAL NOTE

Organizations are getting involved in more and more projects to meet their goals. Knowledge management, which is an invaluable tool in fostering the institutional memory in organizations, has found practical applications in projects and has become a fundamental necessity for the success of projects.

REFERENCES

Amram, Martha, & Kulatilaka, Nalin. (1999). Discipline decisions: Aligning strategy with the financial markets. *Harvard Business Review, 77*(1), 95–104.

APQC. (2002). *Retaining valuable knowledge: Proactive strategies to deal with a shifting workforce.* APQC Best Practice Report.

Boiko, Bob. (2001). Understanding content management. *Bulletin of the American Society for Information Science & Technology, 28*, 8–13.

Bresnen, Mike, et al. (2003). Social practices and the management of knowledge in project environments. *International Journal of Project Management, 21*(3), 157–166.

Brown, J. (1998). Organizing knowledge. *California Management Review, 40*(3), 90–112.

Browne, John Seeley, & Duguid, Paul. (2000). Balancing act: How to capture knowledge without killing it. *Harvard Business Review, 78*(3), 73–80.

Carillo, P. M., Robinson, H. S., Ghasani, A. M., & Anumba, C. J. (2004). Knowledge management in U. K. construction: Strategies, resources & barriers. *Project Management Journal, 35*(1), 46–56.

Choo, C. W. (1999). The art of scanning the environment. *Bulletin of the American Society for Information Science, 25*(3), 21–24.

Chourides, P., Longbottom, D., & Murphy, W. (2003). Excellence in knowledge management: An empirical study to identify critical factors and performance measures. *Measuring Business Excellence, 7*(2), 20–45.

Daft, Richard L. (2008). *Management* (8th ed). Mason, OH: Thomson-SouthWestern.

Davenport, T., & Prost, G. (2002). *Knowledge management case book: Siemens best practices.* New York: Wiley.

Davenport, Thomas H., De Long, David W., & Beers, Michael C. (1998). Successful knowledge management projects. *Sloan Management Review, 39*(2), 43–57.

Davenport, Thomas H., & Prusak, Laurence. (2000). *Working knowledge: How organizations manage what they know.* Boston: Harvard Business School Press.

Denning, Stephen. (2001). The springboard: How storytelling ignites action in knowledge-era organizations. Boston: Buttersworth/Heinemann.

Edum-Fotwe, Francis, & Irani, Zahir. (2003). Management of knowledge in project environments. *International Journal of Project Management, 21*(3), 155–156.

Fahey, L. (1998). Theeleven deadliest sins of knowledge management. *California Management Review, 40*(3), 265–277.

Handzic, Meliha. (2003). An integrated framework of knowledge management. *Journal of Information and Knowledge Management, 2*(3), 245–252.

Hansen, Morten, Nohria, N., & Tierney, T. (1999). What's your strategy for managing knowledge? *Harvard Business Review, 77*(2), 107–114.

Huang, Jimmy C., & Newell, Sue. Knowledge integration processes and dynamics within the content of cross-functional projects. *International Journal of Project Management, 21*(3), 167–176.

Kliem, R. L. (1999). *The role of project management in knowledge management.* Retrieved April 4, 2007, from www.brint.com/members/online/20100210/ projectkm/

Koenig, Michael (2008). The origins and development of knowledge management. *Journal of Information & Knowledge Management 7*(4), 243–254.

Koenig, Michael, & Srikantaiah, T. K. (2004). Knowledge management lessons learned: What works and what doesn't. Medford, NJ: Information Today.

Koskinen, Kaj U. (2004). Knowledge management to improve project communication and implementation. *Project Management Journal, 35*(2), 13–19.

Leonard, D. (1998). The role of tacit knowledge in group innovation. *California Management Review, 40*(3), 112–143.

Liebowitz, Jay, & Megbolngbe, Issac. (2003) A set of frameworks to aid the project manager in conceptualizing and implementing knowledge management initiatives. *International Journal of Project Management, 21*(3), 189–198.

Love, Peter E. D., Fong, Patrick S. W., & Irani, Zahir. (2005). *Management of knowledge in project environments.* Boston: Elsevier.

McInerney, Claire, & Day, Ronald. (2002). Knowledge management and the dynamic nature of knowledge. *Journal of the American Society for Information Science and Technology, 53*(12), 1009–1018.

Nonaka, I. (1991). The knowledge-creating company. *Harvard Business Review, 69*(12), 96–104.

Nonaka, Ikujiro, & Takeuchi, Hirotaka. (1995). *The knowledge-creating company: How Japanese companies create the dynamics of innovation.* New York: Oxford University Press.

O'Dell, C. (1998). If only we knew what we know: Identification and transfer of internal best practices. *California Management Review, 40*(3), 154–175.

Polyani, M. (1967). *The tacit dimension.* New York: Doubleday.

Project Management Institute. (2004). *A guide to the Project Management Body of Knowledge: PMBOK guide.* Hershey, PA,: Author.

Schindler, Martin, & Eppler, Martin J. (2003). Harvesting project knowledge: A review of project learning methods and success factors. *International Journal of Project Management, 21*(3), 219–228.

Senge, Peter. (1990). *The fifth discipline: The art and practice of the learning organization.* New York: Currency/Doubleday.

Srikantaiah, T. K., & Koenig, Michael. (2001). *Knowledge management for the information professional.* Medford, NJ: Information Today.

Srikantaiah, T. K., & Koenig, Michael. (2008). *Knowledge management in practice: Connections and context.* Medford, NJ: Information Today.

Stewart, T. A. (1994). Your company's most valuable asset: Intellectual capital. *Fortune, 130,* 68–74.

Vail, Edmond F., III. (1999). Mapping organizational knowledge: Bridging the business-IT communication gap. *Knowledge Management Review, 39*(2), 10–15.

Valentin, E. K. (2001). SWOT analysis from a resource-based view. *Journal of Marketing Theory and Practice, 9*(2), 54–69.

Wenger, E., McDermott, R., & Synder, W. (2002). *Cultivating communities of practice: A guide to managing knowledge*. Boston: Harvard Business School Press.

Wenger, Etienne C., & Snyder, William M.(2000). Communities of practice: The organizational frontier. *Harvard Business Review, 78*(1), 139–145.

World Bank. (1999). *World Development Report, 1998/1999*. Washington, DC: Author.

WEBSITES

http://wikipedia.org
http://www.apqc.org
http://www.brint.com
http://www.cio.com
http://www.google.com
http://www.icasit.org/km/resources/kmcases.htm
http://www.kmci.org
http://www.kmresource.com
http://www.scip.org
http://www.skyrme.com
http://www.sveiby.com
http://www.tfpl.com
http://www.uts.edu.au
http://www.worldbank.org

12

Aligning Knowledge Strategy with Project Characteristics

Joseph Kasten

There is little doubt that, in the present business environment, knowledge has emerged as one of the most important ingredients of organizational success. There is a large body of literature to testify to this. However, we also understand that knowledge, without a linkage to the strategic direction of the firm, loses some of its value and ability to act as an agent of organizational success. The linkage of organizational knowledge to the strategic plan of the firm is often known as the knowledge strategy. This chapter is concerned with how the organization's knowledge strategy can assist project managers in the successful execution of the project's plans.

Knowledge strategy has been defined as the set of guidelines, rules, or concepts that help to shape the knowledge-related activities of an organization (Kasten 2006). It is very rarely an explicitly defined set of plans. Rather, it tends to be an informal or emergent entity, rarely defined a priori, but rather the result of decisions made over an extended period of time. Knowledge strategy tends to take the shape of the beliefs of the upper management team, or sometimes a single person on the management team who has a vision about how knowledge should be dealt with (Kasten 2009).

Knowledge strategies can exist at the firm, division, or departmental level, though it is unlikely that departmental knowledge strategies could differ widely from those of the firm. Like business strategy, knowledge strategies extend throughout the organization, especially those areas that depend heavily upon knowledge to operate. The more coherent and focused the knowledge strategy is, the more useful and valuable it can be. More importantly, the knowledge strategy cannot be relegated to only certain parts of the organization; it must be pervasive in order to be effective.

This means that projects taking place within a firm are not insulated from knowledge strategy, either. A knowledge strategy in place throughout the organization will also be felt within a project, and this influence might be even more intense given a project's condensed nature. The characteristics of a knowledge strategy, which are discussed in the next section, can have a significant impact on the manner in which a project is executed. The section afterward draws relationships between knowledge strategy types and the types of projects that might benefit from, or be harmed by, their implementation by the parent organization. The final section presents some thoughts for practitioners considering the interactions between their knowledge strategy and project characteristics.

GENERIC KNOWLEDGE STRATEGIES

As defined in the previous section, knowledge strategy is a set of guidelines that help guide an organization's knowledge activities. Like most strategic models, knowledge strategies are not usually quantifiable and must be described by their position in reference to specific sets of qualities. To that end, a model of generic knowledge strategies was developed that helps to describe certain knowledge strategy characteristics (Kasten 2006). The model consists of three independent axes describing the three primary characteristics of knowledge strategy (figure 12.1).

The milieu axis describes the extent to which an organization supports the use of information technology to store organizational knowledge or, on the other end of the continuum, prefers to embed knowledge in the human assets. At one end of the continuum is the firm that emphasizes the use of information technology to store

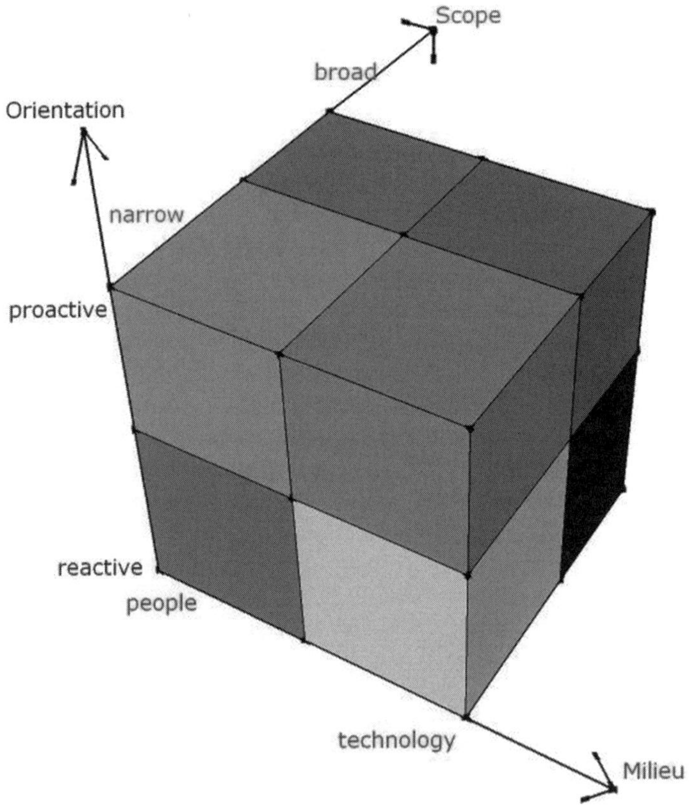

Figure 12.1. Generic Knowledge Strategies

and distribute organizational knowledge. These organizations tend to make great use of knowledge bases, intranets, and possibly expert systems or other knowledge-bearing tools to retain and leverage organizational knowledge. Organizations on the other side of the axis value more the development of human knowledge and might be more inclined to provide extensive training for their employees or make use of mentoring or apprenticeships to help spread tacit knowledge. As with any business situation, there are myriad variations on this and the other strategic variables.

The second axis deals with the organization's orientation toward the development or acquisition of knowledge. Firms that intend to make knowledge development a key part of a strategy meant to gain market share by releasing innovative new products or services, or for whom newly created knowledge is a product unto itself, will likely follow a more proactive knowledge strategy. Organizations whose strategy involves a more conservative approach to product or technology development, preferring to let others take the risk and cost of development, will be more likely to follow a more reactive knowledge strategy.

Finally, those organizations whose knowledge needs tend to center on areas of knowledge directly relatable to current and near future operations are considered to follow a narrow scope knowledge strategy, while those that tend to look beyond current knowledge needs in the hope of finding something useful for present operations or future opportunities will follow a broad scope knowledge strategy. Each of the boxes in the model designates certain combinations of these characteristics and has identifiable characteristics, strengths, and weaknesses, but their individual descriptions are beyond the scope of this chapter.

In the next section, each of these three knowledge strategy dimensions are examined in light of projects and their characteristics.

KNOWLEDGE STRATEGY COMPONENTS AND PROJECT CHARACTERISTICS

Each of the knowledge strategy dimensions put forth in the previous section has some impact on how projects operate. Specifically, certain knowledge strategy characteristics lend themselves to projects with specific characteristics or situations while others do not. In short, certain knowledge strategies are beneficial for certain types of projects while others are not. In this section, we explore each dimension in turn and identify the types of projects they might advantageously be associated with. It should be noted that these are not rules, but simply associations that have not yet been empirically analyzed.

Milieu

When comparing projects or firms across this dimension, it is tempting to convert these labels from technology/human knowledge to explicit/tacit knowledge. This would be a mistake and would cause the misrepresentation of organizational knowledge, which in the case of projects and project management is largely explicit in nature (Reich and Wee 2006). Though tacit knowledge plays a limited role in project management processes (i.e., lessons learned), that knowledge subject to knowledge management procedures is primarily explicit in nature, even if stored in the minds of the project member (Lierni and Ribière 2008).

Technology-Oriented Milieu

Projects that have made a significant investment in information technology (IT) are most likely to benefit from a more technically inclined knowledge strategy. This is not as tautological as it might seem. The well-equipped environment that the project exists in does not exist by accident. It is probably the result of decisions made by either the project management or parent organization management to spend sufficient resources on these tools, and that decision represents the knowledge strategy of the firm in practice. Thus, to take an approach counter to that would represent a departure from organizational norms and, therefore, would have to be appropriately justified.

Projects spanning significant geographical distances benefit from a technologically based knowledge strategy due to the difficulty of transferring knowledge over long distances. Sending computer files of documents or test results electronically is much more efficient than any other means, though we must be careful not to lean too heavily on technologically based communication when it is inappropriate. Care must be taken to ensure proper organizational processes are in place to facilitate these electronic conversations.

The distance between project members does not have to be geographical; it can be organizational as well. Project teams are often drawn from different parts of the organization or from different organizations. These organizational distances make knowledge sharing and application more difficult due to differences in nomenclature, norms, or standard procedures, not to mention the inevitable political issues that arise. A technologically oriented knowledge strategy might produce a more consistently worded and documented knowledge base, thereby reducing individualistic interpretations and conceptions that often arise with human-based knowledge bases. The route to higher levels of consistency consists of discipline in knowledge documentation and storage and substantial depth in the planning of the knowledge base. The less forethought put into knowledge base development and construction, the more likely that the knowledge base will fall victim to inconsistent knowledge content and presentation.

Projects extending between organizations bring with them added stress to the project knowledge base. In addition to those issues arising from the lack of a common language or nomenclature, firms bound together on a project might not find the arrangement altogether comfortable. In some cases, firms that are typically rivals will find themselves teamed on a project and, thus, forced to share organizational knowledge to some degree. The sharing of this knowledge should be controlled to the extent possible, limiting its transference to that necessary to complete the project. Knowledge repositories that are technologically based can be controlled much more effectively than those in which the employee is responsible for personal knowledge access control.

Organizational distance also brings about differences in language, whether driven by different professional disciplines, industries, or countries. Translational requirements are dealt with more effectively when knowledge is technologically based than when it is human based by providing a consistent repository for translated or simplified works as well as providing limited translational services. Though humans are often the best translating tool, especially in a very specialized or technical field, the technical tools used to store knowledge provide a useful method for disseminating translated works consistently and efficiently.

Staged projects are defined as those with varied sets of deliverables due on successive dates, and phased rollout projects have similar deliverables produced over time and/or in different locations (Bower and Walker 2007). In both cases, these projects are likely to involve differing staff throughout their lives, either because of their extended time frame, variable products, or distributed locations. When projects extend over a long time period, personnel turnover is almost unavoidable; therefore, so is knowledge turnover. This is not an artifact of projects alone; organizations of all types face similar challenges. However, project situations, even those of extended duration, face additional challenges due to their relative brevity and isolation that impose potentially larger penalties on employee turnover. Even without considering the issue of employee turnover, projects spread out over a long time face the loss of knowledge due to its very nature. Knowledge that is new or seldom used will not have been committed to the organizational memory and, thus, should be recorded in such a manner that it will not be subject to faulty memories, individual perceptions, or other temporally based threats.

The *Guide to the Project Management Body of Knowledge* (PMBOK) describes the need to capture project lessons learned throughout the life of the project to be of use by future projects (Project Management Institute [PMI] 2004). It is much more effective to capture these lessons and operational knowledge as they occur during the course of the project rather than waiting for the "postmortem" at the end of the project. Project personnel, especially the really valuable ones, tend to get reassigned to other projects or tasks, even before the current assignment is complete. Those that remain might have other project duties to tend to, might not remember the things they have learned, or if they do, these issues might not seem as urgent or important now that the flames have subsided. Knowledge captured at the end of a project, especially one with significant complexity or that has been plagued with problems (which are the projects that produce the most useful knowledge), will often be undocumented, incomplete, or biased, or contain relatively little detail. Capturing knowledge when and where it is created is certainly the most effective, but least convenient, approach to gathering these lessons learned. Technology can assist in this task by providing an easy-to-use method (i.e., electronic forms, audio or video files, or automatic document archiving) for gathering and organizing project management knowledge for future use.

Projects following a technologically oriented approach to knowledge storage and management tend to have a lower threshold for knowledge ownership, simply due to the potential for increased knowledge usage when it exists on the intranet, for instance, than when it remains locked up in an individual's or department's knowledge base. Within the boundaries set for access control by interorganizational requirements, noted above, knowledge stored technologically is much easier to share and leverage. But without the organizational willingness to do so, this knowledge base is likely not being used to its full potential. Thus, organizational preferences and tendencies must be aligned with the technology employed in order to fully extend the usefulness of project knowledge.

People-Oriented Milieu

Unlike projects that are staged or phased in nature, "big bang" projects typically deliver their output all at once and to one customer (Bower and Walker 2007). In these types of projects, human-based knowledge might prove more useful and less cumbersome to manage. Knowledge is necessary throughout the project timeline, which is less likely to be interrupted by phase or product changes, thereby reducing the amount of time during which knowledge is likely to escape or evaporate. The project is more likely to be geographically centralized in nature, thereby reducing the need to transfer knowledge over long distances. Most importantly, the deliverables are likely to be less diverse, requiring a more narrowly defined knowledge base. Knowledge requirements such as these are more conducive to a human-based knowledge system. Knowledge requirements in these situations tend to be more focused and intense, especially as the project nears its conclusion. Though technology can do many things with knowledge storage and application, the human mind is still the best tool for rapid knowledge acquisition, organization, and application, especially within the confines of a project environment.

As discussed previously, projects that are staffed across organizational lines tend to find technological tools useful in communicating knowledge between these organizations. Conversely, projects that stem from one organization or a few with common views and knowledge bases tend to benefit from knowledge strategies that promote human-based knowledge. In this setting, knowledge is more easily shared, and thus new knowledge is more easily created. This is not to say that technology cannot play a role in managing knowledge in these situations as well, but human-based knowledge can play an important role that is much less likely when the project requires multiple, disparate organizations to work together.

The use of human-based knowledge development and application is especially advantageous when the employees working with this knowledge are given sufficient time to completely master and understand the knowledge in their care. Projects with some amount of slack time tend to promote improved knowledge capabilities (Haas 2006). Though slack time on a project is sometimes viewed as a waste or an opportunity to reallocate resources, management teams with a humancentric knowledge strategy might recognize this as an opportunity to build upon already existing knowledge reserves or to leverage existing organizational knowledge to further improve project performance. In either case, projects that continually run with no slack, or at a time deficit, leave very little time to engage the knowledge development processes inherent in project personnel.

By their very nature, all projects involve some level of ambiguity and risk (PMI 2004). However, when the levels of ambiguity of product or process reach a certain point, organizations with a human-centered knowledge strategy might have an advantage. Humans have a much higher capacity to understand the ambiguous nature of complex and dynamic environments and are then better positioned to address these obstacles if the organization has made their personal knowledge base a priority. Organizations that put resources into personnel development and education might be better able to react to dynamic environments, thus providing better performance in the face of ill-defined project goals and pathways (Kasten 2006).

Project risk can be looked at in a similar manner. Risk involves the uncertainty of whether and how external factors might impact the project. The analysis of the likelihood of certain risk factors' occurring, the impact of those risk factors on project performance if they should occur, and what the risk factors are in the first place can all be highly ambiguous concepts. As such, humans with well-developed personal knowledge bases are best equipped to address these risk analyses.

In order for human-based knowledge to be effective, certain organizational variables must be in place. The organizational culture must be conducive to individual knowledge creation and application. Organizational culture can, in some instances, slow or stop the use of organizational knowledge, whether technology or human based, from becoming an organizational and competitive asset (Ajmal and Koskinen 2008). Therefore, it is important both that organizational culture promote the importance of organizational knowledge and learning, and that the culture, as well as formal organizational processes, encourage the development of whatever social relationships are necessary to encourage the growth and spread of organizational knowledge. Research into the concept of "Ba" has demonstrated the importance of culture and social relationships on the success of organizational knowledge creation and application processes (Nonaka and Konno 1998).

Organizational cultures that emphasize individual or departmental knowledge ownership might also benefit from a human-centered knowledge strategy. Knowledge embedded in the human resources of the firm tends to be more personal and intimate in nature, thus fostering the feeling of ownership. Many organizations are trying to free themselves from the concept of knowledge ownership in the belief that freely flowing knowledge encourages innovation and creativity. However, human nature being what it is, employees can still maintain ties to knowledge they have developed or acquired, and in these instances human-centered knowledge provides some level of support. It is unlikely that a project manager can, within the context of the project, change this organizational sentiment, so he or she must work within the confines of the prevailing culture. Thus, a human-based knowledge strategy might be more effective until the staff can be convinced of the benefits of knowledge sharing.

Orientation

Organizations and the projects run within them must choose to be either proactive in their search for knowledge or be content to acquire it secondhand, that is, not to be the developer of new knowledge but rather the applicator of existing knowledge. Firms following a proactive knowledge strategy tend to invest more heavily in research and development and be more willing to develop or acquire industry-changing knowledge in the hopes of gaining a competitive advantage. Reactive firms tend not to be market leaders, but rather exploiters of knowledge first developed by others. Examples of these types of firms abound: the second (and subsequent) bank to introduce ATMs, the second (and subsequent) package carrier to introduce electronic devices to capture package delivery data, or the second (and subsequent) supermarket to scan grocery items at checkout. Projects must also choose whether to develop knowledge or react to the knowledge developed by others. As with the technology/human dimension, there are almost infinite positions for project management to take, but we will examine the endpoints of the continuum here.

Proactive Knowledge Development

Without question, projects that exist to create knowledge or seek to leverage knowledge as their goal must pursue a proactive, or even aggressive, knowledge development orientation. But there exist other project characteristics that complement a proactive knowledge strategy. Projects that battle high levels of ambiguity often benefit from increased knowledge of the project domain, process, or environment. The removal of ambiguity is not always possible and not always productive. From ambiguity, we often derive inspiration and direction, and it can even act as a deterrent to competitors. However, increased knowledge, especially knowledge derived by the project team or acquired specifically for the project at hand, can help project management understand the ambiguities ahead and plot a course through them.

For similar reasons, projects facing substantial risks benefit from active knowledge creation or acquisition processes, as appropriate knowledge can reduce risk profiles and increase the number and effectiveness of tools available to deal with risk factors. Projects with unique deliverables or processes also depend upon proactive knowledge strategies because, by their very nature, there is little knowledge already in existence that pertains directly to them. Their uniqueness demands unique, or, at a minimum, specific knowledge to be acquired and applied.

The existence of a proactive knowledge strategy requires a level of competence and maturity from the project management that might not be necessary when knowledge requirements are not so demanding. Proactive knowledge strategies require a disciplined approach to knowledge that might be difficult to adhere to in the often chaotic project environment. The active acquisition of knowledge means that a balance must be struck between knowledge acquisition/development activities (research, experimentation, etc.) and the other, more mundane project activities such as documentation and budget control. Also, the costs of knowledge acquisition processes must be constantly measured against their benefits. These call for more advanced and mature project management capabilities.

Reactive Knowledge Strategies

As might be expected, a reactive knowledge strategy better supports projects without knowledge-based activities at their core. These projects utilize well-understood and available knowledge in both their project domains and project processes. A reactive knowledge strategy is also better suited to those projects with reduced levels of ambiguity and risk, and usually fit better with projects that are not based on a unique deliverable or process.

Project management teams that are new to project management or have not had an opportunity to build a great deal of trust or cohesion within the project management team are more likely to succeed in a reactive knowledge environment. The stresses inherent in knowledge creation activities seem to find the weak points in management teams of any level of maturity, but new or immature project management teams are particularly susceptible to them. Last, reactive knowledge strategies are more suited to projects with very restricted budgets, especially those in which there is little funding available or allotted to contingency planning. The cost of proactive knowledge acquisition can be high and unpredictable.

Scope

The nature of projects demands that knowledge acquisition be almost exclusively narrow in scope. Projects exist to accomplish one or a few very specific objectives, thus their knowledge needs should also remain very specific. This is especially true as the risks or uniqueness of a project's deliverables and/or processes increase. The only possible exception to this notion is the project with very high levels of ambiguity. Depending on the nature of these ambiguities as well as their intensity, project managers might find that opening the scope of knowledge acquisition could turn up knowledge that, while not immediately obvious as being applicable, can eventually lead to a reduction in uncertainty. In these circumstances, project managers should remember to look for applicable knowledge in other industries, divisions, or projects for knowledge that was developed for other purposes but might be applicable, even groundbreaking, for the problem at hand.

APPROACHING PROJECT KM

In order for a project manager to proceed toward the development of a KM system that supports the needs of both the project and the organization it exists in, a few important steps must be taken or at least attempted. These steps have to do with the project, the organization, and the knowledge involved.

First, it is important that a project manager try to identify and understand the knowledge strategy of the organization in question. This can be a significant challenge for a number of reasons. As mentioned previously, the knowledge strategy of an organization is seldom formalized, waiting on a shelf for the project manager to consult. It is much more likely that the organization's knowledge strategy is an informal, emergent entity that must be understood in the context of the organization's management structure and processes. Understanding the knowledge strategy is difficult enough for a seasoned professional with years of experience in the firm, but very difficult for the less experienced PM. The trend toward external project management teams exacerbates this situation because of the project management team's separation from the parent organization.

Given the propensity for projects to be formed around consortia or joint ventures, the knowledge strategies involved might span multiple organizations, thus complicating further the task of understanding the knowledge strategies involved. Rather than analyzing each of the participating firms, which would probably prove impossible due to schedule, budget, and access restrictions, the PM should determine which of these partners is a major provider or consumer of knowledge and then attempt to understand their knowledge strategies.

At the same time, the project management team should look inward to understand the project's knowledge needs, internal characteristics, and whether the project already has its own knowledge strategy. It is not unusual for subunits of a firm to develop their own knowledge strategies, though these should not stray too far from those of the parent firm. Project managers should ask themselves whether they have demonstrated a tendency to treat knowledge in a certain way, to create or develop knowledge rather than acquire it, or to address knowledge in a predictable manner that, when viewed over time, can be considered a knowledge strategy. This can be difficult for managers to see for themselves, and they might find that an external entity will provide a valuable perspective.

An understanding of the knowledge strategies involved, coupled with the project's knowledge requirements, leads to the possible creation of a project knowledge management system. The characteristics of the KM system should align with these variables. Though that alignment is often difficult to obtain or measure, we can illuminate this relationship with some hypothetical examples. Consider a project that exists within an organization whose knowledge strategy is characterized by a strong attachment to technology-enabled knowledge storage coupled with an aggressive approach to knowledge development and acquisition. The KM system that results from this combination should be comprehensive in its knowledge holdings as well as embody a strong search and retrieval mechanism. The comprehensive nature of its holdings can be interpreted both as its depth, in order to provide knowledge to the level necessary by project participants, and its breadth, thereby fulfilling the knowledge needs of a substantial percentage of project participants. Both of these characteristics are consistent with the system's strong search capabilities, as these should be available for both internal and external knowledge sources. Internal knowledge sources must be well cataloged and indexed, thus improving the system's ability to retrieve documents and other knowledge objects with high levels of precision and recall. External knowledge search capabilities must include the ability to search external knowledge sources both interactively and automatically, continually searching for knowledge that fits the project's knowledge profile, thus contributing to the KM system's depth and breadth.

A firm with a knowledge strategy on the opposite side of the spectrum, with its emphasis on human-centered knowledge storage and development and a more passive approach to knowledge acquisition, would have a somewhat different approach to knowledge management, though not as radically different as might be supposed. These organizations will lean heavily upon internal and external training to ensure their employees are well equipped with knowledge, and the KM system should be configured as a training tool more than as a development tool. This might require a different method of organizing the knowledge in the system or a change in its interface. Knowledge organized for educational purposes often has more intuitive finding aids to support the learning process and will also present knowledge in a method to enhance the synthesis of knowledge, such as using alternate formats (e.g., videos). The search capability of the system, especially the external search capability, must be as robust as that of the previous example to facilitate the location of knowledge developed elsewhere. This firm has decided to follow the rest of the industry, but to do so it must continually scan the knowledge landscape to identify the knowledge it must assimilate to remain viable in the industry. To follow effectively, the firm must maintain a knowledge base that keeps pace with evolving knowledge.

CONCLUSION

Project managers might have little influence over the knowledge strategy of the organization within which a project is domiciled, but knowing what the knowledge strategy is can help align the knowledge requirements of the project and management team with the capabilities of the organization. Understanding how the organization treats the acquisition and development of knowledge should influence which projects are undertaken, how they are managed, and by whom. Differences in how knowledge is pursued, where (or in whom) it is stored, and what it consists of, each aligns with different types of project complexity, risk, length, organization, and management processes. If these alignments can be understood before project launch, it could lead to more successful project outcomes.

REFERENCES

Ajmal, Mian M., and Kaj U. Koskinen. 2008. Knowledge transfer in project-based organizations: An organizational culture perspective. *Project Management Journal* 39 (1): 7–15.

Bower, Douglas C., and Derek H. T. Walker. 2007. Planning knowledge for phased rollout projects. *Project Management Journal* 38 (3): 45–60.

Haas, Martine R. 2006. Knowledge gathering, team capabilities, and project performance in challenging work environments. *Management Science* 52 (8): 1170–1184.

Kasten, Joseph E. 2006. Knowledge strategy drivers: An exploratory study. PhD diss., Long Island University.

Kasten, Joseph E. 2009. Knowledge strategy and its role in the organization: An exploratory study. *International Journal of Knowledge Management* 5 (3): 38–53.

Lierni, Peter C., and Vincent M. Ribière. 2008. The relationship between improving the management of projects and the use of KM. *VINE: The Journal of Information and Knowledge Management Systems* 38 (1): 133–146.

Nonaka, I., and N. Konno. 1998. The concept of "Ba": Building a foundation for knowledge creation. *California Management Review* 40 (3): 40–54.

Project Management Institute. 2004. *A Guide to the Project Management Body of Knowledge* (3rd ed.). Newtown Square, PA: Project Management Institute.

Reich, Blaize Horner, and Siew Yong Wee. 2006. Searching for knowledge in the PMBOK Guide. *Project Management Journal* 37 (2): 11–27.

13

The Role of Organizational Storytelling in Successful Project Management

Kate Marek

In their book *The Social Life of Information* (2000), John Seely Brown and Paul Duguid relate an experience within Xerox Corporation, where the company's leadership was searching for ways to significantly improve the photocopier maintenance function of the organization. Since the company was in the business of photocopier manufacture and upkeep, this was a significant portion of their operation. The general project assignment was to create a new, more efficient work process by designing an expert system, which would be tested and refined over a period of some months before it was launched and all technicians were retrained. The plan mirrored long-standing assumptions from scientific management theories originated in the early twentieth century by Frederick Winslow Taylor (1947); the approach involved scientific study of methods and operations and subsequent standardization, which would then produce the most effective workflow results.

But early in the pursuit of a scientific solution, the experts uncovered an unexpected alternative. A more rigorous and streamlined approach to copier repair and maintenance issues would most likely have little to no effect on the efficiency of the operation. What was needed, they discovered, was more breaks for photocopier technicians. Not just sit-down, get-off-your-feet breaks. What really increased effective maintenance practices was the kind of break where the technicians sat around and had coffee together. They needed more opportunities to share stories.

While photocopier repair narratives may not seem to fit the standard definition of a story (which would include a main character, a plot, a challenge or conflict, and some kind of resolution), one can see how this kind of story could indeed generate quite a bit of interest to someone who held challenges in his or her own daily work life. A retelling of a troubling challenge and the resolution of that challenge would resonate well with someone who might meet that same problem in an upcoming situation and who therefore had a vested interest in listening to tales of success. That listener might never dream of spending time reading yet another manual with diagrams and technical details, and indeed that storyteller's knowledge might never even make it into print. A story can teach, generate, and extend community and can create a common bond among listeners.

This vignette, in itself a story, illustrates an emerging awareness in management theory regarding the power of narrative in the workplace. At its core, project management is all about getting the job done. Pretty straightforward, it seems. It doesn't necessarily require vision, as the project has already been defined within the context of an existing vision. Creativity in itself is not necessarily valued, as too much improvisation may actually derail a project plan. But what *is* necessary for a successful project is human communication and interaction. Along the project's life path, the manager will deal with a variety of people, each of whom may have a stake in the project but may also have his or her own work issues and agendas, perhaps even counterproductive to the project. What a good project needs is a good, unified team. Creating that team is essential. The project manager must get people on board and keep them on board throughout the life of the project. This chapter will investigate one important mechanism for making that happen: the use of organizational storytelling.

WHAT IS ORGANIZATIONAL STORYTELLING?

Organizational storytelling is at once both extremely simple and yet full of complexity and nuance. It can be as simple as an old saying ("The early bird gets the worm") or as detailed and technical as a photocopier technician's description of a sticky repair problem. It's an effort to find a new way to communicate in business, going back to rediscover ancient communication skills that we have systematically marginalized in the workplace. In our industrialized, "just the facts" culture of the nineteenth and twentieth centuries, and then in our hyperautomated society of the past several decades, we have valued logic over intuition, science over improvisation, and numbers over words. Organizational storytelling does not seek to eliminate logic, science, or numbers, but rather to reintroduce the power of narrative to business communication. Countless issues in the workplace involve human interaction and communication; in these situations, stories about real people in real places consistently communicate more effectively than charts, spreadsheets, and diagrams.

THE ZAMBIA STORY

One of the leaders in organizational storytelling is Stephen Denning, who for many years worked in the top levels of management at the World Bank. Denning (2001, 2005, 2007) regularly writes about his own experiences with the use of stories to help steer a new vision of knowledge management at the World Bank in the late 1990s.

As Denning tells the story (2005), the World Bank in 1996 had recently been through a significant change in leadership. As part of the fallout, Denning had been reassigned from his international work to the area of "information" in the firm, a fuzzy and not terribly respected division, in a fairly transparent attempt by higher management to get him out of the way or encourage him to resign. But Denning stuck it out, and indeed he began to see the critical value of information in an emerging era of global knowledge sharing. Denning saw the potential for an international World Bank presence beyond just lending money to developing countries.

If the World Bank could develop and share knowledge resources, its position for twenty-first-century service would be guaranteed.

Denning's resulting dilemma, however, was to get this point across to the top management and ultimately to the organization as a whole. Incorporating knowledge management into the World Bank's mission would require a huge philosophical and psychological shift at all levels of the organization. Through his trial-and-error efforts to generate interest in knowledge management, Denning discovered the power of telling stories about real people in real situations. Denning gave examples, if you will, but fleshed out those examples with just enough substance to generate excitement among his listeners.

Denning's initial success came from his Zambia story. This story relates the experiences of medical workers in Zambia who needed good health information, and they needed it quickly. Denning began telling this story in 1996:

> In June of last year, a health worker in a tiny town of Zambia went to the Web site of the Centers of Disease Control and got the answer to a question about the treatment of malaria. Remember that this was in Zambia, one of the poorest countries in the world, and it was in a tiny place six hundred kilometers from the capital city. But the most striking thing about this picture, at least for us, is that the World Bank isn't in it. Despite our know-how on all kinds of poverty-related issues, that knowledge isn't available to the millions of people who could use it. Imagine if it were. Think what an organization we would become. (Denning, 2005, p. 4)

Denning used that story in a variety of iterations to help the leaders of the World Bank see an emerging need, the inability of the World Bank in its current structure to participate in fulfilling that need, and the potential of knowledge management as an important twenty-first-century corporate strategy to respond to the need. That story was more effective than piles of charts, graphs, and mission statements. It generated ideas without being too specific or too fuzzy. It was a masterpiece of communication.

So what it is about a simple story that can be so effective in an organizational setting? As we think about using this technique at the project management level, it is useful to look more deeply at the variety of applications and techniques of narrative in the workplace. Then we can match aspects of workplace narrative to the specific needs of effective project management.

THE POWER OF STORY

Our standard business narrative, when done well, does a good job of engaging us on an intellectual level. But to really connect with people and inspire them to action, we must go beyond the intellectual and actually touch their emotions. Screenwriter coach Robert McKee says that we can persuade through reason, but that's not good enough

> because people are not inspired to act by reason alone. The other way to reach people—and ultimately a much more powerful way—is by uniting an idea with an emotion. The best way to do that is by telling a compelling story. In a story, you not only weave a lot

> of information into the telling but you also arouse your listener's emotions and energy. ("Storytelling That Moves People," p. 52)

Jerome Bruner describes classic narratives as "templates for experience" (Bruner, 2002, p. 35), calling to mind the universal understanding achieved through stories. Annette Simmons calls storytelling a "pull" strategy rather than a "push" strategy, such as persuasion, bribery, or charismatic appeals (2006, p. 5). Noel Tichy, author of *The Leadership Engine*, writes that all effective leaders have a variety of teachable points of view, but that "these points of view can't just be dry intellectual concepts. To be effective, leaders have to bring them alive so that people can and will act on them. Stories are a powerful tool for doing just that" (p. 43). And Howard Gardner (1996, 2006) speaks of the leader's "story" as an essential part of his or her ability to lead at any given time in history.

Stories have been used throughout history to teach, to share values, and to communicate vision. Great religious leaders such as Jesus and Muhammad were well known to use stories, as are great political leaders (for both good and ill). In American history, we know that Abraham Lincoln, Franklin Roosevelt, John F. Kennedy, Lyndon Johnson, and Ronald Reagan were all master storytellers. Barack Obama's ability to tell stories effectively is one of his greatest communication strengths.

So if storytelling connects us to ideas and to each other, and if it sparks us to action, how can it be used beneficially within the context of effective project management? One good way to approach this is to use a well-articulated project management model and apply specific types of storytelling at each point in the model.

PROJECT MANAGEMENT: APPLYING THE MODEL

Jim Lewis, in his *Fundamentals of Project Management* (2002), defines a project as a "multitask job that has performance, time, cost, and scope requirements and that's done only one time" (p. 2). Lewis calls projects more schedule intensive than regular organizational management. Bringing the various elements of a project together within the target timeline and budget requires careful planning at the outset, before the actual management of the project even begins. Since a key element of projects in an organization is the team-based nature of the work, it is critical that the project manager recognize the value of buy-in from the team members and bring them in at the planning stage for full participation. "Scheduling is certainly a major tool used to manage projects, but it is not nearly as important as developing a shared understanding of what the project is supposed to accomplish" (Lewis, p. 5).

Along these same lines, project management consultants Lewis and Wysocki (2001) emphasize the importance of good communication and interpersonal skills in the successful project manager. Without the ability to motivate and encourage a wide diversity of people, the project simply won't get done. Indeed, Lewis (2002, pp. 2–3) cites alarmingly high rates of project failure or cancellation. How can good project management make a positive difference in the success rate of a project? Through people skills, say Wysocki and Lewis (2001):

> Project managers often have considerable responsibility, yet seldom have any authority over the people on their project teams. This means that the only way they will get

anything done is through the exercise of influence, persuasion, negotiation, and maybe a little begging at times. (p. 37)

STORYTELLING WITHIN THE PROJECT LIFE CYCLE

Lewis (2002) identifies the following phases of a successful project: concept, definition, planning, execution, and closeout. For the project to stay healthy, each of these phases must be appropriately developed and executed, and a good project manager has a range of tools for each stage. Stories can be an important part of that set of tools.

Different stages of the project require different kinds of inspiration and motivation, and thus different kinds of stories. Denning (2001, 2005) has identified a variety of types of organizational stories that are appropriate in different situations. For example, Denning (2001) uses what he calls "springboard stories" to "catalyze understanding." A springboard story, he says, "enables a leap in understanding by the audience so as to grasp how an organization or community or complex system may change" (p. xviii). Thus, a springboard story would be an excellent tool for the concept stage of the project.

Other types of stories as defined by Denning include those that motivate to action, inspire trust, build brands, instill values, create collaborative spirit, transmit knowledge, neutralize gossip, and lead toward the future. Simmons (2006) and Kahane (2007) are two of the many authors who also stress the power of story to influence others. The remainder of this chapter will match Lewis's project phases to appropriate types of stories as developed by Denning and others. This will provide project managers with a template for using stories effectively to successfully lead a project team through the various ups and downs of the project phases. Table 13.1 presents Lewis's project phases (2002, pp. 9–16) alongside actions and appropriate types of stories for each stage.

As you read about the suggested stories, think in terms of very short vignettes. Telling stories may seem quite difficult, but it can be simple, and indeed when using narrative in the workplace, thoughtfully constructed, simple stories are the best kind. For example, review the Zambia story from early in this chapter. When told aloud, that story will take only one to two minutes. The impact of the story does not come from its complexity or its length, but from the shared experience it can convey.

PHASE 1: CONCEPT

Lewis identifies marketing input and survey of the competition as the central activities of this phase of the project. Environmental scanning is another example of an ongoing organizational activity that would produce new ideas and new concepts for products and services. Results from the surveys and scans might indicate a need for innovative products, new services, or a significant change in organizational direction. At this point, managers may or may not actually have been assigned to a specific project, but whoever is in charge will need to inspire people toward new di-

Table 13.1. A Guide to Story Creation and Selection, Based on Elements of the Project Phase

Project Phase	*Phase Activity*	*Type of Story and its Characteristics*	*Desired Listener Response*
Concept • The vision/big idea	• Listen to external signals • Spark action	• Springboard stories • Stories to transmit values	• Inspiration • Shared understanding
Definition • Begin to follow the leader • Visualize and articulate the desired result of the project • Connect this project to the organization as a whole and codify its importance • Come to a consensus among the group as to the exact problem statement	• Build trust • Organizational branding • Consensus building	• "Who I am" stories: Communicating who you are as a leader • Branding stories: Communicating who the company is and how this project fits overall • Stories that influence	• Leader identification and trust • Connection to the bigger picture • Shared commitment; project buy-in
Planning • Develop strategies and timelines; identify resources, logistics, and tactics	• Team building	• Stories that foster collaboration • Stories that stimulate thinking outside the box	• Creating high-performance teams • Allowing for creative problem solving for effective strategies
Execution • Begin work • Respond to challenges and changes	• Implementation • Day-to-day productivity	• Stories that tame the grapevine • Stories that motivate • Stories that influence	• Team remains cohesive • Retention of focus on tasks • Motivated and inspired workers
Closeout • Celebrations • Review • Look ahead	• Evaluation and assessment • Winding down to think about what's next	• Stories that celebrate • Stories that review lessons learned • Stories that lead toward the future • Springboard stories	• Create mutual recognition and shared closure • Create imagination and excitement toward future projects with potential positive impacts for the organization and the customers

rections. Denning's Zambia story is an example of a story that would be considered appropriate here. It is an example of a springboard story, which enables listeners to visualize large-scale transformation and then act on that realization (Denning, 2001). This kind of story is intended to spark action and should describe a successful real-life change from the past while at the same time allowing listeners to imagine a similar success in their own situation. The story should not be too detailed, and it might contain phrases such as "What if . . ." or "Just imagine if. . . ."

This is also a phase to transmit or reinforce the organization's values. A company may post wall signs that proclaim "Let's love our work and enjoy the journey" as a morale booster, but posting the signs can't match the power of a company story relating the time the company president showed up in an Abe Lincoln costume, or the cultural lore of the annual picnic. Denning says stories that transmit values can communicate how things are done in an organization and can be effective when presented as a parable or an event from the past as mentioned above. Another effective type of story for transmitting values is what Denning calls the branding story, which is described in detail in the following section.

PHASE 2: DEFINITION

The definition stage, according to Lewis, is where most projects fail. Pitfalls such as unclear problem definition or disagreements among team members on the statement's interpretation can kill a project before it ever launches. Thus, it is essential that a clear problem statement, vision statement, and mission statement all come out of this stage of the process. It is important now for the project manager to begin to build trust from the team members and to establish her leadership so that she can effectively lead the team through the work of crafting the problem, vision, and mission statements and then achieve consensus and buy-in across the team.

Stories that build trust for the leader can be called "who I am" or "why I am here" stories. Even brief vignettes from the leader's past professional or personal experience can help build relationships and trust. Denning reinforces the value of sharing a strength or vulnerability from one's past, and Gardner (2006) argues that a leader's story is an essential part of his potential to influence. Restaurateur Danny Meyer, famous for his successful New York City restaurants, does a wonderful job of this in his book *Setting the Table* (2008). In telling his own story, Meyer reveals both his successes and his failures and indicates that he actively shares personal life experiences in his daily business life. For example, he writes about opening his first restaurant, the Union Square Cafe. "I struggled mightily with the emotional and technical skills required for . . . leadership as a twenty-seven-year-old first-time leader of my own company" (p. 187). Meyer tells numerous stories of mentors that helped him along the way as he sometimes struggled with management and leadership issues.

Or, if the leader is not comfortable sharing part of his own life, even a short retelling of a story from history, something from the news, or a fable can be effective if it truly reveals part of the leader's personality and values. Simmons writes:

> When a person tells a story about Mother Teresa that reveals that he understands gratitude and the humility of learning from others, we can conclude he is not bound by ego

> and can be trusted to listen to what we have to say. If the story he chooses to tell reveals that he understands self-sacrifice, we feel he can be trusted to blend compassion with desire for self-gain. When we see through a story that someone has learned to recognize his own flaws and not hide in denial, we assume he can be trusted to deal head-on with tough issues rather than pretend things are "just fine." (2001, p. 10–11)

Another type of story effective at this stage of the project is what Denning calls the branding story, or a story that communicates who the company is.

> Just as individuals need trust if they are to lead, so companies need trust if their products and services are to succeed in the marketplace. For customers [*and employees*] to trust a company and its products, they have to know what sort of company they are dealing with, what kinds of values it espouses, and how its people approach meeting customers' needs. (Denning, 2005, p. 14)

A legendary example is the quick, aggressive, and empathetic response of Johnson & Johnson to the 1982 Chicago area Tylenol poisonings, when Tylenol capsules were laced with potassium cyanide and placed back into unsold pill bottles. The story of the Johnson & Johnson leadership's response to this crisis has become a standard model to illustrate company values and branding. While the company lost millions of dollars in the ensuing product recall, it gained decades of positive customer loyalty in a scenario that could have produced the opposite effect if it had been handled poorly. And, it should be noted, the company's response was not based on a cynical read of the more positive ROI of one response over the other, but was a true reflection of the company's values. Stories that are true carry the most impact, and stories that are not true will certainly come back to haunt you.

Stories that influence have applications throughout the life of a project, and they are especially useful at this definition stage of the project. One of the great secrets of influence is to let a person decide for himself what to do; stories can pull someone in rather than force him in. The command and control method of leadership, which can be conceptualized as the "look up, and shout down" method of communication, only serves to alienate people and to make them defensive. People are much more likely to join in if that joining has been their own decision. Stories of influence are caught up in many of the other types of stories—for example, the "who I am" and "why I'm here" stories are preludes to influence, as they create a foundation of trust and relationship from which influence can emerge.

PHASE 3: PLANNING

A key element to successful planning is building an effective team. To foster collaboration, team members must talk to one another. Easier said than done! Using exercises where each team member shares something from his own background (a variation of the "why I am here" story) will provide opportunities for relationship building that will have lasting value for team cohesiveness. And it is essential here to also state the importance of "story listening"—listening to shared stories, as well as contributing a story of one's own, truly builds community. Denning suggests an approach that generates a common narrative around the project's specific goals, starting with one team member's contribution, which generates more stories from the team. "The first story must be emotionally moving enough to unleash the narrative impulse in others and to create a readiness to hear more stories. It could, for example, vividly describe how the speaker had grappled with a difficult work situation" (2005, p. 15). When embarking on this kind of exercise, Denning stresses the importance of an open agenda that does not cut off the developing cooperative narrative. Phrases to begin this kind of story are "That reminds me of the time I . . ." or "Yes, I've had that experience myself. . . ."

Despite efforts to build strong teams, however, project managers may find that all team members are not contributing at the level expected. Learning through a good story can also help managers build skills and understanding.

A fascinating story about team building comes from Malcolm Gladwell (2008), where he explores the decision-making factors involved in selecting professional football quarterbacks and high-quality teachers. Gladwell weaves together two stories from practice (one professional football scout and a teacher evaluation study from the University of Virginia) to very effectively illustrate his ultimate point: you hire good-quality people, put them through rigorous apprenticeships and evaluations, and cut the underperformers. Predictors for success are fuzzy, and those who seem to be the best candidates just may not turn out to be the best performers. Starting the hiring process with the knowledge that as few as 20 percent of the new hires will become permanent team members dramatically shifts the recruitment and retention paradigm, which Gladwell demonstrates to be a much more realistic long-term strategy. This theory is supported by a great deal of complex research, but through the use of storytelling Gladwell presents a very compelling and convincing argument; reading his essay gives project managers a great deal of insight into high-level team building.

The planning phase of the project also involves identifying tactics. Lewis (2002) encourages thinking outside the box at this stage of the project, particularly in regard to brainstorming strategies. An effective story for illustrating the value of innovative thinking is one Lewis relates specifically in regard to replacing outdated strategies for ship manufacture at the time of the Second World War:

> During World War II, defense contractors were under great pressure to build weaponry at an intense level. To accelerate construction of ships and planes in particular, many new assembly methods were invented. Avondale shipyards, for example, worked on finding better ways to build ships. The traditional way had always been to build the ship in an upright position. However, ships built from steel required welding in the bottom, or keel area of the boat, and this was very difficult to do in the traditional model. Avondale decided to build its ships upside down. (Lewis, p. 12)

One can see the power of this simple example of an experience from history, told as a success story of past radical thinking.

PHASE 4: EXECUTION

This phase is where the "real" work of the project gets done, although of course none of this can proceed if the first three steps have not been achieved. At this stage, the project is at risk of derailment due to all kinds of human errors and attitudes, ranging from boredom to exhaustion to sabotage. People come to project teams with their own agendas and backgrounds; in many cases, they come from disparate departments (and report to someone other than the project manager) and may not have the same overall organizational goals as the team itself. If good team building has taken place at earlier project stages, much of this can be avoided. But the project manager still needs to keep the team motivated and focused on the tasks at hand. Stories that will be effective at this stage are stories that motivate and stories that influence.

David Armstrong, in his book *Managing by Storying Around* (1992), tells the story of being inspired by another CEO to give immediate "thank you" gifts to employees who were caught in the act of contributing something special. Armstrong wanted to replicate the idea in his own company. "I started carrying a bunch of $5 bills, which I hand out when someone has done something extraordinary. I had thought about giving out $100 bills, but realized that could cause some problems. If I gave out hundreds, there was bound to be jealousy or resentment" (p. 40). Armstrong is known within his company to be a leader who frequently walks around visiting with employees, and his spontaneous $5 bill reward gifts turned into an internal story told and retold among workers. It was a great way to generate motivation and positive morale. Not everyone has the budget to distribute $5 reward gifts, but this example can encourage project managers to think of ways to generate positive internal stories that keep motivation high.

In addition, this is a time when rumors, always a threat to organizational cohesiveness, can be especially destructive. Denning recommends a specific type of story called "taming the grapevine" stories (2005, p. 15). Rumors can't be ignored, but openly denying them often has the opposite of the intended effect of squelching them. Denning suggests using a story to convince team members that the rumor is unreasonable and untrue.

> You could use gentle satire to mock the rumor, the rumor's author, or even yourself, in an effort to undermine the rumor's power. For example, you might deal with a false rumor of "imminent corporate-wide reorganization" by jokingly recounting how the front office's current struggles involving the seating chart for executive committee meetings would have to be worked out first. Keep in mind, though, that humor can backfire. Mean-spirited ridicule can generate a well-deserved backlash. (Denning, 2005, p. 16)

PHASE 5: CLOSEOUT

The successful completion of a project is a time for celebration and for evaluation. Lewis (2002) suggests a review of what was done well, what should be improved, and lessons learned. A successful project generates its own stories, including tales of individual eureka moments, serendipitous discovery, or comical missteps that led to an unexpected contribution. A new round of the team-building story-sharing exercise would be an excellent way to generate tales about the project in all of Lewis's three categories (what was done well, what should be improved, and lessons learned). Sitting around in an informal story-sharing session is much more likely to generate reflection than a boring PowerPoint presentation of timelines met and missed. An excellent plan would be to schedule a full afternoon's lunch and retreat, with team members charged to bring answers to "My favorite project moment was

. . ." or "I'll never forget the day that. . . ." Ground rules could be established regarding personal remarks, sarcasm, and other potentially destructive comments. Keep it positive, even when reviewing lessons learned.

Danny Meyer (2008) does a good job of reflecting on failures from a positive viewpoint. In *Setting the Table,* Meyer introduces a full chapter on well-handled mistakes with a story about his conversation with Stanley Marcus of Neiman Marcus fame. The men sat next to each other at a dinner one evening, and Meyer shared his frustrations about a new restaurant that was not opening as successfully as he had hoped. Meyer writes:

> "Opening this new restaurant," I said, "might be the worst mistake I've ever made." Stanley set his martini down, looked me in the eye, and said, "So you made a mistake. You need to understand something important. And listen to me carefully: The road to success is paved with mistakes well handled." (p. 220)

Meyer follows up this story with a metaphor of surfers and ocean waves. Mistakes are like waves: your success is not in how well you tame them, but in how well you ride them. Inviting a project team to acknowledge mistakes and discuss how they "rode the wave" is a great way for everyone to learn and to prepare for the next wave.

The final step is to generate stories that lead toward the future. Certainly the project stories from above will lay the groundwork for future narratives. Denning suggests that this preparation toward the next step is another important part of a leader's job and "can help take listeners from where they are now to where they need to be" (2005, p. 17). Stories about the future are, of course, speculative but should ring true enough to inspire the imagination of the listeners. The fact that the future is uncertain, however, can lead to fear of change, so this story must be as positive as possible. Listeners should be inspired and motivated, cycling back to the potential found in the springboard story.

John Kotter and Holger Rathgeber's 2005 best-selling book, *Our Iceberg Is Melting,* is a wonderful example of this kind of story. This allegory centers on a penguin community whose general sense is that things have always been quite good on their iceberg and therefore will continue to be quite good. Most members of the penguin community and its leadership see no need to look for signs of trouble on their iceberg, especially any that might generate significant change. Harvard Business School change guru Kotter and his colleague Rathgeber use the penguin story to illustrate Kotter's eight stages of successful change. In brief, the penguins go through a process of identifying and resolving an urgent need for change, ending up with a successful move to a more secure iceberg and a new attitude toward the future. Telling a brief version of this story could be a great addition to a successful project celebration. Handing out copies of the small book might be even more effective, with the simple admonition, "This has been a terrific success—but let's not be complacent. Read about the penguins and their melting iceberg!" Sharing stories in an organization can contribute to a systemwide understanding and a common culture.

LEARNING THE SKILL

While organizational storytelling may make sense on an intellectual level, many will feel that they themselves simply don't have the skills or the personality to be a successful storyteller. But this is an age-old skill buried in all of us. When you talk about your day to your spouse, tell a colleague about the home run last night at the ballpark, or tell a stranger why you're voting for a particular candidate, you are telling a story. Annette Simmons (2001) encourages "a daily practice" of telling small stories to become more comfortable with the process. She encourages looking for patterns, consequences, lessons, utility, and vulnerability in daily life and then thinking about how to turn something into a story. Simmons suggests also looking for the future experience, turning your daydreams into clearly articulated "what if" stories. She also mentions "story recollections"—find a story that you've loved or a powerful personal or professional memory that you can use to build a successful story.

All the experts emphasize the value of practice. Practice telling stories, and practice listening to stories. Take ideas from the examples in this chapter; use a small book such as *Our Iceberg is Melting,* find stories in biographies like *Setting the Table* or a more focused group of managerial stories such as *Managing by Walking Around.* Find stories in daily reading such as Gladwell's essays in *The New Yorker.* Whether you think of yourself as an introvert or an extrovert, a talker or a thinker, you can be an effective organizational storyteller. The key is to find ideas that connect, communicate, and inspire.

CONCLUSION

Project management is all about leading people through a process. To be successful, the project must be completed on time, within budget, and with a quality product or result. But effective project management goes beyond work breakdown structures, budget analysis, and time estimates. Just as the Xerox photocopier technicians needed more time to share stories, project managers and team members need to make time to share personal and professional stories at all stages of a job. The best project managers are those who enjoy working with a wide diversity of people and who can communicate well at every stage of the project process. Stories are a time-proven method of communication and are an essential tool for knowledge management. Organizational storytelling deserves prime space in the project manager's toolkit.

REFERENCES

Armstrong. D. M. (1992). *Managing by storying around.* New York: Doubleday.

Brown, J. S., Denning, S., Groh, K., & Prusak, L. (2005). *Storytelling in organizations: Why storytelling is transforming 21st century organizations and management.* Boston: Butterworth-Heinemann.

Brown, J. S., & Duguid, P. (2000). *The social life of information.* Boston: Harvard Business School Press.

Bruner, J. (2002). *Making stories: Laws, literature, life.* New York: Farrar, Straus and Giroux.

Denning, S. (2001). *The springboard: How storytelling ignites action in knowledge-era organizations.* Boston: Butterworth-Heinemann.

Denning, S. (2005). *The leader's guide to storytelling: Mastering the art and discipline of business narrative.* San Francisco: Jossey-Bass.

Denning, S. (2007). *The secret language of leadership: How leaders inspire action through narrative.* San Francisco: Jossey-Bass.
Gardner, H. (1996). *Leading minds: An anatomy of leadership.* New York: Basic Books.
Gardner, H. (2006). *Changing minds: The art and science of changing our own and other people's minds.* Boston: Harvard Business School Press.
Gladwell, M. (2008). Most likely to succeed: How do we hire when we can't tell who's right for the job? *The New Yorker, 84*(41), 36–46.
Kahane, A. (2007). *Solving tough problems: An open way of talking, listening, and creating new realities* (2nd ed.). San Francisco: Berrett-Koehler.
Kotter, J., & Rathgeber, H. (2005). *Our iceberg is melting: Changing and succeeding under any conditions.* New York: St. Martin's.
Lewis, J. P. (2002). *Fundamentals of project management: Developing core competencies to help outperform the competition* (2nd ed.). New York: AMACOM.
Meyer, D. (2008). *Setting the table: The transforming power of hospitality in business.* New York: HarperCollins.
Simmons, A. (2006). *The story factor: Inspiration, influence, and persuasion through the art of storytelling* (2nd ed.). New York: Basic Books.
Storytelling that moves people: A conversation with screenwriting coach Robert McKee. (2003). *Harvard Business Review 82*(6), 51–55.
Taylor, F. W. (1947). *The principles of scientific management.* New York: Norton.
Tichy, Noel M. (2002). *The Leadership Engine: How winning companies build leaders at every level.* New York: HarperBusiness.
Wysocki, R. K., & Lewis, J. P. (2001). *The world class project manager : A professional development guide.* Cambridge, MA: Perseus.

14

Friended, Tweeted, Posted

Social Sharing for Project and Knowledge Management

Kyle M. L. Jones and Michael Stephens

"Business is a conversation because the defining work of business is conversation—literally. And 'knowledge workers' are simply those people whose job consists of having interesting conversations."

—David Weinberger, *The Cluetrain Manifesto*

CONVERSATIONS, WEB 2.0, AND SOCIAL SHARING

Knowledge management (KM) at its most granular level can be seen as a process of promoting, creating, and maintaining conversation. Of course, the KM aspect of this conversation is centered on what is important about the conversation and how it is recorded and codified for reuse in the future.

As Weinberger notes, conversation is a key aspect to any business. At micro and macro levels, conversation helps a business communicate internally with employees and externally with consumers. At the micro level it is necessary for employees to be able to discuss their knowledge, lessons learned, and questions they have. Externally, a micro-level conversation allows for individual contact between the business and a singular consumer. Macro-level communication in businesses enables a discussion to be had among large groups of employees internally or a more expansive dialogue to be maintained between the business and potentially its entire consumer base.

The Cluetrain Manifesto examined the idea that "markets are conversations"—conversations are taking place within and outside of business and organizations at micro and macro levels—enabled by the power of the Internet. Published in 1999, the *Cluetrain* foretells the emergence of the social Web a few years later: "A powerful global conversation has begun. Through the Internet, people are discovering and inventing new ways to share relevant knowledge with blinding speed. As a direct result, markets are getting smarter—and getting smarter faster than most companies" (Levine, 2000, n.p.). Now more than ever it is necessary for businesses to have at least a conceptual, but preferably a practical, understanding of the dynamic nature of online conversations and knowledge sharing.

Inventing and sharing relevant and sometimes not-so-relevant information via the social Web (this "new" version of the Internet, as it is sometimes called) has become a popular pastime not only for people but also for businesses, nonprofits, libraries, and other agencies. The implications and uses of social tools in the business or organizational setting has the potential to create connections and points of collaboration across many levels and extend the richness and intricacies of the data/content/knowledge via human participation.

"Web 2.0 is the network as platform, spanning all connected devices," writes Tim O'Reilly, founder and CEO of O'Reilly Media:

> Web 2.0 applications are those that make the most of the intrinsic advantages of that platform: delivering software as a continually-updated service that gets better the more people use it, consuming and remixing data from multiple sources, including individual users, while providing their own data and services in a form that allows remixing by others, creating network effects through an "architecture of participation," and going beyond the page metaphor of Web 1.0 to deliver rich user experiences. (2005, para. 1)

Roush (2005) highlighted the increase in social interaction online via new technologies. He argued that cell phone technology, access to social software, and widespread wireless access to the Internet are creating new forms of self-expression and conversation. Roush labeled this movement "continuous computing." One noted aspect of continuous computing is the prevalence of newer Web tools, such as Weblogs (blogs), search engines, instant messaging, and wikis.

Smith's (2007) "Social Software Building Blocks" is a useful way to understand the affordances of the social tools. Citing early work by Matt Webb (2004) and Stewart Butterfield (2003) and inspiration from *Ambient Findabilty* author Peter Morville (2004), Smith presents seven building blocks as "a solid foundation for thinking about how social software works":

Identity—a way of uniquely identifying people in the system
Presence—a way of knowing who is online, available, or otherwise nearby
Relationships—a way of describing how two users in the system are related (e.g., in Flickr, people can be contacts, friends, or family)
Conversations—a way of talking to other people through the system
Groups—a way of forming communities of interest
Reputation—a way of knowing the status of other people in the system (Who's a good citizen? Who can be trusted?)
Sharing—a way of sharing things that are meaningful to participants (such as photos or videos)

This next incarnation of the World Wide Web has many names: the social Web, social software, the read/write Web, the living Web, and, of course, Web 2.0. Simply put, Web 2.0 might be defined as a set of emerging digital tools that allow users to create, change, and publish dynamic content of all kinds online while other tools syndicate and aggregate this content to those who wish to receive it. Another key element is sharing—the tools of the emerging social Web encourage sharing of content, ideas, and knowledge. The potential for use of these tools in a project management (PM) and KM environment is ripe for exploration. This chapter will explore a set of emerging tools that will enhance and extend projects in a low-cost or no-cost manner.

SOCIAL TOOLS AND THE ENTERPRISE

A recent survey of business use of social tools used within intranets yields a snapshot of the state of KM/PM in 2009, providing a look at the most popular social tools at work within the enterprise. Mills (2009) detailed the results of the research by Prescient Digital Media, noting that "Intranet blogs, wikis and discussion forums are quite pervasive," while other tools seem to be an "afterthought." Some of the findings of the survey of 561 businesses across the globe include:

- 45% have intranet blogs (13% enterprise deployment); 11% have no plans or interest.
- 47% have intranet wikis (17% enterprise deployment); 10% have no plans or interest.
- 23% have intranet podcasts (6% enterprise deployment); 30% have no plans or interest.
- 19% have intranet social networking (6% enterprise use); 20% have no plans or interest.
- 21% have intranet content tagging (9% enterprise use); 24% have no plans or interest.
- 37% have intranet RSS (13% enterprise use); 12% have no plans or interest.
- 46% have intranet discussion forums (19% enterprise use); 9% have no plans or interest.
- 46% have intranet instant messaging (29% enterprise use); 21% have no plans or interest.
- 8% have intranet mashups (3% enterprise use); 45% have no plans or interest.

Social networking has been defined by anthropologists, technologists, and nearly every other professional discipline. So it is no wonder that its definition gets quite convoluted and complex. Without introducing any kind of technological jargon to the definition, social networking can be defined as making connections between individuals and sharing information. And social networking and social sharing software is a great pairing with KM. "Many of us increasingly find that we need to interact, form on-the-fly communities and share self-made content and contributions with our colleagues," said Uwe Richter, vice president for collaborative software company Mindjet. "New technologies to support increased participation are needed" (Richter, 2008). Richter continues his track on social networking and software applications by suggesting that this focus emphasizes a more collaborative knowledge-sharing environment and innovative workplace. Barry Libert believes in social sharing but notes that the "top-down, rigid nature of [current] KM systems discouraged contribution. It was antithetical to the way people want to interact" (Lamont, 2008, pg. 2). Libert does not need to be discouraged for much longer, as KM professionals are seeing the advantages of social networking in KM projects.

Like Uwe Richter, Judy Payne, too, believes in the usefulness of social networking as a knowledge management (KM) tool. Payne (2007) researched twenty public, private, and third-sector organizations to understand how the integration of social software enhanced or inhibited each organization's internal collaboration. She concluded that "social software seems to have the potential to help organizations build the capability of collaboration." Furthermore, "social software is a catalyst for making organizations flatter and more democratic in their behaviour" (Payne 2007, p. 28). Scarff (2006) detailed how specific social networking tools like RSS feeds, blogs, wikis, and social bookmarking were used with much success at IBM, Motorola, Siemens, and Quicksilver. Microsoft, another KM social software success story, has created a four-thousand-employee-strong army of bloggers who not only share their knowledge internally but also externally with their customer base (Boue' 2008, p. 15). Boue' (2008) sums up social software for KM use quite dramatically by stating that it "is about building the equivalent of a town square online—a place where people can meet to share news, ideas and knowledge" (p. 16). KM-related literature suggests that the field is passionate about the integration of social software into the workflow of KM projects.

THE TOOLS

So what tools should be used for social sharing, PM, and general KM initiatives? The answer to that question is, of course, dependent on the needs of the business, its organizational culture, and the purposes that the piece of software might serve. Uhrmacher (2008) suggests that a company should first identify its strengths before adopting a piece of social software. However, this approach ignores opportunities to find new and engaging ways to create and promote knowledge sharing where before, conversation was not taking place. Weaknesses should be used as an opportunity for improvement, while at the same time building on identified strengths.

The following highlights social sharing tools from a wide variety of categories: content syndication and subscription, blogs, open source content management systems (CMS), microblogging, and social networking sites. While generally only one tool is highlighted per category, each category has a plethora of other options not mentioned. Furthermore, the tools discussed represent a shift in communication toward more open lines of access to information in many ways: All are free for use and allow for some kinds of personalization via open source licenses or application programming interfaces (APIs).

RICH SITE SUMMARY/REALLY SIMPLE SYNDICATION (RSS)

RSS is defined as XML-based metadata content from a blog or other source. Web content is created or published in one place to be displayed in other places, such as in RSS aggregators (also called "readers"). Therefore, the easiest way to think of

RSS is as Really Simple Syndication. Whenever the source gets updated, the RSS feed gets updated, and any aggregators that are subscribed to that feed are notified that new content is available.

People who use aggregators to monitor RSS feeds get alerts when new content is added to sites they monitor (Stephens, 2006). From a potential customer standpoint, consumers can use RSS to keep track of newly introduced business products or information. Apple (2009) currently offers over one hundred different feeds for product news and information; additionally, every discussion forum in the Apple support site offers four different feeds (for announcements, all messages, popular threads, and all threads), totaling well over a thousand separate feeds for customers and potential consumers to subscribe to.

RSS is clearly the most transformative tool in social sharing of knowledge. It has the ability to keep customers engaged with a business's brand as those who subscribe to the feed are consistently reminded of what the business has to offer. If KM intranets support RSS, knowledge workers and the wider workforce of a business or organization will be further engaged with internal communications since their aggregators will collect and archive new pieces of conversations as they are published. From a PM perspective, those working on a committee can use RSS in a variety of sites like blogs, calendars, and forums to keep track of deadlines and vital communications.

BLOGS

Delio (2005) urged corporate officers and businesspeople to be aware of the power of this publishing tool. In *Naked Conversations: How Blogs Are Changing the Way Businesses Talk with Customers*, Scoble and Israel (2006) argue that blogs are better than traditional one-way marketing venues because they allow instant two-way communication with customers. They theorize that if a business doesn't provide a blog where customers might interact with the blog authors via commenting, those customers will find a business that does allow two-way communication (p. 143).

In *An Army of Davids*, Reynolds (2006), a professor of law at the University of Tennessee, argues that tools such as blogs allow anyone to have a voice and to compete with the much larger news media. Using blogs, for example, creates horizontal knowledge, defined as "communication among individuals who may or may not know each other, but who are loosely coordinated by their involvement with something, or someone, of mutual interest" (p. 121). Horizontal knowledge offers connections, and the online social tools offer the mechanism for individuals to contribute their opinions about business and consumerism. One recent example involved a blogger who used his cell phone camera to send images of an untidy, disorganized department store to his blog for a post on customer service (McConnell, 2007).

Also in the business sector, popular works such as *The Corporate Blogging Book* by Weil (2006) illustrate the path of best practice for CEOs and companies to take the blogging plunge. Articles as well, such as "Blogs Will Change Your Business" by Baker and Green (2005), urge corporate executives to be aware of the impact of personal publishing on business communication.

DRUPAL, THE OPEN SOURCE CONTENT MANAGEMENT SYSTEM

Srikantaiah (2008) highlights that over one hundred vendors offer CMSs and comments that the CMS "industry is several billion dollars strong" (p. 27). Unfortunately, not all organizations can afford to purchase and implement a CMS even though they understand the value of KM. Knowledge workers need a CMS that is not only cheap, if not free, but a system that is intuitive, flexible, and customizable. One hopeful option would be to explore the world of open source.

According to Black (2007), "The name Open Source came into use in 1998 following the release of the Netscape code. The programmers who collaborated with one another on their own, freely sharing their work on the newly released code, used the name Open Source to describe their unusual openness at the time of tight control of software development by companies" (p. 5). Open source software has become synonymous with the word *free*, and free software is something that these library information professionals need. Many content management systems (CMS) happen to be released to the public with open source licenses.

There are a variety of open source content management systems (CMS) to choose from. Snell (2009) lists more than seventeen different choices for CMSs, a variety of them open source. Of the notable free CMS choices, Snell highlights Drupal and WordPress. Each of these choices has its advantages, but Drupal is known for its extensibility, popularity, stability, and community-backed support forums.

Drupal's extensibility is supported by the use of modules, or plug-ins, that dramatically enhance its principal functions "out of the box." Many of these modules have plug-and-play-like functionality that requires little tweaking for use; others require substantial administration. Development Seed, the designers behind the World Bank's CommNET intranet site, employed Drupal and many KM-focused modules to optimize internal communication and knowledge sharing. Ian Ward (2008) of Development Seed had these KM initiatives in mind as he proceeded on this Drupal project: "[World Bank employees] need to collaborate on projects, share updates and information, and interact easily with other team members. They also wanted to share certain aspects of their work with hundreds of other World Bank staff" (para. 3). Ward's (2008) module-enhanced Drupal implementation has given World Bank employees the ability to easily and quickly create online project groups, maintain their own Web-based schedules, and share virtual space for working on documents (see the resources section at the end of the chapter for all modules used for this project).

WORDPRESS AND BUDDYPRESS

In addition to Drupal, WordPress is one of the leaders in the CMS genre of social software. Created in 2003, WordPress began as a start-up company created "to enhance the typography of everyday writing" (About WordPress, n.d.). In 2005, WordPress introduced its 1.5 version that saw over nine hundred thousand individual downloads; subsequently, WordPress saw nearly four million downloads in 2007. Although WordPress is open to individuals across the world, it has been adopted by companies, too.

WordPress's flexibility and intuitive nature have been key lures for major companies. Commercial institutions like CNN, Fox News, Coca-Cola, and General Electric use the CMS to create conversation internally and externally (Graham, n.d.) "It looks like a website that would have taken six to nine months to create, but it's a blog we made in just a few hours," said Dermot Waters, a senior producer at CNN, about the ease of use of WordPress (Graham, n.d., p. 2). It is important to note that Waters makes a very fine distinction about WordPress by calling it a "blog."

CMSs come in a variety of forms with even more intended purposes. Some are built to be e-commerce sites, while others are simply made to track projects and provide oversight tools for businesses. There are others that are built to provide a platform for communication and documentation; WordPress falls into this category. For better or for worse, WordPress has been tagged as a blogging CMS. But as of late, WordPress has become a contender for the best use of a CMS for PM and KM with its introduction of BuddyPress, a powerful plug-in that transforms WordPress into a custom-built social network.

Just like Drupal has modules, WordPress has plug-ins. These additional installs do everything from enhance WordPress's organization of content to increasing the site's overall usability. In 2007 there were almost three million downloads of 1,384 available plug-ins (About WordPress, n.d.). BuddyPress is a series of plug-ins that allows WordPress to create extended user profiles, adds private messaging functionality, and promotes connections through features like "friending" other site members, groups, forums, and what is called the "activity stream." The activity stream aggregates all content in a BuddyPress installation (About BuddyPress, n.d.).

BuddyPress offers what could be the perfect package for knowledge workers looking to develop an in-house social networking system that promotes communication, has flexible installation options, and personalizes knowledge sharing. The system's highly usable and engaging interface will make training less daunting, and its customizable options will quickly engage workers in much the same way Facebook has for millions of users. By offering a wide variety of communication options (i.e., microblogging, blogging, forums, profiles, and more), PM leaders might find their team members' conversations becoming much more prolific and sustained as opposed to traditional methods like e-mail.

TWITTER

Of all of the tools covered in this chapter, Twitter has had the most prevalent coverage in the mainstream press. Celebrities, political figures, and corporations have adopted the presence/status awareness microblogging Web application as a means to share and communicate. Simply, Twitter enables users to answer a simple question—"What are you doing?"—in 140 characters or less. Users can access Twitter messages—called tweets—via the Web, via an RSS feed, and via text on their cell phones. Lenhart and Fox for Pew Internet and American Life Research (2009) reported that "as of December 2008, 11% of online American adults said they used a service like Twitter or another service that allowed them to share updates about themselves or to see the updates of others" (para. 2).

Fred Stutzman (2007), in his "12-Minute Definitive Guide," divides uses into two areas: social updating and microblogging. Accessing a Twitter user, one might find a status update on his or her day, a message to another Twitterer as part of a conversation, or a bit of wit, wisdom, or everyday minutiae. Composing in 140 characters or less does, at first glance, seem like a hurdle. Updates must be as clear and concise as possible, especially if posting for business purposes. But the limitation on how much can be written is actually an advantage for PM and KM purposes.

Twitter and other microblogging applications can actually encourage employees and knowledge workers to stay engaged with one another. By limiting the amount that can be written, these staffers can update their colleagues on products they are working on, links to information that should be shared, and quick project reminders. Worrying about drafts, composing extensive memoranda, or the general stress of writing is actually reduced by the inherent restrictions of microblogging.

FACEBOOK

As detailed throughout this chapter, social tools afford users the chance to interact, share themselves, and create content. Social networking services (SNS), as defined by Wikipedia (Social Network Service, 2009, para. 1), are "primarily web based and provide a collection of various ways for users to interact, such as chat, messaging, email, video, voice chat, file sharing, blogging, discussion groups." One of the most popular SNSs is Facebook, a site originally conceived for college students but opened to all in 2006. As of this writing, Facebook boasts these growth statistics:

More than two hundred million active users
More than one hundred million users log on to Facebook at least once each day
More than two-thirds of Facebook users are outside of college
The fastest-growing demographic is those thirty-five years old and older

Facebook exemplifies many of Smith's (2007) social software building blocks. Users create a profile page sharing their identity, the system allows presence awareness and status updates, relationships can be created, and conversations can play out between individuals or groups. Sharing is also prevalent: images, videos, links, and feeds from outside the system are possible. Facebook applications, such as those that run the gamut from personal, such as birthday reminders, to the more pragmatic, such as library catalog search apps or enterprise solutions, are included.

Critics of Facebook see this SNS as a place for narcissistic agendas and all-too-easy access to personal and sensitive information for cyberstalkers. The shrewd knowledge worker, however, sees the potential in Facebook as a way for furthering interpersonal connections at the macro and micro levels. At the macro level, KM teams should investigate how to penetrate the two hundred million active users of Facebook to open up the lines of communication about business products and organizational initiatives. At the micro level, PM leaders should motivate their teams to create profiles on Facebook and share their knowledge and information at a higher rate online than they might do in sparse face-to-face meetings. Privacy is of course a concern. If PM leaders have sensitive information they do not want shared with competitors or individuals outside of the company, the PM team members should be instructed on locking down their profiles using Facebook's highly customizable privacy options.

WEIGHING THE BENEFITS

Exploring these social tools yields applications and implications for the field of KM in general and PM specifically. Knowledge workers can utilize open and free tools to advantage while easily carrying on a conversation. More importantly, the use of these tools has the potential to lead to the following benefits.

Humanizing the Conversation

Among the most significant business trends to arise over the past few years has been the humanization of the business face. Typically what is seen between consumers and businesses is a wall unable to be penetrated that hinders communication between these two groups. However, savvy businesses understand that the social Web opens the lines of communication between these once mute groups. By capitalizing on communication trends that humanize and personalize the communication process, businesses can set themselves up for more successful micro and macro communications.

Personalizing the Conversation

Branching off from the discussion to embody a philosophy of humanized micro and macro communication, businesses and KM managers must incorporate ICTs that are personable and customizable. An ICT or technology system that provides a disappointing user experience will severely inhibit both users within the company and the customers outside, which may in fact lessen their desire to purchase goods or services from the company.

Archiving the Conversation

Another benefit of using social tools is the ease of archiving and searching for data as well as the conversations attached to it. Blog comments, wiki histories, and stored media such as podcasts or videocasts provide a way to look back.

Twitter hashtags, for example, group related Twitter posts (called tweets) that via RSS could be archived and saved in a blog format.

Searching the Conversation

Blogs, wikis, and other tools offer varying forms and degrees of search. WordPress blogs can be augmented with a search widget, and many WordPress themes as well as other social tools offer tagging features for making data more searchable.

The mechanisms, however, are not perfect. After attendees at the American Library Association meeting in Denver, Colorado, utilized a hashtag for posts relating to the conference on Twitter, ALA Strategy Guide Jenny Levine (2009) noted that two months later, the tags were no longer appearing in searches:

> So if you were using a hashtag to aggregate content, thinking it would be easier to find it all again in the future, think again. You're going to have to do something more proactive and manual than relying on Twitter's search engine or Google. You'll have to decide what level of ephemeraliness you're comfortable with for that conversation, because you may not be able to get back to it if you let someone else manage access to the archive. In this context, it's a shame so much of the conversation has moved away from blog comments (where individuals can openly archive it) to Twitter and FriendFeed. And if you're a government or archive organization looking to preserve this kind of digital content, the stakes are getting raised on you.

Making the Conversation Transparent

One less tangible, less technical benefit of using social tools in a KM/PM environment is the increased level of transparency provided within the conversation. Early bloggers discovered the tool allowed content-rich conversation beyond corporate control. Singel (2004) noted that blog software company Six Apart wanted to remain as open as possible with blog tools such as commenting and trackback, even in light of negative posts about their 2004 licensing changes.

Thompson (2007) noted that emerging firms as well as big business were discovering the benefits of a more open, honest environment online by allowing employees to participate in the conversation:

> Reputation Is Everything: Google isn't a search engine. Google is a reputation-management system. What do we search for, anyway? Mostly people, products, ideas—and what we want to know are, what do other people think about this stuff? All this blogging, Flickring, MySpacing, journaling—and, most of all, linking—has transformed the Internet into a world where it's incredibly easy to figure out what the world thinks about you, your neighbor, the company you work for, or the stuff you were blabbing about four years ago. It might seem paradoxical, but in a situation like that, it's better to be an active participant in the ongoing conversation than to stand off and refuse to participate. Because, okay, let's say you don't want to blog, or to Flickr, or to participate in online discussion threads. That means the next time someone Googles you they'll find . . . everything that everyone else has said about you, rather than the stuff you've said yourself. (para. 24)

This practice could augment and enhance internal and external conversations. In this new world of open conversation, it seems that companies and organizations can't afford not to participate.

Creating Hyperties within the Conversation

In an essay included in *The Hyperlinked Society*, Smith (2008) defines the concepts of hyperties. Hyperties are those personal, social interactions captured and recorded by location-aware devices and services and logged just as research data might be.

Smith advocates that this type of "life logging" may become widespread, a sort of "pervasive inscription revolution" where we are all co-creating everything: tagged objects, events, data, and so on. Within these networks or clouds of tagged data, others will find and remix data—extending the value to all. Hyperties within a KM/PM context afford connections between workers and between projects.

BARRIERS

Barriers to the effective use and adoption of social tools within a KM/PM environment are also present. In the results of a survey on social tools in business, Mills (2009) noted three issues were prevalent: lack of executive support, lack of IT support, and lack of business case support. The former barriers are tied more to human perception than the limitations of the technologies. The lack of business case support, however, was the most prevalent barrier. Models of success with clearly defined implementation strategies and tangible return on investment data in the business setting are not widely promoted or disseminated. The ubiquity of social networking and growing adoption rates of tools like Facebook and Twitter will, it is hoped, increase KM/PM use and in turn the reporting of the use of these tools in business situations. Sharing successes and failures with these tools and social networking in general is an important step for project managers.

ACTIONS FOR ENHANCING PM/KM WITH SOCIAL TOOLS

1. **Begin with an environmental scan.** Undergoing an environmental scan will allow the business to better understand how its competitors are using micro and macro conversations to interact with their shared consumer base. Usually an environmental scan is multifaceted, but if one has been done previously or other factors inhibit a full scan, a more simplified and focused scan should be completed instead.

2. **Undergo a focused knowledge audit.** Like the environmental scan, the knowledge audit can be focused on the needs of assessing micro and macro conversations internally within a business. By assessing how these types of conversations are already occurring, the business can evaluate their usefulness (or lack thereof) in knowledge transfer.

3. **Complete a SWOT analysis: Analysis of Strenths (S), Weaknesses (W), Opportunities (O), and Threats (T).** Based on the data provided from the environmental scan and knowledge audit, KM workers should complete a SWOT analysis to see whether actually beginning KM projects to enhance micro and macro conversations is valid. While at first glance the SWOT analysis may seem to be an extraneous step, it ties together nicely the data found in the previous two steps and also enhances the value of the project by being scrupulous about the data and the outcome of the project.

4. **Create a *PMBOK Guide* (Project Management Institute publication) project plan.** Now that all initial data has been acquired and an assessment can be made about future changes or adjustments in micro and macro communication, the KM team should assemble and develop a project plan based on the five process groups

outlined in the *PMBOK Guide*. Creating a PMBOK project plan creates significant value for the project as it clearly structures the steps involved.

5. Create a micro and macro communication road map and social media policy. While the PMBOK project plan may take into account the future needs of micro and macro communication for the business, it is stressed that a comprehensive road map be either added to the project plan or created as a separate document. Communication styles change. The social Web is an excellent example of how communication has evolved, and it demonstrates the rapidly changing domain of how people interact. Businesses must be able to respond quickly to these changes, and a well-thought-out road map can assist KM workers in advising businesses on their communication strategies. Sheehan (2009) notes that many employees are already using social media tools in their personal lives. Due to the transition from personal to professional communication with social media, it suggested that a social media policy be composed to address any ambiguity about the purpose and mission of including social media tools in KM and PM workflows.

FUTURE OF SOCIAL SHARING

In 2006, the seminal work *The Long Tail*, by Chris Anderson, asked its readers to consider the economics of limitless choices provided by the Internet. The question was asked of his theory, "Isn't *The Long Tail* full of crap?" Anderson (2006, p. 116) responded, "*The Long Tail* is indeed full of crap." Because of the abundance of unrestricted access to read and write to the Internet, not everything is of exceptional quality, but "it's also full of works of refined brilliance and depth."

The same can be said about social sharing of information via the social tools described herein. Access to open social networks like Twitter, Facebook, and CMSs and blogs that promote conversation may indeed breed not-so-informative dialogues. However, KM professionals understand that it is their objective to create avenues for discussion, break down barriers of communication, and promote sharing of knowledge around projects and organizational goals. Even e-mail, a now ubiquitous communication tool, was at one time questioned and raised concerned brows. With the same scrupulous investigation and exploration that has thrown any apprehensiveness about e-mail aside, knowledge workers must look at these social sharing tools, balance their opportunities with their risks, and attempt Weinberger's "interesting conversations" in new domains.

REFERENCES

About BuddyPress. (n.d.). Retrieved April 29, 2009, from http://buddypress.org/about/.

About WordPress. (n.d.). Retrieved April 28, 2009, from http://wordpress.org/about/.

Anderson, C. (2006). *The long tail: How endless choice is creating unlimited demand.* London: Random House.

Apple RSS Information. (2009). Retrieved June 5, 2009, from http://www.apple.com/support/rss/.

Baker, S., & Green, H. (2005, May 2). Blogs will change your business. *BusinessWeek, 3931*, 56–67.

Black, E. B. (2007). Web 2.0 and library 2.0: What librarians need to know. In N. Courtney (Ed.), *Library 2.0 and beyond* (pp. 1–14). Westport, CT: Libraries Unlimited.

Boue', G. (2008). Don't say web 2.0, say intranet 2.0. *Knowledge Management Review, 11,* 14–17.

Butterfield, S. (2003). No title. Retrieved May 31, 2009, from http://www.sylloge.com/personal/2003_03_01_s.html#91273866.

Delio, M. (2005, March 28). The enterprise blogosphere. *InfoWorld, 13,* 43–47.

Facebook statistics. (2009). Retrieved May 30, 2009, from http://www.facebook.com/press/info.php?statistics.

Graham, J. (n.d.). He's lots of bloggers' best bud. *USA Today,* Retrieved April 27, 2009, from http://www.usatoday.com/printedition/money/20090128/wordpress28_st.art.htm.

Lamont, J. (2008, June). Social networking: KM and beyond. *KM World,* 12–13.

Lenhart, A., & Fox, S. (2009). Twitter and status updating. Retrieved May 31, 2009, from http://www.pewinternet.org/Reports/2009/Twitter-and-status-updating.aspx.

Levine, F. (2000). *The cluetrain manifesto: The end of business as usual.* New York: Basic Books.

Levine, J. (2009). *Twittephemeraliness.* Retrieved May 26, 2009, from http://theshiftedlibrarian.com/archives/2009/03/24/twittephemeraliness.html.

McConnell, B. (2007). The not-so-secret shopper. Retrieved January 31, 2006, from http://www.churchofthecustomer.com/blog/2007/01/notsosecret_sho.html..

Mills, J. (2009). *Intranet 2.0 goes mainstream.* Retrieved May 30, 2009, from http://www.prescientdigital.com/articles/intranet-articles/intranet-2-0-becomes-mainstream.

Morville, P. (2004). *User experience design.* Retrieved June 6, 2009, from http://semanticstudios.com/publications/semantics/000029.php

O'Reilly, Tim. 2005. A compact definition of Web 2.0. Retrieved May 30, 2009, from http://radar.oreilly.com/archives/2005/10/web_20_compact_definition.html.

Payne, J. (2007). Using social software to improve collaboration. *Knowledge Management Review, 10,* 24–29.

Reynolds, G. (2006). *An army of Davids: How markets and technology empower ordinary people to beat big media, big government, and other goliaths.* New York: Nelson Current.

Richter, Uwe. (2008). Putting the participatory culture to work. *Knowledge Management Review, 11,* 5.

Roush, W. (2005). Social Machines. Retrieved May 30, 2009, from http://www.technologyreview.com/article/16236/.

Scarff, A. (2006). Advancing knowledge: Sharing with intranet 2.0. *Knowledge Management Review, 9,* 24–27.

Scoble, R., & Israel, S. (2006). *Naked conversations: How blogs are changing the way businesses talk with customers.* New York: Wiley.

Sheehan, M. (2009). *Crafting your company's social media policy.* Retrieved May 31, 2009, from http://www.hightechdad.com/2009/05/11/crafting-your-companys-social-media-policy/.

Smith, G. (2007). *Social software building blocks.* Retrieved May 23, 2009, from http://nform.ca/publications/social-software-building-block.

Smith, M. (2008). From hyperlinks to hyperties. In Joseph Turow & Lokman Tsui (Eds.), *The hyperlinked society: Questioning connections in the digital age.* Ann Arbor: University of Michigan Press.

Snell, S. (2009). CMS toolbox. *DESIGNM.AG.* Retrieved April 28, 2009, from http://designm.ag/resources/cms-toolbox/.

Social network service. Retrieved May 26, 2009, from Wikipedia, http://en.wikipedia.org/wiki/Social_network_service.

Srikantaiah, T. K. (2008). Knowledge management expansion: Content management, project management, competitive intelligence, environmental scanning, and knowledge audit. In M. E. Koenig & T. K. Srikantaiah (Eds.), *Knowledge management in practice* (pp. 17–41). Medford, NJ: Information Today.

Stephens, M. (2006, August). Web 2.0 & libraries: Best practices for social software. *Library Technology Reports*, American Library Association.
Stewart, B. (2003). *Sylloge*. Retrieved June 6, 2009, from http://www.sylloge.com/personal/2003_03_01_s.html#91273866.
Stutzman, F. (2007). *The 12-minute definitive guide to Twitter*. Retrieved May 22, 2009, from http://dev.aol.com/article/2007/04/definitive-guide-to-twitter
Thompson, C. (2008). *The see-through CEO*. Retrieved May 30, 2009, from http://www.wired.com/wired/archive/15.04/wired40_ceo.html.
Uhrmacher, A. (2008). *35+ examples of corporate social media in action*. Retrieved June 5, 2009, from http://mashable.com/2008/07/23/corporate-social-media/.
Ward, I (2008). *Improving knowledge management at the World Bank with Drupal*. Retrieved June 5, 2009, from http://www.developmentseed.org/blog/2008/nov/03/improving-knowledge-management-world-bank-drupal.
Webb, M. (2004). *On social software*. Retrieved June 6, 2009, from http://interconnected.org/home/2004/04/28/on_social_software.
Weil, D. (2006). *The corporate blogging book*. New York: Portfolio.

RESOURCES

Development Seed's World Bank Drupal modules:

Simile's Timeline Module (http://drupal.org/project/timeline)
Organic Groups (http://drupal.org/project/og)
Spaces (http://drupal.org/project/spaces)
Faceted Search (http://drupal.org/project/faceted_search)
Organic Group Facets (http://drupal.org/project/og_facets)
Context (http://drupal.org/project/context)

IV

Case Studies

15

Constructing Business-Oriented Knowledge Organization Systems (BOKOS)

Denise A. D. Bedford

Organizations achieve their business goals and objectives through functional business processes, programs, and projects. A project is a temporary endeavor, having a defined beginning and end (usually constrained by date, but can be constrained by funding or deliverables [Hodge, 2000]), undertaken to meet particular goals and objectives (Ranganathan, 1937), usually to bring about beneficial change or added value. Programs and functional business processes are longer-term endeavors having a longer planning horizon, with stable, predictable ongoing processes. Projects, programs, and functional business processes require different management knowledge, strategies, and techniques. While there are management differences, projects, programs, and functional business processes all must align to ensure that the organization's decisions on resource allocation, resource investments, and resource utilization are effective, efficient, and aligned with business goals. While this seems obvious and intuitive, it is not always easy to achieve.

The challenge is typically not that an organization lacks a business view, but that it has several views. There may be an accounting view—how funds are allocated or charged within the organization. There may be a legal or evidentiary view—how the organization's legal records are maintained and organized. There may be an administrative view—how the organization's resources are organized to support its work. There may be a technology view—how technology investments are made and applications deployed to support programs, processes, and projects. Each of these views is an important and legitimate perspective. No one, though, is comprehensive or exhaustive. Each is designed to serve a specific purpose or support a specific application. Each can contribute to the design of an integrated and holistic business view.

One of the key tools in aligning projects, programs and business processes is a business-oriented knowledge organization system (BOKOS). This type of knowledge organization system (KOS) can provide the structure for alignment. The BOKOS provides a common view of the organization's business goals and objectives.

VALUE OF A BOKOS

In addition to providing an integrated view of the organization and a structure for harmonizing programs, projects, and processes, a business-oriented knowledge organization system:

- Supports workflow across applications by providing a common definition of business processes and subprocesses
- Supports interoperability by providing an interoperable view into different functional applications
- Enables categorization of information assets from the "business process" perspective
- Defines business-oriented filing structures based on metadata
- Pulls together in a business view content from multiple sources and systems
- Enables the promotion, publishing, and syndication of information assets by business perspectives
- Enables searching for information, data, services, content, and people from a business perspective

Slight Diversion—What a BOKOS Is Not

A business-oriented knowledge organization system is different from a topical scheme. A topical taxonomy describes the subject areas in which the organization is interested:

- Environment
- Agriculture
- Economics
- Education
- Transportation
- Health
- Finance
- Recreation

In contrast, a business-oriented taxonomy would describe how the organization does what it does to achieve its goals—how it conducts its business. A business-oriented taxonomy might look like this:

- Corporate planning
- Human resources management
- Technology support
- Product development
- Customer services support
- Travel support

BUSINESS COMMUNICATIONS AND PROMOTIONSDEFINITION OF A BOKOS

A business-oriented knowledge organization system should represent the organization's business areas, its capabilities, and its processes. It should describe what the organization does to deliver value to its customers or clients and how it does it. It should provide a backbone structure where all of the views described above can find an anchor point.

BOKOS AS A CLASSIFICATION SCHEME

A process of representation and decomposition is used to design a BOKOS for an organization (see figure 15.1). The process begins at the top by defining the organization's business goals and strategies, then progressively decomposes those goals and strategies into high-level capabilities and finally its business processes and tasks. A BOKOS will be specific to an organization at its most elementary levels. At its highest levels—business areas—it may resemble that of other organizations that are engaged in the same business. As we move further down the structure to represent how the organization does what it does, though, the BOKOS will by definition be organization specific.

What kind of a knowledge organization system is best suited to represent a business view?

> The term knowledge organization systems are intended to encompass all types of schemes for organizing information and promoting knowledge management. (Hodge, 2000)

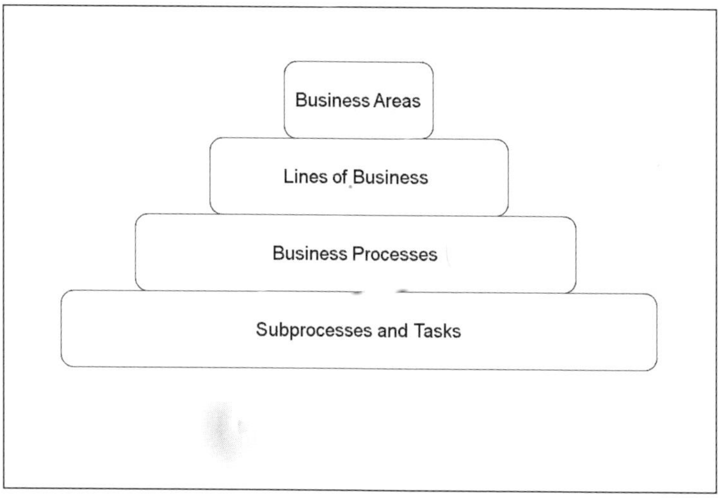

Figure 15.1. BOKOS

The business-oriented knowledge organization scheme is represented as a classification scheme with a hierarchical or a tree structure. In a classification scheme, each level in the hierarchy represents a logical refinement or narrowing of the level above. Classification schemes are used to organize information into collections. Each level in the scheme represents a collection, or set, of information assets. Each refinement of a set creates logical subsets, or a more focused collection.

Classification schemes have a purpose and design foundation. Each level in the hierarchy should have a clear focus and definition. Each level in a classification scheme should be defined and consistently applied. A natural tendency is to allow classification schemes to evolve over time outside of a logical framework. This typically results in a structure that is unbalanced, unpredictable, and essentially unusable for its intended purpose. A disciplined, cross-level approach is critical to designing a BOKOS that will be used to represent the organization's business.

Classification schemes govern the organization of objects into groups according to their similarities and differences or their relation to a "set" of criteria. Classification schemes are in widespread use in everyday life—from grocery stores, to websites, to personal information spaces. Despite this widespread use, there is only one published standard. This standard, ISO 11179-2 Information Technology—Metadata Registries (MDR). Part 2: Classification (2005) provides guidance on the data structures and relationships that should be used to represent a classification scheme. It does not provide guidance on how to create or maintain the values in a classification scheme. Absent a well-defined standard, two sources provide guidance in building a classification scheme: mathematical set theory, and library science classification principles. Mathematical set theory provides the basic concepts of "set" and "membership." A set is thought of as any collection of objects referred to as the members of the set. Members of sets may form subsets and continue to subdivide along specific criteria. Set theory provides us with basic rules for structuring the classification scheme. And S. R. Ranganathan's *Prolegomena to Library Classification* (1937) provides guiding principles of library science classification. Principles provide us with a framework for developing the criteria for a classification scheme.

DESIGNING A BOKOS

A best-practice approach for designing a BOKOS begins with definitions and criteria of each of the levels. The highest level is represented by business areas. Business areas represent the organization's high-level strategy and performance goals. This level is defined by the strategic direction of the organization. This level serves as an aggregation and starting point for aligning lines of business.

The second level—lines of business (LOB)—is defined in terms of lines or groups of products and services. A line of business is defined in terms of lines or groups of products or services that are produced by a set of business processes. Lines of business reflect an organization's strategic choices and levels of business risk and are closely aligned with the organization's performance management. A sample set of criteria for defining a line of business for a BOKOS is presented in table 15.1.

Table 15.1. Criteria for Defining a Line of Business

Criteria	*Application*
Definition	There must be an accepted and published definition of the business line that is accepted by the organization.
Policies and governance processes	There should be a published policy or set of policies pertaining to a business line.
Products and services	Business lines must generate products and services that are required to sustain the organization's business.
Budget	A line of business must have a defined budget line and recurring budget allocations.
Risks	If a line of business is needed to support an enterprise, there is a business risk if it is not available; each line of business should have a business continuity risk rating.
Service standards/metrics	Any product or service line must have published service standards and quality metrics.
Clients/stakeholders	Business lines must have defined clients and stakeholders, internal or external to the organization.
Human resource assets	Lines of business use people to perform work, have a set of core competencies that define the work, have pertinent job profiles, and have human resource assets that sustain them.
Facilities, technology, and information assets	Lines of business are supported by facilities (office space, equipment, and supplies; consume energy; use communication resources; technology assets; data/information assets)
Comparable industrial sector/competencies	Most lines of business within organizations have a comparable external economic product or service line/sector.
Known business processes	A line of business must have one or more associated business processes.
Business area	A line of business must be publicly acknowledged and associated with a business area as defined in the strategic and performance contracts.

The third level describes business processes. A business process is defined as a set of one or more linked procedures or activities that collectively realize a business objective or policy goal, normally within the context of an organizational structure defining functional roles and relationships. Each business process can be further decomposed into multiple business subprocesses or directly into business activities. Sample criteria for business processes are shown in table 15.2.

The fourth level describes either business subprocesses or individual tasks, depending on the granularity of business processes. A business subprocess is defined as a process that is enacted or called from another (initiating) process and that forms part of the overall (initiating) process. A task is a description of a piece of work that forms one logical step within a process. An activity requires human and/or machine resources to support its execution. An activity is the smallest unit of work that is scheduled in a process. When a business activity is executed, a change in the "state" of inputs and/or outputs takes place. Sample business subprocess criteria appear in table 15.3.

Table 15.2. Criteria for Defining Business Processes

Criteria	*Application*
Definition	Has defined conditions triggering its initiation in each new instance (e.g., the arrival of a request) and defined outputs at its completion.
Inputs/outputs	Has defined inputs that are converted directly into outputs at the end of the process.
Business subprocesses or tasks	Can be decomposed into subprocesses or directly to tasks.
Procedures and best practices	Is more likely to be addressed by best practices and procedures than policy statements and governance models. May be represented as a manual or digital procedural model.
Business process model	Can be represented as a business process model, adhering to modeling guidelines.
Budget	A line of business must have a defined budget line and recurring budget allocations.
Risks	Business processes inherit the business risk of their line of business. Changes in business processes are likely to be made as a consequence of the risks to the higher business line.
Service standards/metrics	There may be service standards/metrics associated with a specific business process.
Clients/stakeholders	Business processes generate a product or service for a client or stakeholder, internal or external.
Human resource assets	Both LOB and BP consume human resources, one at a group level and the other at an individual level. They have a set of core competencies that define the work, pertinent job profiles, and human resource assets that sustain them.
Data/information assets	Uses instances of data/information at different steps in the business process/subprocess.
Financial resources	Tracks resources required to produce individual products or services.
Technology assets	May be supported by one or more technical components or by no technology.

HOW IS A BOKOS USED?

A BOKOS provides the values that can be used to tag or profile resources to support "business-oriented" access. Business-oriented access can take the form of reports of program-, project-, and process-level activities, resource allocations, expenditures, and results. Business-oriented access can also take the form of an organizational "services catalog" or internal yellow pages. A BOKOS can support business-oriented searching and navigation structures or even a business view of an organization's intranet. It may also provide a backbone for the organizational filing scheme.

Table 15.3. Criteria for Defining Business Subprocesses

Criteria	*Application*
Definition	A business subprocess is a process that is enacted or called from another (initiating) process (or a subprocess) and which forms part of the overall (initiating) process. A subprocess is useful for defining reusable components within other processes.
Inputs/outputs	Has defined inputs that are converted directly into outputs at the end of the subprocess or task, but the outputs are not finished, final products and services.
Input/output parameters	A subprocess will have its own process definition and may include parameters passed on its initiation and completion.
Functional calls/executables	A business subprocess is represented as a functional call in a business process model and as an "executable service" in a business architecture.
Repurposable/reusable across business processes	Business subprocesses are repurposable and reusable. When variations are needed, they are coded as extensions or parameterizations.
Procedures and best practices	Is more likely to be addressed by a statement in a procedure or practice than an entire procedure or best practice. May be best represented as a manual or digital procedural model.
Business process model	Is represented as a single function call in a business process model.
Budget	Is only tracked at a budget level during a benchmarking or task analysis exercise.
Risks	Changes in a particular step or subprocess will inherit the business continuity value of their line of business parent.
Service standards/metrics	Since there is not a product or service generated in total by a subprocess or step, standards/metrics are not likely to be found.
Clients/stakeholders	Clients/stakeholders may be internal or external. Most clients and stakeholders will be the owners of the next step in the business process.
Human resource assets	Uses small portions of a person's time.
Data/information assets	Uses instances of data/information at the individual step level, and uses them one at a time.
Financial resources	Tracks resources required to produce individual products or services.
Technology assets	May be supported by one or more technical components or by no technology.

MAINTAINING AND SUSTAINING A BOKOS

The creation of a BOKOS is not a one-time effort. As an organization's business changes, its BOKOS must change to serve its purpose. The greatest danger derives not from the change itself, but from variant and unpredictable approaches to governance. Most classification schemes in use today are maintained by an authoritative institution or its issuing body. We rely on that authority to keep the classification scheme up to date and relevant to its intended context. A BOKOS, though, is an organization-specific classification scheme that must be maintained internally.

A clearly defined governance process is the critical success factor. The governance process should address:

- Who can initiate a request for a change
- How requests are made
- What changes in the business will trigger changes in the BOKOS
- What type of changes can be made
- How change requests are evaluated
- Who is consulted as part of the evaluation process
- Who does the evaluation
- How the changes are announced
- How the changes are implemented
- Who serves as the governing authority for the BOKOS

One way to anchor the governance process is to define a series of guiding principles and business rules. Guiding principles do not dictate how the structure is formed but provide a consistent framework for interpretation as the organization's business evolves. Examples of guiding principles might include the following:

- No two classes should overlap or should have exactly the same scope and boundaries.
- Each class in the scheme should be defined in the context of its parent class.
- Classes in the scheme should be exhaustive of their common immediate universe.
- Classes should be presented in a logical order that serves both classification principles and user convenience.

CONCLUSIONS

A business-oriented knowledge organization system is an important tool in managing business information created through programs, projects, and processes. A well-defined BOKOS can provide significant value to an organization. As an internally developed tool, though, a BOKOS requires a clearly defined structure, based on strong criteria and managed through a rigorous governance structure. As organizations automate and integrate all levels of business activity, a BOKOS will become an essential information management tool.

REFERENCES

Hodge, G. (2000). *Systems of knowledge organization for digital libraries. Beyond traditional aurhority files*. Washington, DC: Council on Library and Information Resources. Retrieved from http://www.clir.org/pubs/reports/pub91/contents.html.

ISO 11179-2 Information Technology. (2005). Metadata Registries (MDR). Part 2: Classification.

Ranganathan, S. R. (1937). *Prolegomena to library classification*. Madras: Madras Library Association.

16

Leveraging Information and Knowledge Assets for Project Work

The World Bank Project Profile Pilot

Ana Flavia Fonseca and Arnoldo Fonseca

Recent strides toward a more comprehensive knowledge management framework for project management highlight a growing acknowledgment of the value that can be generated by harnessing these disciplines for mutual benefit. Information and knowledge has always been a staple of project management, at the most primitive level, enabling the status-control function of project managers. Project success has increasingly come to depend upon productive use of information and knowledge for the actual work tasks within projects. Whether through improved data access or more structured methodologies to leverage tacit knowledge, delivering the right knowledge at the right time to the right audience is critical as project cycles have shortened and margins for error have tightened.

Acting upon this goal has nevertheless been challenging. Information and knowledge assets are often difficult to capture and redeploy. Even more structured information assets are often not fully leveraged owing to the costs of adequately integrating them into project workflows and systems. Several factors are changing this, however, opening an opportunity for more effective use of information assets in project work. Shorter project cycles, increased worker mobility, improved capture, and processing paradigms are all facilitating the trade-off toward greater integration and embedding of an organization's knowledge and information assets within project work.

This chapter explores in abstract some issues related to integrating information assets through IT systems into project work and then describes a pilot by the World Bank Group to improve use of its data and information assets within its project management systems.

LEVERAGING INFORMATION AND KNOWLEDGE ASSETS FOR PROJECT MANAGEMENT

Growing Importance of Information and Knowledge in Project Work

Knowledge and information have always been critical for project work, but recent trends are driving visibility of their importance to broader groups of decision makers within some organizations. This growing awareness may help drive efforts toward more deliberate management and utilization of information and knowledge within project work. Some of these trends include the following:

Demographics. Many organizations within developed markets will be facing demographic shifts in their workforce in the future. Years of experience and tacit knowledge that has enabled successful project delivery may gradually "retire." This could have material productivity and execution implications, particularly for project work with long life cycles where experience is gained only across several years. Many organizations have begun human resource initiatives to cope with this longitudinal trend, but depending on their aims, these experience transfer initiatives might not suitably fulfill the needs of project work.

Geographic neutrality. Information technologies have made geography irrelevant for some types of project work. This has yielded twenty-four-hour execution days, where project work is shifted to a new time zone each eight hours to accommodate business hour schedules. Another phenomenon is the use of dispersed operational centers, wherein different parts of a work process chain are performed by geographically independent workers. Such dynamics require greater coordination and greater visibility into projects.

Labor mobility. Increased mobility among workers has led to similar brain-drain effects as demographic shifts, but on a more rapid basis. Mechanisms for information and knowledge retention become particularly important in these cases, as these worker departures tend to cause more immediate disruptions.

Shorter, faster development cycles with less margin for error. Increased global competition, particularly within price-sensitive arenas or those with nominal entry barriers, has resulted in demanding project cycles ever tighter in time line and margin for error or rework. Under these conditions, higher productivity along with greater information transparency becomes critical.

Returns from IT investments. Under recent economic conditions, many leaders are demanding to see productivity enhancements from past investments in IT. Executives are looking to enhance organizational performance with existing assets, and they expect some of the promises underpinning past IT investments to now come true.

The key takeaway from each of these trends is that embedding information and knowledge management practice into the project work itself can help to ensure successful future delivery of project deliverables. This is because these practices and the increased richness of information that would follow should make workers more productive and projects less prone to common sources of failure. This goal has always been present, but with more pronounced urgency, resources to realize this goal are being more actively deployed.

Broader Obstacles for Project Work Enrichment

Several obstacles exist to undercut project work through enriched IT systems. Some of these are organizational in nature and thereby require a broader set of approaches to overcome. Another set of obstacles has more to do with the pragmatic concerns of implementation.

Organizational obstacles underlie any effort for change and as such are a topic well covered within literature focused on change within people, processes, structures, and related arenas. Some common organizational obstacles pertinent to enriched IT include:

Executive ownership and expectations. Executive ownership of initiatives is clearly important and well recognized as important for overall change success. Beyond inspirational and monetary/resource support, executives need to have realistic expectations, and recent expectations have been built high on the promises of IT.

Employee and process myopia. Employees and processes have their common patterns. Changes to these must be managed well in order to avoid difficulties getting buy-in, maintaining support, minimizing problems, and retaining/enhancing overall performance levels. In addition to existing practices, new processes will need to be created to fit the needs of an enriched environment. New processes are often required to allow an enriched environment to exist, and existing modes of work may thwart these new processes. Special support and attention must be taken to allow these new processes to emerge and take root.

Resource scarcity. Resources are important, both to implement as well as to support an enriched environment on an ongoing basis. Too often, IT-based resources are allocated on a "package implementation" basis, wherein a buildup is followed by drastic cutback following installation of new software. Implementing an enriched environment requires a process-oriented view, where the goal is to ensure a long-term evolution and adaptation to fit business-driven needs.

Inaction toward enriched project work environments has also been driven by pragmatic obstacles related to available IT capabilities. Some of these obstacles include:

Identification of information assets and knowledge assets for project enrichment through IT. Organizations have many intangible assets, but there is often no method to enable these to be captured, processed, and repurposed through an IT system. Often the most valuable intangible information and knowledge is contained within workers themselves, making this task intractable on a regular basis.

There have been no clear, winning solutions for translating such intangible assets to forms easily used by IT systems. There have been several attempts, through collaborative environments or through processes that encourage workers to capture and catalog as they perform their daily work. The search for a winning solution is likely to continue until IT systems are themselves intelligent enough to interface with humans in a manner that is transparent and nonimposing.

Another common problem involves focusing on those assets that really are most valuable for project work. Often, in order to score early wins, IT implementations only capture "low hanging fruit" information, but these are not necessarily ones providing outsized value to project work. While seemingly a good idea from an implementation standpoint, the "low hanging fruit" approach can often lead to false and unmet expectations by users and can numb them from using such systems in the future. It is important to make a good-faith effort at addressing the key needs of workers in some fashion, even if implemented in a manner that is less than ideal.

Existing systems and system change. Many existing systems were not designed and built in a manner that can easily leverage the diversity of information and knowledge types existing within the enterprise IT infrastructure. Their design at the time was well intentioned, since they were purposed on very specific processing tasks. The problem is that many information and knowledge assets are not simple, and often flexibility is important, since tomorrow's data file formats are unknown at present. This is a key obstacle for many organizations that cannot justify reengineering of their systems, and opens up the need for adequate intermediary mechanisms that mediate existing system capabilities with new needs.

Algorithmic sophistication. Commercially available and affordable packages that can effectively scan, capture, repurpose, interpret/infer, and reuse information and knowledge types are not accessible to most organizations. At present, it is difficult for many organizations to justify such costs, especially if their core business or activity does not hinge substantially upon information flow. Furthermore, knowledge is generally not yet well understood as an asset by many organizations. Advanced processing systems tend to be found only within information and knowledge-intensive industries like financial services.

Culture and learning. Although organizational in nature, many programs fail because system limitations and requirements were not able to meld to natural human interaction and patterns of work. Part of the reason projects phased through small modular rollouts are more successful is that they enable human adaptation to the new system and its process over time.

Clearly, those seeking to enrich project work environments through IT by leveraging information and knowledge assets need to be realistic about the fact that there is no clear solution at present. Contemporary implementations are bridging points to provide increasingly enriched environments. Nonetheless, by understanding longitudinal trends and anticipating the needs of project work both today and tomorrow, it is possible for organizations to develop information and knowledge management practices through which progressive efforts may be made to enrich project work environments through IT.

Some key principles and criteria can already be derived, including the need for flexibility, the need for conveying information at specific points in time to target audiences, the needs for systems to understand project processes so that they can accurately effect actions that generate value. As this chapter will illustrate, it is possible to leverage approaches from information management and knowledge management disciplines and presently available technologies to craft mechanisms for enriching environments.

In the next section, we will explore how the World Bank Group has begun to think about this issue through its own pilot of an enhanced project portal system.

WORLD BANK GROUP PROJECT PORTAL PILOT CASE STUDY

The World Bank Group is a multinational development bank operating across 185 member countries providing loans, grants, and other assistance across a variety of purposes, including investments in education, health, public administration, infrastructure, financial- and private-sector development, agriculture, and environmental and natural resource management. It concurrently runs or oversees several hundred development projects throughout the world across these disciplines. As a result, project work is both a core activity within the bank as well as relatively complex in nature.

Goals and Summary of the Approach Taken

Goals of the Pilot

The goal of enriching project work environments was tested through a pilot conceived in 2004. At the time, it was anticipated that future tools and technologies would provide a superior offering to what was then available. As a result, the pilot aimed at achieving two goals: (1) to act as a proof of concept for increased contextualization of project information from existing bank sources, and (2) to provide a "logical" foundation for future efforts. Contextualization would enable users working on projects to experience a more responsive and customized interaction experience from bank systems. This contextualization would also help set the stage for empowering bank systems to become more able to find solutions—knowledge (rather than just more information)—to users' problems. In many respects, the implementation proposed for the pilot was simplistic and not by any means a showcase of information processing. It was unique, however, in its scope as a large-scale attempt to tie together cross-enterprise information for enriching project environments.

The Notion of Contextualized Information in Project Work: The Project Profile

The notion of "contextualized project information" extends beyond well-structured project data to include unstructured metadata embedded within actual work products utilized and produced during the project life cycle. These would include reports, documents, and other communications that capture more qualitative aspects of projects. Operationalizing contextualization requires both a processing step, discussed below, as well as a suitable data structure to make such "context" easily accessible. Dubbed the project profile, this data structure contained or referenced standard data, such as project name, start dates, and other structured details as well as the unstructured data culled from project-related artifacts.

The pilot developed a first version of this profile, which would capture basic project information and some semistructured metainformation. Tying project information across multiple structured data sources was a challenge in and of itself, and enrichment from semistructured sources was consequently limited. As an example of the latter, the pilot's profile captured the fact that a project had "lessons learned" associated with it as well as the topical areas related to these lessons. It would not capture or try to understand the specific lessons themselves, however. To balance its usefulness with the difficulty of implementation, the pilot's project profile was constructed to address a defined set of queries deemed useful for project workers, thereby providing projects with limited but valuable contextual information.

Subsequent versions of the profile would increase the breadth of information collected. This progressive information enrichment should facilitate future IT technologies and interfaces to deliver enhanced user experiences and levels of productivity.

Using IT to Deliver Contextualized Information

For the pilot, leveraging information and deriving knowledge contained within the project profile essentially meant enabling the bank's project Web portal, the

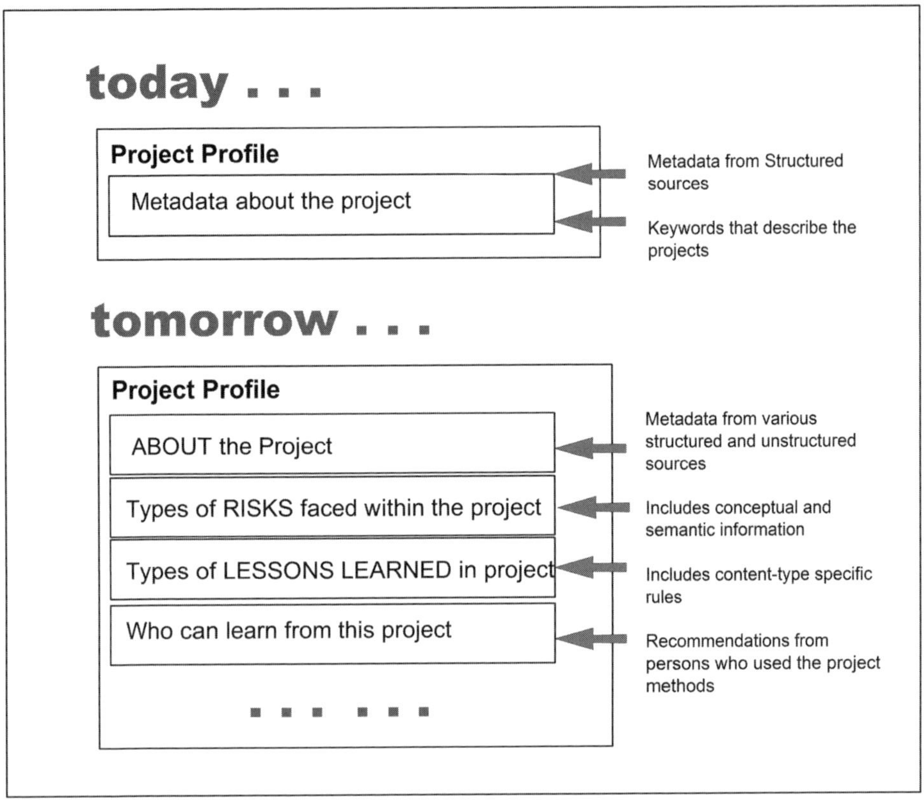

Figure 16.1.

project portal, to deliver answers to a target set of questions. The project portal is a Web-based portal system through which workers can view and track at a high level the progress of projects. The pilot enriched project information in a manner that was tangible and valuable for project workers. More importantly, it enabled direct demonstration of the value that contextual information could provide at the project level.

Key Steps in the Project Profile Pilot

Several steps were necessary to operationalize the pilot. At a high level, key steps involved:

1. Review of existing project work within the organization
   a. Understand key project processes
   b. Uncover potential gaps of value for project workers
2. Map of existing and potential pools of data
   a. Identify existing and potentially new pools of project information
   b. Narrow down information sources for pilot

   c. Map information and knowledge sources to subset of questions/needs by project workers
3. Generations of context information for projects
   a. Generate a project profile
   b. Use profile to endow project and objects with context
   c. Generate a search-focused profile from the project profile
4. Making referential information accessible through the project portal

The first step of the pilot involved a review of existing practices and needs related to project work within the bank. Many bank project are circumscribed to a rigid set of rules and practices, yielding a well-defined project life cycle. This facilitated discussions with actual project workers regarding perceived gaps with the information and knowledge that existing project IT systems provided to them. These workers were asked what types of information and knowledge could help them with parts of their project work and could be conveyed through a medium like the project portal.

Following this first step, a review of bank structured data sources was conducted to identify those which contained project-related information. Based on the project life cycle review in the first step, additional reports, documents, and unstructured information sources were identified as containing value-added information and able to reflect knowledge accumulated over time. The life cycle review highlighted several routine, semistructured pieces of documentation generated along project execution that could be automatically mined for information.

A subset of these structured and semistructured information sources was then identified for use in the pilot. Key criteria for inclusion included ease of integration into the pilot and how reliable and value-added each source was. An example of valuable data sources not included in the pilot were recommendation-related systems in which users disseminate "what works" and other experiential knowledge; this type of information was deemed too complex for the pilot, although likely invaluable for future iterations of the project profile. Many project-related documents that were included nonetheless contained important pieces of knowledge, such as lessons learned, important considerations, risk trade-off discussions, and other qualitative items. Taken together, these documents could provide valuable insights relevant to ongoing and future bank projects.

For the pilot to drive tangible value to users, a subset of the gaps/needs identified by project workers was then mapped to information fields from chosen data sources. This mapping was composed of standardized querylike procedures. The mapping often did not address the need directly, but provided some directional information that could still be useful to facilitate the search process by users. It is worthwhile to note that as not all projects had the same information sources available to them, mappings tried to avail themselves of many often redundant information fields in order to arrive at some level of response.

In the next phase of the pilot, contextual project information that was generated from culling of information and application of the querylike rules yielded the creation of the project profile. Figure 16.2 illustrates an extended version of this process. The image proposes that the project profile could be used to engender individual information objects with contextual information. This aspect, while part of the pilot's conceptual development, has not yet been implemented.

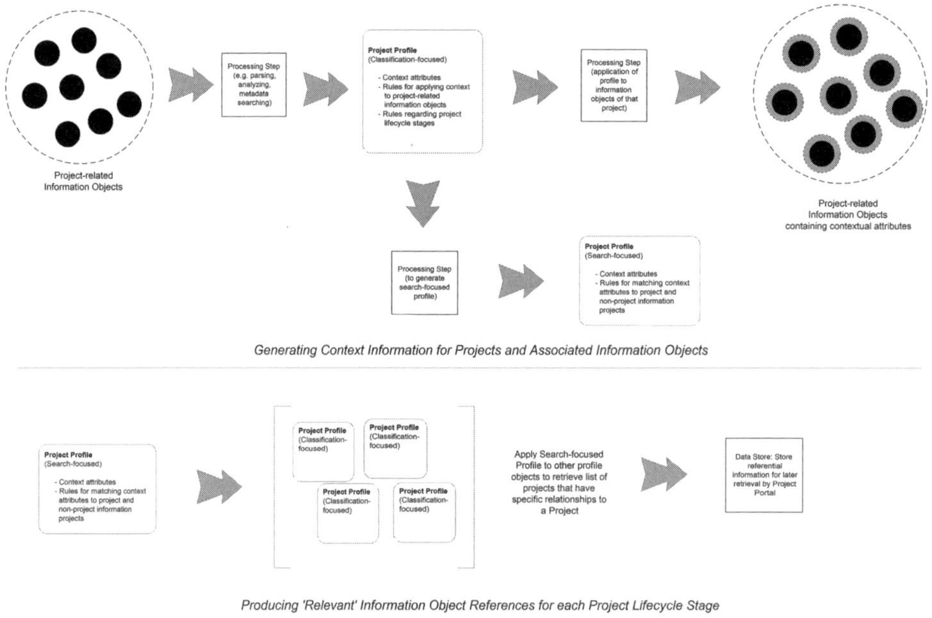

Figure 16.2.

Subsequent steps involved using this profile to enrich the bank's project-related systems. Specifically, the pilot aimed to enrich the bank's project portal. The project portal was enhanced by inclusion of answers derived from the predefined questions the profile was constructed to answer.

Project Profile Design

The pilot version of the project profile was conceptually organized around three types of information:

- Structured data from structured data systems like SAP and its Business Warehouses
- Keywords extracted from project documents
- Concepts or topical descriptors extracted from project documents

In addition, the profile contained rules that shaped how data was used for achieving various goals, such as deriving answers to predefined user questions. For ease of implementation, the profile did also contain actual results from these questions or queries, facilitating retrieval but necessitating the ongoing refreshing of stored data over time. More advanced or real-time implementation approaches were considered and are possible, but these were deemed unnecessarily complex, particularly since bank project information tends not to change very rapidly.

Ultimately, the goal was to design a profile that enabled users to introspect projects through various facets, depending on defined needs. This was and in many cases is still a shift from the approach taken by most systems, which aim to collect information that describes only a project but not important contextual dimensions of the project (such as risks, outcomes, impact, lessons learned, etc.) in a continual and automated fashion. Making these contextual dimensions available through the project portal was a first step in unlocking the knowledge generated by bank projects and making it available to enrich subsequent projects. Whether a sales campaign or internal supply-chain activity, many "projectlike" activities within most organizations are able to achieve this contextual dimension only through ad-hoc, manual efforts wherein analysts perform the integration and synthesis aspects.

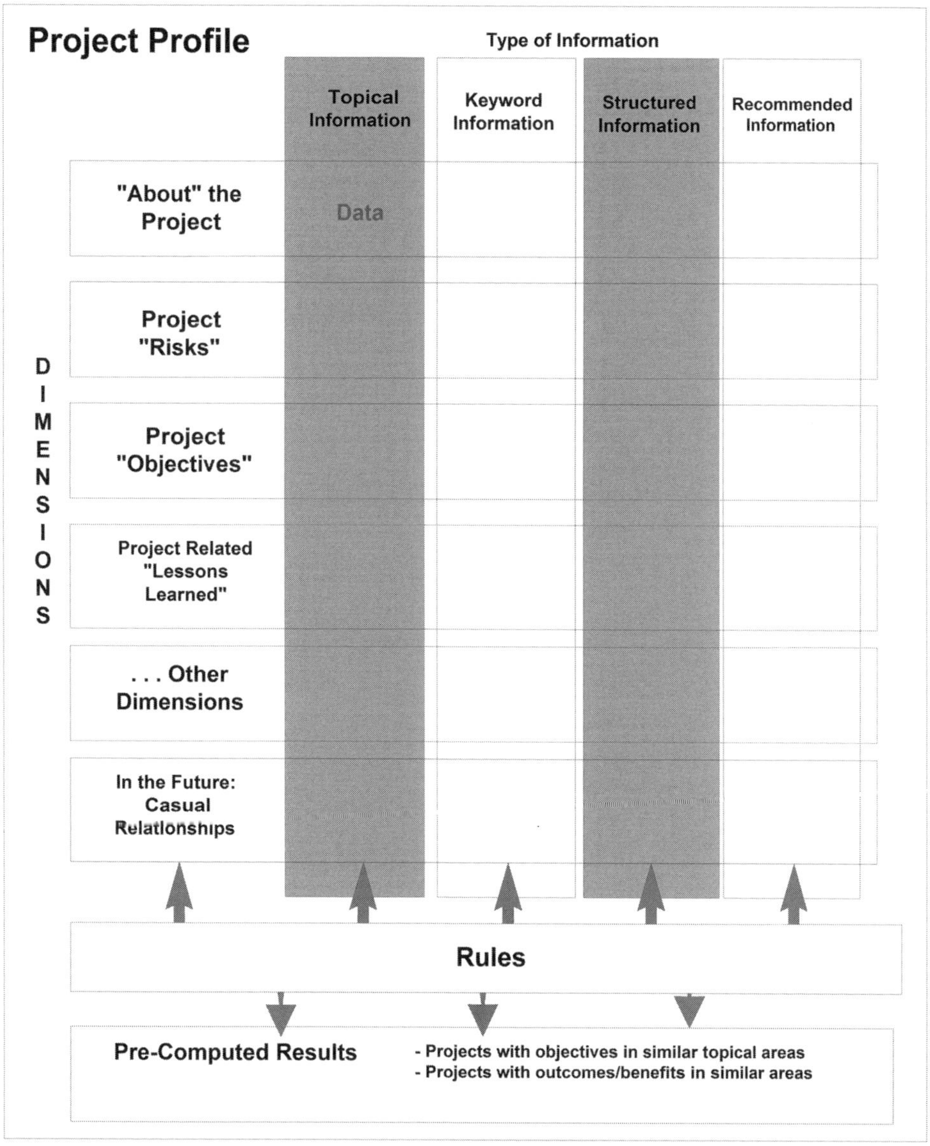

Figure 16.3.

As the conceptual drawing of the pilot's project profile in figure 16.3 suggests, the profile would store or make accessible various data across various different project "contextual domains," such as its "risks" and "benefits." As discussed, underpinning these contextual domains were data drawn from project document extraction, structured information, and other sources. Since the profile would be used primarily for back-office purposes and to mitigate complexity of the pilot, relatively no work was done in the pilot to improve or consolidate pieces of information that were redundant or "noisy."

For the pilot, a set of twenty-three document types and enterprise data repositories were used as data sources, based on our review of a typical project life cycle. Some notes and caveats included:

- These sources represented the main documents/repositories associated with projects.
- Among these sources, information retrieved from structured data stores (like SAP) acted as primary or authoritative sources for data elements for which they have been identified as a source.
- These sources were in part selected because they contained pertinent information for answering specific questions defined for the pilot. Furthermore, they tended to have some common internal structure (i.e., a standard or required outline of sections or table of contents), which facilitated machine-based introspection.
- Many of the data sources not included in the pilot were either too technical in nature or too informal in nature. In the former case, documents that were too technical (e.g., lending documents such as financing plans) did not provide information broadly descriptive enough for the needs of the profile; their language and substance did not represent what most users would be looking for when searching for related projects, lessons learned, and other dimensions. In the later case, documents that were too informal (e.g., project team e-mails) would have been too difficult for then existing content extraction software to quickly comprehend; these would have required one to follow progressions of previous e-mails in order to understand the context, nature, and subject matter of the discussion.

Generation of the Project Profile

A key challenge in the creation of the project profile was the information acquisition process, both from structured and unstructured sources. Each data source presented a unique list of peculiarities that had to be dealt with in order to arrive at usable results.

Structured Data Sources

Most organizations store standard and company-specific project information within centralized repositories and databases. The difficulty here is generally less about data integration and more about identification of relevant sources, interpretation of data, and quality of the data. For the bank, several project-related data are stored within the enterprise SAP system as well as task-/function-specific systems. One of the benefits from a review of a typical project life cycle was the identification of which systems were the authoritative stores for different data elements.

Unstructured Data Sources

Many of the pilot's data sources were formal documents and other semistructured sources. These contained factual data as well as important nuggets of knowledge that could provide important insights for project workers but that had typically been filed away and uncovered only through specific inquiry. In order to obtain usable information from these sources, the pilot employed a concept extraction and keyword extraction application software engine called Teragram.

Teragram is an advanced natural-language-processing software product leveraging an extensive data dictionary and linguistic rules to provide more comprehensive answers to questions. Teragram was acquired and integrated into the SAS platform of software in 2008. The software itself has several processing capabilities, but the pilot focused on use of its concept extraction and keyword extraction functionality. Concept extraction in this case meant mapping of keywords found within a text document to categories/facets predefined by a thesaurus of terms. Teragram was configured to use the bank's standard thesaurus as well as some industrial sector-focused vocabularies. Keyword extraction involves the identification of terms from text that are usually deemed as nontrivial or of frequent usage.

Concept and keyword extraction provided a means for primitive capture and conversion of knowledge to a form easily usable by the pilot. As discussed, the pilot did not aim toward providing definitive answers to questions but rather more toward providing indicative answers—for instance, identifying projects with learning in similar topical areas rather than providing the lessons learned themselves. Concept and keyword extraction helped to "boil down" knowledge contained within documents (like lessons learned, risks, etc.) into common concepts and searchable keywords, which facilitated the pilot's implementation and integration into systems like the project portal. As such, this approach balanced the enrichment of projects with pilot constraints.

Different data sources employed concept and/or keyword extraction in varying degrees. The selection of whether to use concept extraction versus keyword extraction (or a combination) was primarily based on the text analyzed vis-à-vis anticipated goals (driven primarily by the questions the pilot's profile aimed to answer). In general, concept or keyword extraction was not applied throughout the entirety of documents, but rather to specific segments of documents identified during the data sources identification phase. As will be discussed below, different questions the pilot aimed to answer required use of different, specific segments within documents.

Concept extraction using Teragram had shortcomings that preclude its use in many situations. These included the following:

- Concepts derived using Teragram were limited to those facets predefined by the thesaurus in use. Consequently, the extractor was not able to "adapt" concepts to a text, but rather force-fitted the text to its predefined set of concepts. While allowing the software to adapt concepts from a text presents obvious advantages, the performance of the software coupled with the drive toward simplicity of the pilot led to a conscripted set of concept choices. However, since the pilot aimed to address specific questions, this approach provided adequate results.

- Many bank thesaurus keywords serve multiple concepts. For instance, "education" can describe both the education sector as well as the "public health" facet. Analysis of sample extractions from bank documents demonstrated that this issue led to concepts that were only descriptive half of the time.
- Concepts were selected based on the frequency of keywords related to that concept. Since the semantic meanings of texts were not part of the concept selection process, there were apt to be significant margins of error. This was particularly true for texts that were more verbose or wide ranging in subject matter. Teragram has semantic concept extraction capabilities, but these were not fully available at the time of the pilot's initial implementation.

Keyword extraction also had some shortcomings:

- Teragram keyword extraction was able to cull the more nontrivial keywords. However, it was not able to distinguish the importance of different words. Keyword frequency was the sole means for scoring keyword importance, but this can be misleading since some terms that are used sparingly can be crucial to the meaning of a text. As a result, a conservative approach was utilized wherein all keywords extracted by Teragram were viewed equally. For the purposes of the pilot, keyword extraction was most effective over shorter text segments. Long texts tended to generate long keyword lists that diluted the relevance of different keywords.
- Keyword-based matching is inherently limited, since it limits the search space to only those keywords extracted. Concept-based matching abstracts keywords into common analogs; this enables documents with dissimilar keywords to nonetheless be paired if their keywords are analogous to each other. Keyword-based matching requires that the source and target texts contain the same or highly similar descriptor keywords. As a result, keyword-based matching is effective only when one can make the assumption that the words used in both source and target documents will be significantly similar or exactly the same.

These limitations were generally remedied by tailoring the use of concept or keyword extraction to each query and to each data source. Texts selected as sources were generally focused on relevant subject matter and tended to be short. Concept extraction was generally used in cases where the goal was to determine general topical areas rather than substantive meanings. Keywords were used in cases where texts were determined generally to be composed of precise wording or where keyword matching was believed to be satisfactory.

Delivering Value to Project Workers

As discussed, the pilot was focused on delivering tangible value to project workers by endeavoring to address qualified information and knowledge gaps. Many of the gaps the pilot was able to address involved facilitating the search for similar historical experience by way of identifying similar past projects with similar risks, lessons learned, and so on. Usually, this process is achieved through manual work and is limited by a researcher's past experiences and word of mouth. Since project success can be appreciably improved by learning from past experiences, identification of "similar projects" was deemed by most project workers interviewed as having high value. Some of the queries the pilot's profile addressed were:

Find projects that have similar aspects to a given project—

1. Find projects with objectives in similar topical areas.
2. Find projects with outcomes in similar topical areas.
3. Find projects with failures in similar topical areas.
4. Find projects with successes in similar topical areas.
5. Find projects with similar types of methodologies.
6. Find projects with risks in similar topical areas.
7. Find projects with indicators in similar topical areas.
8. Find projects with problems in similar topical areas.
9. Find projects with similar types of results.
10. Find similar types of projects.

Find aspects from other projects that could be useful for a given project—

11. What were the topical areas of lessons learned used in similar projects?
12. What previous projects were used in the project design?

To derive answers to the above questions, several queries, dubbed "search-type rules," were crafted. Each of the questions above had its own search-type rule, and some questions referenced results from other questions. For the most part, search-type rules defined both the data elements that should be utilized as well as how these data should be processed. These results were generally then matched against those from other projects in order to identify "similar projects" along a desired dimension.

These queries were a first and crude attempt at arriving at suitable answers. Anticipating that over time these rules would be supplanted by more sophisticated data processing algorithms, the rules themselves are not as important as is the overall type of architecture that is created through the use of such rules. In this approach, individual data needs are uncovered through individual code rules. This is in contrast to more typical structured data approaches wherein filtration of data from standardized data "views" tends to predominate. The implementation approach taken here is only one of many. A popular analogous approach could have implemented such rules through autonomous computer agents or "bots."

Since these queries were based on documents and data that are produced during the life cycle of projects, these queries would have to be refreshed periodically. This is particularly true as projects ended or began a new phase of their life cycle. Ideally, this process of metadata replenishment would be performed each time a relevant new data source, such as a new project document, became available or each time a project moved to a new stage in its life cycle. In practice, the pilot opted for the simpler refresh policy of periodic reconstitution of "open" project profiles.

Example of Query from Contextualized Environment

Below is an example of a search-type rule that tried to pair a given project with other projects whose outcomes addressed similar topical areas. Topical areas in this context denoted subject matter, such as children's health or small business development. Some of the acronyms used refer to specific types of bank project documents.

Find projects with outcomes in similar topical areas

Data/criteria
Source
Project benefits

- PAD (Section B.3 or C.3 "Benefits and Target Population")
- Staff appraisal report (section IV, "Benefits")
- ISDS (section I)
- Memorandum and recommendation of the president ("Benefits" section)

Cost-benefit/effectiveness
PAD (section E)
Outcomes expected

- Implementation completion report (section 4.1)
- Implementation completion memorandum (section C, "Main Outcomes")
- PCR (section 4.1, "Outcome/Achievement of Objectives")
- PPAR (section 2, "Objectives and Implementation of Assessed Projects" for the project in question)

Unexpected outcomes
Project performance assessment report (section 2 and annex A)
Factors affecting outcomes

- Implementation completion report (section 5)
- Project performance assessment report (section 2)

Performance ranking: outcomes
ICR or PPAR's "Performance Ranking: Outcomes" rating

1. Run Teragram over the "project benefits" (PAD/SAR) and "cost benefit/effectiveness" (PAD) fields to extract keywords from these fields (not using any taxonomy).
2. Match keywords retrieved in step 1 with keywords derived from the "Outcomes expected" (ICR, PPAR), "Unexpected outcomes" (PPAR) and "Factors affecting outcomes" (ICR, PPAR) information of other projects.

3. Retrieve the twenty projects with the highest match rate that results with matching keywords in steps 1 and 2, prioritized based on how well the items are matched.
4. For each project retrieved in the previous step, display for users the value of the "Performance Ranking: Outcomes" (ICR or PPAR) variable, if this is available (usually only for closed projects). The rational here is that display of this rating will help to guide users as to the usefulness of the retrieved project in meeting its outcomes. Depending on the intended use of the retrieved information, this dimension may/may not be important. For instance, positive ratings could denote beneficial or at least positive outcomes.

Schema for query "Find projects with outcomes in similar topical areas"

Rationale:

- This query matches the expected benefits of the source project with the outcomes achieved by other projects as a basis for finding projects with similar outcomes.
- The source project is normally active and consequently usually does not have any (or has few) final outcomes achieved. As a result, we use expected benefits as a proxy for the outcomes one expects to achieve through the source project.
- Projects for which users are seeking should have outcomes that it is hoped will help users. As a result, their "Outcomes expected" and other end-of-project criteria should contain data.
- The performance ranking is displayed for matched projects to enable users to easily identify those projects that may have had positive or negative outcomes. Attempts to more accurately isolate "positive/beneficial" outcomes or "negative/bad" outcomes through the use of concepts or keywords have not proved effective. Use of a human-driven ranking system (such as the outcomes rating being used) seems to be the best/highest-quality alternative.
- It is important to note that the twenty-concept limitation imposed in step 3 could be changed based on findings from the implementation of the pilot. This quantity was arbitrarily determined.

Tying the Profile to Project Workers' Interface

The bank's project portal system was chosen as the vehicle through which to enable questions addressed by the project profile to be made available to users. As a Web-based system, the portal generally operates with a requirement of fast-response Web pages. This was part of the impetus leading the pilot's project profile to contain pregenerated/precalculated answers to the target set of questions. By computing

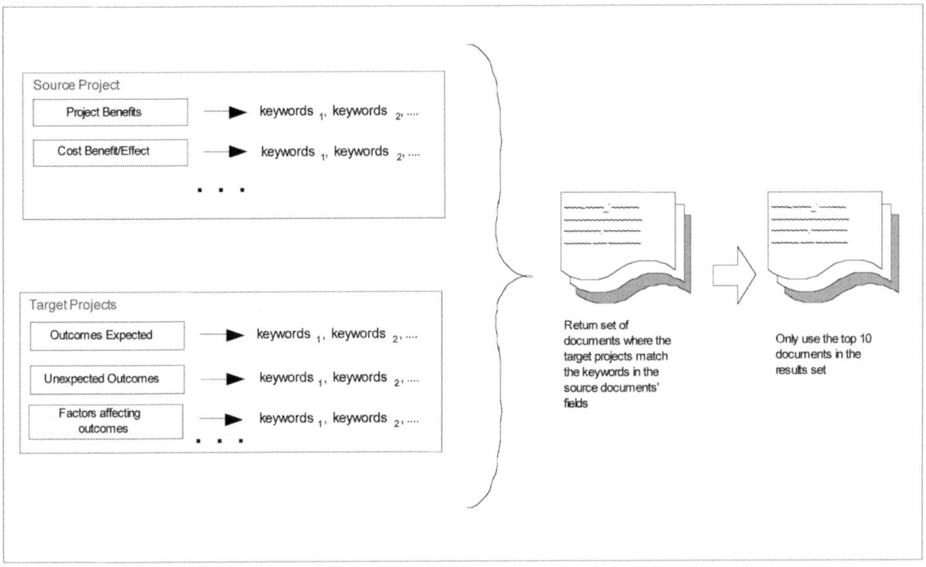

Figure 16.4.

answers to all questions up front, project portal Web pages were not taxed by this process in real time.

Beyond the project portal, the pilot did envisage the possibility of other modes of use for its contextualized project information, although these were not implemented. Specifically studied were document context browsing capabilities and "search-box" integration.

Document Context Browsing

Because the project profile encapsulated rules that address data across the whole project life cycle, it would be well positioned as a source for engendering context information about project-related objects. In other words, the profile could help IT systems and users to better understand the "what is" rather than just "what contains" of a particular document or other object. This could help augment how users browse for information and knowledge acquired during the steps of the project cycle rather than solely browse by title, date, or topic; systems could offer more natural relationship descriptions, such as "browse by documents/objects that resulted from the project approval meeting. . . ."

Although several implementation options for this are possible, the simplest would be to use the project profile as a type of pseudonym for object context. In other words, the profile would contain the necessary information enabling browser systems to retrieve necessary information on demand. Beyond ease of implementation, a benefit of this approach is that it avoids the creation of another data structure containing lists for browsing software. Documents would be able to "request" contextual information from the profile at the same time as browsing software would be able to identify those documents having desired relationships.

Search Processes

The search process represents a clear arena for the use of contextualization and therefore for uncovering knowledge contained in contextualized objects. As figure 16.5 suggests, contextual information within the profile could in the simplest scenario be added to the search space of queries. This is particularly true of search engines that focus on identification of documents or other objects as results (in contrast to those simply searching Web pages with links to documents).

Outcomes of the Pilot

Many of the more important queries identified by the pilot based on more straightforward data sources were implemented into the project portal, as was expected. These queries were precalculated, and their results set made available through a users' click on a hyperlink in the project portal page of each project. More recent initiatives enforcing the need for improved "operations results" has reincited urgency for the benefits the pilot promised, and some of its concepts are now being integrated into an operations portal, which tracks projects in a broader context of bank work processes.

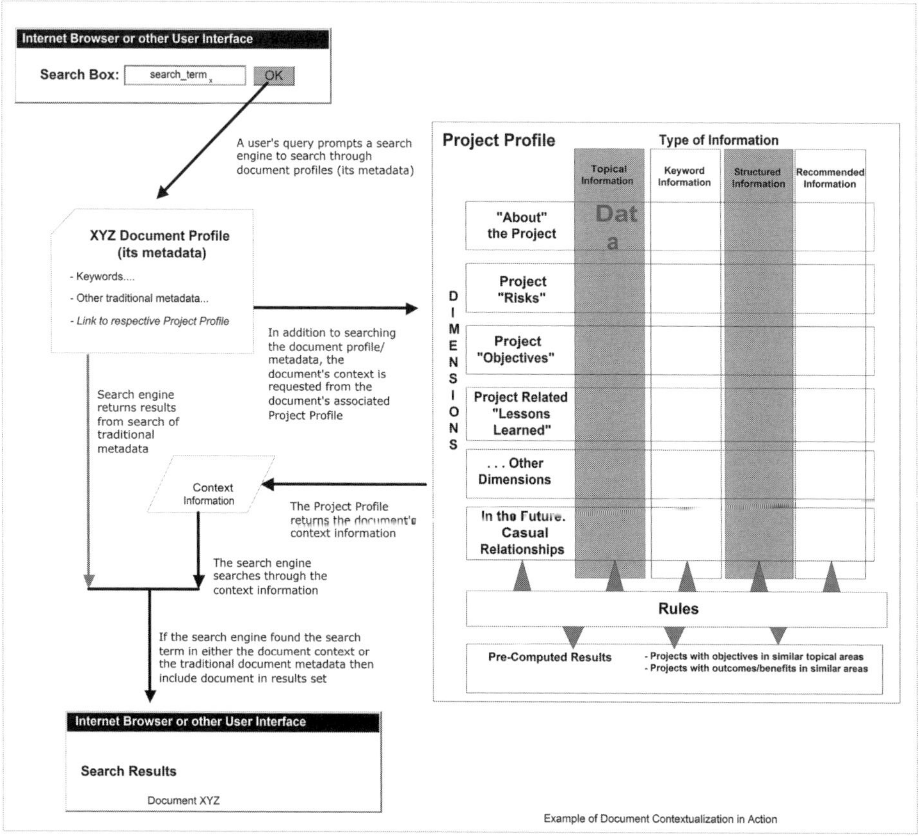

Figure 16.5

The key challenge to implementation of the pilot has been difficulty in data extraction from the structured and semistructured data sources. This has been partly a technical difficulty, but also a data management difficulty, wherein the expansive operations of the bank have made centralization and control of project data objects difficult to cull. In addition, the cross-sectional nature of the pilot and its goal of enriching existing systems has required much more extensive reviews and approvals as part of the bank's data management schema than originally anticipated. As a result, the human resources necessary to tune results, analyze data sources and data definitions, and review related technical aspects have been greater than anticipated, and hence full implementation of all the concepts recommended have proceeded more gradually than anticipated.

CONCLUSION AND FUTURE CONSIDERATIONS

As this chapter has described, the World Bank has begun to enrich its project work environment through more extensive use of its data, information, and knowledge. Capturing better contextual information about projects helps project-related systems in their goal to deliver the right information and knowledge to the right person at the right time. Untangling knowledge embedded within documents and other data objects presents a clear opportunity to leverage value already being generated to improve project success and address future challenges organizations will face. Initiatives like this pilot are only a modest first step. Clearly we would expect that at some point the promises of IT would be realized through improved artificial intelligence, improved natural-language processing, and more facile and accurate indexing, structuring, repurposing, and repackaging of information independent of direct human intermediation. While the technologies will without a doubt provide more advanced implementations of the approach discussed in this chapter, it is equally probable that some of the underlying principles embodied by the pilot will not change.

17

Knowledge Management at Infosys

An Assessment

T. Kanti Srikantaiah

RATIONALE

Knowledge management is becoming increasingly important in meeting the objectives of any large organization. As an interdisciplinary field, knowledge management is a product of the 1990s, with many practitioners in such disciplines as business, engineering, information science, management, communications, and education. KM embraces those disciplines and treats knowledge as an entity dynamically embedded in networks, processes, repositories, and people. This has led to managing knowledge at various stages, such as creation, capture, codification, organization, sharing, and application. The reasons are many: first, the advancement of technology; second, the exploding nature of information; third, organizations competing for projects in order to survive; fourth, the increasing nature of collaboration and regulatory reforms; and fifth, an evolving management style, focusing on increasing productivity with fewer resources. Today, on a global basis, the investment in knowledge management has grown to several billions of dollars. In the United States, organizations such as Accenture, IBM, GM, World Bank, and others have benefited by implementing knowledge management systems. The benefits, among others, include increased productivity, enhanced cost savings, avoidance of redundancy, minimization of similar mistakes, greater efficiency, improved quality, and so forth.

Infosys as an organization has implemented many knowledge management tools and techniques for the benefit of Infoscions and the organization. Through its humble beginnings in the 1980s, Infosys has become a leading IT organization with more than one hundred thousand employees in seventeen countries. The number of projects in Infosys has grown tremendously, from a handful in the 1980s to around five thousand in 2008/2009. These projects acquire a high volume of new and reusable knowledge. They generate a high volume of further knowledge, which, if not properly managed, results in a loss of productivity and added costs. Infosys realized this potential problem early and has set up various KM applications to access and share knowledge with enhanced effectiveness.

This chapter provides a description of the efforts by Infosys to capture and share knowledge, a summary of key findings through analysis of information gathered, and gaps and issues identified in the current KM system.

BACKGROUND

The growth of Infosys is phenomenal. Infosys, founded in 1981 with seven people, expanded to more than 150 employees in 1991. Today, the organization employs over one hundred thousand people all over the world, across thirty locations in seventeen countries. The Bangalore campus alone has twenty-six thousand employees. Infosys is the second-largest IT firm in India and is the first Indian firm to be listed on NASDAQ. Most of the company's clients are from Fortune 1000 companies located in North America, Europe, and the Asia-Pacific region. Naturally, the company operates globally, with eight development centers in India, five in North America, and one each in the United Kingdom, East Asia, and Australia. In addition, several marketing offices have been established in other countries.

Among the staff, 70 percent are software engineers and program analysts, 12 percent are project managers (PMs) and special project managers (SPMs), 8 percent are group project managers (GPMs) and delivery managers (DMs), and 10 percent are from human resources, the KM group, finance, administration, and other areas. The repeat business of Infosys is 97 percent, a level that speaks highly of the organization's credibility. As of January 2009, Infosys had a total of 586 clients.

During the company's first decade, the revenue was less than US $4 million, but over the next few years Infosys grew at a compounded rate of 70 percent. In U.S. dollars, the revenue of Infosys in FY05–06 was $2.35 billion; in FY06–07 it was $3.1 billion; in FY07–08 it was $4.1 billion; and in FY08–09 it was $4.6 billion to $4.7 billion. Historical milestones at Infosys are listed in table 17.1. Similarly, Infosys growth is displayed in graphic form in figure 17.1.

The Infosys industry segmentation has stayed more or less uniform, with the exception of growth in transportation and insurance. This segmentation by industry for the five years covering 2004–2008 is displayed in table 17.2.

EVOLUTION OF KNOWLEDGE MANAGEMENT AT INFOSYS

On a global level, knowledge management is becoming increasingly important to meeting organizational objectives with the investment of billions of dollars. Infosys, possessing a result-oriented culture, initiated knowledge management in 1999 with strong support from senior management. Infosys has accomplished a great deal in the area of knowledge management due to the creativity and hard work of its KM group. The Infosys vision of knowledge management is of an environment "where every action is fully enabled by the power of knowledge; which truly believes in leveraging knowledge for innovation; where every employee is empowered by the knowledge of every other employee; which is a globally respected knowledge leader."

Infosys defines knowledge management as "people, process, and technology directed towards the harvest and reuse of organizational knowledge." The company

Table 17.1. Infosys Evolution

Date	*Infosys Milestone*
1981	Led by N. R. Narayana Murthy, seven young people start a small company in Pune with US $250 and a dream to create quality software First client: Data Basics Corporation in New York
1983	With the MICO engagement, moves to Bangalore
1987	Opens its first international sales office in Boston
1987–1990	Over one hundred employees work on-site and offshore; global delivery mode is evolving Moves into Europe Labinf and Reebok France
1992	Strategic business units set up
1993	Goes public and shares wealth with its employees—the ESOP has arrived
1994	Corporate headquarters moves to Electronic City; development center opens
1995	First European office is opened in the United Kingdom, with global development centers in Toronto and Mangalore
1996	Infosys Foundation formally launched
1999	Touches the US $100 million mark and is listed on the NASDAQ; becomes the twenty-first company in the world to be accredited the CMM level 5 standard
2000	Banks 2000 relaunches as the Finacle suite of products; revenue grows to US $200 million.
2001	Murthy is rated among Time/CNN twenty-five most influential businesspeople in the world; Infosys is rated best employer by Business Worlde/Hewitt
2002	Offers secondary ADS offering; grows to 345 clients across industry verticals; launches WIBTA—with the Wharton School—program
2003	Expands operations in Pune and Chennai; sets up new centers in Thiruvanantapuram
2004	Becomes a billion-dollar company; acquires Expert Information Services Pty. Limited, Australia; establishes Infosys Consulting Inc.; grows to four hundred-plus clients and about twenty-nine thousand employees
2005	Selected for the Global MAKE Hall of Fame
2006	Celebrates its twenty-fifth anniversary; revenues cross US $2 billion; employee strength 52,000-plus
2007	Crosses the US $3 billion revenue mark
2008	Crosses the US $4 billion revenue mark

Source: Adapted from Infosys display.

believes that all organizational learning can be leveraged in delivering advantages to the customer and that all Infosys employees (Infoscions) should have the full backing of the organization's learning behind them. Infosys's knowledge management motto is "Learn Once, Use Anywhere!"

Infosys's key objectives for knowledge management are:

- Better quality—taking best practices from small pockets in the organization and institutionalizing them throughout the organization
- Better revenue productivity (reuse, cycle time reduction, virtual teamwork)—enabling the company's global delivery model and dispersed teams
- Reduced risk—diversifying into new technologies, domains, geographical areas, services, and resource interchangeability
- Greater market awareness

Infosys Technologies – v2

- 55+ quarters of continuous growth (top- and bottom-line), meeting analysts' estimates
- Zero debt; $4+ billion in revenue
- 97% repeat business; 90+% on-time delivery

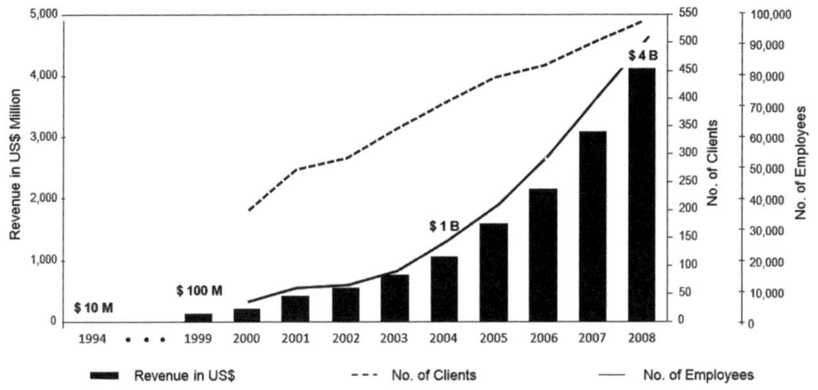

Figure 17.1.

- Higher revenue growth
- Increased customer satisfaction

The knowledge management program in Infosys has evolved in many ways to fulfill the objectives of the organization:

1992: Body of knowledge (BOK)
1995: Online technical bulletin board
1996: Corporate intranet unveiled
1997: Online sales and marketing system introduced

Table 17.2. Industry Segmentation

	2008	*2007*	*2006*	*2005*	*2004*
Manufacturing	14.7	13.5	13.9	14.4	14.8
Banking, financial services and insurance	35.7	37.4	36.0	34.6	14.8
Banking and financial services	28.5	30.2	28.5	25.2	23.7
Insurance	7.2	7.2	7.5	9.4	12.9
Telecom	21.6	19.3	16.5	18.5	16.6
Retail	11.8	10.0	10.1	9.8	11.6
Energy and utilities	5.2	5.3	4.7	3.2	3.0
Transportation	2.5	2.4	5.1	7.6	7.1
Others	8.5	12.1	13.7	11.9	10.3
Total	100.00	100.00	100.00	100.00	100.00

Source: Infosys. Annual Report (2008).

1998:	Project leader toolkit introduced
1999:	KM initiative formalized
	People Knowledge Map (PKM)
2000:	Publication process
	Genesis of the KM identity at Infosys
	Integrated KM portal launched
	Satellite servers added at global locations
2001:	KM road shows are conducted in different DCs (development centers)
	KM DC Champions network identified
	Launch of B and P activities
	Integrated project management (IPM) tool integrated with the KM system
	Employee skill system (ESS) integrated with the KM system
	Electronic bulletin board integrated with the KM system
2002:	Launch of KM in projects
	Discussion forums Web interface launched
	KM processes integrated with the delivery processes
	KM prime role was introduced
	Knowledge alliance is initiated
	First KM road show in United States is hosted
	Recognized as Asia's Most Admired Knowledge Enterprise (MAKE)
2003:	Launch of KM discussion forum anchors
	Integration with IPM
	Dedicated promotion space
	Various communities of practice formalized across the organization
	Recognized as the Globally Most Admired Knowledge Enterprise (MAKE) and Asia MAKE
2004:	KM patrons network established, focusing on deployment at IBU (integrated business units) level
	KShop available on extranet
	On-site presence strengthened
	Data sharing on quarterly DC KM performance through KSTATS
	Recognized as the Globally Most Admired Knowledge Enterprise (MAKE) and Asia MAKE
2005:	KM for key accounts
	KM metrics report for IBUs introduced
	KM R&R program relaunched
	KM benefits assessment initiated
	RSS feeds launched
	Increased focus on tacit knowledge sharing
	Recognized as the Globally Most Admired Knowledge Enterprise (MAKE), Asia MAKE, and India MAKE
2006	Pilot for KM for IBUs
	KM networks at DC piloted
	Search engine reframed to use Microsoft SharePoint 2003 platform
	Launch of MasterMinds
	Asia MAKE award and India MAKE award

2007	SME (subject matter experts) review of content mandated; new review process launched
	Integrated deployment framework along with measurement and metrics formulated
	KM newsletter launched
	Publication workflow changed to incorporate mandatory review
	Recognized as the Globally Most Admired Knowledge Enterprise (MAKE), Asia MAKE, and India MAKE
2008	Integration with IPM+ completed
	Recognized as the Globally Most Admired Knowledge Enterprise (MAKE) and India MAKE
2009	(planned) My KShop, personalization for taxonomy and content types, to be launched; PKM to be completely reframed; FRISCO delivery

CAPTURING AND SHARING EXPLICIT KNOWLEDGE

BOK

In 1992, the education and research (E&R) department, which had the mandate of "empowering people through knowledge," was given the responsibility to set up an organization-wide repository focusing on experiential learning. Body of knowledge (BOK) was implemented. Infoscions contributed BOK material with a review mechanism to screen content, applicability, and presentation aspects. A user-friendly template was set up to record experiential knowledge. In 1997, it was reposted as a Web-based application with HTML content and made available to staff through the intranet.

Technical Bulletin Board/Discussion Forum

In 1995, Infosys launched a companywide e-mail system and a technical bulletin board. The bulletin board was a dynamic knowledge-sharing forum where employees could post queries and offer/receive responses. Although the forum had no owner—and there was no imperative to participate—it was still very active. Typically, a posted question would receive one or more responses within minutes.

This is now known as the discussion forum. Today, the discussion forum is also called the knowledge exchange, which brings in the collaborative feature by giving Infoscions an option to post their technical queries and get responses in the most relevant technical forum.

SPARSH

In 1996, the companywide intranet "SPARSH" was in place, promoting the sharing of knowledge. Most of Infosys information was posted to this companywide intranet functioning as the central information portal. It consists of several thousand nodes spread throughout the global development centers (DCs) and marketing offices. Sparsh facilitated Geo, IBU, department Web pages, and personal Web pages with bulletin boards, as well as technical discussions connecting to other available knowledge mechanisms. Objectives included (a) motivation—making people want to share knowledge, (b) facilitation—making it easier to use, and, (c) awareness—making people aware of the KM architecture that has been created and their roles in using it. Infosys has tried to capture its knowledge base in a very intensive manner through this intranet. The Sparsh home page has a pull-down menu under appropriate categories and useful links to other sites, as shown here:

My Links
Communications @ Infy
Telephone Directory
Email
AHD
ICICI Bank
Inbay
Leave System
Library
Payana
PRidE
Performagic
PayWorld
Exception Authorization
Claims System
Infy Mailers

GDM

The underlying framework for the new organizational structure was the global delivery model (GDM). Infosys developed this model on the principle of distributed project management, that is, executing the project at multiple locations with flawless integration.

Sales teams at each business unit would bid for software projects in their respective markets. Once a project was landed, a technical team from the project delivery unit attached to that business unit would travel to the client's site to assess project requirements. Based on the project requirements, a team would be assembled at the software development center attached to that business unit to develop the software solution. Alternatively, if the project requirements dictated, a virtual team would be assembled from multiple software development centers worldwide. After the software was developed, the technical team would revisit the client to install the software as well as handle maintenance and training-related issues.

GDM enabled Infosys to operate as a virtual corporation that could work across multiple time zones on a twenty-four-hour work cycle. Other advantages included:

- Scalability—software engineers at all locations had access to organizational resources, helping them respond swiftly to client requirements.
- Reduced cost of completing a project.

The company pioneered the global delivery model (GDM) for development of customized software solutions, which is based on the principle of taking work where it can be done best, makes the most economic sense, and carries the least acceptable risk. Infosys innovation with the globally distributed client work resulted in attaining level 5 of the Capability Maturity Model ten years ago. It also has won the Most Admired Knowledge Enterprise (MAKE) awards at the global level, Asian level, and Indian level for many years.

However, all corporate functions, such as finance, planning, marketing, quality, HR, education and research, and information systems, are based in Bangalore, India.

PKM

Infosys realized that because of the organizational growth, informal mechanisms for getting to know experts were no longer adequate. In response, E&R (education and training) developed a knowledge directory to be called People Knowledge Map (PKM) that pointed out experts within the organization. The registration of experts to PKM was voluntary and based on the idea that it would attract highly enthusiastic registrants, ensuring high credibility for PKM. A taxonomy was developed to represent knowledge, and the People Knowledge Map was based on the self-policing model. Today, a multilevel taxonomy of topics exists to reflect Infosys content with 3,600 nodes.

The People Knowledge Map was developed as an expert locator—a company "yellow pages" for finding people. Self-proclaimed experts list themselves in the directory and classify their level of skill/expertise according to a knowledge hierarchy, which comprises four levels and more than 1,200 topics. Since the credibility of this system is critical, it includes only people who are willing to participate—that is, people willing to share their knowledge—and not those who are experts but who do not have the time or inclination to take part.

Today, the People Knowledge Map operates as an application where Infoscions faced with problems can locate a resource link to find the experts in their problem area. They can get complete details regarding the relevant experts and their areas of expertise before contacting them for help.

KMail and K Plugged

KMail is an automated e-mail-response system for communities. It captures and archives all e-mails sent through mail-id-KMail@infosys.com within its repository. It also builds and maintains a repository of archived conversations. Further, it sends automated replies to the user queries sent by e-mail with relevant search results from its repository. Thus, KMail acts as an intelligent intermediary between the users and experts. The number of queries sent to the experts is reduced, and users get immediate responses to queries. Overall, it reduces e-mail traffic and network usage. Ultimately, KMail helps in developing a dynamically growing knowledge base to promote learning and reuse across the organization to assess knowledge exchange among users. Currently, KMail has 6,500 such users. Most queries receive a quick response from the archives or a somewhat longer response from the experts.

K Plugged is another tool to assist Infoscions. It deals with case studies resulting in projects. About eighty to eighty-five KM practices are available through this application.

BLOGS AND TEAM WIKIS

InfyBlogs, the intranet blogging platform, was launched on April 26, 2006. More than 13,000 users have since registered with InfyBlogs, and the number keeps growing by the day. The back-end code for this is from LiveJournal, an open source blogging software. It has been extremely beneficial to users. There are about fifteen thousand to twenty thousand individual blogs and about fifty community blogs in Infosys.

Similarly, Team Wiki is an intranet wiki portal started in 2007 and managed by the KM group. TeamWiki runs on the TWiki engine. A wiki is a Web 2.0 platform to create, share, and remix content. "Wiki" systems are fundamentally editable Web pages. It is a fun and useful way of communicating asynchronously over the Web for many existing intranet and public Internet sites. It aims to provide a transparent way to publish and exchange ideas with others over the Web. There are about two hundred communities participating in Team Wikis. There is a plan to integrate Team Wikis with the K-Shop portal (see below). At present, these wikis are functioning without any taxonomy.

K-Shop Portal

In 2000, the "integrated K-Shop portal" was introduced to access content/information and experts, link to key workflow applications, and provide subscription and customization capabilities. Each content type has its own home page. A content rating system, based on the knowledge currency unit, provides a measure of quality for content in the K-Shop repository. A subscription capability allows users to subscribe to specific types of content and receive e-mail notification on new content. Customization features enable users to reconfigure their home page to show only the topics in which they are interested. K-Shop search is central to the knowledge management activities. By navigating through the search knowledge assets link, a search for the required knowledge asset can be carried out in many different ways. Various options to filter the search results apart from keywords enable users to access artifacts more easily. K-Shop has been integrated with the internal project management system (IPM +) that provides information on projects undertaken by Infosys. K-Shop hosts the information as project snapshots where the users can view the generic details of every project.

The knowledge currency unit (KCU) scheme associated with the K-Shop portal, a key factor in promoting and providing incentive to knowledge sharing at Infosys, serves four purposes: visibility, reward, rating system, and level of activity. The KCU is a composite measure of the quality of a K-Shop document and is based on the number of times the document has been viewed by users and users' ratings of that document. When a document is first submitted to the repository, an SME reviews it and assigns it a certain number of points. Over time, as users look at the document, they can also assign points. The composite KCU is updated nightly. Every employee can view his or her own KCU score through a private activity-reporting system.

Project management emerged as an important and relevant area. The KM group began developing an IT-based project learning system (PLS) where project managers could submit a detailed account of their learning from a project.

Later, because of the environment, PLS was modified for an existing integrated project management (IPM) system to ask for project-related information that had a low proprietary knowledge component. Originally, IPM was a tool for project life cycle management. The KM group altered IPM to require a brief project summary and information regarding project's quality indexes. The project managers provided the project summary, while the quality department provided the quality indexes after the project audit.

With the employees encouraged to do their part in knowledge creation, it was top management's turn to fulfill its responsibility. This led to the creation of two knowledge-creating units: the domain competency group (DCG) and the technology competency group (TCG). DCG had a business focus and was assigned the role of creating new knowledge in various industry domains. It had experts on various domains such as aerospace, banking, e-commerce, insurance, manufacturing, retail, and telecommunications.

TCG was technology focused and had the responsibility of creating new knowledge in various technical domains. A key subsidiary of TCG was the software engineering and technology laboratories (SETLabs), which developed novel software engineering methodologies and technological architectures for Infosys's project teams worldwide.

To involve global locations in the knowledge creation exercise, knowledge-generating divisions were added to all practice units. These divisions gained access to the latest technical and functional knowledge from their local environment. This knowledge was then supplied to DCG and TCG. These two units then coordinated with the education and research department and the management development center to disseminate newly acquired knowledge through their training programs. A display of project categories in IPM+ (KM Group) is shown here for reference:

- Service Delivery Management Plan
- Project Profile (SLA refers to service-level managers)
  - Overview
  - Contacts
  - Project Scope
  - Charter Information
  - Deliverable
  - SLA-Based Deliverables
  - Non-SLA-Based Contractual Commitments
- Assumptions
- Process Plan
  - Deviations
  - Scope Change Management
  - Project Processes
- Project Estimates

- Effort Estimate
- Services in Scope
- Service Window

Quality Management Plan
- Measurement Plan and Process Goals
- Project Health Goals
- Strategies

Overall Benefits
Supplier Details
Intergroup Dependency
Staffing Plan
- Roles and Responsibilities
- Staffing Plan
- Shift Schedule

Training Plan
- Training Requirements

Risk Mgmt Plan
- Risk Plan

Communication Plan
- Communication and Reporting Plan
- Escalation Plan

Capacity Plan
- Hardware Details
- Network Details
- Security Details
- Software or App Details

Service Continuity Plan
- Requirement Analysis and Strategy Definition
- Implementation
- Operational Management

Service Improvement Plan
Security Plan
Details
Comments
Workflow
Traceability
Attachments
Activity Log
Previous Versions

FRISCO

The KM group at Infosys has been working on a solution framework (FRISCO) for knowledge management. The solution is intended for deployment in customer KM engagements, an area that is of late eliciting a high level of interest among Infosys customers. FRISCO will comprise a set of product and vendor independent knowledge management (KM) functions that can be readily customized and deployed in customer organizations. The framework facilitates cost optimization through enabling the integration of any (existing or new) product chosen by the customer, for example, search engine, content management system, or collaborative platform. The framework adds key KM functionality that is typically not available in the individual components and products that go into a complete KM solution. Essentially, the KM functions in FRISCO enable an organization to manage knowledge at the knowledge level. The framework provides nine areas of key functionality: KM data management services; knowledge classification management services; knowledge search and browsing services; knowledge capture, aggregation, and delivery services; collaboration management services; knowledge quality and maturity assessment services; KM metrics and measurement services; knowledge security management services; and KM promotion management services.

Others

Many other repositories at Infosys do not fall under the KM group. There are repositories under the quality group emphasizing "reuse." They include ENCORE, TOOLS, and PRIDE. They deal with project knowledge/information. Similarly, SETLabs have repositories that include thought papers, frameworks, technologies, academic collaboration, and research activities. They assist project work in performance engineering techniques and emerging technologies. Most projects have their own portals managing project knowledge. Many of these groups manage knowledge in those repositories well, although they do not label them as knowledge management activities. There is also the M+ repository, which includes useful demographic and background information on Infosys.

KM ARCHITECTURE

As the new market demand emerged, Infosys realized that its organizational structure of 1998 was cumbersome for scalability. There was a need to make the system flexible so that it could respond to the new demands. With the technology changing rapidly and the business models becoming outmoded quickly, a new market environment was needed.

In 1999, Infosys determined that sharing knowledge in the organization improves the knowledge situation and helps in scalability. To further this concept, a steering committee with full-time directors and several unit heads was formed. A working group was also formed to develop mission and objectives for KM at Infosys. The strategy for knowledge management stressed four aspects of KM: (a) people, (b) process, (c) content, and (d) technology.

People areas included understanding the expectations from all quarters of the organization and managing these expectations, determining the responsibility of the organization for making KM happen, and defining specific roles to collectively own those responsibilities.

Process areas included ensuring the quality and relevance of content, making content generation easier, maintaining the content over time, measuring the usage of the KM initiatives, and the benefits to the organization from the usage.

Content areas include understanding the scope (the context of content) and the limitations, understanding the role of tacit knowledge, and appropriate taxonomy for classification and retrieval to fulfill user needs.

Technology areas include investment to support KM applications, feasibility of developing technology systems internally, and designing the appropriate technological architecture.

The four pillars of people, process, content, and technology are serving Infosys well as a strong foundation in terms of KM architecture.

KM AWARDS

As already noted, for recognition of knowledge management applications and innovations, Infosys has won several awards at the global level, Asian level, and India level. It has won five global MAKE (Globally Most Admired Knowledge Enterprise) awards in 2003, 2004, 2005, 2007, and 2008. It has won six Asia MAKE awards in 2002, 2003, 2004, 2005, 2006, and 2007. It has won four India MAKE awards in 2005, 2006, 2007, and 2008.

The company has been assessed at level 5 of the SEI and CMM (Capability Maturity Model) in 1999 and at level 5 of the PCMM (People Capability Maturity Model) in 2002.

KNOWLEDGE FLOWS

Infosys realized that constraints for knowledge flow were impacting the effectiveness of the new GDM (global delivery model)-based organizational structure. The success of GDM structure was contingent on seamless knowledge sharing across a dispersed global workforce.

Despite the robust communication infrastructure connecting Infosys's global locations, knowledge flows across various locations were conspicuously absent. Each location operated as a knowledge silo. An Infoscion outside India trying to work out a solution to a problem separately could be unaware that the solution to that problem already existed in Bangalore or in another field office, thus creating redundancy issues. If "reuse" was in place, access to knowledge would be readily available, and this would not have happened. This reflects on scalability. Staff working on projects should be able to extract knowledge, and the project should have the maximum capacity utilization and real-time access to Infosys knowledge resources through well-established knowledge flows. The World Bank and other organizations have instituted a virtual system to share knowledge using intranets and realizing knowledge as a core commodity. For example, could a staff member in Beijing, China, working for the company headquartered in Washington, D.C., be made aware of work by another staff member of the organization in Valparaiso, Chile, and respond authoritatively to a request for a proposal and be awarded a contract? This scenario is possible through knowledge management.

Through knowledge management, scalability should facilitate Infosys response to project opportunities. This requires a knowledge management system, which can gather knowledge quickly from different domains and disseminate it effectively to appropriate personnel.

By late 2002, most Infosys employees had begun using the KM system. At this time, the KM group made the critical decision to integrate the stand-alone applications, which were previously left untouched, to include the following:

- Integrated project management (IPM)
- Employee skill system (ESS)
- Electronic bulletin board

With this consolidation, Infosys's KM system emerged as a robust consortium of IT-based applications for knowledge creation and sharing. Employees could visit the KM system to access various forms of documented knowledge, such as previous client proposals, client case studies, technical white papers, project summaries and snapshots, and even reusable codes. They could visit bulletin boards to view and participate in various technical as well as nontechnical discussions. Additionally, they could search the discussion archives for previous discussion threads. All this was done with explicit knowledge through an emphasis on the short time line and standard templates. However, there was a lot more work to be done in handling tacit knowledge.

A case was cited where an account manager was able to deliver a well-developed proposal on a short time line because the template details were already available in a companywide repository. If it can be proved that KM thus provides a competitive advantage for Infosys, it can add value to KM measurement.

Over the years, Infosys regularly thought proactively. If answers to many organizational problems were "stored" in the KM system, why not proactively provide solutions to clients? Account managers could begin to work with clients to anticipate future problems based on the experiences of past Infosys clients. This truly could make KM a core competency of Infosys and give the company a competitive advantage in the marketplace.

The software delivery apparatus of the company is organized by geos (geographical units), IBUs (integrated business units), and a few units that each focus on a single global client account. A domain competency group (DCG) exists and is responsible for building expertise in vertical domains, such as manufacturing, retail, financial services, and so on. This domain knowledge is vital to deliver solutions to meet clients' business expectations. SETLabs exists for the purpose of addressing the building of competency in horizontal technology areas such as enterprise solutions, infrastructure, performance and security, and so on.

SUMMARY OF KEY FINDINGS

Structural capital is composed of the mechanisms in place to take advantage of knowledge capital, mechanisms such as IT that stores, retrieves, and communicates knowledge. This is well established at Infosys. The concept of intellectual capital reflects the importance of valuing and nurturing people who carry knowledge in their heads. Building on past successes with securing explicit knowledge, Infosys needs to develop appropriate methodologies to satisfy this requirement. It has been reported from the "balanced score card" studies that an organization's tangible assets—cash, land, and buildings; plant and equipment; repositories; and other balance sheet items—are substantially less valuable than the intangible assets—patents, staff know-how, and so on—not carried on the books. Here, the skills, capabilities, access of expertise, values, and loyalties of staff are significantly important. Recently, it has been understood that intangible assets are the driving force for the growth, sustainability, and success of any organization.

The Delphi Group analysis points out that a survey of more than seven hundred U.S. companies shows that only a small portion of corporate knowledge is in sharable form. The majority is in employee's brains and documents not easily shared.

Learning and sharing tacit knowledge are social activities. Accordingly, processes for capturing knowledge must fit the culture of the organization. Organizations must create a conducive environment where people connect with one another and share their tacit knowledge. Staff should see the connection between sharing knowledge and the business plan; management should influence staff to collaborate and share; knowledge sharing should be integrated with people's work processes through knowledge-sharing events; the rewards and recognition system should be aligned with sharing knowledge.

Project Knowledge

Projects are generated by exploring opportunities through OTR (opportunity through receipt), and engagement managers take the leading role. The sales unit deals with the new customers. Once documents are signed, delivery managers handle producing a project code (an eight-letter code) and planning the project. All knowledge relating to the project is entered under this code. CIMBA, an online system, assists in recording all opportunities and makes that information available on a need-to-know basis. There is no mechanism to capture knowledge before the RFI or RFP is produced.

Project work is the core activity of Infosys. Also, project knowledge is the critical knowledge Infosys should manage well to increase productivity, meet time lines, and save on costs. Currently, there are two hundred accounts with five thousand projects. Each medium and large project is equipped with KM prime (every project has a person in charge of KM, titled KM prime) and a KM plan. There are roughly 2,000 KM primes, which means three thousand projects do not have KM primes. Each project also has a quality manager from the quality group. The delivery manager and quality manager make sure the project is on track and the deliverables are met within the time frame. The project people use IPM+ as an important tool to record and access project knowledge. It is accessible on a need-to-know basis. IPM+ includes a standard project profile with basic information on projects drawn from the RFP and other documentation. However, associate knowledge/information objects on projects may not be uniform in projects. Regarding "reuse" for knowledge management, many areas need depth analysis. These include, for example, determining whether knowledge is accessed before the project starts, whether knowledge is captured during the project on a continual basis, and whether all knowledge is captured when the project is closed.

All project profiles should contain several descriptors and appropriate metadata. Each query should generate context information for projects and associated knowledge/information objects. One could use a profile to align projects and objects with context. The system should be able to find (a) similar aspects and objectives in other projects, (b) related outcomes in other projects, (c) failures in like projects, (d) successes in comparable projects, (e) analogous methodologies in projects, (f) parallel problems in project areas, (g) projects with corresponding types of results, (h) approximating risks in projects, (i) lessons learned in like projects, (j) other projects used in the project design, and (k) aspects from other projects that could be useful for a given project. A depth analysis is needed in the project area to determine the knowledge access, knowledge-sharing activities, and KM effectiveness. A typical IBU KM network is provided in figure 17.2 for reference.

Note that the dotted line signifies reporting with K primes and KM network reporting from PM, DM, and BU head to KM champion and KM patron, and the solid line indicates reporting to the KM group.

PLES AND ATYPICAL NEEDS

Some units in Infosys have different needs in terms of knowledge management. PLES is such an example. Unlike software development, where most KM activities are concentrated, PLES has engineering requirements. It has designed its own portals to meet its knowledge needs, and they are more customer specific. Like projects, PLES has file servers for each account. These servers work to capture lessons learned, including mistakes, for the benefit of the organization. The needs of such units require a full review to make knowledge management work.

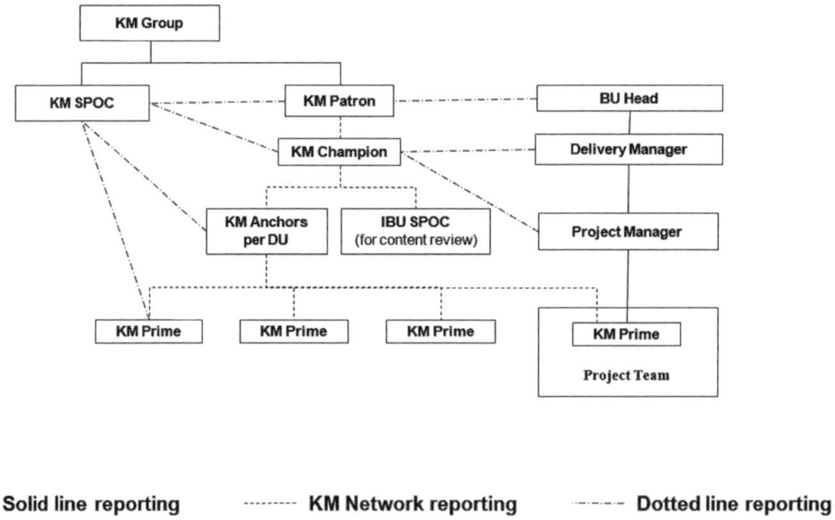

Figure 17.2.

QUALITY GROUP

The quality group deals with three areas, which focus on knowledge management: ENCORE, TOOLS, and PRIDE. Their emphasis is on "reuse." The target is to meet 5 percent of "reuse" in all projects, cutting delivery time and costs, and increasing productivity. In the quality group, the software engineering process group (SEPG) has an important role to play. There are plenty of knowledge management activities in the quality group, although they are not labeled as knowledge management. A greater degree of collaboration is needed between the quality group and the KM group to benefit Infoscions and the organization as a whole.

CERTIFICATE PROGRAMS

All Infoscions working in operations have to successfully complete two certificates, one in technology and one in domain (or project management), per year for their career paths. This is an incentive, and if they do not comply, they suffer for it in their appraisal and promotions. This carrot-and-stick approach is working well for the organization. This program deals with a high volume of knowledge/information, and KM portals and other repositories are invaluable. The KM group can provide additional initiatives to enhance this program from the knowledge management perspective.

SETLABS

SETLabs deal with thought papers, frameworks, technologies, academic collaboration, and research activities. The labs help the verticals as well as the horizontals in the organization. About three hundred to four hundred experts in labs in Bangalore fill the gap with the latest knowledge to support accounts. Their emphasis is on performance engineering techniques and emerging technologies. SETLabs is filled with knowledge management activities, and its core work is on knowledge. A greater degree of collaboration is needed with the KM group to maximize the return on SETLabs services.

ILI

ILI (Infosys Leadership Institute) deals more with tacit knowledge through mentoring and coaching. Mentorship includes the "Leaders Teach" series and is divided into tier 1, tier 2, and tier 3. Tier 1 leadership is mentored by board members; tier 2 leadership is by tier 1 members; and tier 3 leadership is by tier 2 members. The philosophy in mentorship is that a high percentage of knowledge is derived from self-realization, a smaller portion from differing experiences, and a negligible portion from classroom training. For example, In tier 1 mentorship, 70 percent comes from self-realization, 20 percent from differing experiences, and 10 percent from classroom training. These ratios change for tier 2 and tier 3 mentorships.

Coaching includes training in self-improvement. It includes training in public speaking and making effective presentations. The emphasis is on projects drawn from case studies and technical knowledge. Some popular focused coaching areas include how to chase large deals and how to write winning proposals.

There is plenty of knowledge management work in ILI, largely tacit knowledge-sharing activities. KM group can provide a solid support for ILI work through repositories and KM tools and techniques.

TR

The Mysore center trains sixteen thousand Infoscions recruited every year, starting in June. Training is held for eighteen weeks: one week of induction, one week of soft-skills training, seven weeks of foundation training, eight weeks of technology training, and one more week of soft-skills training. In this training period, trainees are introduced to KM through an awareness session, which lasts for sixty to ninety minutes. Training also deals with a "Campus Connect" program, connecting to more than 512 engineering colleges and helping them to revise their curriculum to meet industry needs. Training is filled with knowledge management activities—for both explicit and tacit knowledge. There is a need to improve KM participation in the training area. The KM group can play an important role in enhancing training.

BPOS

At Infosys, a good deal of work is done through BPOs (outsourced call-center operations). They include seventeen thousand staff dealing with fifty accounts. They have their own internal KM systems to satisfy their needs, for example, Panorama, which is similar to Sparsh, K-Mine, which is similar to K-Shop, and so on. They have their own quality team, training material, and so on. They are not integrated into the mainstream KM applications of Infosys. They have twelve portals, six for vertical and six for horizontal. The KM group can share its expertise to assist BPOs in their knowledge management work.

OTHER KEY FINDINGS

Sparsh is the gateway to knowledge for all Infoscions connecting with many links.

K-Shop has an important role to play in capturing knowledge across the organization and disseminating knowledge to Infoscions, supporting seven verticals and eight horizontals. As of January 1, 2009:

- K-Shop has 36,682 documents, with content submission of 1,645 per month, 64,092 users accessing K-Shop, 6,336 users published in K-Shop, and 3,636 users reviewing K-Shop documents. Documents viewed per work-hour averaged 629. K-Shop has 3,600 nodes in the taxonomy for information retrieval.

- There were 12,842 project snapshots. There were 11,451 KMail conversations, and 7,368 users accessed KMail. There were 13,374 Team Wiki Web pages, and 24,680 users accessed Team Wiki.
- Total KCUs (knowledge currency units) awarded were 1,274,983. There were 1,706 users who had more than a hundred KCUs.
- PKM has fifty-thousand records of staff created on a voluntary basis. The records need weeding and fine-tuning to make the system work for the organization. The connection with the skill center database is not effective.

Approximately 5 percent of the budget is spent on knowledge management, learning, and research in the organization. Resources for the KM group need to be added for improved services.

KM activities are distributed all over the enterprise, including SETLabs, the quality group, projects, ILI, training, certificate program, and KM group. More collaborative work is needed to strengthen the KM program in the organization.

KNOWLEDGE SHARING

At Infosys, KM applications have been incremental. The KM group needs to motivate Infoscions with experience to share their knowledge quickly because that knowledge is critical for the organization. In general, project scheduling is tight. PMs and others are focused on delivery, while treating knowledge sharing as secondary in importance. The KM group needs to educate them by pointing out how KM helps them in performance. It has also been observed that contribution to KM repositories is high whereas retrieval from the repositories is low. Perhaps the taxonomy for retrieval is not sufficiently specific enough to retrieve the documents Infoscions need. There is no effective quality control mechanism for inclusion in KM repositories.

From the project side, when accounts compete with one another, knowledge sharing becomes difficult—except generic knowledge. In addition to IP, staff attitude (behavior) has a bigger role to play in knowledge-sharing activities. Since many medium and large projects have their own repositories, staff does not bother to contribute to the centralized repositories causing problems in knowledge management. Also, the institution has not made knowledge sharing mandatory. At this point, a one-stop approach to meeting all knowledge needs does not exist. Many project staff still create knowledge from scratch, although much knowledge is readily available at their fingertips. This behavior needs to be addressed. PMs should attempt knowledge sharing and access to facilitate delivery. In general, the requirements of two artifacts to be posted in the repository is not effective as there is a tendency to post two artifacts at the last minute because of time pressure and other priorities, to avoid penalty in appraisals. This also results in a lack of quality postings.

CAPTURING TACIT KNOWLEDGE

Infosys is rich in tacit knowledge. Much of the work gets done through tacit knowledge in the organization. Some Infoscions network with others who have experience in similar work to take advantage of their tacit knowledge. Capturing tacit knowledge contributes to the richness in content of explicit knowledge. Many major and leading organizations have invested in capturing tacit knowledge to benefit the organization. Following are some selected tools those companies have employed in capturing tacit knowledge.

Oral History Program

Infosys should consider establishing such a program to serve the institutional memory and assist staff members in their work. The oral history program can be initiated as follows. Conduct interviews of carefully selected individuals. The average duration for the interview can be adjusted and agreed upon before hand. Formulate questions based on primary and secondary source material covering Infosys work and previous work experience. Infosys tenure, lessons learned, best practices, and concluding personal reflections can be addressed. Interviewees are given a set of questions for review prior to the interview. Once the transcript is prepared, interviewees will review it and then finalize the transcript. The primary focus and emphasis should be within the broader institutional objective of building a knowledge bank. The contents can then be disseminated via the website in the form of descriptive summaries. This program is generally focused on board members, senior managers, and senior SMEs. This will be extremely valuable for capturing the institutional memory.

Mentoring

Mentoring can facilitate the transfer of tacit knowledge from seasoned employees to new recruits, which benefits both parties. A pilot effort can be made by selecting pairs of mentors and their protégés and recording the experiences. Some of this work is already being done at ILI (Infosys Leadership Institute). The KM group can collaborate with ILI and expand to cover other areas of knowledge management in the organization.

Coaching

Coaching helps staff to develop their skills, capabilities, and performance potential in order to achieve individual and business goals. Coaching helps in capturing the tacit knowledge of experienced staff. This is also in practice through ILI and training at the Mysore center. The KM group needs to collaborate with the coaching activities to share with other Infoscions.

DEBRIEFING

Debriefing is a systematic process that gives staff members the opportunity to reflect on their experiences and identify lessons learned. In turn, this enables them to share knowledge and helps to create an operational knowledge base for improved quality in projects and program design and implementation. Debriefing is done in one-on-one or team interviews after assignments to capture and disseminate lessons learned. Elements include facilitating the interview of the selected subject and identifying critical issues to be addressed during sessions. It will also help to discuss experiences and identify what worked, what didn't work, and why. The interview can be videotaped and made available to the debriefee subject for approval and editing before dissemination to users. Then the video can be edited and made available in its entirety or via shorter clips. Documents and other resources referred to during the debriefing can also be linked, highlighted, and made available.

Debriefing can help learning before, during, and after tasks. It can help in sharing critical information about task processes and achievements to help reduce the possibility of future failures. At the same time, debriefing can point to available knowledge resources and identify knowledge gaps. Debriefing can help management understand what works so that improvement of quality can be established at entry and exit. At Infosys, debriefing is given by the PM to stakeholders, through a PowerPoint presentation, after the completion of a project. However, since debriefing is not done on a continual basis and with sufficient depth, there is knowledge loss for the organization. The KM group can facilitate debriefing sessions to capture knowledge in full.

Communities of Practice

Communities of practice are an effective approach to capturing and sharing tacit knowledge. The knowledge exchanges in communities take place, for the most part, at informal levels. This approach is to connect those who need to know with those who do know and collect what is learned to share both internally and externally with clients, stakeholders, and partners around the world. It is felt that neither connecting nor collecting could be effectively conducted unless communities of practice were in place. At Infosys, blogs and Team Wikis are fulfilling this aspect to some extent. The COEs (communities of excellence) are not as effective as communities of practice. A list of COEs is shown here:

21CN Forum (access restricted)
Business Intelligence—BACOE
CME Service Fulfillment COE
COE for Mining Domain
COEs in IMS
COEs in PE
Centre for Engineering Competence & Excellence of PLES
Enterprise Content Management
Enterprise Solution—Oracle COE
Enterprise Solution—CRM COE
ES HCM COE Portal
Flex COE @ Infosys China
IP Multimedia Subsystem (IMS) COE at Product Engineering
IVR-CTI-Speech Centre of Excellence
J2EE
Mainframe COE @ Infosys China

Maintenance Center of Excellence (MCoE)
MFG EDI CoE
Microsoft Technology Center (MTC)
Perl CoE Procurement Practice Portal
Project Management COE (PMCOE—formerly known as PMCC)
RETL MFCOE (Mainframe Center of Excellence)
Telecom Billing Packages COE
Web Services/SOA
Wireless Network CoE at Product Engineering

More vigorous communities of practice are needed to make this a dynamic process by providing incentives. The KM group can facilitate expanding COEs to communities of practice. These can be developed around thematic groups.

GAPS AND ISSUES

Some gaps occur in knowledge management and have issues resulting from them. These gaps need to be addressed properly. They include:

- At Infosys, user needs assessment needs to be strengthened to understand the current needs.
- A knowledge audit has not been performed in the organization.
- There is no KM newsletter inviting Infoscions to participate and communicate their activities in the organization.
- Organizational mandatory requirements to capture knowledge and share knowledge do not exist.
- Debriefing in projects does not have a holistic approach and results in knowledge loss.
- As artifacts in repositories increase, there is no clear methodology to monitor the quality of artifacts.
- There are hundreds of portals all over the organization serving local needs. No collaboration exists with the KM group.
- At client locations abroad, access to the Infosys network does not exist.
- Currently, KM is of secondary importance in operations. With the introduction of FRISCO searching across all contents, giving a semantic context is possible. At that time, the situation may change.
- Regarding COEs, technology COEs are stronger and have a greater degree of collaboration. Some domain COEs needs strengthening. PMCOE (Project Management Center of Excellence) works well in the enabling area. Communities of practice do not exist. Tacit knowledge sharing is difficult.
- A standardized, controlled vocabulary does not exist to meet the needs of all Infoscions.
- Taxonomy at the KM group includes the following subareas: technology, 2,331; application domain/industry verticals, 768; methodology/service offering, 292; Finacle, 136; soft skills, 105; strategic sourcing, 39; project management, 31;

culture, 23; and others, 22. However, this is not standardized as various other taxonomies exist in the organization.

KM MEASUREMENT

The KM group has designed many tools to measure the impact of KM in the organization. Periodic surveys facilitate an understanding of the KM impact. R&R as incentive promotes measurement (KCU is a good example). Various statistical analyses have been added for KM metrics. However, metrics needs to be done at the IBU level, HBU level, delivery-unit level, and project level. Ad hoc user surveys indicate positive responses. Saving through "reuse" is highlighted. Percentage of knowledge assets reused in coding, tools, and K artifacts is impressive. Benefits from K artifacts are viewed as both short-term and long-term outcomes.

At Infosys, measuring results from the knowledge management effort is tackled on three fronts: metrics, surveys, and anecdotal information. Quantitative metrics help the company map knowledge management results into traditional project and company measures, such as productivity, defect rate, and schedule adherence. For example, Infosys has been able to show that projects with employees that have more KCUs also have a better success rate

Infosys tracks return on capital employed, economic value added, annual training cost per employee, and efficiency. While the company believes these are valuable measures—and has seen improvements in each area since implementing a formal knowledge management program—it does acknowledge that knowledge management is only one attributable factor in such results.

The knowledge taxonomy has developed into a robust structure encompassing more than seventeen hundred nodes and representing more than thirty-six thousand knowledge assets covering various industries, technologies, and project management topics.

- One in every four employees has contributed at least one knowledge artifact to the central knowledge repository.
- Thousands of employees regularly participate in knowledge exchanges on the discussion forums.

CONCLUSION

In general, knowledge management applications at Infosys demonstrate hard work, creativity, and innovation by the KM group. In the past nine- to ten-year period, knowledge management has also received support from senior management. Winning MAKE awards at the global, Asian, and Indian levels for many years proves the recognition of solid KM work at Infosys. However, some areas can be strengthened for increased returns. They could include conducting a knowledge audit exercise, improving the K-Shop portal, enhancing training, capturing project knowledge in full, developing a controlled vocabulary authority file, and appointing a CKO to manage all knowledge management activities.

REFERENCES

Dalkir, Kimiz. (2005). *Knowledge management in theory and practice.* Burlington, MA: Elsevier.

Davenport, T. H., & Prusak, L. (1998). *Working knowledge: How organizations manage what they know.* Boston: Harvard Business School Press.

Drucker, P. (1998). The coming of the new organization. In *Harvard Business Review on Knowledge Management.* Boston: Harvard Business School Press.

Infosys. (2008). *Annual report.*

Kochikar, V. P., Mahesh, K., & Mahind, C. S. (2002). Knowledge management in action: The experience of Infosys Technologies. In *Knowledge and Business Process Management.* Hershey, PA: Idea Group.

Kochikar, V. P. (2000). Learn once, use anywhere. *Knowledge Management Magazine, 4*(1).

Kochikar, V. P. & Suresh, J. K. (2004). Towards a knowledge sharing organization: Some challenges faced on the Infosys journey. In M. Rao (Ed.), *Annals of Cases on Information Technology* (Vol. 6) (pp. 244–258). Hershey, PA: Idea Group.

Nonaka, I., & Takeuchi, H. (1995). *The knowledge creating company: How Japanese companies create the dynasties of innovation.* New York: Oxford University Press.

Polanyi, M. (1966). *The tacit dimension.* Garden City, NY: Doubleday.

Srikantaiah, T. Kanti, & Koenig, Michael E. D. Koenig (Eds.). (2008). *Knowledge management in practice: Connections and context.* Medford, NJ: Information Today.

Suresh, J. K., & Mahesh, K. (2006). *Ten steps to maturity in knowledge management.* Oxford: Chandos.

Sveiby, K-E. (1997). *The new organizational wealth: Managing and measuring knowledge-based assets.* San Francisco: Berret-Koehler.

18

Knowledge Management in Software Service Projects Ecosystem

A Perot Systems Case Study

C. S. Shobha and Bhanu Kiran Potta

Much has been heard, spoken, experienced, and written about knowledge management (KM). Yet making KM operational continues to pose significant challenges to CKOs, CIOs, and other operations leaders across organizations. This chapter attempts to throw light on making KM operational at the project level in software service delivery environments.

THE ECOSYSTEM

Software applications are becoming more complex and important to the daily operations of enterprises and governments around the world. Keeping the balance of productivity enhancements, maintenance requirements, and an adequate return on investment presents a bigger challenge every year—especially when combined with the need for agility, scalability, availability, and predictability. Designing, building, deploying, supporting, maintaining, and keeping lights on for software applications are critical endeavors that are accomplished through software projects. The Perot Systems application solutions group delivers its services to customers globally through a variety of software services projects. There is an essential need to build an ecosystem that leverages knowledge in and around these projects.

To improve overall project results and better serve customers, our applications solutions group set up a knowledge management office (KMO). Our journey started with the following objectives:

- To elevate knowledge work to a key focus direction
- To integrate KM into daily workflow and long-term planning
- To extract maximum value from the collective learning of project teams
- To make the organization an attractive choice for knowledge workers
- To deliver innovative solutions to customers on a sustainable basis

Before setting up the knowledge management office, the team used preliminary ecosystem knowledge audits, which clearly revealed the critical role that project teams played in managing and delivering projects to make KM truly operational. As a result of these findings, the KMO focused 50 percent of its attention on institutionalizing project-level KM in delivery groups. The remaining 50 percent of the focus was on KM initiatives for other shared services groups, including marketing, sales and sales support, HR, and other organizational-level functions.

THE EVIDENT I–P–O CYCLE

In a software services ecosystem, project teams form the delivery engine that takes software requirement specifications as the input to churn out new or updated software applications and/or software services. This input–process–output cycle is outlined in figure 18.1.

While the attention usually centers on successful completion of projects, most software services ecosystems miss out on another critical input–process–output cycle that is a key contributor to project success. For most initiatives, this cycle takes place alongside project delivery, but often these two facets do not align effectively. In most cases, the people coming onto a project team possess acceptable levels of knowledge, which forms the input. As each team member begins to use his or her existing knowledge while collaborating and sharing skills with other project team members, the team member begins acquiring new knowledge from others, and most importantly, the whole group co-creates new knowledge together as a team. The knowledge process is now in action. From a knowledge output perspective, people emerging from the project team now possess new and/or improved knowledge capabilities. A long-term synergy is created for each member by the interactions and exchanges within the team.

KNOWLEDGE DIMENSIONS IN SOFTWARE SERVICES PROJECTS

It is evident that there is positive transformation of knowledge levels for just about any team in a successful project. To best ensure the success of a project, managing knowledge is planned and executed effectively. Effective KM processes are all the more essential in a software services projects ecosystem. To fully appreciate the power of combining key knowledge dimensions, let's examine a software services project that adopts knowledge best practices.

Customer knowledge. Knowledge about the customer includes the following aspects: industry context, business drivers and challenges, leadership and manage-

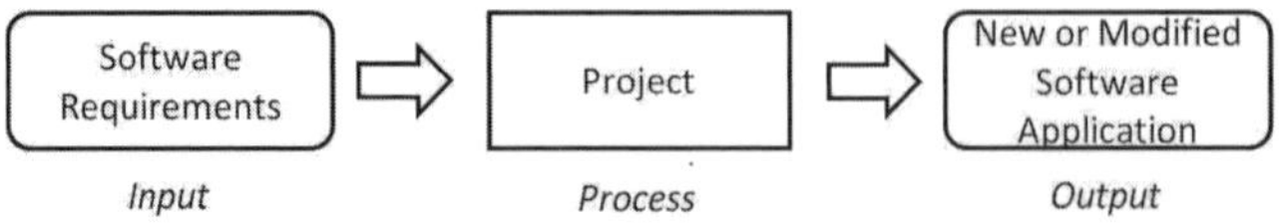

Figure 18.1. Software Services Input–Process–Output Cycle

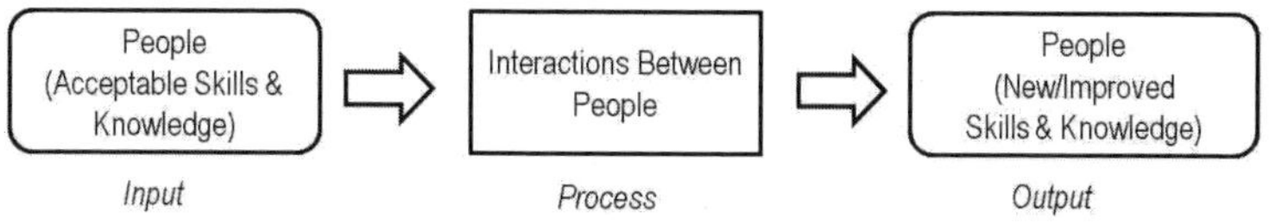

Figure 18.2. People in Software Services Input–Process–Output Cycle

ment culture, critical business policies and processes, decision-making process, appropriate and correct escalation paths and communication preferences, key stakeholders and their work style preferences, specific business challenge(s) that the project needs to address, acceptance criteria and success definitions of the project, and more.

Domain knowledge. Domain knowledge includes a deep understanding of the customer's line of business. Full domain knowledge includes answers to the following questions: How does the business operate? What are the models and policies at the industry level? What are the relevant details and specific functional level awareness process steps? What are the business rules and drivers in the domain in which the application or software services will operate?

Knowledge of the software application(s). Application knowledge includes the following: architecture and design; database design and structures; various modules, interfaces and dependencies; application-specific coding guidelines, test cases, unit-testing, and system-testing processes; infrastructure specifications, setup, and deployment processes; support, maintenance, and enhancement of processes per the customer; and user guides, specifications, and past experience (including knowing the error database log, lessons learned, etc.).

Knowledge of technology/tools. This knowledge includes familiarity with the technology tools used to develop, deploy, or test the software application, such as programming languages, databases, interface APIs and markup languages, and any other tools either integrated into the application (for example, a flash player) or used in the project (for example, Rational Rose, Unified Modeling Language, test director, etc.).

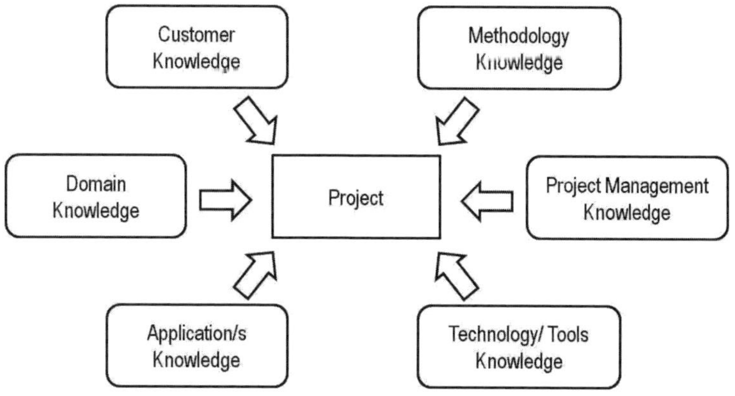

Figure 18.3. Knowledge Dimensions in a Software Services Project

Project management knowledge. This knowledge encompasses an understanding of the project management processes within the client and the service provider organization, including PM guidelines, rules, governance models, communication processes, and risk management. Effective project management approaches include planning documents, established methodologies, workshops, status reporting, tracking, auditing, meeting minutes, management presentations, stakeholder involvement reports, project metrics, and relationship notes.

Methodology knowledge. This dimension includes knowing your own company's and the customer's standard operating procedures, life cycle documentation, and project life cycle processes around development, migration, testing, support, and maintenance.

A key element to note is that each knowledge dimension is subject to continuous changes, and each change has a ripple effect on other knowledge elements. The challenge is to effectively manage change, comprehend the status change events, and relate them effectively to other knowledge elements. This alignment requires sophisticated systems and disciplined process steps along with a deep understanding of each knowledge element.

KNOWLEDGE CHAMPIONSHIP

In all successful software service projects, we observe that knowledge dimensions are well managed by the project team, which enables it to consistently deliver successfully. The challenge, then, is to enable effective management of all dimensions of knowledge at a level of consistency across the organization, thus ensuring project successes across the board, leading to more satisfied customers. Perot Systems "knowledge champions" act as the pivots points for KM in projects.

A knowledge champion (KC) is a part-time role taken on by a member of the project team. The KC of a project is generally chosen by the project manager and works closely with the project manager to address the knowledge management and skill development needs of the group and the project as a whole. Apart from managing all six knowledge dimensions of a software service project, the KC looks into the following areas among many other KM initiatives.

Project induction. Implement a systematic and detailed induction and material process for the project. The project induction process includes instituting training delivery mechanisms such as self-read, instructor-led, shadow hands-on, reverse shadow hands-on, and more. The content for these training programs comes from documentation and artifacts developed for each of the knowledge dimensions, including lessons learned, known issues, and resolutions.

Expertise mapping. Record and baseline the knowledge and skills inventory within the project team for each team member and for the team overall. Conduct knowledge and skills gaps analysis, and execute fulfillment initiatives. Identify go-to experts in several knowledge and skills areas that are critical to the project. Frequently update the knowledge and skills inventory and keep tabs on any increase/decrease in levels to identify potential deficiencies. Update the team with new knowledge and skills that may come up during the project.

Knowledge sharing sessions. Set up regular and reoccurring knowledge-sharing sessions during the project (perhaps weekly, biweekly, or as needed). Proactively use the knowledge and skills area gaps identified from the expertise mapping and plan the topics for these sessions accordingly. Quite often, the KC ensures that a major milestone or problem addressed is followed by a session to allow discussion and information sharing pertaining to that topic. At Perot Systems, the project teams create self-study groups for team learning to teach and learn particular knowledge sets and to prepare for external certification exams on those competencies.

Project case study. Even before the project begins, proactively start documenting the progress in the form of a case study from a successful engagement perspective, both from customer and project management viewpoints, and from a technical superiority angle. The case study can be used in the future during other project inductions internally and by sales support teams externally to demonstrate capability, establish best practices, identify lessons learned, and serve as testimonials to success.

Reusability and innovation. The KC, along with the project manager, also addresses possible reuse functionality of knowledge in the project. At the beginning of a project, the organization's library of archives is reviewed for two primary reasons: first, to evaluate whether completed project knowledge and/or materials from previous initiatives can be reused in the current project, and second, to identify whether the new project can contribute to the level of the organization's library in any way. While reuse potential is being evaluated, the team takes extreme care to stand up to and honor all contractual IP aspects. Even when IP is owned by the customer, there is a fair chance that multiple projects being delivered to the same customer may be able to leverage and reuse items between themselves. The KC also keeps an

Table 18.1. Knowledge Champions Nurture

KC Life Cycle	*Nurturing Action Steps*
Identification	• KC identification is a joint activity involving the project manager and KMO. • A KC is identified from among the team members, keeping in mind important aspects such as initiative, professional demeanor, and identified career path.
Orientation	• A new KC undergoes a detailed orientation on KM practices, KM procedures, and other operational nuances. • All new KCs are exposed to and mentored by experienced KCs.
Ongoing support	• KCs are provided continuous support from the KM core team and senior KCs. • Monthly KC conclave forums discuss common challenges and exchange possible solutions. • Senior delivery leaders interact with the KCs at least on a quarterly basis to ascertain the overall alignment of KCs to common goals. • A monthly newsletter is published that showcases the exceptional work done by KCs and also provides a platform for upgrading their knowledge base.
Moving up/ becoming a coach	• After project completion, KCs may opt to move into a role at an account or a practice level or transition to a partial presence to coach new KCs as needed.

eye open for possible innovation opportunities. Innovations can be breakthrough or incremental, product/tool or process/service, and internal to the organization or open to the customer.

Capture best practices/known errors. The knowledge champion will also facilitate in the creation of systems, keeping a watch on capturing lessons learned and identifying and recording best practices. Tracking and sharing what works and what does not work related to knowledge on a specific project can provide significant benefits in long-running projects.

At Perot Systems, knowledge champions are nurtured continuously to develop capabilities and be in the best position to make frontline KM a reality. A great deal of attention is paid to how each KC facilitates catalyzing knowledge actions within project teams. Any gaps are quickly supported and filled.

KM PROCESSES AROUND SOFTWARE SERVICES PROJECTS

We identified critical knowledge actions and embedded these action steps into the standard operating process for projects. This helped us bring project management consistency across the board and make KM truly operational inside projects. Compliance to process actions is verified through routine audits and progress checks. Once KM actions are embedded in the processes, even a new or first-time project manager can ensure completion of best practice actions and will not miss or overlook them.

Table 18.2. KM Processes

Project Phase	Knowledge Action Step
Feasibility	• Use the case study repository to identify and demonstrate capabilities and as testimonials. • Draw from lessons learned and expert connects for better planning, assessment, and estimations. • Identify possible experts for consultation(s).
Initiation	• Identify project knowledge champion as guided by KM procedure. • Create project knowledge repository.

Planning	• The KC in collaboration with the project manager defines a KM plan for the project in consultation with the KMO if needed.
	  • Draw up expertise inventory map and knowledge fulfillment plans.
	  • Identify and record reuse opportunities.
	  • Initiate project case study and induction kit.
	• Draw from lessons learned and case study repository.

Execution	• KC executes the KM plan along with all its components and tracks it closely. • KC reports on the KM plan monthly to project manager and quarterly to KMO. • Project manager reviews the KM plan on a frequent basis to bring in required alterations.
Shutdown	• Final update of project case study, induction kit, reusable items list, lessons learned, and other key artifacts. • Final update of project knowledge repository.

BEST PRACTICES AIDING KM IN SOFTWARE SERVICES PROJECTS

Our journey in making KM operational has led us to believe that the following best practices have contributed significantly to success.

Knowledge leadership and common vocabulary. We put in place a highly engaging and compelling KM vision and mission, along with goals and objectives, both of which included visible senior management participation and buy-in. The KM guidelines in the form of values, beliefs, and assumptions were widely publicized. Consistent flow of leadership messages and communication around KM was orchestrated to keep KM top of mind for frontline staff. The KM program was branded and had its own logo that various members performing knowledge actions could relate to and associate with in a unified manner. These communication-building activities helped to reinforce that *knowledge is power* and knowledge management supports using that power to gain business advantages, reduce learning curves, decrease defects, improve efficiencies, enhance innovations, add value, and delight customers.

Nurture knowledge skills. We focused and continue to focus special efforts to teach, seed, and nurture smarter and faster knowledge skills throughout our staff, knowledge champions, and project managers. The capability gains enable greater KM benefits in projects for both our company and our customers. In this stage, the usage of library and e-learning platforms increases, mentoring is at its best, physical spaces such as meeting/conference rooms are constantly occupied, traffic to the portal increases, and there is greater participation in various modes of learning and sharing.

Align KM with project goals. We worked with the KCs and project managers to align KM initiatives at the project level to both strategic and operational project goals and objectives. Key components included establishing a deep understanding of project objectives along with the strengths and weaknesses within the team from the knowledge viewpoint. This alignment made it easier to engage the project teams' attention to the importance of KM activities within the project and to the importance of KM for the organization overall.

Online collaborative platform for project teams. With more and more project teams being dispersed across the globe, there was a greater need to put in place an online collaborative platform for project teams on our KM portal. These repositories are called "project spaces," and project team members worldwide can capture, store, and share knowledge and collaborate in real time on various project aspects. This not only helps in making KM possible in a multilocation team environment, but it also helps promote team bonding despite the distances and remoteness. We have used Web 2.0 features extensively for this collaboration on the virtual platform.

Involve customers in KM and innovation. We have seen the benefit of opening up internal KM and innovation endeavors to customers. Once the project team and the customer's team become a collaborative and cohesive unit, the knowledge sharing and co-creation often increase significantly, and innovation is better and more focused. Customers also start seeing the project teams as valuable partners rather than contracted staff augmentation workers.

Connect with knowledge resources outside of the project. It has also proved to be a strong proactive measure to connect with experts and knowledge resources outside the project team, either inside or outside the organization or the customer team. These collaborations help promote proactive sharing of earlier lessons learned and provide opportunities to identify past issues and resolutions that can save precious time and effort. Building basic project familiarity through an extended team also provides added resources in case an issue proves to be a continuing challenge for the core project team. Communities of practice are highly effective methods to get other people connected across projects on a specific topic. While knowledge seekers go out and look out for knowledge in repositories, communities of practice provide more interactive forums to ask questions of experts and allow the experts to answer them or reach out to others for discussion. Many subject matter experts have built considerable credibility over time and may have a large following within a certain industry or topic area. Their input may help drive improved organizational decisions and help promote collective decision making. Business leaders who work with experts and are skilled in applying their knowledge and experience often make the best decisions for their organizations.

Create visibility, reward, and recognize. Identifying and creating visibility for project successes is a significant role of KM/innovation initiatives. This recognition can be a powerful motivator for the project team and instill a greater desire in other teams to embrace KM programs. An effective visibility and reward system can also be used positively to motivate those who already believe in the power of KM and as a pressure point for those who have not yet bought in. Either way, increasing the focus on desired KM behaviors will positively influence the overall ecosystem and create an energized environment based on desired knowledge behaviors. It also cannot be overlooked that access to a greater knowledge base can be a reward in itself.

Interaction between project and organizational KM. It is vital to create synchronous interactions between project-level and organizational-level KM because both of them have difficulty functioning alone effectively in a software services environment. While organizational KM initiatives focus more on culture building, project-level KM focuses more directly on returning benefits to the project, customers, and thereby back to the organization. The different groups needed to enable a strong KM culture are senior leadership, KM team, quality/process team, domain/technical SME groups, infrastructure team, training team, human resources team, legal team (copyrights, IP, policies, etc.), and others.

Investment and perseverance. Wilkins and Dyer (1988) suggest that culture "is [composed] of the values, competencies, and beliefs of a group of people that strongly influence whether and how organizational strategies are implemented." Building an ecosystem with the desired KM culture requires investment and perseverance. Investment in terms of time, effort, money, and senior management participation is an important element to achieve success. Long-term perseverance is also demanded from the KM custodians and senior management as the organization proceeds to build a culture and awareness that is ideal for KM programs to flourish. It will not surprise anyone to hear that not all environments respond in the same manner to stimuli. Building meaningful KM within an organization often requires many tiny steps, some high-level mandates, and a few process changes with roll-back features. Some of the investments needed in this journey are:

Creation of IT systems—investments in hardware, software, and networking
Creation of physical spaces such as training rooms, meeting rooms, lecture halls, auditoriums, and so on

Investment for setting up infrastructure for audio/video/Webcasting systems
Investments for rewards
Investment for ongoing operation of KM initiatives, which may include transportation, meals, incentives, and more
Investment for knowledge assets such as books, CBTS, e-learning, journals, periodicals, memberships to industry forums
Sponsorship in external events—seminars, conferences, and the like
Publication of books, journals

EVOLVING TO KNOWLEDGE CYCLES AROUND SOFTWARE SERVICES PROJECTS

At the Perot Systems application solutions group, our KM journey started twenty-four months before writing this chapter. In the pilot phase, we had just a handful of knowledge champions with nurturing support from the knowledge management office, but without any established KM processes in place. During the six-month pilot program, we experimented with various KM actions and gauged outcomes to determine which we would develop into standardized processes that we called KM action steps. After the pilot phase, we moved to the segmented rollout phase, which lasted another nine months. In this phase, we expanded the number of KCs and identified segments where the processes could be embedded into and implemented with the KM action steps. After seeing significant benefits from the segmented rollout phase, we moved to a full rollout phase. In the full rollout phase, a few enhancements were made to the KM actions steps based on the experiences from the previous phase. Nine months after the full rollout phase started, we had our critical projects cocooned in a knowledge cycle (figure 18.4). This cycle yielded efficiencies through reductions in time to capture information/knowledge, a decrease in defects, a reduction in risk materialization due to proactive mitigations, an increase in productivity, an increase in deliverable quality, an increase in customer satisfaction, an increase in the organizational knowledge base, and more.

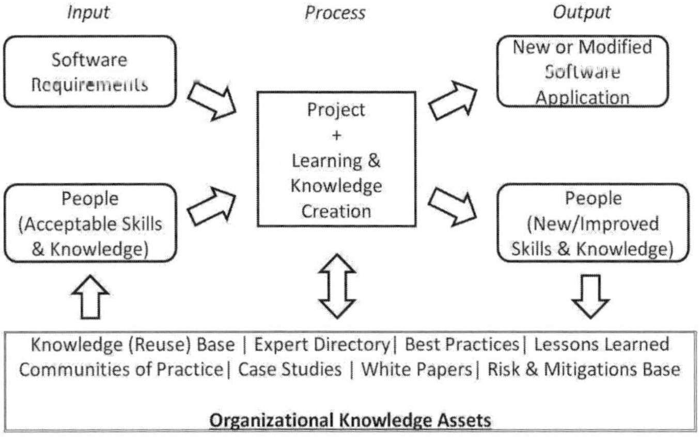

Figure 18.4. Knowledge Cycle

TRANSFORMATIONS IN PROJECT CONSTITUENTS

During our journey, we have been able to successfully implement critical KM-flavored transformations and raise KM mind share throughout various project constituents, including team members, team/project leads, project managers, and delivery heads. Figure 18.5 depicts these interactions and some of the key interventions that resulted in successful transformation.

These transformations helped us to deeply root knowledge behaviors across the organization and to further expose/share/expand KM gains and benefits with customers. Establishing and instilling a more robust KM culture helped create the added advantage of further supporting our company goals of delivering value and customer success with each project.

KNOWLEDGE ACTIONS DEMOGRAPHY

Our recent KM ecosystem survey within the Perot Systems application solutions group highlighted some interesting and welcome facts around the consistency of KM at the frontline in our ecosystem. Some of the findings from the survey include the following:

1. Forty percent of respondents participated in at least two types of project-level KM activities.
2. Ninety-one percent of respondents felt that project knowledge champions are well recognized and respected in their project teams.
3. Eighty-six percent of the respondents who are not knowledge champions at present wanted to take up this role at the next available opportunity.
4. Seventy-five percent of the KM initiatives are seen as delivering value to the organization by more than 80 percent of the respondents.

From the survey we were also able to understand basic employee knowledge-action demography at the project level.

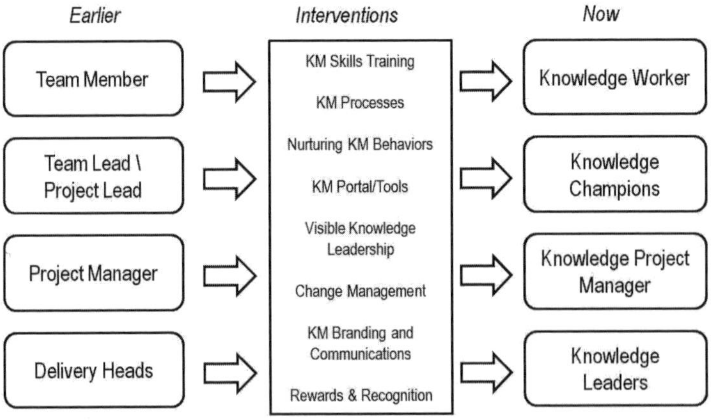

Figure 18.5. Transformations in Project Actors

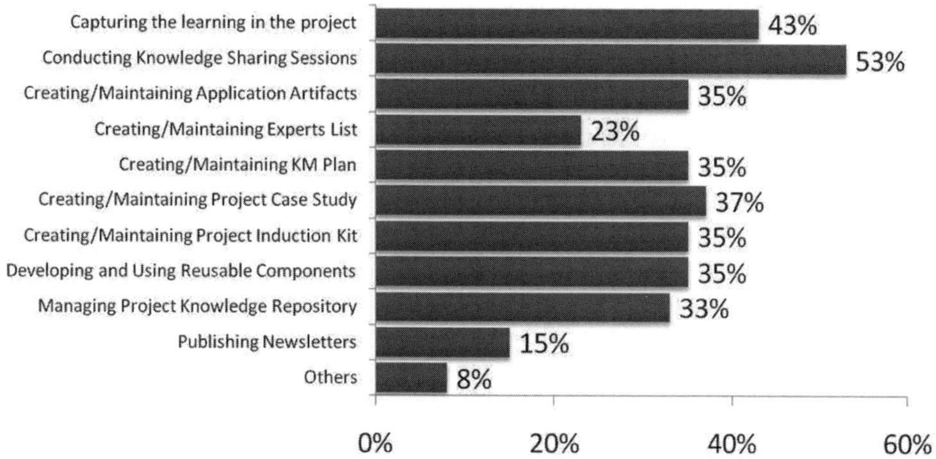

Figure 18.6. Employee Knowledge Action Demography at Project Level

CONCLUSION

To evolve to this stage in our KM program in just two years is exciting and gratifying for the Perot Systems team. This continuous journey for the KM custodians at Perot Systems is designed to make knowledge management effective and actionable at the project level, which not only benefits those within our company who deliver services but also our customers. A useful metric for the scale of these accomplishments is that we have progressed from seven knowledge champions in the pilot phase, to forty-two in the segmented rollout phase, to 125 in the full rollout phase. Our knowledge management office relied on resources both within our organization and from outside. Achieving success required significant expertise in implementing, communicating, and demonstrating commitment to KM through change management, engineering culture transformation, creative communication strategies, and advisory communications to senior management. The leaders and team members who worked on this program were energetic problem solvers, sensitive to people issues, and they showed respect to and an inherent interest in all individuals.

REFERENCE

Wilkins, A. L., & Dyer, W. G. (1988). Toward Culturally Sensitive Theories of Culture Change. *The Academy of Management Review, 13*(4), 522.

19

KM and PM

Case Studies and Learnings from the Infotech Sector

Madanmohan Rao

Global IT firms are successfully leveraging KM to capture best practices, improve project management, nurture innovation, enhance customer service, reuse software code, and expand across boundaries of technology generations and varying maturity levels of markets.

In fact, information technology (IT) companies feature very prominently in the list of winners of awards such as the annual Most Admired Knowledge Enterprises (MAKE) awards, conducted by Teleos in association with The KNOW Network. IT companies account for the largest single industry sector in MAKE rankings over the years and across regions. Thus, the IT sector would seem to be a good focus in this chapter to examine project management applications and impacts.

A range of IT companies have evolved sophisticated strategies to manage content in the project context. These include EDS's Techlore technical knowledge repository, EMC's Knowledgebase for tech support, Fujitsu Consulting's ProjectFinder, i2's knowledge base and project workbench, knowledge asset editors at Infosys, and i-Flex's Project Closure Documents (PCD).

SAS has formally designated knowledge support officers who assist busy employees in creating, editing, and translating knowledge assets. Improper planning at an earlier stage led to rampant database proliferation and knowledge clutter at Fujitsu Consulting, which was subsequently rectified. Digital content-management platforms have completely transformed the merged entity SunPhil, which had an archaic paper-based environment prior to merger.

PROJECT MANAGEMENT: ENHANCEMENTS VIA KNOWLEDGE MANAGEMENT

KM has been applied to a number of corporate strategic and operation activities, ranging from scenario planning and IP-led acquisitions to project management and expertise retention.

The collection of essays by Malhotra (2001) offers insights into how KM practices can differ according to the nature of the organization: project based (e.g., construction industry), umbrella corporations (e.g., GE), virtual business communities (e.g., the Linux movement on the Internet), and the multidirectional network (e.g., lobbies of small and medium-size enterprises in Taiwan).

Though IT-sector companies are the most numerous of any category in the MAKE awards, companies in the non-IT sector as well have leveraged KM and cross-functional networks to enhance project performance. In this section, we review some of the KM strategies for project management in non-IT companies; the remainder of the chapter focuses on the IT product and services sector.

For instance, knowledge portals and a PeopleNet expertise directory are used to connect projects, people, processes, and communities at ChevronTexaco.

The Bank of Montreal has used social network analysis to determine who shares information and point out likely interventions. "The groups initiate a knowledge fair to share information between teams. Cross functional teams are formed to address new project demands, and leadership forums encourage greater sharing among team leaders," says Richard Livesley, head of KM at the Bank of Montreal, speaking at the KM Asia 2002 conference in Singapore.

Dixon (2000) identifies five key categories of lesson sharing in large companies: serial transfer, near transfer, far transfer, strategic transfer, and expert transfer. They differ in terms of who the intended knowledge receiver is (same or different from the source), the nature of the task involved (frequency and routine), and the type of knowledge being transferred (tacit/explicit).

Examples of near transfer include Ford's Best Practice Replication in the vehicle operations division (each plant receives five to eight best practices per week via the intranet), Texas Instruments' Alert Notification System for wafer fabrication yields (managed via e-mail and newsgroups on the "ShareIt" intranet site), and Ernst&Young's PowerPacks (collections of best proposals, presentations, and articles pushed from the corporate knowledgeWeb databases onto consultants' laptops).

Examples of far transfer include Chevron's Capital Project Management (with online forums as well as physical movement of project managers to spread learned lessons across the company).

Examples of expert transfer include Buckman Lab's TechForums (started in 1992, monitored by librarians and sysops, and supported by editorial help in producing weekly summaries of discussions), Tandem Computer's Second Class Mail (for tech support), Chevron's Best Practices Resource Map (a yellow pages of employee resources), the World Bank's internal help line, and Ernst&Young's knowledge stewards.

KM capacity at NASA is built via training and mentoring via the Academy of Program and Project Leadership, which hosts classes, team-targeted training, just-in-time online learning, storytelling activities, and intelligent authoring tools for experts and communities of practice for project managers, according to Jeanne Holm, chief knowledge architect at NASA, speaking at the KM Asia 2002 conference in Singapore.

Syngenta's KM initiative has focused on saving money in project management via solutions ranging from content formats and shared vocabularies to knowledge behaviors and a revamped intranet. "Buy-in is necessary from the IT department but

KM is not necessarily high on their agenda," cautioned Pauline Stewart, knowledge manager at Syngenta, speaking at the KM Pharma 2003 conference in London.

Consulting firm Bain and Company has an elaborate KM system consisting of the Bain Virtual University (BVU) for online courses coupled with the Global Experience Centre (GXC). Its content assets include the core global toolkit (launched in 1999), codified insights into industry verticals (launched in 2000), and sanitized summaries of client projects, video modules of case study reviews, staff profiles, and external market research.

CASE STUDY 1: I2

Supply chain software leader i2 moved quickly from informal collaboration mechanisms to formal knowledge codification strategies in areas ranging from software engineering to constraint theory. i2's founders, Sanjiv Sidhu and Ken Sharma, believed in applying technology and best practices to eliminate inefficiencies in business.

This belief, percolating throughout i2 since its inception in 1988, is also reflected in its knowledge management initiative—applying technology and best practices to encourage increased productivity within i2. Its knowledge base and project workbench help product developers and marketers in India and the United States improve upon software quality for its products and supply chain performance for its customers.

i2 has viewed the intellectual capital within the company as being its competitive advantage and has emphasized the management of knowledge ever since its inception. Although knowledge was earlier managed on a more informal basis, i2 has focused on ways to codify, store, and exchange knowledge in the form of presentations, white papers, and other collateral.

The quantum of knowledge, however, is so vast that the company now depends on a formal KM practice to discover these knowledge assets as well as source, codify, and store new ones so that critical knowledge can be disseminated and socialized throughout i2.

In 1998, the i2 India corporate communications team was given the charter to manage information for internal as well as external purposes. At that time, this was not seen as a KM initiative, but it soon grew into one. This team was responsible for developing the i2 India intranet that soon become the main repository from which knowledge assets were accessed. The department would soon also become responsible for managing e-learning projects for products and solutions.

The corporate communications department soon evolved into the knowledge management department responsible for KM as well as technical documentation. The formal i2 India SCM knowledge management team comprises twelve people, nine of whom form the SCM technical documentation team. The team is managed by a design expert, a technical architect, and a documentation expert.

The KM effort for the i2 India operations began in 1997 and was supported by the software engineering process group (SEPG). This group plays a critical role in the KM effort at i2. Other support comes from veterans in software development and project management.

KM leaders are appointed from various regions, and their performance in KM implementation is included in their quarter-end appraisals. Knowledge-centric strategies have been successfully used to position the company's products for medium-size companies instead of just Fortune 500 giants, by leveraging knowledge assets to develop scaled-down products, speed up implementation time, and educate customers via e-learning modules. The company identifies e-learning, cognition studies, and organizational learning as key productivity areas to watch out for in the future.

The global solution delivery (GSD) organization at i2 has an established KM practice. The GSD Web-based knowledge base is available to every i2 consultant, whether on-site or off-site. The knowledge base has been developed using a comprehensive database that contains everything needed by a consultant to implement i2's solutions in the shortest possible time. Its content includes customer information, case studies, and tools and tips that allow each consultant to be extremely productive, thereby helping customers achieve rapid ROI.

In addition to this knowledge base, the GSD organization also uses a project document library for documentation management and a collaboration website for individual projects called the i2 project workbench.

The i2 India metrics site (http://www.sujitpavithran.com/web/i2_india_metrics.htm), developed under the aegis of the software engineering process group (SEPG), was launched in 1998. The objective of this site was to share metrics captured for each product group in the demand chain management group, now a part of the supply chain management development organization.

This site continues to be used by product teams, as it is the space where performance metrics for each product group can be reviewed. Besides an overview of the product and related team information, this site captures metrics that reflect performance levels of each team member and product group. These metrics can be further sliced and diced in order to reflect the efficiencies or lack thereof of the product teams.

This information transforms into powerful knowledge when the product team leaders, managers, and other team members make their strategic and tactical plans to institute better processes and benchmarking levels and create better products.

CASE STUDY 2: I-FLEX

Financial software and services firm i-Flex (now Oracle Financial Services Software Ltd.) has launched a combination of enterprisewide strategic KM initiatives as well as smaller individual initiatives of a more tactical nature. As is the case with other leading software firms, i-Flex's KM initiative is heavily based on process automation, as per the capability maturity model (CMM) framework developed by the Software Engineering Institute (SEI) at Carnegie-Mellon University.

i-Flex has unveiled a plethora of schemes and tools on its i-Share KM portal—like the QuBase repository of methodologies, the Promotr project-tracking tool, project closure documents (PCD), the i-CleaR corporate learning repository, QPati quiz program, i-Suggest process improvement suggestion scheme, K-Forum for employees to seek solutions on unresolved issues, business intelligence monitoring contextualized with respect to i-Flex's positioning, and K-Webcast conferences with i-Flex experts hosted on the intranet called i-Opener.

Within the i-Flex process knowledge framework, QuBase is the ever-growing intranet-based repository of methodologies, processes, standards, templates, checklists, guides, tutorials, and other useful information that practitioners use in their day-to-day work.

Promotr, the other automation component, is designed as an environment that addresses the monitoring and tracking needs of projects along parameters such as size, effort, schedule, and quality. It also facilitates capture and analysis of data generated from the projects executed by the organization to assess the process capability of the organization at any point of time.

This capability, on parameters such as productivity, defect density, defect leakage, effort slippage, and schedule slippage, is published annually in the form of the i-Flex baseline report. The knowledge that is inherent in this data is then used by i-Flex to achieve greater levels of accuracy in estimating and planning for future projects, as well as to refine the processes to achieve higher levels of performance.

i-Flex also has an institutionalized mechanism of capturing the experiences and learnings of projects that the organization executes. These are captured at the end of each project, in the form of the project closure document (PCD). The PCD is deployed through the organization's learning repository, i-CleaR, which documents management lessons learned during the project as well as process recommendations. These are used by relevant projects as inputs to enable better planning and management of ongoing projects.

As a first step toward the creation of a centralized i-Flex knowledge repository, the company created a technology platform called i-CleaR (i-Flex Corporate Learning Repository). i-CleaR was developed in house, selected ahead of seventy other tools that were thoroughly evaluated by i-Flex's software engineering practice group (SEPG).

i-CleaR is a tool tailored to the company's requirements and is being constantly upgraded based on user feedback and requirements. Using this tool, documents can be categorized using a logical relationship. The actual relationship depends on the specific categorization scheme that is employed. Documents uploaded into i-CleaR can be classified under various categories: ownership (e.g., sales, product groups), location (e.g., New York office), type of document (e.g., proposals), or data sensitivity (e.g., confidential). Comprehensive search facilities and reporting, high-security control and access rights, and strict audit trails are other features of this tool. i-CleaR today has become i-Flex's centralized knowledge repository.

Creating a collaborative culture in an organization is critical to the success of any KM program. By allowing a wider range of employees to take advantage of knowledge that has previously been available only to limited groups, i-Flex is introducing a culture of collaborative participation and making the knowledge creation process more effective by leveraging multiple skills across projects and geographical locations in i-Flex.

The KM team introduced several programs and roles that could create a new organizational culture in i-Flex furthering collaboration and sharing of knowledge and effectively leveraging the intellectual assets of the company. These include knowledge mentors as well as knowledge champions. K-champion role is an institutionalized role mandatory in all development projects in i-Flex. The K-champion ensures that every project collects reusable collateral from the project, codifies it, and publishes such information (including tacit information) in the central repository for further reuse.

i-Contribute is another collaborative program undergoing a pilot implementation that attempts to maximize the utilization of resources across projects. In this initiative, a project manager may decide to auction noncritical tasks using this platform, depending on his requirement and on constraints such as overstretch. The task is then open for bid from the participating groups.

OTHER IT SECTOR PROFILES

A range of other large IT companies, such as Fujitsu Consulting, Siemens, Accenture, Oracle, and Sun, as well as smaller ones, such as Context Integration, also leverage KM in the project context, as briefly surveyed in this section.

Formal KM practices at Fujitsu Consulting (FC) actually got off to a bumpy start, with rampant database proliferation, inadequate budgetary support, multiple technical platforms, and cultural confusion. Things got back on track with awareness programs, top-level support, the knowledge access system (KAS) portal, a results chain model for realizing benefits, formation of a community called "The Knowledge Underground," and a global knowledge support office (KSO), which works around the clock in different time zones. FC's KM practice has helped increase the quality and consistency of work, decreased the cost of proposals, and delivered a measurable improvement in gross margin via tools like ProjectFinder. Upcoming trends to watch include the use of handheld wireless devices in the spread of KM at multiple "trigger points."

Siemens Information and Communication Networks (ICN) devised a business development KM practice called ShareNet in 1999 to help share project knowledge across technologies and markets in different stages of maturity. The company reports more than 150 knowledge management projects worldwide. Siemens's ShareNet—linking thirteen thousand telecommunications sales and marketing experts in more than eighty countries—is the most notable of these projects.

Sales staff members find themselves playing the role of strategy management consultants who have to be able to interpret trends and design new opportunities together with the customer. ShareNet helps tap and share local innovation in different parts of the world via project debriefings, manuals, codified databases, structured questionnaires, chat rooms, and hotlines. Technically based on OpenText's LiveLink, it is used by seven thousand sales and marketing staff.

IT and offshore services giant Accenture implemented a Lotus Notes–based KM system in 1992. In its early years, it was beset with problems like information overflow, duplication, and redundancies. Today, the Knowledge Xchange system has a standardized architecture and design and is accessed by seventy thousand professionals to share information on project methodologies, sales cycles, current engagements, and other client learnings. Over 3,600 databases exist, and 250 knowledge managers are responsible for reviewing the content and selecting best practices. These are synthesized into special Web sections, and expert directories and external references are provided as well.

Though decentralized processes for harnessing intellectual capital were in place for over a decade, Oracle's formal KM-centered program kicked off in 1997. Its success relies on a network of change agents—including KM leads, domain mentors, and portal managers. Web-based project libraries have helped consultants readily find reference material and decreased the number of technical assistance requests from customers. Thirty percent of Oracle EMEA employees are members of the eighty communities of practice, or "Professional Communities," and more than 70 percent of the members say that their communities add value to their performance. Technology is not just another enabler for KM but a key one; technology-assisted platforms such as My.Oracle.Com, GlobalXchange, knowledge areas, and community areas help KM concepts to be put into action. Future steps include extending KM beyond the enterprise via the Oracle Technology Network (OTN) and Oracle Partner Network (OPN).

Sun Microsystems Philippines (SunPhil), a joint venture between Sun Microsystems and erstwhile distributor Philippine Systems Products, was formed in 1999. Digital KM platforms can have a transformative power in environments where paper and face-to-face meetings constituted the bulk of knowledge transfer. Sun technology was used to launch the SunPhil corporate portal and its knowledge management system, with features like document rating, profiling and filtered search, and collaborative authoring. The time taken to prepare proposals and project documentation has been reduced tremendously, and innovative approaches are being explored to harness information mobilization and real-time expert contact via personal digital assistants (PDAs) and short-message services (SMS; the Philippines, after all, is the world's SMS capital). SunPhil professionals are now partnering with clients, sharing their homegrown experience, and expertise in the area of KM. SunPhil is even taking the KM message to the national level through its active support of the Knowledge Management Association of the Philippines (KMAP).

E-business solutions provider Context Integration launched a KM platform called Intellectual Assets Network (IAN) in 1997, initially based on Lotus Notes and Verity. It has developed a client collaboration environment called PETE (Project Enablement Team Environment). Parts of the system can be downloaded to employee laptops. The portal links to introductory documents called road maps, learning documents called curriculum paths, and project artifacts.

DISCUSSION

In this section, we review contributions by KM in project management and identify other emerging trends in this practice. KM is one of many strategic and operational steps in an organization and is continually shaped by new approaches to business strategy, workforce behaviors, and emerging IT tools, especially now in the area of Web 2.0 tools for collaboration.

Tiwana (2002) outlines a "knowledge management toolkit," a practical ten-step road map to KM implementation. At the same time, KM is not a "fix-it-all" technology, not just a smarter intranet, not a seductive "silver-bullet" solution, not a canned approach, and not a one-time investment, Tiwana cautions.

The ten steps of Tiwana's KM road map can be grouped into the following four phases: infrastructure evaluation, KM system development, deployment, and evaluation. Technology enablers must be harnessed for knowledge finding (e.g., search, employee yellow pages), creation (collaboration), packaging (digital publishing), applying (classification), validation (CoPs), and reuse (project record databases).

Kim Sbarcea and Rui Martins (in Rao, 2003) call for a change in conceptualization of project management (a key activity in sectors like IT) as befits the transition from an industrial age to an information- and knowledge-driven age. This change includes a novel typology of knowledge: expectational, immediate, transformational, and transdisciplinary knowledge.

Firsthand research from QAI India shows that KM tools have been successfully used in project management, brainstorming activities, and networking knowledge workers but have been less successful in crisis management and large-scale organizational redesign. Challenges have been observed in failure to control KM infrastructure costs, inability to integrate multiple IT tools, developing solutions without seeking external professional help, and not properly aligning KM tools and solutions with business needs. Future trends include the use of systems thinking, pattern theories, and social network analysis.

In addition to the Internet and intranet, the emergence of tools for peer-to-peer communication, mobile access, instant messaging, and Web services are all having an influence on collaborative platforms and methods. Collaborative tools can facilitate a practice (how people work together to get the job done) as well as a process (the explicit or formal definition of how work should be done). Key observations include the proliferation of project-based collaboration tools in the market (such as Zoho, Google Docs, ProjectSpaces, Telligent, Huddle) and the importance of a leadership role in encouraging collaborative solutions to knowledge work.

Beerli, Falk, and Diemers (2003) compare and contrast the codification ("stocks") approach to content management with the connection or personalization ("flows") approach of bringing employees together for project work. "Companies using the codification strategy are facing the problem of information overflow and the increasing difficulty of structuring the vast collections of documents. On the other hand, those adopting only the personalisation strategy cannot cope with the challenge of speed in the new economy," according to the authors.

They also address the important issue of quality of information assets (via three parameters: comprehension, contextualization, and valuation) in work environments of tight budgets, pressures on time, shortening half-lives of knowledge, and rapidly changing classifications or indexes. Information in such settings must be useful, usable, dependable, sound, well defined, unambiguous, reputable, timely, concise, and contextualized.

Within organizational settings, social network analysis (SNA) is emerging as a powerful tool for mapping knowledge flows and identifying gaps in project settings. SNA can be used to reinforce existing flows and improve knowledge integration after activities like mergers and acquisitions. Methods used can be qualitative (e.g., employee surveys) or quantitative (e.g., analysis of transactions such as e-mails or phone calls or information artifacts such as documents and search strings).

Natural-language techniques, visualization tools, and recommender systems can be harnessed here, leading to actions like identifying key individuals for retention or expanded roles or creating teams for cross-organizational and cross-functional projects. Direct applications of SNA include process redesign, role development, and improved collaboration between knowledge seekers and providers.

The focus on networks in the twenty-first-century knowledge workplace is increasing because networks are where people engage, networks are where work happens, and networks are where knowledge lives, according to Rob Cross, author of "The Hidden Power of Social Networks," speaking at the KM World 2003 conference in Santa Clara.

Typical roles in organization networks include central people, peripheral people, boundary spanners, and knowledge brokers. "Network structure can facilitate or impede effectiveness of knowledge workers," Cross says.

Social network analysis (SNA) can help identify central people, connectivity levels of individual knowledge workers, diversity of subgroups, and level of organizational interconnectivity. "Getting things done often depends less on formal structure than on informal networks of people," Cross observes. Many companies have top management teams but not top management networks.

Successful SNA depends on metaknowledge of employees, access to colleagues, frequency and intensity of interaction, and levels of trust. SNA has implications for organizational leadership, social ecology, relational development, and network planning. Tools like SNA can be used to analyze and improve numerous kinds of networks, such as advice networks and even energy networks. "Position in the energy network can be a much higher predictor of performance than expertise or use of informational networks. Employees connected to energisers tend to perform better," according to Cross.

Models and theories from disciplines like complex adaptive systems can be deployed in the area of storytelling and case studies as ways of capturing project learnings. Organizations such as IBM's Cynefin Centre have developed classifications of knowledge work into categories like known, knowable, complex, and chaotic, focusing not just on storytelling but on narrative analysis for collaborative sense-making and decision-making inputs.

Tools like participatory observation, anecdote circles, deep immersion, organizational metaphors, and naive interviews are useful in this regard. Storytelling is used to promote knowledge sharing at NASA, via the Transfer Wisdom Workshops and the Project Management Shared Experiences program conducted by the Academy of Program and Project Leadership (APPL).

In terms of narrative structuring, tools like "knowledge blogging" (or k-logs, a term coined by John Robb, president of Userland) have a lot of potential. "Stories are a good framework for sharing information, meaning and knowledge. Blogs encourage story-telling and foster understanding because they usually offer context," according to Darlene Fichter, library coordinator at the University of Saskatchewan Library, speaking at the KM World 2003 conference in Santa Clara.

"Knowledge blogs help encourage brain dumps, exploration, and think-aloud behaviour. They create connected content, break down silos, allow comments, and can also be treasured as useful searchable archives," she observes.

Besides, over time, blogs are self-rewarding. "Often bloggers report that they discover their own interests and refine their perspectives. It leads to peer recognition," according to Fichter.

K-logs are also a useful, low-cost, and flexible tool for competitive intelligence (CI), according to Arik Johnson, managing director of Aurora WDC, speaking at the KM World 2003 conference in Santa Clara.

Well-designed CI blogs can help collect, analyze, package, and deliver current awareness and early warning of competitive and regulatory developments for sales staff and top managers. Blogs help write thought pieces to guide the organization on a strategic path. Bloggers can collect and connect information and provide useful overlays of context.

Blogging has enough critical mass and momentum and will soon be integrated with other KM tools in project settings. We are now seeing a new phase in this growth with the proliferation of microblogging tools such as Twitter.

REFERENCES AND RESOURCES

Bahra, Nicholas. (2001). *Competitive knowledge management*. New York: Palgrave Macmillan.

Beerli, Alfred, Falk, Svenja, & Diemers, Daniel. (2003). *Knowledge management and networked environments: Leveraging intellectual capital in virtual business communities*. New York: AMACOM.

Brown, John Seely, & Duguid, Paul. (2000). *The social life of information*. Boston: Harvard Business School Press.

Collins, Heidi. (2000). *Corporate portals: Revolutionizing information access to increase productivity and drive the bottom line*. New York: AMACOM.

Davenport, Thomas, & Prost, Gilbert. (2002). *Knowledge management case book: Siemens best practises*. Wiley/Publicus.

Davenport, Thomas, & Prusak, Laurence. (2000). *Working knowledge: How organizations manage what they know*. Boston: Harvard Business School Press.

Denning, Stephen. (2001). *The springboard: How storytelling ignites action in knowledge-era organizations*. Boston: Butterworth-Heinemann.

Dixon, Nancy. (2000). *Common knowledge: How companies thrive by sharing what they know*. Boston: Harvard Business School Press.

Figallo, Cliff, & Rhine, Nancy. (2002). *Building the knowledge management network: Best practices, tools and techniques for putting conversation to work*. New York: Wiley.

Frappaolo, Carl. (2002). *Knowledge management*. Oxford: Capstone Publishing.

Gamble, Paul, & Blackwell, John. (2001). *Knowledge management: A state of the art guide*. New York: Kogan Page.

Honeycutt, Jerry. (2000). *Knowledge management strategies*. Redmond, WA: Microsoft Press.

Kluge, Jurge, Stein, Wolfram, & Licht, Thomas. (2001). *Knowledge unplugged: The McKinsey & Company global survey on knowledge management*. New York: Palgrave Macmillan.

Koulopoulos, Thomas, & Frappaolo, Carl. (1999). *Smart things to know about knowledge management*. Oxford: Capstone.

Malhotra, Yogesh. (2001). *Knowledge management and business model innovation*. Hershey, PA: Idea Group.

Newell, Sue, Robertson, Maxine, & Swan, Jacky. (2002). *Managing knowledge work*. New York: Palgrave Macmillan.

Rao, Madanmohan. (2003). *Leading with knowledge: Knowledge management practices in global infotech companies (The KM chronicles, travelogue 1)*. New Delhi: Tata/McGraw-Hill.

Rao, Madanmohan. (2004). *Knowledge management tools and techniques: Practitioners evaluate KM solutions (The KM chronicles, travelogue 1)*. Boston: Reed Elsevier.

Sbarcea, Kim. (2002). *Rethinking knowledge*. Chatswood, Australia: Lexis/Nexis Butterworths.

Tiwana, Amrit. (2002). *The knowledge management toolkit: Orchestrating IT, strategy and knowledge platforms*. Upper Saddle River, NJ: Prentice-Hall.

Index

About the Contributors

Ms. A. Latha is associate vice president at Infosys Technologies Limited and is currently responsible for all operations of the KM function at Infosys. She has been with the education & research department of Infosys (which hosts KM) for more than sixteen years and has donned various roles in education and learning during this period. Her interests include corporate education models, design, development, and deployment of KM solutions, and integration of KM with education to realize the organization's charter of providing all its employees with an ecosystem promoting effective "anytime, anywhere learning." She has a bachelor's degree and a master's degree in engineering from the PSG College of Technology, Coimbatore, India.

Franz Barachini is associate professor of computer science at the Technical University Vienna and founder of the management consulting company BIC-Austria. He is also cofounder of the Vienna International School of Thought (VIST). His main research interest today is knowledge management, process management, and strategic management, in which he has published books and more than fifty peer-reviewed papers.

Denise Bedford is currently a senior information officer at the World Bank in Washington, DC. At the World Bank she serves as practice lead for business architecture and is a core member of the operational and knowledge systems program and the enterprise search team. Her responsibilities include development of the bank's core metadata and content type strategies, management of ontology, taxonomies, and the World Bank's multilingual topic thesaurus, and development and operationalization of the bank's semantic analysis technologies. In addition to the World Bank, she has held positions at NASA, Intel Corporation, Stanford University, the American Mathematical Association, the University of California, University of Michigan, and University of Southern California. She is adjunct faculty at Georgetown University, University of Tennessee, and Kent State University, where she teaches a variety of courses in information architecture, knowledge management, systems and project management, and semantics/semantic applications. Her educational background includes a BA in history, Russian language and literature, and German language and literature; an MA in Russian history; an MS in librarianship, and a PhD in information science.

Dr. Yun-Ke Chang is an assistant professor in the School of Communication and Information at Nanyang Technological University. She teaches information technology–related topics and research method courses. Her research areas include search engines, digital image retrieval, website evaluation, human-computer interaction, human visual perception, learning organization, and knowledge management. Dr. Chang also has served in several academic program committees of international conferences and as a paper reviewer for journals.

Ana Flavia Fonseca is currently a senior technical adviser to the University of Joao Pessoa–UNIPE, Brazil. Dr. Fonseca teaches knowledge management at the UMUC and also provides consulting services in information and knowledge management. Before retirement, Dr. Fonseca was the chief information architect and information services manager for the World Bank in Washington, DC.

Arnoldo Fonseca was formerly principal, Defonseca Consulting, in the area of information and knowledge management. Presently, he is a business manager at a Fortune 500 industrial and chemicals company.

Dr. Suliman Hawamdeh is a professor and the program coordinator of the master of science in knowledge management program at the University of Oklahoma. He was the founding director of the first knowledge management program in Asia at Nanyang Technological University in Singapore. He is the author of several books on knowledge management. He is also the editor of the *Journal of Information and Knowledge Management (JIKM)* as well as the book series on innovation and knowledge management published by World Scientific. He is the founding chair of the International Conference on Knowledge Management (ICKM). Additional information on Dr. Hawamdeh is available at www.Hawamdeh.net.

Kyle M. L. Jones is currently the library IT specialist at Elmhurst College's A. C. Buehler Library in Elmhurst, Illinois. He earned his master's in library and information science from Dominican University in 2009 with honors. He can be reached at http://thecorkboard.org.

Dr. Joseph Kasten is an associate professor in the computer information systems department of Dowling College. Professor Kasten's current research interests include the strategic application of knowledge in organizations, especially transportation and health care, and the use of project management techniques to improve alignment of software with an organization's goals. His past research has been published in *Knowledge Organization* and *International Journal of Materials & Product Technology*, as well as the proceedings of the International Conference of System Dynamics, Decision Sciences Institute, and the Production and Operations Management Society. Prior to joining academia, Joe was a senior engineer for the Northrop Grumman Corporation, where he helped develop both military and civilian aircraft as well as information systems for the United States Navy. When not involved in research or teaching, Joe and his family spend their time traveling the country in their RV, paddling their canoe, and hiking.

Michael E. D. Koenig is professor and former and founding dean of the College of Information and Computer Science at Long Island University. His career has included senior management positions in the information industry: manager of research information services at Pfizer Inc., director of development at the Institute for Scientific Information, vice president–North America at Swets & Zeitlinger, and vice president of data management at Tradenet; as well as academic positions: associate professor at Columbia University, and dean and professor at Dominican University. His PhD in information science is from Drexel University, and his MBA in mathematical methods and computers and MA in library and information science are from the University of Chicago. His undergraduate degree is from Yale University. He is the author of more than 100 peer-reviewed publications and recipient of the Jason Farradane award for outstanding work in the field of information.

James E. Lightfoot spent over twenty-three years as a consultant. Within those years, he provided expert and professional services for Fortune 500 companies. He provided services as a senior consultant, data base administrator, system programmer, and application programmer. He led management efforts and coordinated system migrations and implementation for large databases for multinational groups, for example, companies such as Charles of the Ritz, Citibank, American Express, IBM, Con Edison, Westinghouse, GTE, Publix Supermarkets, Florida Power & Light, Whirlpool, and PSE&G. James obtained his bachelor of science degree in mathematics with a minor in economics from Long Island University (LIU) in 1975. He obtained his master's in business administration from the University of South Florida (USF) in 2006.

Kavi Mahesh is a principal consultant with the knowledge management group at Infosys Technologies Limited, Bangalore. He is also a professor of computer science at PES Institute of Technology, Bangalore, India. He was previously with Oracle Corporation, USA and New Mexico State University. His areas of interest are knowledge representation and management, epistemology, ontology, and classification studies. He has published two books and authored over fifty papers and book chapters and holds an MTech in computer science from the Indian Institute of Technology, Bombay (1989), and an MS (1991) and a PhD (1995) in computer science from Georgia Institute of Technology.

Kate Marek, PhD, is an associate professor at Dominican University's Graduate School of Library and Information Science. Kate comes to graduate education from a long and diverse career in library practice, which began formally with her MLIS from Rosary College. Before receiving her PhD from Emporia State University, Kate worked in a private law library, an academic library, and a public middle-school media center. In addition, she spent five years as a library consultant with an emphasis on technology development in libraries. Kate's interests and expertise include technology development in information services, information literacy issues, information policy, and using literature in professional education.

Dr. Miguel A. Morales-Arroyo is lecturing in the School of Communication and Information at Nanyang Technological University, where he is a research fellow. Dr. Morales received his bachelor's degree in EEE, his master's degree in system engineering, and his PhD in information sciences. His research area is in decision-making process and problem-solving methods, including identifying stages and factors related to the nature of collaborative projects. He has served on several academic program committees of international conferences as well as being a paper reviewer for journals.

Siegfried Neubauer is founder of the management consulting company ACM Quadrat Ltd. and cofounder of the Vienna International School of Thought (VIST). His main spheres of activities are learning organizations, strategic management, and change management. He also gives lectures on universities of applied sciences and is author and coauthor of management papers and books.

Bhanu Kiran Potta has over thirteen years of mainstream industry experience in rendering successful capability-building programs in global enterprises as well as public sector organizations in areas like knowledge management, innovation management, competence development, education/knowledge/learning technology management (products and services), and organization change management. Currently, as the associate director of the knowledge management group at Perot Systems, Bhanu provides leadership and strategic direction to the application solutions business unit's global knowledge management program. Bhanu also provides strategic consulting/advisory for reputed organizations and frequently writes on enterprise knowledge management, Web 2.0, education 2.0, social networking, community engineering, knowledge leadership, and related topics.

Dr. Madanmohan Rao is a KM consultant and author from Bangalore. He is the editor of the book series *The Knowledge Management Chronicles*. He is the cofounder of the Bangalore K-Community, a network of KM professionals. Madan was formerly the communications director at the United Nations Inter Press Service Bureau in New York and vice president at India World Communications in Bombay. He graduated from the Indian Institute of Technology at Bombay and the University of Massachusetts at Amherst with an MS in computer science and a PhD in communications. Madan is a frequent speaker on the international conference circuit and has given talks and lectures in over sixty countries around the world. Madan is also world music editor for *Rave* magazine.

Gabriel de las Nievas Sánchez-Guerrero is a professor in the systems engineering department at National Autonomous University of Mexico (UNAM). Dr. Sánchez-Guerrero received his PhD (Hons.) in systems engineering from UNAM. His research areas include heuristic techniques for participatory planning, systems evaluation, and brief intervention processes in organizations. His current research is focused on participatory evaluation using heuristic techniques.

C. S. Shobha is a senior management professional with twenty-two years of experience in the information-technology industry in critical success areas such as software delivery (ten years) and operations management (twelve years). She operationalized several innovations in quality, knowledge management, training, talent management, project management competency, and risk management. Currently Shobha is working as senior director, quality and operational excellence, applications solutions at Perot Systems, leading organizational quality and knowledge management programs. She has been responsible for the company's achieving ISO 9001, CMM, CMMI, ISO 27001, and ISO 20000 certifications. She is an active member of communities in quality, knowledge management, and innovation in Bangalore, and has spoken at several industry forums and conferences. She has led many consulting engagements for customers in the United States, Europe, and Asia in the area of quality and knowledge management.

Taverekere (Kanti) Srikantaiah, director and professor, Center for Knowledge Management at Dominican University, joined the Dominican faculty in 1997. Before joining Dominican, Kanti had a distinguished career at the World Bank, where he headed varied and important assignments in the areas of information management at headquarters in Washington, DC (and also at the World Bank's field offices in Africa and Asia). Prior to joining the World Bank, Kanti worked on building a strong and advanced academic background in sciences as well as in social sciences. He worked at the Library of Congress as an area specialist and taught at the California State University, Fullerton, California, as an associate professor. He has taught as an adjunct faculty member at the Catholic University of America in Washington, DC, Syracuse University, University of Wisconsin at Madison, University of Maryland at College Park, University of Maryland University College, and Kent State University in Kent, Ohio. His areas of specialization include systems analysis, taxonomies, business process management, organization of knowledge, management of information repositories, environmental scanning, information audit, project management, and knowledge management.

Dr. Michael Stephens is assistant professor in the Graduate School of Library and Information Science at Dominican University in Illinois. He spent over fifteen years working in public libraries while developing a passion for technology and the human connections it affords. His recent publications include two ALA Library technology reports on Web 2.0, the monthly column "The Transparent Library" with Michael Casey in *Library Journal*, and other articles about emerging trends and technology. Michael also maintains the popular blog "Tame the Web." He received an IMLS doctoral fellowship at the University of North Texas, was named a *Library Journal* Mover and Shaker, and received the 2009 Association of Library & Information Science Educators Faculty Innovation Award as well as a 2009 University of North Texas Rising Star Alumni Award. He is the 2009 CAVAL Visiting Scholar, researching the effect of learning 2.0 programs in Australian libraries. Michael speaks nationally and internationally on libraries, technology, and innovation. He is fascinated by library buildings and virtual spaces that center on users, content, digital creation, and encouraging the heart.

J. K. Suresh, associate vice president, heads knowledge management for the Infosys group of companies headquartered at Bangalore, India. As the principal knowledge manager for Infosys, he has been instrumental in spearheading effective KM practices across the organization that has elicited global acclaim in recent years. He has authored around fifty publications in the areas of aerospace engineering, application performance testing, design methodologies for Web-based systems, and knowledge management. He has deep secondary interests in the fields of education, history, and philosophy of science, social psychology, and epistemology. He obtained his BTech and MS (engineering) from the Indian Institutes of Technology at Kanpur and Madras, respectively, and a PhD from the Indian Institute of Science, Bangalore, India.

Michael J. D. Sutton, an assistant professor at the Bill and Vieve Gore School of Business at Westminster College, brings a unique view to his passion of knowledge mobilization (KM). He is currently a lead member of a team structuring a new bachelor of business administration educational degree completion program. His comprehensive career in senior corporate and consulting positions encompasses nearly four decades associated with business planning, business process management, administrative renewal, education, knowledge management, management consulting, coaching, mentoring, and institutional memory management. He has acquired extensive experience in educating, teaching, managing, technically structuring, and leading strategic business initiatives and new business ventures. He was a practice director for over fifteen years, concentrating his analytical, leadership, management, systems-thinking, and team-building talent in the emerging field of knowledge management in preparation for achieving his PhD in KM late in life. Michael has provided innovative consulting services to a range of clients, from Microsoft Corporation, United Nations agencies, and numerous departments of the Canadian federal government, to the U.S. Department of the Navy.

Dr. Deborah E. Swain, PhD, is interim associate dean and assistant professor at the School of Library and Information Sciences at North Carolina Central University in Durham, NC. She has over twenty years of experience in process engineering, organizational design, business and technical training, and managing information projects for corporations such as IBM, AT&T, and Lucent Technologies/Bell Labs. In 1999, she completed her doctorate in information science at the University of North Carolina at Chapel Hill. She also has an MA from UNC-CH in English and a BA from Duke University. Her areas of academic research are knowledge management, collaboration, and health informatics. Dr. Swain has presented papers and workshops at conferences for the ASIS&T, ICKM, ALA, NCLA, NCHICA, STC, and IEEE on knowledge management, electronic health records, the National Library of Medicine, use cases, database design, computer interfaces, information retrieval/indexing, online help design, expert systems, quality and process auditing, business communications, and software engineering. She is now involved in research on social network analysis and tools for knowledge sharing in health care and emergency management.

Charles A. Tryon is a nationally respected educator and popular symposium speaker. Chuck founded Tryon and Associates in 1986 to provide seminar training and consulting that helps organizations and individuals develop predictable and repeatable approaches to modern project management, knowledge management, and business requirements. The strategies presented in Mr. Tryon's seminars are used by thousands of professionals in hundreds of organizations across the United States, Europe, and Canada. His client list includes many top one hundred companies. Chuck and his wife, Tresa, reside in the Tulsa, Oklahoma, area. They have two grown daughters, Amanda and Casey. When not teaching, writing, or attending classes at OU, Chuck tries to find time for his favorite things in life, spoiling grandchildren, playing golf, and scuba diving . . . but not usually at the same time.

Dr. Stephanie M. White, a Woodrow Wilson Fellow, is a professor and member of the doctoral committee in the College of Information and Computer Science at Long Island University; she teaches courses in computer science, software and systems engineering, and information studies. Her research interests are in software and systems engineering, with emphasis on requirements management, systems modeling and analysis, and the interaction among systems and software engineers. Previously she was principal engineer of requirements and architecture for the Northrop Grumman Advanced Technology and Development Center in Bethpage, New York. During her twenty-year career at Grumman, she was principal investigator on a number of research contracts provided by Naval Research Laboratory and other agencies.